COLLEGE
STUDENT PERSONNEL
SERVICES

COLLEGE
STUDENT PERSONNEL
SERVICES

Edited by

WILLIAM T. PACKWOOD, Ph.D.

Director of Evaluation and Research
Louisiana Health and Human Resources Administration
Associate Professor, School of Social Welfare
Louisiana State University
Previously, College Student Personnel Program Coordinator
University of Iowa

Forewords by

Theodore K. Miller, Ed.D.

Associate Professor and Coordinator of the
Student Personnel in Higher Education Preparation Program
Director of the Student Development Laboratory
University of Georgia

and

Clyde A. Parker, Ph.D.

Professor of Educational Psychology
Chairman of the Department of Social, Psychological, and
Philosophical Foundations of Education
University of Minnesota

CHARLES C THOMAS • PUBLISHER
Springfield • Illinois • U.S.A.

Published and Distributed Throughout the World by
CHARLES C THOMAS • PUBLISHER
Bannerstone House
301-327 East Lawrence Avenue, Springfield, Illinois, U.S.A.

© *1977, by* CHARLES C THOMAS • PUBLISHER

ISBN 0-398-03638-1

Library of Congress Catalog Card Number: 76-54847

With THOMAS BOOKS *careful attention is given to all details of
manufacturing and design. It is the Publisher's desire to present books that
are satisfactory as to their physical qualities and artistic possibilities and
appropriate for their particular use.* THOMAS BOOKS *will be true to those
laws of quality that assure a good name and good will.*

Printed in the United States of America
C-1

Library of Congress Cataloging in Publication Data

Main entry under title:
College student personnel services.

   Bibliography: p.
   Includes index.
   1. Personnel service in higher education. I. Pack-
wood, William T.
LB2343.C614   378.1'94   76-54847
ISBN 0-398-03638-1

CONTRIBUTORS

BETTY BLASKA is an M.A. student in College Student Personnel and Counseling and a Special Research Assistant in Education at the University of Iowa. She received her B.A. from the University of Wisconsin, Madison.

MICHAEL DANNELLS is a doctoral student in College Student Personnel and Counseling and a Teaching Assistant at the University of Iowa, where he previously was a Special Research Assistant in Education and Assistant Coordinator for Programming at the Counseling Service. He received his B.S. from Bradley University.

TERRY F. GANSHAW was a doctoral student in College Student Personnel and Counseling at the University of Iowa where he was also Graduate Assistant for the Chairman of the Division of Counselor Education, Associate Editor of the *Journal of College Student Personnel,* and winner of the 1975 American College Personnel Association's Graduate Student Essay Contest. Previously he was a Graduate Assistant in the Office of Student Activities at the University of Rochester, where he also obtained his B.A.

GEORGE D. KUH received his Ph.D. from the University of Iowa, his M.S. from St. Cloud State College, and his B.A. from Luther College. Presently he is an Assistant Professor in College Student Personnel Administration at Indiana University. Previously he was an Assistant Professor in College Student Personnel and Counseling and Assistant Director of the Drug Counseling Program at the University of Iowa and an Assistant Director of Admissions at Luther College.

WILLIAM T. PACKWOOD received his Ph.D. from the University of Minnesota and his B.A. from Yale University. He is presently Director of Evaluation and Research for the

Louisiana Health and Human Resources Administration and Associate Professor in the School of Social Welfare at Louisiana State University. Formerly he was Associate Professor in Counselor Education and Coordinator of the College Student Personnel Program at the University of Iowa.

MARLIN R. SCHMIDT received her Ph.D. from the University of Iowa, her M.A. from Columbia University, and her B.A. from Grinnell College. Presently she is Assistant Professor in Counselor Education, Coordinator of the College Student Personnel Program, and Associate Director of the Drug Counseling Program at the University of Iowa and is a member of the Executive Council of the American College Personnel Association. Previously she was an Assistant Professor in Counselor Education at the University of Florida.

LYNETTE DANIELS SCHNEIDER received her Ed.S. and M.A. in College Student Personnel and Counseling at the University of Iowa, her M.A. in American History and B.A. at the University of California at Los Angeles. Presently she is an Instructor in Career Information and the Psychology of Women at Northwestern State University of Louisiana's Extension Program at Fort Polk, Louisiana. Previously she was a counselor and instructor at community colleges in Salinas and Monterey, California and Cedar Rapids, Iowa.

DEDICATION

to my wife
GINI
in appreciation of her patience,
insistence, and professional assistance

to my sons
KIRK, TED, and MATTHEW
in appreciation of all those times I said no

to my
GRADUATE STUDENTS
for whom the book was conceived and especially those
without whose commitment and high degree of
professionalism the book would not have been written
and
to the memory of
TERRY F. GANSHAW

FOREWORD

Higher education as an American institution is in transition. Perhaps it has ever been thus. After all, institutions, like human beings, develop and change over time as they interact with their environments. Likewise, the component parts of subunits which go to make up the larger institutional system are similarly undergoing change. We are, in other words, dealing with a dynamic entity when we concern ourselves with the process of higher education. This comprehensive volume focuses careful attention upon one of the very important aspects of that process, namely, college student personnel services.

In recent years some have begun to question the nomenclature of higher education, especially the term "student personnel" which has come into generic usage to describe the sector of activity and service with which this book so admirably deals. In a posthumously published statement to the profession ironically entitled "Student Personnel — All Hail and Farewell!", Burns Crookston makes the following proposal. The term

> *student personnel work* should be given its due and retired into history. Efforts should be made in the professional literature and in other communications not to use the term to describe contemporary programs, services, or concepts. Although it is legitimate to use the term in its proper definition to refer to specific functions such as placement, it is recommended that a ten-year moratorium be placed on any such public use of the term, after which presumably there should be no mistake as to its proper meaning and usage (1976, p. 29).

It is highly unlikely that the Crookston proposal will be acted upon in the immediate future, but it does point to the importance of our nomenclature and to the communication difficulties which ensue from a too broad definition of traditional terminology.

As you begin reading this book, however, you will probably become cognizant of the fact that the authors have diligently held to the traditional and appropriate definition of student personnel. They deal intimately and in depth with nearly all of the key college student personnel service functions which have evolved over the years and which represent the components which go to make up the student affairs administrative subdivision responsible for coordinating and implementing the non-academic curriculum so essential to the development of the total student. What the authors do best, perhaps, is to give the reader not only a clear description of the substance of each service area, but a real sense of the evolutionary processes which have made them what they are today.

It is essential that all practitioners possess both an understanding of our professional antecedents and a sense of the profession's mission for guiding our work into the future in ways which will increasingly enhance the full development of the students who encounter our people and programs. This book does a fine job of facilitating this needed understanding and moves the reader toward clarifying a sense of mission, particularly within the individual service areas under consideration. Whether one is an established practitioner or a student preparing to enter the field, this book has something important to say to you. It represents the most comprehensive descriptive statement of student services to be published in the past decade and a half and will likely become "must" reading for students in student affairs practitioner training programs throughout the country.

College spans the years of late adolescence and young adulthood for a majority of our students although more and more we are seeing other adults who are seeking to utilize post-secondary educational resources for their own betterment. All of these people have important developmental needs which require attention. If the education and development of the total person is considered an important part of the mission of higher education, then increased attention on the part of student service practitioners and student affairs programs toward achieving this goal is essential.

Institutions and organizations, just as human beings, have a propensity for development and change over time. Lippitt and Schmidt (1967) have postulated three stages of organizational development including birth, youth, and maturity. It appears to me that the field of student affairs is currently in the throes of moving from the stage of youth to the stage of maturity according to their model. For the past several decades programs of student services have been gaining stability and have established organizational patterns to maintain that stability within the higher education community. Although student affairs practitioners may often tend to be somewhat crisis oriented and reactive, there has been an increasing emphasis upon becoming proactive and devising developmentally engendering programs for students. The desire to establish a positive reputation in the campus community and to develop pride in our work and accomplishments has also been important, and seeking ways to review and evaluate our efforts has become paramount. This book reflects all of this and focuses attention not only upon what we have become but also upon how it has come about.

In addition, this book raises a number of important questions as to what the profession is to become. This is the key to entering into the stage of organizational maturity. According to Lippitt and Schmidt we begin this advanced stage with the critical concern of how to achieve uniqueness and adaptability and the key issues of whether and how to change. It is my contention that student affairs programs, as subunits of institutions of higher learning, are particularly faced with these concerns and issues at this time. Student affairs leaders know that they cannot rest on their laurels for having developed student service programs of excellence alone, for today's students and society are calling for more. Although the foundations have been laid, there is much more to be accomplished before the superstructure is complete, and new blueprints are needed now.

This book outlines the state of the art to date and should be a useful vehicle to aid the practitioner in preparing for achieving the important next steps essential to moving us wisely and effectively into the future.

This book is not designed to specifically give direction to the profession for the future, however, as it is a treatise outlining where the field, as a developing entity, is at present. This book, coupled with the recently published *The Future of Student Affairs: A Guide to Student Development for Tomorrow's Higher Education* (Miller & Prince, 1976) sponsored by the American College Personnel Association, should give the reader a truly comprehensive view of where the field of student affairs has been, where it is presently, and where it may be going in the future. No panaceas are involved herein but a comprehensive overview of an important element of higher education in America is delineated intelligently, systematically, and interestingly. An important body of knowledge in the area of college student personnel services has been developing over the past half century and this book rates well in attempts to describe this knowledge in meaningful ways.

Perhaps the student personnel services' approach to facilitating the growth and development of college students is in its final stages and may evolve into a more mature and complex entity in the years to come. This, in all likelihood, is going to happen for development, whether human, organizational, or cultural, tends to occur by moving from simpler to more complex forms over time. By the turn of the Twenty-First Century the term "college student personnel services" may be relegated to the historical archives of higher education but the functions involved will continue to be very much with us as well as others yet to be identified and institutionalized.

The United States of America has only recently celebrated its second century of existence. The dream that it represents, however, goes back to the beginnings of mankind with the desire to be free and responsibly self-determining beings. The goal of educating and developing the whole person is a derivative of this dream as are the many social institutions which have been established over the years to aid in its achievement. Perhaps this dream can never become reality. Perhaps the feelings of purposefulness alone, which derive from having a goal to seek, are adequate to sustain us. Whatever the truth might be, those of us involved with the education of our society's constituents must continue to strive to more effectively achieve our goals and objectives. We cannot do it alone, however, as collaboration by all involved is essential. Students, faculty, administrators, student service specialists, student development educators, and others can, together, better meet the needs of all. College student personnel services has a place in this process. This book aids significantly in delineating what that place has been and what it can be.

Theodore K. Miller
University of Georgia

REFERENCES

Crookston, B. B. Student personnel — All hail and farewell! *Personnel and Guidance Journal*, 1976, *55*, 26-29.

Lippitt, G. L., & Schmidt, W. H. Crises in a developing organization. *Harvard Business Review*, 1967, *45*(6), 102-112.

Miller, T. K., & Prince, J. S. *The future of student affairs: A guide to student development for tomorrow's higher education*. San Francisco: Jossey-Bass, 1976.

FOREWORD

$\mathbf{A}$ BOOK of this scope needs to be viewed from
several perspectives. Not since 1961 (Mueller) has anyone attempted to present under a single cover all of the significant
research, opinion, and experience related to college student
personnel work. Because of the depth and breadth of the book
it is important to reflect on the historical and cultural perspectives as well as the current status of student personnel work.

About thirteen years ago, Cowley (1964) addressed the largest
college student personnel organization (ACPA) at its annual
convention in San Francisco. He titled his remarks "Reflections
of a Troublesome but Hopeful Rip Van Winkle." Because he
had been removed from active participation in the field for
some thirty years, he approached his remarks as though awak-
ening from a long sleep. Most cogently he remarked:

> I'm delighted with the enormous growth of student
> services as epitomized by such facts as these: the
> numbers of men and women in these services have mul-
> tiplied at least 25 times; the institutional budgets for
> your programs have grown from a few thousand dollars
> to more than a million in a number of universities and
> have increased proportionately in most small colleges;
> and the membership of this association has grown from
> 91 in 1934 to 3,200 last year.
>
> These and other advances "pleasure" everyone who has
> been or is now engaged in your area of higher educa-
> tional activity; but it seems to me, the debit side of the
> ledger very considerably outbalances the credit side. For
> example: this Association [ACPA] and the three dozen
> or so others devoted to student affairs in colleges and
> universities are currently struggling with the same
> problems that afflicted them 25 years ago. Here and

there a bit of headway has been made, but in the main the confused and vexatious situation of the past continues to prevail (p. 66).

At first one may wonder that the problems had not changed during those years of sleep. Upon reflection it is easier to see why. Universities are communities of scholars, including both professors and students. The students enter, study, and leave. Professors tend to stay awhile longer; thus professors are always confronted with new students who bring the same "old" problems. Some of these problems include how an environment is created which is most conducive to students' learning and professors' teaching; what is important for a student to learn; how does an institution meet the needs of the students; and how can students best be supported (economically, psychologically, and physically) while they learn. From the beginning these have been the problems that student personnel workers have accepted as their concerns.

To illustrate how these concerns reappear let me select two. The first was the creation of a service at the University of Minnesota in 1916 to meet the vocational needs of women (Williamson & Sarbin, 1940). Rather remarkably the 1970's have presented higher education with nearly the same conditions, so much so that the same justification would be applicable.

A program [was] developed for the vocational advising of women. . . . Assistance for women . . . may be attributed to at least three factors: (1) women students were eager to acquire information about many new occupations which were being opened to them; (2) the emphasis on vocational education was filtering up from the secondary schools; and (3) the Feminist movement was going in high gear.

A series of vocational conferences were held for women. . . . The Board of Regents created the office of Vocational Counselor for Women, with duties defined as follows:

"1. To make a study of vocations open to college

women, the qualifications required, the opportunities, the remuneration, the conditions of work, etc.;

"2. To study the qualifications, interests, and preparation of women students upon entering and during their course in the University;

"3. To confer personally with students about their plans and to advise them in their choice of studies in preparation for their vocations.

"4. In every way possible ... to promote women students seriousness of purpose and an intelligent appreciation of their duties and responsibilities as University graduates" (p. 17).

This proposal was made twelve years before similar services were established for men.

Those persons who instigated that first vocational guidance service for women may have seemed farsighted, but they were doing what seemed the most appropriate thing for them to do — that is, identify the special needs of students and provide a service for meeting these needs.

A second example is the need to adopt admissions policies that will minimize student mortality. Compare a note in a 1975 ACT bulletin ("Retention Gets Attention") with a paragraph from a 1928 report of a University of Minnesota committee (Patterson).

Student retention will be the theme for a series of three special seminars, which for the second consecutive year are sponsored jointly by ACT and the National Association of College Admissions Counselors (NACAC) .... "Student retention has been chosen for the theme of the 1974-75 seminar series because it is emerging as one of the most, if not *the* most, critical issues in higher education today" ("Retention Gets Attention," 1975, p. 1).

* * *

Of those who attempt some form of higher education, if they apply for admission to the older endowed colleges, one-half or two-thirds or four-fifths of them are rejected on the basis of entrance criteria. Of those who enter the University of Minnesota a little over half eventually graduate from some school or college. Thirty per cent do not reach the sophomore year. . . . The twenty per cent who are certain to fail amount to 300 or 400 in one of the large state universities. *These individuals can be identified by name before entrance.* (Patterson, 1928, pp. 6-7).

Both examples show the repetition of themes with which student personnel workers are familiar. They are specific illustrations of the larger concern expressed very early in the first attempt to present a comprehensive, integrated approach to student personnel work (Williamson & Sarbin, 1940).

This, then, is the objective of the personnel phase of higher education — to assist in the alleviation of those conditions which interfere with students' development; to assist in increasing the effectiveness of the University's instructional program; and to facilitate students' progress toward intellectual, social, moral, and emotional maturity (p. ii).

However, student personnel work as it is described by Packwood et al. is an American peculiarity. Nowhere in the world have there been the resources in either money or personnel to provide the elaborate superstructure described in this book. In most countries students have been left to fend for themselves (because by now they should be adults and not need such assistance) or faculty have provided assistance in the course of their regular duties (because of a commitment to education of the whole person).

As an example of an attempt to transport the enterprise to a new culture, American consultants were requested, in the mid-1960's, to assist faculty in Indian universities and colleges to improve student services. While some of us who worked in that project considered it successful in its ten-year duration, we were struck by the differences in India and the United States. After ten years of development, only a few colleges employ professionally trained counselors, almost all hostel Wardens are full-time faculty, there are very few full-time deans of students, and student activities are limited to a few departmental clubs on most campuses.

In reading the present volume from that perspective I was overcome by the apparent affluent state of American higher education. As if the brick and mortar differences were not sufficient, the number of persons required to man a student services program as described in this volume would be greater than the number of faculty on most Indian campuses. It is important to keep in mind our abundant resources as we consider the multiple ways we have attempted to meet student needs in this country.

Still a third perspective might be helpful: What has happened between 1964 when a troublesome but hopeful Cowley passed on his reflections and publication of this volume? For one thing we have passed through the very tumultuous period of student activism of the late sixties. That experience shook many people into the realization that the days of *in loco parentis* were over; that students' rights could not be ignored; that universities were socio-political institutions; and that students expected an education fitted to their needs as defined by them. The response from the student personnel leadership was a focus on student development as a goal for the field.

Cowley had observed in 1964 that

> regardless of whether you like or dislike the term complementary functions, the fact stands out clearly that the distinguishing characteristic of all the members of all the groups in your field is this: you serve students in various non-curricular ways. In short you are student service officers. . . . You should not only accept this fact but also, welcome and, indeed, broadcast it (p. 68).

Partly as a reaction to the student services image as reflected by Cowley, the American College Personnel Association has led the movement to refocus the field on the original goals stated in the 1939 ACE Student Personnel Point of View. The ACPA project, Tomorrow's Higher Education, has been a three-phase attempt to define the meaning of student development, to describe projects exemplary of student development, and to suggest organizational strategies to implement them. Such a re-emphasis is very much needed, but in promoting it we must not overlook the more basic services required. Having initiated some of this thought in the late sixties I was pleased to be reminded that student development was the concern of the entire university and that someone had to tend to the business of administering policy and providing services.

Packwood reflects that vision in his introduction when he says

> Without first being a service specialist, one cannot become a student development specialist or behavioral scientist. . . . Both specialists are professionals, the latter is preferable — an ideal (p. xxvi).

My own current view is that a complete student personnel program includes all three functions: policy formation and implementation, student services, and educational programming (student development). However, to include all three functions is not enough. Each of those functions can be carried out from either a static, status-quo position or from a dynamic growth facilitating one. For example, policies can be written to preserve the institution in its present form so that it continues to serve students as they are. Or policies can be written which will require students to undergo changes consistent with the liberating purposes of the university. Does one, for example, have coed dormitories? How does one decide? In the early 70's when students were choosing to live off campus some colleges turned to coed dormitories because they could attract more students, others avoided them because of public fears of increased cohabitation. Very few persons responsible for policy asked, "What happens to the psycho-social development of students when they live in mixed dorms?" It is only when we ask such questions and base policy on the answers that we can have a truly developmental institution.

Or in the area of services: one can have a financial aid office that provides financial support for students and collects loan payments, or one can have a financial aid counseling program that stimulates students to consider the implications of long-term loans, alternative ways of financing an education, and the problems of budgeting for college.

Similarly a college can provide cocurricular activities that fill students' free time and leave them relaxed but unchanged. Alternatively, using a developmental perspective, a co-curricular activity program can be aimed at encouraging students' ability to better manage their emotions and better integrate their emotional and intellectual selves.

Multiple examples of the application of these principles can be found today in higher education such as living-learning centers, internships, student development centers, and universities without walls. If Cowley were to reflect now on the past thirteen years he would see large changes in the ways that student personnel workers were carrying out their responsibilities, and he would see enormous changes in the amount that has been written about students and how to assist them in their education. This book is a masterful presentation of the accumulated knowledge about serving and working with students. It brings together what is important to know and presents it systematically and clearly. I am hopeful that in another ten years there will be as much to say about *student development* as these authors have had to say about *student services*.

Clyde A. Parker
University of Minnesota

REFERENCES

Cowley, W. H. Reflections of a troublesome but hopeful Rip Van Winkle. *Journal of College Student Personnel*, 1964, *6*, 66-73.

Mueller, K. H. *Student personnel work in higher education*. Boston: Houghton Mifflin, 1961.

Patterson, D. G., et al. The Minnesota student personnel program: Organizing student personnel services. *Educational Record*, 1928, *9*(7), 3-40.

Retention gets attention with seminar series. *Activity*, 1975, *13*(1). Iowa City, Iowa: American College Testing Program.

Williamson, E. G., & Sarbin, T. R. *Student personnel work*. Minneapolis: Burgess Publishing, 1940.

PREFACE

COLLEGE student personnel services are an integral part of all institutions of higher education. When an institution admits a student, it provides a college student personnel service. The relationships established among the various services offered to students by higher education institutions are provided by college student personnel professionals, who are guided by the Student Personnel Point of View. This Point of View, expressed by E. G. Williamson's committee in 1949 (American Council on Education Studies), is based on the assumptions that students' individual differences are planned for, that each student is considered a functioning whole, and that students should be met at their particular point of development (Wrenn, 1951). These assumptions serve as the basis for the profession's emphasis on student development in the provision of services (see Brown, 1972).

All services provided students by an institution are the province of the college student personnel worker. However, the line between those functions which are college student personnel functions and those which are not is unclear. Thus college student personnel functions may be performed by noncollege student personnel workers, as when faculty members provide counseling. Maintenance of the facility and the preparation and serving of food are not considered college student personnel functions, but both are services which support the college student personnel program and both may be impacted by college student personnel policies.

Academic deans are primarily administrators, but they influence the college student personnel program when they make decisions or policies, for instance, on admissions. In one sense the president of the college is the chief college student personnel worker, but in reality most of his or her responsibilities in this area are delegated.

Higher education institutions in the United States come in a variety of types. In 1975 there were 2,747 institutions and 10,223,729 students (Grant & Lind, 1976; see also Golladay, 1976). Of these institutions 158 were universities, 1,586 were four-year colleges, and 1,003 were two-year colleges. Public institutions (as opposed to private) accounted for 44 percent of the 2,747 institutions with 59 percent of the universities, 22 percent of the four-year colleges, and 76 percent of the two-year colleges. Seventy-five percent of all college students attended public institutions. Unless otherwise indicated, the word *college* is used throughout this book to refer to the various kinds of public and private institutions: universities, liberal arts colleges, teacher's colleges, religious colleges, community colleges, and vocational-technical institutes.

The college student personnel program at an institution is influenced by the variables which make up that institution. Size of the student body is perhaps primary. Usually, the larger the institution, the larger the percent of the budget allotted to student services, the more programs offered by the services, the greater the differentiation and specialization of the services, and the better the training of the college student personnel workers. The type of institution and the kinds and needs of students admitted also influence the program. For instance, prospective teachers may have different needs and require different programs than future engineers. An institution's educational philosophy, traditions, and purpose may require different programs, such as demanding a more religious character rather than a vocational or cultural one. Geographic location may influence the program, as when community resources are not available to a rural college. A college student personnel program also is affected by the mix of commuter versus resident students and younger versus older students. The degree of support from administrators, faculty, students, parents, alumni, and the community is also important. Given the variety of institutional needs, one of the challenges of the college student personnel profession is to develop a program that is responsive to each one of those needs.

There is no one ideal college student personnel program. Standards of good practice have been developed by the profession, but for the most part these are flexible and suggestive in nature. Like the institutions it serves, the college student personnel field is diverse, with a multitude of viewpoints and practices. This book is written to convey the dominant professional viewpoint and at the same time to present those views which differ.

It is the editor's aim to present an issue and an idea for research on every page. In most cases the issue is explicit and the research idea is implicit. Research in the college student personnel field is reported in this book as it relates to the issues. Most of the research findings are qualified, however, because of substantial limitations in design. Small sample sizes, unrepresentative samples, small return rates from samples, lack of control of relevant variables, and data collected from only one institution are the rule. These limitations are omitted not only because they would greatly expand the book, but also because the data even with their limitations are all that is available. In all cases, the reader is referred to the original report of the data to determine their validity.

This book was written for beginning students in college student personnel graduate training programs. Practitioners, particularly those new to the profession, may also find ideas and resources for programs and administrative policies. A book of this breadth is limited to a general, introductory overview of college student personnel services, but each chapter is based upon a thorough review of the literature and provides a ready means for accessing the literature.

Many college student personnel workers are hired because they are experts in a given service or can do the job in the service that the college wants done. The basis for employment then is professional and technical skill, just as a surgeon is hired for surgery. Of course there is much more than the skill of surgery that is included in the professional surgeon's activities. That "much more" for the college student personnel worker becomes the implementation of student development principles.

College student personnel workers can, as they have throughout the profession's history, make the job bigger and better. To do the job and to do it bigger and better requires commitment of a professional magnitude. Nothing less will see the college student personnel worker through an eighteen-hour day. It requires professional knowledge and skills or a willingness to acquire them. It requires interest in and satisfaction from getting the technical aspects of the job done well. It requires a strong role definition with the ability to articulate it and act according to it. Then, after the job is being performed well, are the professional resources again drawn upon to do the job better: to move, say, admissions or financial aid into a student development framework. Without first being a service specialist, one cannot become a student development specialist or behavioral scientist (see Berdie, 1966; Miller & Prince, 1976; Parker, 1971, 1973, 1974; Parker & Morrill, 1974). Both specialists are professionals, the latter is preferable — and ideal. This book is designed to introduce the reader to the service specialties with the behavioral science introduction provided by inference.

It is the position of this editor that a coordinated college student personnel program on each campus is a necessity. Whatever the organizational structure, the services on each campus must have a coordinated and articulated philosophy which is appropriate to the goals of the institution and the needs of the students. Anything less, and on the majority of campuses it is less, is disadvantageous and unprofessional. The reviews of literature in this book underscore the amount that each service speciality has to offer the others and the advantages cross communication would bring to the whole.

W.T.P.

REFERENCES

American Council on Education Studies. *The student personnel point of view* (Series 6, No. 13). Washington, D.C.: Author, 1949.

Berdie, R. F. Student personnel work: Definition and redefinition. *Journal of College Student Personnel*, 1966, 7, 131-136.

Brown, R. D. *Student development in tomorrow's higher education: A return to the academy*. Washington, D.C.: American College Personnel Association, 1972. (Student Personnel Monograph Series No. 16)

Golladay, M. A. *The condition of education: 1976 edition*. Washington, D.C.: United States Government Printing Office, 1976. (National Center for Educational Statistics, HE 19.314:976)

Grant, W. V., & Lind, C. G. *Digest of educational statistics: 1975 edition*. Washington, D.C.: United States Government Printing Office, 1976. (National Center for Educational Statistics, HE 19.315:975).

Miller, T. K., & Prince, J. S. *The future of student affairs: A guide to student development for tomorrow's higher education*. San Francisco: Jossey-Bass, 1976.

Parker, C. A. Institutional self-renewal in higher education. *Journal of College Student Personnel*, 1971, *12*, 405-409.

Parker, C. A. With an eye to the future ... *Journal of College Student Personnel*, 1973, *14*, 195-201.

Parker, C. A. Student development: What does it mean? *Journal of College Student Personnel*, 1974, *15*, 248-256.

Parker, C. A., & Morrill, W. Student development alternatives. *Journal of College Student Personnel*, 1974, *15*, 163-167.

Wrenn, C. G. *Student personnel work in college*. New York, Ronald Press, 1951.

ACKNOWLEDGMENTS

I WOULD like to express my appreciation to Al Hood for his assistance in the initial phases of the book and his continued support throughout.

Special thanks are due to Reta Litton, Ginny Volk, Norma Shatshat, Beverly Tircuit, and Delores Hebert for their typing of the initial drafts and to Bill Binney, Jim Burke, Pat Carretta, Corinne Hamilton, Judy Hendershot, Bob Leahy, Ann Matthews, John Moore, George Wallman, Pete Wirtz, and Jim Wockenfuss for their ideas and the publications and resources which they generously offered.

I am deeply grateful to my parents Ted and Julia Packwood for all they gave and provided to make this book possible and in particular to my mother for her tireless efforts in the preparation of the final draft.

W.T.P.

CONTENTS

Contents

Contents   xxxiii

Contents

Contents

Chapter   Page

Professional Activities 85

Contents

Chapter   *Page*

COLLEGE
STUDENT PERSONNEL
SERVICES

CHAPTER 1

ADMISSIONS

George D. Kuh

HISTORY

ALTHOUGH similar activities were performed by the "major beadle" in the medieval university (Smerling, 1960) and later by the office of the archivist (Lindsay & Holland, 1930), the creation of specific positions for coordination of new student admissions was the direct result of expanding duties of college registrars (Arbuckle, 1953; Brubacher & Rudy, 1968; Fine, 1946; Perry, 1970a). Unlike the evolution of admission requirements, comparatively little is known concerning the function of the admission office prior to the early 1900's because of its haphazard development (Perry, 1970a).

Preformative

College admissions in America began with the founding of Harvard in 1636 (Arbuckle, 1953). During this early, preformative period (Bowles, 1956), admissions was exclusively a faculty province. The purpose of colonial colleges was to train a select group of men for the clergy (Arbuckle, 1953; Brubacher & Rudy, 1968; Fine, 1946), and most institutions' formal admission requirements were limited to a working knowledge of Latin and Greek (Broome, 1903). As a result, the admissions process was simple, consisting of an oral examination of the applicant's character and background conducted by the president or senior tutor during the spring term prior to enrollment (Brubacher & Rudy, 1968; Fine, 1946).

As secondary education expanded in America, the scope of college entrance requirements broadened to include arithmetic, added by Yale in 1745, and geography (Bowles, 1956; Fine, 1946). Academies, because of their curricula which provided a

3

balance between the classics and newer subjects such as science, soon replaced grammar schools as the primary source of college applicants (Bowles, 1956). By 1870, English grammar, ancient history, geometry, and physical geography were common college entrance requirements (Brubacher & Rudy, 1968; Fine, 1946), and the first admissions officer (Haley, 1960) and possibly as many as five registrars were appointed (Perry, 1970a).

Civil War to World War II

The technological revolution, considered a cause of the Civil War (Bowles, 1956), permanently altered the structure of the American educational system. A new form of secondary education emerged, the public high school (Bowles, 1956), and modern languages such as French and German were added to admissions requirements and became characteristic of the transition to modern public education. The participation of farmers and technicians in higher education was encouraged by the Morrill Act of 1862, resulting in colleges being more receptive to less traditional curricula. Knowledge of factual material soon became an important admission requirement and each college developed its own entrance examination. Concurrently, the use of high school transcripts became widely accepted and was acccompanied by a rapid rise in the number of registrars (McGrath, 1936).

As a result of numerous debates between various groups of colleges, entrance requirements achieved greater standardization in the Twentieth Century (Bowles, 1956) though few colleges actually adhered to them in selecting students (Brubacher & Rudy, 1968). In the East, the College Entrance Examination Board (CEEB) designed the *Scholastic Aptitude Test (SAT)* to estimate candidate potential and aptitude (Bowles, 1956; Brubacher & Rudy, 1968; G. A. Cramer, 1970).

In the Midwest and West, increasing uniformity among public schools and adoption of the Carnegie Unit as a quantifying measure of secondary school coursework resulted in another form of standardization (Brubacher & Rudy, 1968; Jencks & Riesman, 1968). Higher education became involved in an "accrediting procedure whereby the university examined high schools and decided upon their fitness to prepare students for admission" (Bowles, 1956, p. 30).

The increasing complexity of public high school offerings and the continuing diversification of college programs required further specialization of the registrar function and the appointment of admissions directors. Many other student service areas were also created during this time, a phenomenon often described as the "personnel movement" (Brubacher & Rudy, 1968).

Up until the turn of the century, colleges had been content to draw their students from a relatively narrow geographical region. In the late 1920's, however, leading eastern universities began to recruit nationally. Their success not only enabled them to become more selective in choosing among candidates but also upset the fine balance between applicant supply and demand (G. A. Cramer, 1970). The paradoxical increase in eastern selectivity during the Depression combined with the need of institutions elsewhere to enroll enough students to fill dormitories resulted in a growing number of admissions officers appointed for recruitment purposes (Thresher, 1966).

The Present

The conclusion of World War II and the G. I. Bill of Rights had a tremendous impact on higher education. Because of a profound miscalculation in the projected number of veterans who would enroll in post-secondary education, unprepared colleges were inundated with students (Bowles, 1956).

Although entrance requirements became fairly uniform in the 1950's, they were also flexible, "making it possible for any high school graduate to apply to any college" (Bowles, 1956, p. 33). As enrollments in nearly every college increased, admissions officers found themselves elevated to positions of importance in college administrative hierarchies (Sanders, 1973). The search for talented high school students gained momentum on a national level (Thresher, 1966), and the literature describing the complexities of college admission became voluminous

(Sanders, 1973).

As the postwar baby boom produced ample applicant pools, admissions officers became more than recruiters and recorders, with time to devote to such things as the interaction of student and environmental press (Astin, 1965; Pace & Stern, 1958). The *American College Testing Program (ACT)* became a popular entrance examination alternative, especially among public institutions in the Midwest. Recruiting efforts remained important, however, particularly those directed toward disadvantaged minority youth during the 1960's (Kurland, 1967).

While the Vietnam conflict tended to inflate enrollments into 1970, afterwards the impact of many college-age youth selecting alternatives other than college, a slowed economy, and the community college explosion were felt by many four-year college admissions offices. As a result, recruitment again became the major theme. Specialization among admissions 'staff was common as different individuals coordinated freshman, transfer, veteran, and disadvantaged student admissions. As many smaller institutions struggled to remain open, admissions equalled or surpassed most other collegiate functions in importance. Larger state-supported universities, previously reluctant to participate in most recruiting activities, reconsidered the manner in which the institution's image was presented by the admissions office.

DEFINITION

College admissions includes those policies and procedures which provide for students' transition from secondary to postsecondary education. All admissions policies are based on the inherent belief that the educational experience offered by the institution will benefit certain individuals (Thresher, 1970). Faculty determined admissions policies and academic qualifications (G. A. Cramer, 1970; Kastner, 1962; Thresher, 1970), considered an institution's most important expression of educational philosophy (Linton, 1967), are translated into action by the admissions office (Shaffer & Martinson, 1966).

Purpose

The purpose of admissions is to serve as the major conduit between a college and the society that generates or sustains it (Thresher, 1970). Admissions personnel are responsible for communicating the public benefits of higher education, such as an enlightened electorate and democratic ideals, as well as the private benefits, such as intellectual gains, increased earning power, and development of individual abilities (Brubacher & Rudy, 1968). As the initial contact between an institution and its clientele, the admissions office must impart a proper image to the institution's many constituencies (Dunn, 1967; Garland & Wilson, 1970). The need for clear and effective communication also generalizes to admissions publications, such as catalogues, brochures, and written correspondence (Canterbury, 1975).

As a result, the admissions office is an internal liaison with faculty, student, and alumni groups as well as external liaison with prospective students, parents, and high school counselors. As an internal liaison, the admissions office must interpret secondary schools and community and junior colleges to faculty and administrators so that order and continuity in institutional programs are maintained (E. S. Wilson, 1970a). As an external liaison, the admissions office must articulate curricular innovations and institutional policies and practices to the feeder institutions (see Yanitelli, 1975).

Recruitment of students has always been considered a legitimate admissions function (G. A. Cramer, 1970; Shaffer & Martinson, 1966) and has been emphasized during various periods: during the Depression; in the early 1950's to fill private college residence halls and to search for talented youth; in the 1960's to increase minority representation (Snyder, 1954; Thresher, 1966); in the 1970's to attract students able to afford the spiraling cost of private education. While humanitarian concerns are often served in the process, the fact remains that fiscal stability is dependent on student enrollment (Barton, 1973; Johnson, 1969, 1973). Admissions offices are the first of the college constituencies to feel the effect of a disintegrating economy, war, population shifts, and birth rate fluctuations (Mueller, 1961).

To a large extent effective recruiting is dependent upon the educational goals to be served as well as the supply and demand of prospective students (see Finn, 1973). Definitions of recruiting range from elaborations of educational philosophy to highly sophisticated marketing techniques. Characterizing the former are Trent's (1966) suggestions that recruitment should be reviewed and treated as a developing process of education, not merely a screening process; should consider an individual's needs and personality; and should result in a new student profile, a mix of students with various ability levels and interests.

Marketing is that business activity which directs the flow of goods and services from producer to consumer. Those who urge inclusion of principles of marketing in recruitment and admissions (Barton, 1973; Johnson, 1973; Wolf, 1973) suggest that (a) institutional plans be adjusted for emerging trends, such as offering more vocational programs; (b) admissions policies and practices be oriented toward the needs of applicants, such as reducing the length of applications for adult students; and (c) the mission of the institution be matched to the segment of the market to which the institution appeals (Wolf, 1973; see also Barton, 1974; Meeth, 1970).

In communication and recruitment, one important variable which can have a dramatic impact on an institution is applicant quality (Millett, 1962; Mueller, 1961). Perry (1970a) contends that the quality of students determines in large measure the reputation of the institution. Others believe the reputation of the institution or the saliency of its image determines applicant quality (Clark, 1960; Snyder, 1954). While the latter may be the most credible explanation, the issue is moot as the influence of an admissions office on institutional policy is often less than that of state and federal statutes (Hooten, 1971).

Legal Basis

Each state is responsible for its educational programs. For the most part, legislatures and courts have been reluctant to interfere with admissions practices provided they are commensurate with the stated goals and purposes of the institution. While admission cannot be prohibited or denied because of race or creed (Lowry, 1970), sex discrimination is permissible if it is provided for in the institution's charter and is integral to the institution's educational philosophy (Horle & Thompson, 1968). Except for a rash of racial segregation cases during the 1950's (Jacobson, 1963), judicial intervention has been limited. However, Title IX of the Education Amendments of 1972 may increase the number of civil court tests concerning college admission policies.

Generally, public institutions must conform to state statutes in selecting students. Some states require every applicant be admitted (Bakken, 1968) while others permit each institution to determine its own standards (Horle & Thompson, 1968; Lowry, 1970). The courts' refusal to adjudicate private college admissions matters has furthered the sectarian goals of private education (Bakken, 1968; Beaney, 1969; Jacobson, 1963) and has virtually assured them of complete autonomy in selecting students (Bakken, 1968; Dunham, 1965; Portman, 1971).

Authority

The authority to determine admissions policy is derived from the governing board of an institution. Governing bodies of state-supported institutions are usually a facsimile of a state board of control and, in the private sector, a board of trustees (Bakken, 1968). In some cases, governing boards determine specific admissions criteria; generally, however, the board delegates its authority to faculty (Perry, 1970a).

Most institutions have an admissions committee comprised of faculty, student personnel professionals, students, and others to determine specific admissions criteria (Shaffer & Martinson, 1966). Although various campus constituencies have input, faculty influence is usually most pervasive (Meder, 1954; Perry, 1970a). As a result, a spirit of colleagueship must exist between faculty and admissions personnel in order to function as "partners in the enterprise not utensils" (Linton, 1967, p. 27).

ADMINISTRATION

Admissions offices rarely report directly to faculty or governing boards. Perry (1964) found that 50 percent of admissions directors reported directly to the president, with the remainder reporting to the provost, academic vice-president, academic dean, and vice-president for student affairs. In another survey, half of eighty-six admissions directors were part of the academic administration, while 25 percent reported to student affairs officials (Gibson & Thomas, 1971).

Admissions Policies

Although admissions policies vary from college to college, they can be grouped into three major categories: open, selective, and competitive (Bowles, 1954).

Open Admissions

Rationale and support for open admissions has roots in the Morrill Act of 1862 which provided accessibility to higher education for lower socioeconomic groups (Carnegie Commission, 1970). The Second Morrill Act theoretically extended this opportunity to racial minorities through its separate but equal provision (Jaffe & Adams, 1972). Today, open admissions promises to include those who have been frozen out of postsecondary education due to lack of money or previous academic achievement (Smith, 1972).

Open admissions frequently connotes "the absence of any standards of academic performance in ... determining the admissibility of a prospective student" (Munday & Rever, 1971, p. 90). Most open admissions policies, however, do include some minimum requirements, usually a high school diploma or its equivalent. Nevertheless, the egalitarian promise implicit in the open admissions philosophy threatens proponents of the meritocratic system of higher education. Those who support meritocracy argue that: talent should seek its own level

(Tonsor, 1971); only those who qualify and are able to benefit should attend college (Babcock, 1971); open admissions is incompatible with quality education (Agnew, 1970; Tonsor, 1971); motivation is lacking among lower class youth likely to be admitted by an open admissions policy; huge expenditures of resources are necessary for remedial and tutorial assistance (Chalmers, 1972; Munday & Rever, 1971; Nisbet, 1972); and the diversity of American higher education will be reduced.

Those who reject elitism in higher education emphasize the incompatibility of selection within democracy (Carnegie Commission, 1970; Healy, 1971) because it: perpetuates existing differences between rich and poor (Astin, 1971; Karabel, 1972); evidences more concern for insuring wealthy and distinguished alumni than with education itself (Astin, 1971); and serves as a talent scout for business and industry (Karabel, 1972). Egalitarian proponents contend that if institutions really educate and support open admissions students, academic and graduation standards need not be lowered (Karabel, 1972).

Three models of open admissions presently exist: Midwestern, California, and CUNY. Several large midwestern state universities, such as Ohio State University, admit any high school graduate in the state. Because remedial programs are typically not provided, attrition tends to be high — sometimes as great as 50 percent of the freshman class — and the open door becomes a revolving door.

The California Master Plan (Master Plan Survey Team, 1960) is a differential access model, as high school graduates in the top fifth of their class have access to state universities, those in the top third may attend state colleges, and all others with diplomas may enter community colleges (Jaffe & Adams, 1972).

City University of New York (CUNY) considers both class rank and applicant college preference and is also a differential access model (Strauss, 1971). Almost 80 percent of the 35,000 freshmen enrolled under the open admissions policy entered the college of their first choice (Jaffe & Adams, 1972; Strauss, 1971). CUNY differs from the other two models, however, in that it has provided remedial and other support services for its students (City University of New York, 1969; Jaffe & Adams, 1972; Rosner, 1970; Strauss, 1971; University Commission on Admissions, 1969; Zeller, 1972). A program of such magnitude is not without problems (Kaplan, 1972; Libo & Stewart, 1973), but the fear that it would reduce the quality of CUNY education has not been determined (Hyman, 1972; Kaplan, 1972).

While 27 percent of four-year colleges and 18 percent of universities claim to practice some form of open admissions (Creager, 1973), nearly all two-year community colleges have adopted an open admissions philosophy (Creager, 1973; Huther, 1971). Actually, the growth of the community college and acceptance of the concept of open admissions are nearly synonymous. In reality, however, admission to specific programs within two-year colleges is often selective (Blocker, Plummer, & Richardson, 1965; Gleazer, 1968).

Selective Admissions

These policies work to prohibit those who cannot perform at a satisfactory academic level from entering a particular institution or a program within an institution (Bowles, 1954). Such policies require that the criteria used in choosing applicants as well as the objectives for doing so be defined. Suggested objectives include: to help the student discover the right college, to help the college attract the best students, and to assure a place in higher education for those who show promise of significant societal contribution (Thresher, 1968).

Selective institutions frequently use minimum loss strategies, which provide accept-reject cut-off points (Bogue, 1968) coupled with prediction formulas (Hall & Coates, 1973; Hills & Klock, 1965) to reduce the probability of accepting students who will not succeed academically. At best, however, such institutions can account for only about 40 percent of the variance in college grades. Actually, it appears that accuracy of prediction may be more closely related to the proportion of students accepted by the institution than individual applicant characteristics. For example, a college which accepts nearly all of its applicants based on predictor variables can have almost as effective a selection procedure if candidates were chosen at random from its applicant pool. A college which accepts about half of its applicants using the same variables will tend to make a lower proportion of correct admissions decisions but a higher proportion of correct rejections (Whitney & Boyd, 1971).

Even more frustrating is the realization that, in spite of all these efforts, some of the most highly qualified students are forced to leave the most selective colleges because of academic failure (Gordon, Lane, & Mendenhall, 1970). Apparently, selectivity may not result in colleges choosing the most appropriate students. In any event, the more selective colleges continue to attract the best students (Fincher, 1968). College grade point average has been found to be a very poor indicator of a student's later contribution to society (Gable, 1972; Fincher, 1968; Hoyt, 1966). The utility of prediction is therefore appreciably diminished if the criterion considered predictive of later success fails to do so. Apparently, selectivity has little societal value (Astin, 1969a; Thresher, 1968, 1970).

The most vocal proponents of selectivity are college faculty (Brubacher & Rudy, 1968; Jencks & Riesman, 1968). They are likely to support criteria which select students similar to themselves in background and ability. This phenomenon coupled with increasing selectivity could decrease diversity among the college student population (Whitney & Boyd, 1971), though some have disputed this theory (Hills, Gladny, & Klock, 1967).

Competitive Admissions

Unlike open admissions in which virtually everyone qualifies or selective admissions which screens out those least qualified, competitive admissions picks candidates from an applicant pool in which almost all are highly qualified (Bowles, 1954). The rationale for this policy stems from two of the "frozen assumptions" in college admissions: because selection is inherently good, more selection is better; and recruit as many good students as possible (Thresher, 1968). Many large state universities were at one time as competitive as the more prestigious eastern private schools. However, as the demand for higher education increased, state institutions became fearful of legislative censure and refrained from raising admissions standards to any great degree. As a result, the private sector of American higher education is generally considered more competitive and presently only thirteen of the 160 most selective institutions are public (Jencks & Riesman, 1968).

Astin (1969a) has renounced what he considers to be the folklore of selectivity by citing the research on students at competitive schools. He reports that able students are more likely to return to college than not; any student, regardless of quality of academic preparation, is less likely to drop out of a competitive college than a less selective one; and the chances of bright students surviving the college are *not* better at a less selective institution.

Several competitive institutions have eliminated some traditional requirements such as entrance examinations (Moll, 1973) while others have employed different, more subjective criteria, such as diversity of applicant interests and unusual backgrounds (Tavris, 1974; Whitla, 1965). Underlying these efforts is a new value in American higher education. Rather than placing a premium on picking winners (Astin, 1969a), admissions personnel are selecting applicants most likely to be favorably influenced by educational programs (Chickering, 1971; R. Nelson, 1966).

Viewed globally, however, the degree of selectivity exercised by a college or university is minor compared to the range of choice available to the prospective college student. As a result, more admissions decisions are made outside an admissions office than in one (Thresher, 1970).

Admissions Procedures

The process by which prospective students gain admission to institutions of higher education has been described as the "great sorting" (Thresher, 1966, p. 3). The procedures which make up this process are operationalized admissions policies. Therefore, the three most commonly used sets of admissions procedures — open door, rolling, and regular — correspond to the open, selective, and competitive admissions policies discussed above.

Open Door

This method, in which virtually all applicants are accepted, can create unusual and demanding problems for an institution (Hoy, 1970a). Faculty appointments, program planning, and budget are all directly related to number of new students, which is difficult to accurately predict when virtually anyone may enroll. Sensitivity to the educational needs of the community or student pool is crucial.

Rolling Admissions

This procedure, favored by most high school counselors (Amsden, 1965; Blai, 1968), advises candidates of admissions decisions (accepted, rejected, waiting list) within two to four weeks after completing an application. Clearly defined admissions criteria are required as selection cannot be based on a comparison of all candidates. A successful rolling admissions system is also dependent on accurate yearly predictions as to the number of candidates who will matriculate.

Regular Admissions

Sometimes described as cut-off/reply date, regular admissions requires applications to be completed by a predetermined date, e.g. February 1st, with the understanding that admissions decisions will be announced on or shortly after another date, e.g. April 15th. Acceptance of an offer of admission must be communicated to the admissions office prior to yet another specified date, e.g. May 1st.

Regular admissions procedures were common to most institutions during the 1960's as colleges preferred to choose the best candidates from their complete applicant pool. The procedures were troublesome for the candidates, however, because notification dates were not uniform from college to college and many students were expected to make a commitment to an institution before learning of their status at others. The CEEB and its member institutions championed adoption of the May 1st Candidate Reply Date which standardized regular admissions procedures (Garland, 1970).

Early Decision

This option is sometimes made available by institutions employing the rolling or regular admissions models. Early decision enables applicants to be appraised of their eligibility prior to a specified fall date, e.g. December 1st. Decisions are based on candidates' high school grades through the eleventh grade which are as predictive as performance through high school graduation (Elton, 1965). A nonrefundable deposit typically accompanies acceptance of an offer of admission and candidates are expected to withdraw applications to other institutions (Garland, 1970; Hoy, 1970a).

A corollary program is the Early Evaluation Procedure introduced by eastern institutions. Because these colleges practice competitive admissions, they adhere to a candidate reply date. However, if a candidate requests Early Evaluation, participating institutions will provide a tentative assessment of chances for admission without a commitment from either institution or applicant (De Fiore, 1973).

Deposits

Many institutions require some sort of financial commitment from the student indicating intent to enroll. The deposit guarantees a place in the incoming class and, upon matriculation, is credited to the student's account. In some institutions, deposits may also reserve on-campus housing. Prior to a predetermined date, deposits may be refundable. In order to reduce confusion and avoid misunderstanding, deposit policies need to be clearly defined and articulated to prospective students and parents (Garland, 1970).

Quotas

Estimating the appropriate number of students to admit each year so that an optimal number matriculate each fall is a difficult assignment. The task was even more challenging during the 1960's when the multiple application phenomenon, students submitting applications to several colleges to ensure an acceptance, was at its zenith (Bean & Centra, 1973).

In order to reduce anxiety about projecting class size, admissions personnel encouraged consideration of a national clearinghouse concept similar to that employed in Great Britain (Crossland, 1965; Hanford, 1965). This approach generated far less support than the single application method (SAM) in which an applicant was able to apply simultaneously to several colleges within a consortium. SAM applications are reviewed by the designated institutions in the order of applicant preference with the first offer of admission precluding consideration by the remaining institutions (Harmon, 1964).

Assuming there are no unusual factors operating, a reduction in the number of multiple applications usually serves to reduce the error estimate in calculating the total number of acceptances needed to reach the quota goal. The optimal number of new students for the coming academic year is usually determined the preceding fall by the president with the counsel of other administrative officials. The director of admissions is responsible for calculating the number of students to be admitted in order to attain the goal.

The standard rule of thumb is to accept twice as many students as desired. A more acceptable approach begins by computing the total number of acceptances during the past year. By dividing the number of deposits that year into the total number of acceptances, the deposit percentage can be calculated. The product of this percentage and the new quota are the number of students which must be accepted to reach the new student goal. After comparing these calculations with those of several preceding years to note trends, the director informs the staff of the new target and initiates discussion as to how the goal can be attained (Garland, 1970).

Application Forms

Each institution designs its own application blank in order to generate pertinent candidate information (Ockerman, 1973). When the completed application is received by the admissions office, it marks the beginning of formal communication between the institution and the candidate (Smiley, 1954). It is unclear as to whether information required by admissions practices enjoys privileged communication status. Unless explicitly stated otherwise, it is possible admissions information may be subpoenaed by the civil courts ("Admissions records," 1969). Although an application may request racial and religious identification, candidates cannot be required to comply nor can the absence of this information influence the admissions decision.

A basic core of information is common to most applications (Hoy, 1970b; Smiley, 1954): identification by name; names of parents or guardians; sex; mailing address; family background, such as number of siblings and parental employment; previous educational experience; and applicant interests. Other information often requested includes candidate marital status, parents' marital status, hobbies, motivation for attending college, other colleges under consideration, religious preference, and need for financial assistance.

Required information from sources other than the candidate includes secondary school records indicating courses, grades, high school rank, and standardized test results, and recommendations from counselors, teachers, principals, and clergy. While the high school transcript is of vital importance to the selection process, personal recommendations are considered to be of questionable value (Byer, Altmeyer, Bell, & Blodget, 1976; J. W. Robinson, 1966). Almost all institutions require an application fee of $15 to $25 to underwrite the cost of application processing. Although application fees can serve to discourage applications from students of low socioeconomic status, fee waivers are often granted (Haines, 1975).

Admissions Interviews

The on-campus interview allows the candidate to ask specific detailed questions of credible information sources and the institution to solicit additional, more subjective information from the candidate (Scott, 1968; E. S. Wilson, 1970b). In order to project a balanced view of the institution, prospective students should be encouraged to meet with faculty (Scott, 1968; E. S. Wilson, 1970b) and current students (Sternberg, 1973).

The value of the interview in evaluating candidates has not been determined. The predominantly subjective evidence which does exist indicates that interviews are favorable to candidates. Yale University, which interviews approximately 25 percent of its applicants, discovered that the acceptance rate for those interviewed is 7 percent higher than for those not interviewed (Sternberg, 1973). While interviews do not represent spent money, they do require a substantial investment of professional staff time. Nevertheless, candidates continue to incorrectly place a disproportionate weight on its outcome and the interview practice persists (Bucci, 1967). Allen's (1968) conclusion best summarizes the usefulness of the interview as an appraisal device: Candidates are sometimes granted admission on the strength of an interview, some in spite of it, but very few are rejected based on it.

Entrance Examinations

Most institutions use the results of either the *SAT* or *ACT* when predicting first year grade point average. The *ACT* is considered to be more curricular or subject oriented while the *SAT* is considered more factor oriented (Weston & Lenning, 1973). The bulk of the recent research indicates that prospective students should not be required to take both *SAT* and *ACT* (Sassenrath & Pugh, 1966). The tests' predictive validities are similar enough so that most institutions can use either one in prediction formulas (Lenning & Maxey, 1973; Passons, 1967; Weston & Lenning, 1973).

Psychiatric Evaluation

Previous psychiatric care is of questionable importance to the accurate prediction of success in college (Farnsworth, 1968; Masterson, 1968). Even so, many admissions personnel desire this information (Noland, 1971). Apart from the questionable ethical and legal implications of such a procedure, two issues seem to be important in reaching appropriate decisions: Does the candidate's therapist recommend admission (Kiernan, 1968)? Does the institution have the appropriate psychological resources to support the individual (Dudley, 1968)? Most institutions accept students with previous psychiatric care but usually reserve the right to determine whether an individual can cope with collegiate stress (Albert, 1971, see Mental Health section).

Prediction

By combining high school rank with the results of an entrance examination, the admissions office can maximize the number of academically successful students and deny admission to those likely to encounter scholastic difficulty and eventually drop out (Whitney & Boyd, 1971). The regression model of prediction is most appropriately used if selectivity is the institutional goal. Other models such as the equal opportunity model described by Cole (1972) seem to be more meaningful and defensible when the social benefits of education are thought to be considerable. No matter which model is chosen, periodic reevaluation of the preferred formula is necessary to protect against misleading predictions (Hills, Bush, & Klock, 1966).

While the high school record is generally accepted as the best single predictor of success in college (Cramer & Stevic, 1971; Ivey, Peterson, & Trebbe, 1966; Lavin, 1965; Weiss, 1970), the multiple correlation method which includes a battery of intellective variables usually provides the most accurate prediction (Lavin, 1965; Weiss, 1970). The average multiple correlation is about +.55 (Fishman, 1962). While this method is the most common approach, more than half the variance in academic performance remains unexplained (Lavin, 1965). Attempts to reduce the amount of variance have met with little to moderate success.

Although slight increases in predictive validity have been found from multiple correlations which have included personality dimension measures, the results are not conclusive (Fishman, 1962; Ivey, Peterson, & Trebbe, 1966). If the goal of prediction is to be maximum utility to the individual, however, nonintellective variables may be particularly useful (Lunneborg & Lunneborg, 1966). The greatest hope for improving prediction may resolve around assignment of different weights to various variables as some differential weighting formulas have produced correlations in excess of +.85 (Weiss, 1970).

One variable which has often been weighted differentially is sex. According to the Walster, Cleary, and Clifford (1970) study males are preferred candidates. Because women typically achieve at higher levels in secondary school (Northley, 1958; Phelps, 1973), many prediction formulas often include a correction for differences in achievement. McBee and Suddick (1974) conclude, however, the use of sex weighted predictive formulas is not only discriminatory but unwarranted as well. After taking into account initial differences, a regression of predicted average on first year actual grades of men and women produced no significant differences (McBee & Suddick, 1974).

Another source of variance in predictive formulas may be due to differences inherent in secondary school grading policies (Aiken, 1964). Shields (1970) hypothesized that predictive validity could be increased if certain secondary school characteristics were considered by the formula. For the most part, researchers have met with frustration in those efforts (Watley & Merwin, 1967). Even if significant correlations were to be found, it is doubtful whether they would be of practical or economic value.

Information Processing

Efficient collection, storage, and analysis of admissions data require a systematic and computerized admissions process.

Computerization is not synonymous with impersonalism; in fact, an efficient, well-conceived information processing system can increase the degree of attention each candidate receives (Hoy, 1970b) by reducing time-consuming paper work and allowing the admissions staff more freedom to individualize decision making (Bingham, 1970; "Impersonal Computers," 1968; Hoge, 1968). The required computing capacity will vary with the size of the institution and the expectations of the system (Hoy, 1970b). Although packaged programs are available, specific needs are best met by developing individual institutional programs (Chalmers & Carroll, 1972).

Although the compilation and reproduction of admissions data is of value to other student services such as the registrar and housing ("Computer Program," 1971), the most important computer service may be periodic admissions reports. The activities of both admissions office and applicant are recorded and reproduced weekly (Hoge, 1968; Shutt, 1967). An accurate summary of the number of applications, acceptances, and deposits by geographical area enable the admissions officer to continually evaluate the admissions program.

Information processing has influenced college admissions on a national level in the form of computer matching. Students desirous of computer selection complete a detailed questionnaire concerning their special needs and interests. Participating institutions also provide information to the computer service. The computer matches the students' expressed interests with institutional characteristics and provides a list of compatible colleges to each student. Although the value of this approach to college selection has not been evaluated, the accuracy of information provided by both student and institution is a potential problem (Walton & Mathis, 1967).

Budget

The director of admissions is charged with developing a budget which will enable the office to efficiently and effectively serve the institution. Admissions budgets usually comprise about 2.5 percent of the total institutional budget with a slightly lower ratio in public institutions. Approximately 40 percent of the budget is for professional salaries, 23 percent for support personnel salaries (secretarial, student help), 17 percent for printing, 10 percent for travel, 5 percent for campus visits, 2 percent for office supplies, and 3 percent for other expenses (Chenowith, 1969). Perry (1970b) has offered a detailed orientation to admissions costs and budgeting practices.

Admission of Special Student Groups

High School Students

Early admission differs from the concept of early decision discussed earlier in that students enroll in college prior to high school graduation, usually after completing the eleventh grade. The popularity of this practice was widespread during the early and mid-1960's, declined somewhat during the late 1960's (Hoy, 1970a), and increased once again in the early 1970's (Babbott, 1973). Although early admission students comprise less than 3 percent of the college population, 79 percent of the 378 institutions surveyed (Babbott, 1973) had provisions for admitting students at the end of the eleventh grade. Two thirds of the responding institutions employ higher standards when considering early admission applicants. Selective colleges are more likely to have a higher proportion of early admission students and are likely to use more liberal admissions criteria (Babbott, 1973).

Few institutions conscientiously follow-up early admissions students (Babbott, 1973). However, the few studies which have assessed their development are favorable though generally inconclusive. The progress of students who begin college prior to the senior year of high school seems to be comparable to that of classmates of equal ability (Babbott, 1973; Ekstrom, 1964; Pressey, 1967). Only a few students consider their early admissions experience to have been a handicap (Pressey, 1967).

Transfer Students

Admissions practices which affect students who transfer from one institution to another usually fall under one of three broad categories: accreditation, evaluation, and articulation (G. C. Wilson, 1970).

Most institutions have been suspect of transfers from nonaccredited schools and usually employ more stringent academic requirements (Adelphi University, 1967). This practice was most common during the rapid growth of the community college (Priest, 1966).

The collegiate function responsible for evaluating transfer credit seems to be dependent upon the size of the school and the number of annual transfers. In larger institutions which commonly receive in excess of 400 transfers per year, the admissions office assumes the transfer responsibility. Institutions which receive less than 200 transfers per year often delegate evaluation of credit to the registrar. According to L. M. Thomas (1971), transfer credit should be evaluated by an admissions officer with the appropriate experience and training.

Although a few have higher standards, most schools require transfers to have a *C* average (Knoell & Medsker, 1965; Winandy & McGrath, 1970). The establishment of a minimum grade average and thorough consideration of a variety of individual factors seems to be an acceptable practice (Hoy, 1970c). Apparently, previous college grade point average is the single best indicator of transfers' scholastic success (Burke, 1973; Gleazer, 1968; Wray & Leischuck, 1971). Also widely documented is the phenomenon of transfer shock. Students are likely to experience a .5 drop in grade point average after transferring from a two-year to a four-year institution (Hills, 1965; Knoell & Medsker, 1965; Young, 1964). Recovery to the prior achievement level, however, is just as likely as is the shock itself (Hills, 1965).

Articulation, the sharing of information with students and agencies or institutions to insure that students transfer from one level to another with a minimum of confusion (O'Banion, 1971), is at once a process and an attitude (Gleazer, 1968). For the most part, institutional policies and procedures have been marked by disparity (Winandy & McGrath, 1970). The rapid development of the two-year community college underscored the need for clear channels of communication between institutions (Gleazer, 1968; Hoy, 1970c; Meskill, 1971). Four-year institutions have typically been reluctant to state formal transfer policies. Indeed, in 1970, half could not offer an institutional definition of transfer students (Winandy & McGrath, 1970). Because almost 25 percent of the transfer population are reverse transfers (students who transfer from four- to two-year schools), clearly articulating institutional policies seems to be important to all segments of higher education. Menacker (1975) and J. H. Nelson (1966) consider these issues and offer explicit guidelines for developing articulation procedures.

Minority Students

Even though the number of minority students enrolled in colleges and universities has increased appreciably (Crossland, 1971; Sedlacek, Brooks, & Mindus, 1972; Sedlacek, Lewis, & Brooks, 1973) a gross underrepresentation still exists in relation to the proportion of minorities in the population. Among the numerous barriers to higher education (testing, poor preparation, lack of financial resources, racial discrimination), traditional admissions requirements may be the most formidable (Astin, 1969b, Crossland, 1971).

The dramatic increase in the number of minority students was accomplished through adoption of more flexible admissions requirements. Once admitted, however, minority students were expected to perform like the typical college student (Astin, 1969b). It soon became evident that special programs were needed to introduce and acclimate the minority student and higher education to each other. As a result, a number of programs designed to assist minority students flourished during the late 1960's (Crossland, 1971). Although most institutions continue to actively recruit minorities, the number of special programs has decreased, particularly at private institutions (Sedlacek, Lewis, & Brooks, 1973).

The question of whether college entrance tests are valid predictors for minority applicants escapes resolution. Some studies suggest the *ACT* and *SAT* are biased against minorities (Borup, 1971; Clark & Plotkin, 1963) while others indicate such tests have comparable predictive validity for both minority and white students (Cleary, 1968; Pfeifer & Sedlacek, 1971; Temp, 1971). Others expect minority achievement to be overpredicted (they will be predicted to perform better than they actually do) if predictions are based on the typical college student's experience (Kallingal, 1971; Pfeifer & Sedlacek, 1971). Still others encourage development of separate systems of prediction for the various subgroups of college-bound students (Bowers, 1970; Cramer & Stevic, 1972; Harris & Reitzel, 1967; Temp, 1971). Because it is difficult to generalize from these results, admissions officers must determine the validity of minority entrance requirements for their respective institutions as well as exercise care in establishing predictive differences among subpopulations of various groups of college-bound students (Davis & Temp, 1971).

Adult Students

In a study designed to determine admissions procedures for adult students, 75 percent of forty-four institutions used the same criteria to evaluate both adults and high school applicants. Less than half considered nonscholastic, practical experiences in their predictions, and not one college employed a specialist to coordinate adult admissions. Admissions practices seem geared primarily for applicants of typical college-going age (18 to 21) and experiences (Waters, 1971). For most persons over twenty-five, traditional admissions criteria may be misleading as high school rank and references are usually outdated. Because entrance examinations such as the *ACT* and *SAT* are not constructed to evaluate the nontraditional characteristics of adult learners (Allyn, 1969; Brandenberg, 1974), it is likely other criteria may serve as more appropriate bases for evaluation.

The *College Level Examination Program (CLEP)* is among the most popular nontraditional admissions criteria used in determining adult admission (Arbolino, 1968; Waters, 1971). The *CLEP* is comprised of two separate tests: the General Exam which assesses general or liberal arts preparation comparable to two years of undergraduate education in English, composition, mathematics, social sciences, natural sciences, history, and humanities; and Subject Exams which are more closely related to specific disciplines (Allyn, 1969).

Adult students admitted on the basis of *General Educational Development (GED)* test results have exhibited similar rates of attrition and levels of achievement when compared with traditional students (Sharon, 1972). Other measures such as the *Adult College Aptitude Test* may be more appropriate for evaluating adult learners. However, until admissions officers support such exploratory evaluation efforts, discriminatory practices in adult admissions will continue (Brandenberg, 1974; Waters, 1971).

Foreign Students

Applicants from foreign countries can be naturalized Americans attending overseas dependent schools or citizens of a country other than the United States. At times, applications from naturalized Americans being educated abroad are mistaken for those of foreign students. As a result, these students may be required to take the *Test of English as a Foreign Language (TOEFL)* rather than the appropriate entrance exam required of U. S. nationals (Sweeney, 1967). In addition, some institutions committed to a foreign student quota have rejected American citizens erroneously classified as foreign students. Because many overseas dependent schools are not approved by U. S. accreditation associations, a student's chances for admission may be reduced (Phillips, 1972). Cardinale (1971) offers a number of suggestions designed to ameliorate the admissions problems of American dependents schooled overseas.

The complexity of foreign student admissions is related to the increase in the number of foreign students enrolled in American higher education. In 1945 only 7,000 attended postsecondary institutions in this country (Dremuk, 1966). Over

144,000 foreign students are now enrolled (R. E. Thomas, 1974). In order to reduce confusion and standardize the process, the Institute of International Education developed the Applicant Information Service (AIS) to compile up-to-date information from participating colleges and coordinate applicant interviews in their home country (Strain, 1965). Other sources of general foreign student admission information include a handbook (Institute of International Education, 1973), the Cultural Affairs Office of the U. S. Embassy in a particular country (R. E. Thomas, 1974), and the educational officer of the country's embassy located in Washington, D. C. (Kelson, 1973).

Foreign admissions policies are now fairly uniform (Sweeney, 1967). Most institutions have established an overall admissions policy which enjoys administrative support (National Association of Foreign Student Affairs, 1966; Sweeney, 1967). The centralized foreign student admissions operation coordinated by a foreign admissions specialist or foreign student advisor strongly advocated by the National Association of Foreign Student Affairs or NAFSA (1966) has become a reality. In some settings, the number of applications from foreign students has necessitated creation of a separate foreign student admissions committee (Sweeney, 1967).

Increased application fees and overseas mailing charges have prompted foreign student admissions specialists to use a preliminary application. If an applicant appears promising based on preliminary information, completion of a more extensive application including test scores and transcripts is encouraged by the admissions office (NAFSA, 1966; Sweeney, 1967). NAFSA (1966) has proposed a model for foreign admissions procedures.

While the verbal score of the *SAT* is generally considered to be more predictive for American college students than the mathematics score, the converse seems to be true for foreign students (Howell, 1968; Kelson, 1973). Because of language differences, the predictive validity of the verbal portion is decreased, thereby increasing the importance of the mathematics score. As a result, the *TOEFL* is often substituted for the verbal portions of college entrance exams (Kelson, 1973; Sweeney, 1967).

Graduate Students

Graduate and professional school admission practices differ appreciably from the typical undergraduate college admission process. While graduate college admission is usually coordinated by the office of admissions, individual graduate and professional programs assume the major role in decision making (Harvey, 1971). Less than 15 percent of admissions officers report having a voice in graduate admission decisions (Burns, 1970). Administrative details such as record collection and enforcing deadlines were usually performed by either a dean's office (Harvey, 1971) or the central admissions office. Recruitment of prospective students is low key at best and nonexistent at worst.

Because individual departments determine admission standards, it is difficult to assess specific requirements. However, most graduate programs do state minimum requirements which must be satisfied before an applicant is considered (Burns, 1970; Harvey, 1971). An application, transcript of all previous undergraduate and graduate work, letters of recommendation, and some graduate admission test scores (40% of graduate institutions require the *Graduate Record Examination — GRE*) are usually required. The undergraduate record seems to receive the greatest weight in determining admission. Although these criteria are commonly used, their predictive validity remains obscure primarily because most graduate school and individual graduate programs do not keep accurate records concerning their enrollment.

PROGRAMS

Even though a growing proportion of college-bound students manifest nontraditional characteristics, the typical college-bound student (17 to 18 years of age, coming directly from high school) constitutes the largest single source of new students each year. The two most popular methods used by admissions officers for meeting with prospective college students are described below.

College Day/Night Programs

These programs are designed to complement the secondary school guidance program by distributing information from a number of different colleges with a minimal amount of disruption (Perry, 1967; Wagner, 1972). Although Hull (1973) encourages ninth graders to participate, commitment to the concept of planning for college does not seem to crystallize until the junior or senior year (Cramer & Stevic, 1969; Seron, 1967). The typical College Day or Night format includes 30 to 45 minute sessions during which the admissions officer briefly describes general institutional offerings and entertains specific questions from students and parents. Often the College Day begins with a general orientation period and ends with an informal coffee hour (Wagner, 1972).

Some College Day programs have been modified in an effort to minimize the emphasis on recruitment (Perry, 1967; Wagner, 1972) and maximize precollege guidance. One method invites representatives from different types of colleges to participate in panel discussions concerning the various aspects of college selection, such as admissions requirements, financial aid, and housing. Others have invited representatives to participate in small group discussions with students not necessarily considering their particular institutions (Wagner, 1972). The Dade County Public Schools (1971) in Florida integrated college planning into the curriculum by introducing a course designed to gather relevant college information and facilitate the students' self-selection of an appropriate post-secondary educational option. Most college planning programs are supplemented by periodically revised college information books (e.g. Einstein, 1967, 1970; Lovejoy, 1970).

Sporadic efforts to evaluate the effectiveness of the College Day have not produced conclusive results. One survey of participating high schools indicated over 85 percent of students, counselors, and administrators wanted such programs to continue (Cross & Hocker, 1971). Others tend to be less enthusiastic (LaBaugh, 1974; Perry, 1967; Wagner, 1972).

High School Visits

A recruiting practice used by almost all admissions offices is
the high school visitation (Yaw, 1973). Several weeks in advance, the admissions officer requests a specific period of time
to visit with students interested in learning more about the
college. The visit can be publicized in a variety of ways including school announcements, bulletin board displays, and
postcards, and often results in an exchange of information not
only between college and prospective student but also between
college and secondary school (Amsden, 1965). High school
counselors can receive feedback concerning former students as
well as have pertinent college information updated (L. Robinson, 1969).

The increasing demands placed on the secondary school
counselor in the areas of career, vocational, and drug
counseling (Hull, 1973) coupled with an increased emphasis on
student recruitment has become burdensome for some guidance
staffs. Requests for a reduction in the number of high school
visits have become common (Lindahl, 1973; Logan, 1966). An
alternative method of improving school-college relations is the
college visitation or counselor reception. High school counselors are transported to the college and offered a tour of the
campus as well as an opportunity to visit with students and
receive answers to questions about campus life (S. Cramer,
1966; Garland & Wilson, 1970; Savides, 1967).

Whether recruitment activities such as high school visits result in new students is not certain. In fact, Yaw (1973) discovered negative relationships between many admissions
activities and two quantitative objectives of the admissions office: the number of individual applications received and the
number of new students enrolled. Because these activities are
costly in terms of financial and human resources (LaBaugh,
1974), the small amount of evidence in this area is surprising
(Peterson, 1968).

College Choice

Basic to all admissions programs is the assumption that they will favorably influence the prospective student's choice of a college. Although general spheres of influence have been isolated, perhaps the most accurate summarization of the college selection process is that it is done in a haphazard manner (Kurland, 1967). Some have attempted to bring order to the process (Hammond, 1965; Hills, 1964) but no evidence exists to suggest they have been successful.

Richards and Holland (1965) have factor analyzed student explanations of college choice and their conclusions seem to be supported by other research (Bowers & Pugh, 1973; Morrison, 1968; Stordahl, 1970; Thompson, 1965). Choice of college seems to be affected by four categories of influence: (a) Intellectual — consideration of scholastic standards and faculty reputation; (b) Practicality — desirable location, reasonable cost, distance from home; (c) Advice of Others — parents, alumni, counselor, peers; and (d) Social Emphasis — social atmosphere, athletics, coeducation, fraternity/sorority (Richards & Holland, 1965).

Although few agree as to the single most important influence, geographical propinquity must be one of the more important determinants (Berdie, 1954; Douvan & Kaye, 1962) as over 80 percent of college-going students remain in their home state (Thresher, 1968, 1970). Others suspect prestige (Holland, 1958) and the interaction of the social and practicality factors (Stordahl, 1970) as being most influential. If this question is to be decided based on the bulk of evidence, advice of others may be the most pervasive influence (Bentley & Salter, 1967; Kerr, 1962; Kuh, Redding, & Lesar, 1972; Kurland, 1967; Stahmann, Hanson, & Whittlesey, 1971). K. Wilson (1971) estimates two thirds of college students first learned about their institution through parents, counselors, peers, teachers, or relatives.

Parents are often considered extremely influential (Kuh et al., 1972), especially parents of low socioeconomic status (Douvan & Kaye, 1962). As parental income increases, however, students are more likely to be influenced by intellectual considerations

(Mickelson, 1967). Parents may also be influential in decisions not to attend a particular college (Anderson, Mathieu, & Krueger, 1973). Admissions officers are not considered especially influential (Anderson et al., 1973; Peterson, 1968; K. Wilson, 1971) although continued contact with the admissions office may be related to stability of choice over time (Ruch, 1967).

The source of the most accurate information eludes consensus. Some have suggested high school counselors provide the most valuable assistance (Fredrickson & Fonda, 1971; Kerr, 1962, 1963) while Stahmann et al. (1971) contend college students are the most accurate sources of information. The admissions officer's role is also unclear: One study reported admissions personnel were the most accurate information source (Kuh et al., 1972); another concluded they were the poorest source (Carine, 1974).

Certainly the potential exists for admissions officers to become more accurate sources of college information. Becoming cognizant of the factors which exert influence on various groups of college-bound students and clearly communicating specific institutional characteristics to the appropriate audiences are two steps toward this end (Day, 1976). Generally, parents are interested in financial considerations, geographical location including transportation, and academic concerns. Students, on the other hand, place greater weight on informal advice concerning social and cultural factors (Bowers & Pugh, 1973). Because students are also greatly influenced by others, a special effort should be made to include parents and significant others in college planning discussions (Miller, 1976). Currently enrolled students may be in the best position to provide social and cultural information to prospective students and should be utilized not only as campus tour guides (K. Wilson, 1971) but as home town liaisons during vacations as well (Simmons, 1969).

PERSONNEL

Males are overrepresented as admissions directors in public

institutions as well as among all universities (95%) and colleges (79%). The median age for male directors is forty-three and for females, fifty. Median length of service is five years. A greater proportion of directors in public institutions majored in education while private college directors were more likely to have been humanities majors. About 60 percent attended the institution which they represent (King, 1969).

According to Perry (1964), most directors perceived their present level of preparation as inadequate for the responsibilities of the position. About 15 percent hold either the Ph.D. or Ed.D., 53 percent the M.A., and 27 percent the B.A. Doctorates are more likely among public institutions. About half hold faculty rank (Hauser & Lazarfield, 1964; King, 1969; Perry, 1964) while a much smaller proportion have both rank and tenure (Bucci, 1971; King, 1969). Only 14 percent teach in addition to their admissions responsibilities (Bucci, 1971).

Tasks

The duties of admissions personnel are many and varied. After reviewing the literature, Fletcher (1962) offered this list of admissions tasks: public relations, human relations, recruitment and selection of students, service agent, high school-college relations, precollege guidance, evaluation of transcripts, preparation of promotional materials, appraisal, research, policy formation, office management, budget, correspondence, public speaking, and alumni relations. Since this list was compiled, familiarity with data processing systems has also become advantageous (Hooten, 1971). Some tasks are more appropriate for the director, such as budget and office management. Others, such as recruitment and precollege guidance, are more directly the responsibility of staff members (Hauser & Lazarfield, 1964).

Personal Characteristics and Training

Personal qualities such as friendliness, poise, and educational beliefs seem to take precedence over previous training in psychology or education when selecting admissions personnel

(Fletcher, 1962; Hauser & Lazarfield, 1964; Perry, 1970a). However, in order to acquire the credibility and experience necessary to participate in policy determination and enjoy colleagueship with faculty (Anderson, 1970; Fletcher, 1962; Linton, 1967; Perry, 1970a), graduate work seems to be a necessity. The following is representative of the training and experience thought to be most relevant by admissions officers: guidance and counseling, group dynamics, personnel management, human relations, psychology, philosophy and history of education, humanities, public relations, curriculum and higher education, and statistics and research design (Hauser & Lazarfield, 1964; Perry, 1964).

Because degree programs in college student personnel administration provide for experiential learning in many of these areas, it seems to be an appropriate area of graduate study (Perry, 1970a). Given the increasing diversity and complexity of the admissions director's responsibilities, coursework through the doctorate has been encouraged (Fletcher, 1962; Perry, 1970a). Although counseling per se is an infrequent activity among admissions officers (Jorgenson, 1967), the term "admissions counselor" is widely used. Formal preparation in student personnel work would do much to dispel the controversy which surrounds this title and increase the credibility of professional staff (Sheffield & Meskill, 1974).

In-service training on an institutional level can provide specific information necessary for the orientation of the aspiring professional (Hohengarten, 1973). Moss (1972) suggests an admissions in-service training program include an overview of: the mission and philosophy of the institution, enrollment projections, organizational sturcture, financial aid resources, ratio of on-campus to travel time, length of recruiting trips, existing recruitment and selection procedures, and seminars with academic department heads.

At the state, regional, and national levels, suitable learning experiences for both the experienced and inexperienced admissions officer are provided through workshops sponsored by the American Association of Collegiate Registrars and Admissions Officers (AACRAO), Association of College Admissions Counselors (ACAC), College Entrance Examination Board (CEEB), American College Testing Program (ACT), American College Personnel Association (ACPA), and American Personnel and Guidance Association (APGA). Since 1959, summer institutes designed to bring the inexperienced admissions officer into contact with the issues and challenges inherent in college admissions have been sponsored by CEEB (Perry, 1970a).

Ethics

The National Association of College Admissions Counselors (NACAC) has adopted a "Statement of Good Practices" (1973) which outlines professional behavior. Although common sense and honesty in college-applicant communication has always been encouraged (Eddy, 1967), proper perspective may become distorted during periods of increased emphasis on recruitment. To recognize potential problems, Woodward (1973) offered this rule of thumb: If the economic survival of the institution becomes more important than the educational guidance of the student, the practice in question is probably unethical.

RELATIONSHIPS TO OTHER SERVICES

The offices of the registrar and admissions have performed similar record collection tasks throughout the history of higher education. Gibson and Thomas (1971) found that over two thirds of the colleges responding combined admissions and records into one office. Sharing the same data bank optimizes storage space by eliminating duplication of information. This arrangement is more common among larger, public institutions (Gibson & Thomas, 1971). Ascertaining from admissions data the number of prospective students contemplating majors in various academic disciplines enables the registrar to anticipate scheduling problems and to assign advisors.

Reciprocal relationships must also be developed between the admissions office and financial aid, housing, and orientation (Arthur, 1975).

REFERENCES

Adelphi University. *Survey of 150 private and public institutions.* Unpublished manuscript, Author, 1967.

Admissions records aren't legally confidential, Maine court rules. *College Board Review,* 1969, *71,* 21.

Agnew, S. T. Toward a "middle way" in college admissions. *Educational Record,* 1970, *51,* 106-111.

Aiken, L. R. Rank in high school graduating classes of various sizes as a predictor of college grades. *Journal of Educational Research,* 1964, *58,* 56-60.

Albert, G. College admission for the emotionally disturbed. *Journal of Contemporary Psychotherapy,* 1971, *4,* 49-52.

Allen, W., Jr. Admissions interviews don't have to be a total loss. *College Board Review,* 1968, *70,* 15-17.

Allyn, N. C. *Evaluating adults for further study.* Paper presented at the National Seminar on Adult Education Research, Toronto, Canada, February, 1969. (ERIC Document Reproduction Service No. ED 026 612)

Amsden, R. Good and bad admissions practices as seen by high schools. *National Association of College Admissions Counselors Journal,* 1965, *11*(1), 3-6.

Anderson, D. L. Innovation is your responsibility, too! *College and University,* 1970, *45,* 177-180.

Anderson, J. F., Mathieu, D. T., & Krueger, A. H. Non-matriculation. *National Association of College Admissions Counselors Journal,* 1973, *18*(3), 16-20.

Arbolino, J. Not the traditional student but almost everyone else. In College Entrance Examination Board (Ed.), *College admissions policies for the 1970's.* New York: Editor, 1968.

Arbuckle, D. S. *Student personnel services in higher education.* New York: McGraw-Hill, 1953.

Arthur, S. Should the admissions office do it alone? *National Association of College Admissions Counselors Journal,* 1975, *20*(1), 30-31.

Astin, A. W. *Who goes where to college?* Chicago: Science Research Associates, 1965.

Astin, A. W. The challenge of open admissions: The folklore of selectivity. *Saturday Review,* December 29, 1969, pp. 57-58, 69-70. (a)

Astin, A. W. *Racial considerations in admissions.* Paper presented at the meeting of the American Council on Education, Washington, D. C., 1969. (b)

Astin, A. W. Open admissions and programs for the disadvantaged. *Journal of Higher Education,* 1971, *42,* 629-647.

Babbott, E. A year early: What 378 colleges say about admitting students right after their junior year of high school. *College Board Review,* 1973, *87,*

7-10; 32-33.

Babcock, R. S. Commentary: Who should attend college? In P. R. Rever (Ed.), *Open admissions and equal access.* Iowa City, Iowa: American College Testing Program, 1971.

Bakken, C. J. *The legal basis for college student personnel work.* Washington, D. C.: American College Personnel Association, 1968. (Student Personnel Monograph Series, No. 2)

Barton, D. W., Jr. If the customers don't buy, the institution will die. *National Association of College Admissions Counselors Journal,* 1973, *17*(3), 9-12.

Barton, D. W., Jr. Taking the scare out of the student scarcity. *National Association of College Admissions Counselors Journal,* 1974, *19*(2), 4-7.

Bean, A. G., & Centra, J. A. Multiple college applications. *Journal of College Student Personnel,* 1973, *14*, 537-543.

Beaney, W. M. Some legal problems of higher education. *National Association of Women Deans and Counselors Journal,* 1969, *32*, 162-169.

Bentley, J. C., & Salter, S. College freshmen view counselor help in college selection. *Personnel and Guidance Journal,* 1967, *46*, 178-183.

Berdie, R. F. *After high school — what?* Minneapolis: University of Minnesota, 1954.

Bingham, R. D. A computerized model to individualize admissions at a large university (Doctoral dissertation, Pennsylvania State University, 1970). *Dissertation Abstracts International,* 1970, *31*, 2676A-2677A. (University Microfilms No. 70-24,144)

Blai, B., Jr. Pressures and practices in college admissions. *College and University,* 1968, *43*, 167-177.

Blocker, C. E., Plummer, R. H., & Richardson, R. C., Jr. *The two year college: A social synthesis.* Englewood Cliffs, N. J.: Prentice-Hall, 1965.

Bogue, E. G. Application of a minimum loss strategy in selection of cutoff points in college and university admissions. *College and University,* 1968, *43*, 131-142.

Borup, J. H. The validity of the American College Test for discerning potential academic achievement levels — ethnic and sex groups. *Journal of Educational Research,* 1971, *65*, 3-6.

Bowers, J. Comparison of GPA regression equations. *Journal of Educational Measurement,* 1970, *7*, 219-225.

Bowers, T. A., & Pugh, R. C. Factors underlying college choice by students and parents. *Journal of College Student Personnel,* 1973, *14*, 220-224.

Bowles, F. H. Admission. In College Entrance Examination Board (Ed.), *College admissions.* Princeton: Editor, 1954.

Bowles, F. H. The evolution of admissions requirements. In College Entrance Examination Board (Ed.), *The interaction of school and college.* Princeton: Editor, 1956.

Brandenberg, J. B. The needs of women returning to school. *Personnel and*

Guidance Journal, 1974, *53,* 11-18.

Broome, E. C. *A historical and critical discussion of college admission requirements.* New York: Macmillan, 1903.

Brubacher, J., & Rudy, W. *Higher education in transition.* New York: Harper, 1968.

Bucci, F. A. Counseling in admissions: A devil's advocate view. *National Association of College Admissions Counselors Journal,* 1967, *12*(4), 12-13.

Bucci, F. A. How important are registrars and admissions officers? *College and University,* 1971, *46,* 191-198.

Burke, B. H. Changing needs in transfer admissions: Build policy from the data. *College and University,* 1973, *48,* 69-79.

Burns, R. Are we far apart? The graduate record examination board study of graduate admissions. *College and University,* 1970, *45,* 686-700.

Byer, J. M., Altmeyer, D., Bell, G. B., & Blodget, D. F. Tell us how. *National Association of College Admissions Counselors Journal,* 1976, *20*(3), 29-33.

Canterbury, R. M. The admissions process. *National Association of College Admissions Counselors Journal,* 1975, *20*(1), 9-16.

Cardinale, A. Getting into American colleges: Difficulties face graduates of overseas dependents schools. *College Board Review,* 1971, *90,* 25.

Carine, E., Jr. How students find out about college. *College Board Review,* 1974, *90,* 25.

Carnegie Commission on Higher Education. *A chance to learn: An action agenda for equal opportunity in higher education.* New York: McGraw-Hill, 1970.

Chalmers, E. L. Open admissions — one century later. In Council for Basic Education (Ed.), *Open admissions: The pros and cons.* Washington, D.C.: Editor, 1972.

Chalmers, J. A., & Carroll, J. T. A flexible student reporting system for registration and admission offices. *College and University,* 1972, *47,* 184-193.

Chenowith, G. A survey of budgetary and management practices among admissions offices in American colleges and universities. *National Association of College Admissions Counselors Journal,* 1969, *14*(1), 2-14.

Chickering, A. W. The best colleges have the least effect. *Saturday Review,* January 16, 1971, pp. 48-50; 54.

City University of New York (Ed.). *Admissions policy of the City University of New York, statement of policy by the Board of Higher Education.* New York: Editor, 1969.

Clark, B. R. College image and student selection. In T. R. McConnell (Ed.), *Selection and educational differentiation.* Berkeley: University of California, 1960.

Clark, K. B., & Plotkin, L. *The Negro student at integrated colleges.* New York: National Scholarship Service and Fund for Negro Students, 1963.

Cleary, T. A. Test bias: Prediction of grades of Negro and white students in integrated colleges. *Journal of Educational Measurement,* 1968, *5,* 115-124.

Cole, N. S. *Bias in selection.* Iowa City, Iowa: American College Testing Program, 1972. (ERIC Document Reproduction Service No. ED 066 117)

Computer program available to aid in admissions. *College Board Review,* 1971, *82,* 25.

Cramer, G. A. Admissions as a profession. *College and University,* 1970, *45,* 273-280.

Cramer, S. A critical look at college visiting. *College Board Review,* 1966, *60,* 15-17.

Cramer, S., & Stevic, R. Research on the transition from school to college. *College Board Review,* 1969, *73,* 22-30.

Cramer, S., & Stevic, R. Research on the transition from school to college. *College Board Review,* 1971, *81,* 32-38.

Cramer, S., & Stevic, R. Research on the transition from high school to college. *College Board Review,* 1972, *85,* 32-37.

Creager, J. A. *Selected policies and practices in higher education.* Washington, D. C.: American Council on Education, 1973.

Cross, W., & Hocker, P. College admissions planning: A professional service for students. *National Association of Women Deans and Counselors Journal,* 1971, *34,* 153-159.

Crossland, F. E. Politics and policies in college admissions. *Phi Delta Kappan,* 1965, *46,* 299-302.

Crossland, F. E. *Minority access to college.* New York: Schocken, 1971.

Dade County Public Schools. *So you want to go to college?* Miami, Fla.: Author, 1971. (ERIC Document Reproduction Service No. ED 070 015)

Davis, J. A., & Temp, G. Is the SAT biased against black students? *College Board Review,* 1971, *81,* 4-9.

Day, R. W. Echoing voices and deaf ears. *National Association of College Admissions Counselors Journal,* 1976, *20*(3), 10-12.

DeFiore, L. The ivy group turns over a new leaf. *College Board Review,* 1973, *88,* 7-8; 23-24.

Douvan, E., & Kaye, C. Motivational factors in college attendance. In N. Sanford (Ed.), *The American college.* New York: Wiley, 1962.

Dremuk, R. Will we be admitting foreign students in 1975? *National Association of College Admissions Counselors Journal,* 1966, *11*(4), 4-8.

Dudley, D. The college applicant who has had psychiatric care. *National Association of College Admissions Counselors Journal,* 1968, *13*(1), 11; 17-18.

Dunham, S. Some legal decisions which have influenced American collegiate admissions. *College and University,* 1965, *41,* 49-60.

Dunn, A. The college admissions office as a public relations function.

National Association of College Admissions Counselors Journal, 1967, *12*(3), 1-3.

Eddy, E. Pretense and honesty in college admissions. *School and Society,* 1967, *95*, 415-417.

Einstein, B. W. *Guide to success in college.* New York: Grosset & Dunlop, 1967.

Einstein, B. W. *College entrance guide.* New York: Grosset & Dunlop, 1970.

Ekstrom, R. B. Early admission to college. *Journal of Educational Research,* 1964, *57*, 408-412.

Elton, C. F. Three year high school average as a predictor of college success. *College and University,* 1965, *40*, 165-167.

Farnsworth, D. The college applicant who has had psychiatric care. *National Association of College Admissions Counselors Journal,* 1968, *13*(1), 10; 12-14.

Fincher, C. Studies in college admission. In E. Schietinger (Ed.), *Introductory papers on institutional research.* Atlanta: Southern Regional Education Board, 1968.

Fine, B. *Admission to American colleges.* New York: Harper, 1946.

Finn, R. Suggested new trends in educational recruiting. *National Association of College Admission Counselors Journal,* 1973, *18*(3), 11-12.

Fishman, J. A. Some socio-psychological theory for selecting and guiding college students. In N. Sanford (Ed.), *The American college.* New York: Wiley, 1962.

Fletcher, W. G. The admissions officer: Educational Solomon or pariah. *College and University,* 1962, *38*, 23-31.

Fredrickson, R., & Fonda, T. College admissions assistance by secondary school counselors. *Personnel and Guidance Journal,* 1971, *49*, 383-389.

Gable, R. K. College admissions procedures: The prediction of success. *National Association of College Admissions Counselors Journal,* 1972, *17*(2), 15-17.

Garland, G. C. Admissions — freshman class quota. In A. Knowles (Ed.), *Handbook of college and university administration — academic.* New York: McGraw-Hill, 1970.

Garland, G. C., & Wilson, E. S. Admissions — public relations. In A. Knowles (Ed.), *Handbook of college and university administration — academic.* New York: McGraw-Hill, 1970.

Gibson, H., & Thomas, J. E. Doing your own thing. *College and University,* 1971, *46*, 139-147.

Gleazer, E. J. Recognizing the expanding role of junior colleges in higher education. In College Entrance Examination Board (Ed.), *College admissions policies for the 1970's.* New York: Editor, 1968.

Gordon, E. W., Lane, H. W., & Mendenhall, T. C. Admissions policy: Implications and consequences. *Liberal Education,* 1970, *56*, 270-291.

Haines, R. W. Student recruitment practices: A survey yields some surprises.

National Association of College Admissions Counselors Journal, 1975, *20*(1), 35-37.

Haley, A. F. An analysis and critique of the full-time director of admissions in American colleges and universities (Doctoral dissertation, Boston University, 1960). *Dissertation abstracts,* 1961, *21,* 3323-3324. (University Microfilms No. 60-6489)

Hall, R. L., & Coates, C. J. Prediction of academic success for special program and regularly admitted college freshmen. *College and University,* 1973, *49,* 14-18.

Hammond, J. S. Bringing order into the selection of a college. *Personnel and Guidance Journal,* 1965, *43,* 654-660.

Hanford, G. A new *RX* for our admissions ills. *College Board Review,* 1965, *57,* 6-8.

Harmon, L. R. College applications: Multiplication versus cooperation. *National Association of Women Deans and Counselors Journal,* 1964, *27,* 71-73.

Harris, J., & Reitzel, J. Negro freshman performance in a predominantly non-Negro university. *Journal of College Student Personnel,* 1967, *8,* 366-368.

Harvey, J. *Graduate school admissions.* Washington: ERIC Clearinghouse on Higher Education, 1971.

Hauser, J., & Lazarfield, P. *The admissions officer.* New York: College Entrance Examination Board, 1964.

Healy, T. S. Commentary: Who should attend college? In P. R. Rever (Ed.), *Open admissions and equal access.* Iowa City, Iowa: American College Testing Program, 1971.

Hills, J. R. Decision theory and college choice. *Personnel and Guidance Journal,* 1964, *43,* 17-22.

Hills, J. R. Transfer shock: The academic performance of the junior college transfer. *Journal of Experimental Education,* 1965, *33,* 201-215.

Hills, J. R., Bush, M., & Klock, J. A. Keeping college prediction equations current. *Journal of Educational Measurement,* 1966, *3,* 33-34.

Hills, J. R., Gladney, M. B., & Klock, J. A. Nine critical questions about selective college admissions. *Personnel and Guidance Journal,* 1967, *45,* 640-647.

Hills, J. R., & Klock, J. A. Setting cutoff scores in selective admissions. *Journal of Educational Measurement,* 1965, *2,* 97-102.

Hoge, W. The use of data processing in the admissions process at the moderate-size college. *National Association of College Admissions Counselors Journal,* 1968, *13*(1), 9; 35.

Hohengarten, F. The admissions officer: A focus on preparation and competence. *National Association of College Admissions Counselors Journal,* 1973, *18*(3), 8-10.

Holland, J. L. Student explorations of college choice and their relation to college popularity, college productivity and sex differences. *College and University*, 1958, *33*, 313-320.

Hooten, D. E. The admissions function in public urban colleges and universities. *College and University*, 1971, *47*, 63-69.

Horle, R. F., & Thompson, J. T. Legal and political implications of policies governing admission to publicly supported institutions of higher education. *College and University*, 1968, *43*, 274-285.

Howell, J. J. On the meaning of SAT scores obtained by foreign students of non-English language background. *College and University*, 1968, *43*, 225-232.

Hoy, J. C. Plans for the admission of new first-year students. In A. Knowles (Ed.), *Handbook of college and university administration — academic*. New York: McGraw-Hill, 1970. (a)

Hoy, J. C. The mechanics of admission. In A. Knowles (Ed.), *Handbook of college and university administration — academic*. New York: McGraw-Hill, 1970. (b)

Hoy, J. C. Admission of the transfer student to upperclass standing. In A. Knowles (Ed.), *Handbook of college and university administration — academic*. New York: McGraw-Hill, 1970. (c)

Hoyt, D. P. College grades and adult accomplishment. *Educational Record*, 1966, *45*, 70-75.

Hull, B. J. Vanishing high school visitation. *National Association of College Admissions Counselors Journal*, 1973, *18*(3), 23-24.

Huther, J. W. The open door: How open is it? *Community and Junior College Journal*, 1971, *41*(7), 24-27.

Hyman, S. C. The open admissions freshman at the City University of New York. In Council for Basic Education (Ed.), *Open admissions: The pros and cons*. Washington, D. C.: Editor, 1972.

Impersonal computers personalize selection. *College Management*, 1968, *3*, 52.

Institute of International Education, *Handbook on U.S. study for foreign nationals*. New York: Author, 1973.

Ivey, A., Peterson, F. E., & Trebbe, E. S. The personality record as a predictor of college attrition: A discriminant analysis. *College and University*, 1966, *41*, 199-205.

Jacobson, S. Judicial review of college admission policies. *Journal of Higher Education*, 1963, *34*, 432-437.

Jaffe, A. J., & Adams, W. Two models of open enrollment. In L. Wilson & O. Mills (Eds.), *Universal higher education*. Washington, D. C.: American Council on Education, 1972.

Jencks, C., & Riesman, D. *The academic revolution*. Garden City, N. J.: Doubleday, 1968.

Johnson, D. L. Can your admissions program fill the empty beds on campus? *College and University Business*, 1969, *46*, 57-62.

Johnson, D. L. Managing change in admissions. *National Association of College Admissions Counselors Journal*, 1973, *17*(3), 13-16.

Jorgenson, D. The counseling aspects of admissions. *National Association of College Admissions Counselors Journal,* 1967, *12*(4), 9-11.

Kallingal, A. The prediction of grades for black and white students at Michigan State University. *Journal of Educational Measurement,* 1971, *8*, 263-265.

Kaplan, B. Open admissions: A critique. *Liberal Education,* 1972, *58*, 210-221.

Karabel, J. Open admissions: Toward meritocracy or democracy? *Change,* 1972, *4*(4), 38-42.

Kastner, E. C. The registrar and director of admissions. In G. P. Burns, (Ed.), *Administration in higher education: Their function and coordination.* New York: Harper, 1962.

Kelson, D. So you know nothing about foreign admissions. *College and University,* 1973, *48*, 578-585.

Kerr, W. D. Student perceptions of counselor role in the college decision. *Personnel and Guidance Journal,* 1962, *41*, 337-342.

Kerr, W. D. High school counselors and college information. *Journal of College Student Personnel,* 1963, *5*, 45-48.

Kiernan, I. The case for psychiatric evaluation and reporting prior to admission to college. *National Association of College Admissions Counselors Journal,* 1968, *13*(2), 16-17; 25.

King, F. P. The director of admissions and registrar as reflected in the mirror of brass. *College and University,* 1969, *45*, 95-100.

Knoell, D., & Medsker, L. *From junior to senior college: A national study of the transfer student.* Washington, D. C.: American Council on Education, 1965.

Kuh, G. D., Redding, A. J., & Lesar, D. J. Counseling the transfer: Does it make a difference? *National Association of College Admissions Counselors Journal,* 1972, *16*(4), 16-19.

Kurland, N. D. *Transition from school to college.* Durham, N. C.: Duke University, 1967. (ERIC Document Reproduction Service No. ED 013 378)

LaBaugh, T. D. Alternatives to college days and nights and high school visitations. *National Association of College Admissions Counselors Journal,* 1974, *18*(4), 8-10.

Lavin, D. E. *The prediction of academic performance.* New York: Russell Sage Foundation, 1965.

Lenning, O. T., & Maxey, E. J. *ACT* versus *SAT* prediction for present day colleges and students. *Educational and Psychological Measurement,* 1973, *33*, 397-406.

Libo, K., & Stewart, E. Open admissions: An open-and-shut case? *Saturday Review,* January, 1973, pp. 54; 57-58.

Lindahl, C. But is recruiting really obsolete? *College Board Review,* 1973, *89*, 6-9.

Lindsay, E. E., & Holland, E. O. *College and university administration.* New York: Macmillan, 1930.

Linton, C. College deans look at admissions. *National Association of College Admissions Counselors Journal*, 1967, *12*(2), 24; 26-28.

Logan, F. The trouble with school visiting. *College Board Review*, 1966, *59*, 23-24.

Lovejoy, C. E. *Lovejoy's college guide*. New York: Simon and Schuster, 1970.

Lowry, R. A. An analysis of court cases concerning the authority of colleges and universities to establish policies pertaining to the admission, dismissal, control, and graduation of students (Doctoral dissertation, University of Pittsburgh, 1970). *Dissertation Abstracts International*, 1970, *31*, 2130A. (University Microfilms No. 70-20,329)

Lunneborg, P. W., & Lunneborg, C. E. The differential prediction of college grades from biographic information. *Educational and Psychological Measurement*, 1966, *26*, 917-925.

Master Plan Survey Team. *A master plan for higher education in California, 1960-1975*. Sacramento, Calif.: State Department of Education, 1960.

Masterson, J. F. The college applicant who has had psychiatric care. *National Association of College Admissions Counselors Journal*, 1968, *13*(1), 10; 12-14.

McBee, M., & Suddick, D. Differential freshman admissions by sex. *National Association of Women Deans, Administrators, and Counselors Journal*, 1974, *37*, 75-77.

McGrath, E. J. *The evolution of administrative offices and institutions of higher education in the United States, 1860-1933*. Unpublished doctoral dissertation, University of Chicago, 1936.

Meder, A. E. Admission and the college. In College Entrance Examination Board (Ed.), *College admissions*. Princeton: Editor, 1954.

Meeth, L. Innovative admissions practices for the liberal arts colleges. *Journal of Higher Education*, 1970, *41*, 535-546.

Menacker, J. *From school to college: Articulation and transfer*. Washington, D. C.: American Council on Education, 1975.

Meskill, V. P. Transfer student performance and admissions policies for transfers. *National Association of College Admissions Counselors Journal*, 1971, *16*(2), 23-24.

Mickelson, H. I. Parental factors influencing college selection (Doctoral dissertation, Colorado State College, 1967). *Dissertation Abstracts*, 1967/68, *28*, 2449A-2450A. (University Microfilms No. 68-440)

Miller, I. Accountability in the face of pressures. *National Association of College Admissions Counselors Journal*, 1976, *20*(3), 5-7.

Millett, J. D. *The academic community*. New York: McGraw-Hill, 1962.

Moll, R. W. Optional *SAT*. *College Board Review*, 1973, *86*, 10-13; 38-41.

Morrison, J. R. Factors influential in college selection. *Clearing House*, 1968, *42*, 265-270.

Moss, D. Workshop for new admissions officers. *College and University*, 1972, *47*, 714-716.

Mueller, K. *Student personnel work in higher education*. Boston: Houghton-

Mifflin, 1961.

Munday, L. A., & Rever, P. R. Perspectives on open admissions. In P. R. Rever (Ed.), *Open admissions and equal access.* Iowa City, Iowa: American College Testing Program, 1971.

National Association for Foreign Student Affairs. *Selection and admission of foreign students guidelines.* Cleveland, Ohio: Author, 1966. (ERIC Document Reproduction Service No. ED 024 063)

Nelson, J. H. Guidelines for articulation. *Junior College Journal,* 1966, *36*(6), 24-26.

Nelson, R. An admissions man's guide to college organizations. *College Board Review,* 1966, *61*, 14-20.

Nisbet, R. Some skeptical observations on open admissions. In Council for Basic Education (Ed.), *Open admissions: The pros and cons.* Washington, D. C.: Editor, 1972.

Noland, R. L. Damaging information and the college application. *Personnel and Guidance Journal,* 1971, *49*, 544-554.

Northley, A. S. Sex differences in high school scholarship. *School and Society,* 1958, *86*, 63-64.

O'Banion, T. *New directions in community college student personnel programs.* Washington, D. C.: American College Personnel Association, 1971. (Student Personnel Monograph Series, No. 15)

Ockerman, E. Application for admission — who needs it? *College and University,* 1973, *48*, 231-236.

Pace, C. R., & Stern, G. G. An approach to the measurement of psychological characteristics of college environments. *Journal of Educational Psychology,* 1958, *49*, 269-277.

Passons, W. R. Predictive validities of *ACT, SAT,* and high school grades for first semester GPA and freshman courses. *Educational and Psychological Measurement,* 1967, *27*, 1143-1144.

Perry, R. R. *The admissions officer.* Toledo: University of Toledo, 1964.

Perry, R. R. Admissions communication by T.V. — better than college nights. *College and University,* 1967, *43*, 39-46.

Perry, R. R. The office of admissions — role of the administrator. In A. Knowles (Ed.), *Handbook of college and university administration — academic.* New York: McGraw-Hill, 1970. (a)

Perry, R. R. Admissions department costs and budgeting. In A. Knowles (Ed.), *Handbook of college and university administration — academic.* New York: McGraw-Hill, 1970. (b)

Peterson, D. How high school visits influence college admissions. *College Board Review,* 1968, *68*, 8-9; 18.

Pfeifer, C. M., & Sedlacek, W. E. The validity of academic predictors for black and white students at a predominantly white university. *Journal of Educational Measurement,* 1971, *8*, 253-261.

Phelps, M. O. Sex still makes a difference. *College and University,* 1973, *48*, 90-91.

Phillips, D. Admissions problems of overseas independent schools' students. *College Board Review*, 1972, *83*, 30-32.

Portman, D. N. *Authority and admissions policy at 118 American colleges and universities.* Syracuse, N. Y.: Syracuse University, 1971. (ERIC Document Reproduction Service No. ED 052 714)

Pressey, S. "Fondling" accelerates ten years after. *Journal of Counseling Psychology*, 1967, *14*, 73-80.

Priest, W. On the threshold of greatness. *Junior College Journal*, 1966, *37*, 6-8.

Richards, J. M., & Holland, J. L. *A factor analysis of student explanations of their choice of a college.* Iowa City, Iowa: American College Testing Program, 1965. (ERIC Document Reproduction Service No. ED 016 994)

Robinson, J. W. Academic double talk: Phrases of praise. *College and University*, 1966, *41*, 168-172.

Robinson, L. How to give feedback on students' progress. *College Board Review*, 1969, *73*, 19-21.

Rosner, B. *Open admissions at The City University of New York.* Chicago: American Association for the Advancement of Science, 1970. (ERIC Document Reproduction Service No. ED 050 676)

Ruch, C. Participation in selected guidance activities and the stability of college choice. *National Assocation of College Admissions Counselors Journal*, 1967, *12*(4), 21-24.

Sanders, J. The new admissions scene. *College Board Review*, 1973, *87*, 4-6; 29-32.

Sassenrath, J. M., & Pugh, R. Relationship among CEEB, *SAT* and *ACT* scores and GPA: A replication. *Journal of Educational Measurement*, 1966, *3*, 37-38.

Savides, H. Counselors' summer visits to colleges — an untapped familiarization resource. *National Association of College Admissions Counselors Journal*, 1967, *12*(4), 19-20.

Scott, R. Faculty assistance in admissions. *National Association of College Admissions Counselors Journal*, 1968, *13*(3), 27-28.

Sedlacek, W. E., Brooks, G. C., & Mindus, L. A. *Black and other minority admissions to large universities: Three year national trends.* College Park: University of Maryland, 1972. (ERIC Document Reproduction Service No. ED 061 409)

Sedlacek, W. E., Lewis, J. A., & Brooks, G. C. *Black and other minority admissions to large universities: A four year national survey of policies and outcomes.* College Park: University of Maryland, 1973. (ERIC Document Reproduction Service No. ED 075 740)

Seron, M. S. Analysis of factors which determine choice of college among urban, suburban, and rural high school students (Doctoral dissertation, Northwestern University, 1967). *Dissertation Abstracts*, 1967/68, *28*, 4060A. (University Microfilms No. 68-3221)

Shaffer, R., & Martinson, W. *Student personnel services in higher education.* New York: Center for Applied Research in Education, 1966.

Sharon, A. T. *Validity of the tests of General Educational Development for admission of non-high school graduates to higher education.* Princeton: Educational Testing Service, 1972. (ERIC Document Reproduction Service No. ED 064 304)

Sheffield, W., & Meskill, V. P. Admissions counselors or recruiters? *Personnel and Guidance Journal,* 1974, *52,* 521-525.

Shields, J. F. High school origin as a variable in predicting freshman grades for the purpose of admission (Doctoral dissertation, University of Maryland, 1970). *Dissertation Abstracts International,* 1971, *31,* 5803A. (University Microfilms No. 71-13,192)

Shutt, B. Indiana University goes to computer-based admissions. *College and University,* 1967, *42,* 181-185.

Simmons, A. Students in recruiting and selection. *National Association of College Admissions Counselors Journal,* 1969, *14*(3), 25.

Smerling, W. H. The registrar: Changing aspects. *College and University,* 1960, *35,* 180-186.

Smiley, E. K. The application. In College Entrance Examination Board (Ed.), *College Admissions.* Princeton: Editor, 1954.

Smith, M. Varieties of open admissions. In Council for Basic Education (Ed.), *Open admissions: The pros and cons.* Washington, D. C.: Editor, 1972.

Snyder, R. K. Recruiting. In College Entrance Examination Board (Ed.), *College admissions.* Princeton: Editor, 1954.

Stahmann, R. F., Hanson, G., & Whittlesey, R. Parent and student perceptions of influences on college choice. *National Association of College Admissions Counselors Journal,* 1971, *16*(2), 21-22.

Statement of good practices. *National Association of College Admissions Counselors Journal,* 1973, *17*(3), 3.

Sternberg, R. J. Cost-benefit analysis of the Yale admissions office interview. *College and University,* 1973, *48,* 154-164.

Stordahl, K. E. Student perceptions of influence on college choice. *Journal of Educational Research,* 1970, *63,* 209-212.

Strain, W. H. Which foreign students should U. S. institutions admit? *Phi Delta Kappan,* 1965, *46,* 332-335.

Strauss, R. S. Open admissions 1970: The audacious experiment. *Teachers College Record,* 1971, *72,* 513-518.

Sweeney, L. Administration of foreign student admissions. *College and University,* 1967, *42,* 433; 446.

Tavris, C. What does college do for a person? Frankly, very little. *Psychology Today,* September, 1974, pp. 73-76; 78; 80.

Temp, G. Validity of the *SAT* for blacks and whites in thirteen integrated institutions. *Journal of Educational Measurement,* 1971, *8,* 245-251.

Thomas, L. M. Award of transfer credit: Policies and practices. *College and University,* 1971, *47,* 30-35.

Thomas, R. E. So you want to recruit foreign students. *National Association of College Admissions Counselors Journal*, 1974, *19*(2), 11-13.

Thompson, G. R. Factors influencing college choice among seniors in selected suburban high schools (Doctoral dissertation, University of Colorado, 1965). *Dissertation Abstracts*, 1966, *26*, 6519. (University Microfilms No. 66-3291)

Thresher, B. A. *College admissions and the public interest.* New York: College Entrance Examination Board, 1966.

Thresher, B. A. Frozen assumptions in admissions. In College Entrance Examination Board (Ed.), *College admissions policies for the 1970's.* Princeton: Editor, 1968.

Thresher, B. A. Admissions in perspective. In A. Knowles (Ed.), *Handbook of college and university administration — academic.* New York: McGraw-Hill, 1970.

Tonsor, S. J. Commentary: Who should decide who goes to college. In P. R. Rever (Ed.), *Open admissions and equal access.* Iowa City, Iowa: American College Testing Program, 1971.

Trent, J. W. A new look at recruitment policies. *College Board Review*, 1966, *58*, 7-11.

University Commission on Admissions. *Report and recommendations to the Board of Higher Education of the City of New York.* New York: City University of New York, 1969. (ERIC Document Reproduction Service No. ED 035 373)

Wagner, T. E. The college night program: An alternative. *National Association of College Admissions Counselors Journal*, 1972, *16*(4), 22-24.

Walster, E., Cleary, T., & Clifford, M. Research note: The effect of race and sex on college admission. *Sociology of Education*, 1970, *44*, 237-244.

Walton, W., & Mathis, B. The college suggestor — a system of descriptive information about colleges. *Association of College Admissions Counselors Newsletter*, 1967, *5*, 5-8.

Waters, E. The other generation gap: Admissions procedures for adult students. *Journal of College Student Personnel*, 1971, *12*, 464-466.

Watley, D. J., & Merwin, J. C. An attempt to improve prediction of college success by adjusting for high school characteristics. *American Educational Research Journal*, 1967, *4*, 229-240.

Weiss, K. P. A multi-factor admissions predictive system. *College and University*, 1970, *45*, 203-209.

Weston, R. J., & Lenning, O. T. Prediction at a highly selective institution after corrections have been made for selection: *ACT* versus *SAT*. *College and University*, 1973, *49*, 68-76.

Whitla, D. Admission to college: Policy and practice. *Phi Delta Kappan*, 1965, *46*, 303-306.

Whitney, D. R., & Boyd, N. W. Limiting effect of predictive validity on the expected accuracy of admissions decisions. *College and University*,

50   *College Student Personnel Services*

1971, *46*, 180-190.

Wilson, E. S. Admissions — internal liaison with administration, faculty, student, and alumni groups. In A. Knowles (Ed.), *Handbook of college and university administration — academic.* New York: McGraw-Hill, 1970. (a)

Wilson, E. S. Special problems of admissions. In A. Knowles (Ed.), *Handbook of college and university administration — academic.* New York: McGraw-Hill, 1970. (b)

Wilson, G. C. The impact of transfer admissions in the next decade. *College and University,* 1970, *45*, 266-272.

Wilson, K. Your image is showing. *College and University,* 1971, *46*, 620-634.

Winandy, D. H., & McGrath, R. A. A study of admissions policies and practices for transfer students in Illinois. *College and University,* 1970, *45*, 186-191.

Wolf, J. Marketing admissions. *College Board Review,* 1973, *89*, 2-4; 23-24.

Woodward, T. M., Jr. Ethics in student recruitment in the 1970's. *National Association of College Admissions Counselors Journal,* 1973, *17*(3), 1-3.

Wray, F. E., & Leischuck, G. S. Predicting academic success of junior college transfers. *College and University,* 1971, *47*, 10-16.

Yanitelli, V. R. A president looks at the admissions office. *National Association of College Admissions Counselors Journal,* 1975, *19*(3), 14-15.

Yaw, E. J. *A survey and evaluation of college and university recruitment activities.* Skokie, Ill.: National Association of College Admissions Counselors, 1973.

Young, W. Admission of the transfer student. *Personnel and Guidance Journal,* 1964, *43*, 60-62.

Zeller, B. College education for all? *Today's Education,* 1972, *61*(3), 46-49.

CHAPTER 2

FINANCIAL AID

MICHAEL DANNELLS

HISTORY

STUDENT financial aid began in this country
in 1643 when Lady Ann Mowlson of London gave Harvard
College

> the full and intire somme of [one] hundred pownds ... to be
> and remaine as a perpetuall stipend for and towards the
> yea[rly] maintenance of some poor scholler (Morison, 1935, p.
> 309).

Since that event "student aid has been central to the history of
the American college and university" (Rudolph, 1962b, p. 2). In
fact, the "American college has been giving itself away ever
since" (Rudolph, 1962b, p. 1).

First Two Hundred Years

From the founding of Harvard College to the Civil War,
charity funds or the "meager endowments available for students
unable to pay their way" (Rudolph, 1962b, p. 4), along with
the tuition remissions, came out of colleges' operating incomes.
These funds were used to keep a few poor students among the
affluent student bodies, so that charges of elitism and snobbish-
ness could be refuted and so that able students could be recruited (Moon, 1963; Rudolph, 1962a). During the mid-1800's,
the recruiting function of student aid hit its peak, and student
enterprise and part-time work were common.

Civil War to World War II

After the Civil War, "a new burden [was placed] on the

51

tradition of student aid: the increasing desirability of a college education argued forcefully for the maintenance of equality of access to that education" (Rudolph, 1962b, p. 6). States began funding scholarship programs and private colleges obtained sizable endowments for scholarships from the self-made millionaires of the age. By the early 1900's sizable scholarship funds for grants, loans, self-help dormitories, and student employment agencies were an integral part of American higher education (Moon, 1963; Rudolph, 1962b).

Since the Civil War, continually rising costs, increasing societal need for post-secondary education, and the financial inability of colleges to handle the entire cost of education have contributed to the increasing role of federal and state governments in aiding needy students (Meade, 1972). Despite these forces, the federal government was slow in developing programs of direct aid to students (Adams & Stephens, 1970). It was not until the country was well into the Depression in 1933 that the Federal Emergency Relief Administration began the temporary Student Work Program, which in its ten-year existence served approximately 600,000 students and 1,500 out of 1,700 eligible colleges, but which met with limited success because of administrative difficulties at the institutional level (Adams & Stephens, 1970; Nash, 1968a).

Federal aid to graduate education started in 1938 with fellowships given by the National Cancer Institute (Nash, 1968b). But apart from the Student Work Program and Student War Loans, a small lending program which ran from 1942 to 1944, federal involvement in direct aid to students did not really begin until the end of the war and the Servicemen's Readjustment Act of 1944, better known as the G. I. Bill.

The Present

The G. I. Bill was the first substantial federal government support program without a financial need criterion (Van Dusen & O'Hearne, 1973). Fifteen million veterans were eligible for this program. As a result, enrollments in higher education doubled from 1.3 million to 2.6 million, and from 1946 to 1947 about one half of all college students were veterans. Because of administrative difficulties and a feeling that colleges had increased tuition to take advantage of money from the G. I. Bill, when the act was extended to Korean War veterans in 1952, the tuition payments were made directly to the veterans rather than to the institutions.

In 1958 the National Defense Education Act (NDEA), which probably would never have passed but for Sputnik and the use of the "defense" label (Cohen, 1968; Kaufman, 1972; McCormick, 1972), financially helped more than 1.5 million college students in its first decade of existence (Rothschild, 1968) and was probably the first real step toward making equal opportunity for higher education an economic reality (McCormick, 1972). Although conceived as an emergency measure to remedy serious deficiencies in higher education, the National Defense Student Loan Program, which was the act's major thrust, became the first long-term federal program to aid undergraduates (Nash, 1968b).

In 1964 the Economic Opportunity Act established the College Work-Study Program. One year later the Higher Education Act broadened student eligibility under the College Work-Study Program, provided grants for the needy through the Educational Opportunity Grants Program, and established the Guaranteed Student Loan Program, the largest federal program of all (McCormick, 1972; Nash, 1968b).

The Higher Education Amendment of 1972 gave student assistance "unprecedented federal endorsement" (Brugel & Hofmann, 1974, p. 11) by continuing the previous programs and establishing the Basic Education Opportunity Grant Program (Brugel & Hofmann, 1974). "But the unique contribution of the act of 1972 is that it states unequivocally that every American is equally entitled to post-secondary education" (Caldwell, 1975, p. 32).

States also developed financial aid programs, the earliest of which occurred in New York in 1913 and Oregon in 1935. Most state scholarship programs began in the 1950's, and in 1972 twenty-two states, those with the largest numbers of college students, had such programs (Meade, 1972). By 1974 another six states had adopted comprehensive financial assistance programs (Boyd, 1975).

DEFINITION

Student financial aid has been defined as:

> any direct, material effort made by a segment of society, other than the family, which serves either to reduce the student's expense of college attendance or to minimize the pressure of such expense on the student while in college (Moon, 1959, p. 342).

This definition does not include funds or services given to the institution, such as governmental subsidies and private endowments, which indirectly benefit students through tuition reduction.

Since the growth of the concept of need as a criterion for student financial aid, a more specific definition is:

> any [direct] means available to offset or to diminish the expenses normally incurred by an individual who lacks the resources needed to cover his [her] expenses while he [she] is in college (Van Dusen & O'Hearne, 1973, p. 8).

This definition is congruent with the opinion that if there is no show of need the recipient is getting a reward and not aid (O'Hearne, 1973).

Three Forms of Aid

Student financial aid is typically divided into grants, loans, and employment (Mueller, 1961; Panel on Student Financial Need Analysis, 1971; Van Dusen & O'Hearne, 1973; Wrenn, 1951). Grants are frequently called scholarships, prizes, awards, or grants-in-aid and represent "a simple transfer of resources to students and involve no repayment" (Panel on Student, 1971, p. 77). There are at least five different forms of grants, which as a group will be called gift aid in this chapter. The term grant will be reserved for those grants or gift aid based solely on need.

A second form of gift aid is honor scholarships given on the basis of some academic performance criterion, which is probably the most widespread, nonfinancial criterion. A third and related form of gift aid is graduate fellowships which are given on the basis of high intellectual ability (Wrenn, 1951) or the possession of some talent related to the recipient's graduate work, such as research or writing ability.

A fourth form of gift aid is tuition remission or the practice of not charging full tuition. These discounts or waivers are usually given to some children of an institution's faculty. This practice is common in private colleges (93%) but unusual (13%) in public institutions (Ingraham & King, 1965). Tuition remissions have faculty recruiting and retention value for the institution and help support underpaid faculty, but they may make the faculty callous to tuition hikes, place the faculty in a psychologically dependent position, favor faculty with children over those who do not have children, and smack of favoritism (Wilbanks, 1972).

The fifth form is service awards, which are based on recognition of a special ability and require performance of a service, such as playing football or trombone playing. Given today's emphasis on the need principle and the growing recognition that intercollegiate athletics, and even musical and dramatic performances to some extent, are big business for institutions, such service awards might be more appropriately considered employment (Mueller, 1961).

Of all service awards, athletic scholarships are probably the most well known. Some believe that aid of this type should not be considered a part of student financial aid. Wrenn (1951) said about athletic scholarships:

> Unless [they] are administered by the financial-aids office under general scholarship policies, they should not be called "scholarships" but be recognized frankly for what they are, a subsidy for the athletic program (p. 367).

Rudolph (1962b) says that they and other

> hidden forms of assistance useful in the care and feeding of athletes ... [are not] consistent with the concern for opportunity, service, and serious academic purpose that characterized student aid at its best (p. 9).

Gift aid has also been categorized as general, regional, and special (Feingold, 1955). General gifts are those awarded without attention to the recipient's religion, residence, course of study, and so on. Regional gifts are those that stipulate preference for recipients coming from a particular school or a certain region. Special gifts are "conditioned by one or more stipulations such as religious affiliation, ancestry, place of employment, organizational membership, professional intentions or course of study" (Feingold, 1955, p. 13). Many of the latter category run counter to civil rights legislation and the need principle and are no longer permissible today.

Loans are "sums of money offered with the requirement that they be repaid in whole or in part, with or without the payment of interest" (Van Dusen & O'Hearne, 1973, p. 13). Loans may be obtained through a commercial lending institution, in which case they are not usually considered financial aid, or through the college, which has as its major source of funds the federal and state governments. Loans may be short-term for emergency or petty cash purposes and small in amount or they may be long-term, in which case they are typically repayable when the borrower graduates or leaves school (Van Dusen & O'Hearne, 1973).

Student employment need not be defined except to the extent that ordinarily only certain kinds of jobs are considered financial aid; for example, part-time jobs and jobs secured through the college. Jobs held by students in support of their expenses may be funded through the institution or from outside (Van Dusen & O'Hearne, 1973).

Packaging refers to the relative mix of the three types of aid given to a student at any one time and is closely related to need. If a student needed $500 to meet expenses for a given semester, that need could be met in a variety of ways. It could be covered completely by gift aid; by a combination of gift aid and a loan; or by a combination of gift aid, a loan, and a part-time job; and so on. Thus, there are seven different mixes that can be offered to students.

Purpose

Student financial aid serves three masters: society, the institution, and the student. Unfortunately, what serves one master does not necessarily serve the other two. Society wants "education of the maximum number of its citizens to the maximum extent possible for each" (Prentice, Hill, & Nelson, 1971, p. 570), and it wants to reduce the talent loss from higher education that financial barriers create (West, 1963). Thus the specific goal of financial aid from a societal point of view is to help the needy (Mueller, 1961), although there is considerable disagreement on just which needy should be aided and how they can best be helped.

The real difficulty arises between institution-serving and student-serving uses of financial aid. Gross (1966) expresses this conflict in terms of the administrative and the personnel views of financial aid administration. The administrative view has as its purpose the meeting of institutional objectives, such as attracting students (especially the academically talented ones), filling dorm spaces, and enhancing the public image of the college (Moon, 1966; Mueller, 1961; Sidar, 1966). The institution must meet these objectives to some degree before it can meet student service objectives (Allen, 1967).

The personnel view gives primary attention to the needs of the students (Gross, 1966). Two important principles of awarding aid stem from this approach. The financial aid package should be tailored to the needs of the individual student (Allen, 1967; Babbidge, 1960; Bingham, 1970; Burns, 1963; Hage, 1973; Mueller, 1961; Sidar, 1966; Van Dusen, 1966; Van Dusen & O'Hearne, 1973) and the receipt of aid should be a part of the student's learning experience (Allen, 1967; Babbidge, 1960; Mueller, 1961; Van Dusen, 1966; Wrenn, 1951).

Until recently, student aid was based more on enhancing institutional interests than students' interests (Henry, 1969; Moon, 1965). But the "systemization of need analysis brought a virtual end to scholarships as 'prizes' to the bright and diligent" (Johnstone, 1973, p. 13) and severely curbed the once prevailing practice of institutional competition for promising students by offering them different amounts of financial assistance. Nevertheless, the practice continues (Davis, 1968; Moon, 1966; Owen, 1970; cf. Henry, 1969); the difference today is that colleges compete through the mix of the aid package. This practice conflicts with the need principle because the use of aid as a recruitment tool often dictates that brighter students, who can most easily handle the burden of a loan or job, get disproportionate amounts of grant money (Bingham, 1970; Davis, 1968). It also leads to candidates choosing a college on the amount of grant money in the aid package rather than for its educational offerings (Bingham, 1970).

FINANCING HIGHER EDUCATION

Ever since Lady Ann Mowlson's gift to Harvard, students in American higher education have had their education subsidized either through private philanthropy, underpayment of faculty, or governmental support (Rudolph, 1962a). This last source of support has become increasingly important as rising costs, inflation, and diminishing nongovernmental sources of income (Marmaduke, 1971), combined with increasing demands for equal opportunity in education as the great socioeconomic equalizer, have hit higher education. By the late 1960's 20 percent of the financial support of higher education originated in federal coffers and 18 percent of those funds went for student aid (Carnegie Commission, 1968). This use of federal funds is generally defended on the basis that the college graduate job market is continental and the country as a whole benefits from it (Carnegie Commission, 1968). As long as the goals of large enrollments, equal opportunity, and the social benefits of higher education are agreed upon, governmental support to higher education institutions coupled with low tuition and primary emphasis on grants is the logical system of financing (Bowen, 1971).

However, the current crisis of purpose in higher education and the lack of consensus on its aims has resulted in much controversy over how it should be financed (Bowen, 1971). Those who emphasize the private benefits of education, efficiency, balanced public budgets, and equity, prefer a system of finance that entails high tuition, primary use of loans, and limited governmental support for higher education.

These two views, concerning whether education provides public or private benefits, give rise to three alternative patterns or models for financing higher education: full-cost pricing in which education is priced at its full cost, say $40,000 for a year's tuition rather than $3,000; free public education in which education is free with society paying the cost; and the conglomerate model or the present mixed approach which uses some aspects of each model (Bowen 1971).

Within the present conglomerate model, the question remains as to the crucial role of the federal government. There are several methods of federal funding of higher education: (a) categorical aid in which specifically defined projects are funded through grants, contracts, and loans; (b) noncategorical aid to institutions through grants; (c) direct grants or loans to students; (d) tax relief to parents or students for educational expenses; (e) revenue sharing with states for compensation of state monies spent in aid to higher education; and (f) the eclectic approach, or some combination of the above (Orwig, 1971a; Wolk, 1968). Currently, the last alternative prevails with the mix being a combination of the first three.

Basic Assumptions

Financial aid has been provided for higher education because it is assumed that lack of sufficient finances is one of the major obstacles to obtaining a college degree in this country (Doermann, 1971; Rivlin Report, 1969). It has been estimated that lack of funds prevented 569,000 men (96,500 black) and roughly the same number of women from going to college within one year of their high school graduation in 1969 (Doermann, 1971). However, money is but one of several important factors in determining college attendance (Doermann, 1971; Jencks, 1971) and completion.

Lack of money is frequently overrated as an obstacle because it is a socially acceptable reason given by the individual to mask lack of motivation to attend or persist in college (Henry, 1963, 1965; Iffert, 1958; Nash, 1969). Iffert (1958) found financial reasons to account for only 15 percent of withdrawals and Nash (1969) concluded from his research review that motivational factors are much more important than finances in determining college attendance. However, family financial power, in that it is extremely interrelated with motivational variables, does correlate highly with college-going behavior (Henry, 1965).

A second basic assumption is that higher education is a primary method of socioeconomic equalization. In the broad sense of wealth redistribution, Jencks (1971) provides a convincing argument that the assumption is incorrect. Between 1945 and 1965, despite an average increase of 1 percent per year of young people going to college, there has been no significant redistribution of wealth in our society. Thus, Jencks reasons, it appears that "mass higher education has *no* significant effect on the size of the various social strata" (p. 73). Yet in the more narrow sense of the individual who attends college, higher education may open many socioeconomic doors.

Direct Versus Indirect Aid

Accepting the premise that federal aid should be available to students, the next question concerns the means of transmittal (Tombaugh, 1972; Trimble, 1969). There are two broad options: direct and indirect aid. Direct aid, such as the G. I. Bill and the educational benefits of Social Security, goes from the governmental agency to the individual student. Indirect aid channels money through the institutions, generally in the form of noncategorical support (Tombaugh, 1972; Trimble, 1969).

Recently there has been increased advocacy of the direct aid option (Newell, 1970; O'Hearne, 1970; Rivlin Report, 1969; Roose, 1970). Arguments in support of direct aid to students include: (a) It is the best alternative for promoting equality of educational opportunity (Hansen & Weisbrod, 1971; Panel on Financing, 1973; Rivlin Report, 1969; Roose, 1970; Windham, 1972). (b) It would result in the most efficient and flexible use of limited resources (Hansen & Weisbrod, 1971; Roose, 1970; Tombaugh, 1972; Trimble, 1969) because persons who do not need the support are not subsidized (Hansen & Weisbrod, 1971). (c) It promotes educational diversity by helping ailing private higher educational institutions (Morrison, 1970) and by allowing students more freedom of choice and more consumer power (Hansen & Weisbrod, 1971; Tombaugh, 1972; Trimble, 1969). (d) It would result in a minimum reduction of talent loss to higher education because it is a more efficient means of support (Rivlin, 1961) and because high school students would know in advance of college attendance the availability of aid funds.

Arguments against direct aid are: (a) It would require a central federal agency and a huge bureaucracy (Tombaugh, 1972). (b) Support for the individual would be more certain only if the funding were open-ended like the G. I. Bill (Tombaugh, 1972). (c) Private schools, because the grants would cover a greater percentage of the cost at public institutions, would face declining enrollments (Tombaugh, 1972). (d) Increased student consumer power might lead to ugly competition between schools (Tombaugh, 1972; Walkup & Hoyt, 1975). (e) It would encourage students to become, or try to appear, independent from their parents sooner (Hansen & Weisbrod, 1971). (f) The incentive for parents to work and save for their children's education would be reduced (Hansen & Weisbrod, 1971). (g) The evidence is insufficient that direct aid is a more efficient means of allocating financial resources (Thackery, 1971). (h) The higher tuition levels that would result from direct aid "would destroy the illusion that education can be had cheaply, therefore, discouraging low and lower-middle class youth from obtaining a college education" (Winter, 1973, p. 171).

The arguments for indirect aid to students and continued institutional support are: (a) It is the best way to strengthen specific types of education and higher education generally (Rivlin, 1961; Rivlin Report, 1969). (b) The present system means less bureaucratic paper-shuffling for financial aid personnel (Tombaugh, 1972; Trimble, 1969). (c) Need analysis is more simple, consistent, and flexible under the present arrangement than it would be with direct aid (Tombaugh, 1972; Trimble, 1969). (d) Institutional aid is necessary to "preserve strong institutions with diverse structures and emphases" (Young, 1970, p. 307).

Income Contingent Loans

One of the direct aid alternatives of financing higher education is that of income contingent loans, also called deferred tuition, tuition postponement, and pay-as-you-earn or "PAYE." As Johnstone (1972) defines it:

> an income contingent contract stipulates at the time of borrowing, only the repayment burden, expressed as a percentage of future income, and the upper limits on repayments and payment periods. The actual interest rate, repayment period, and total dollars repaid will vary in accordance with individual income (p. 4).

Because high income borrowers pay back more than low income borrowers, thus spreading or sharing the risk, income contingent loans represent an extension of the insurance concept of risk mutualization (Lamson, Johnson, & Lundeen, 1971; Rauh, 1972; Rivlin Report, 1969).

The limitations of the current conventional loan programs which income contingent loans are designed to remedy are high annual payments if the debt is large, a disproportionate burden of payment in the first few years of repayment, high risk for the student borrower, and limited available private credit (Johnstone, 1972). The main advantage of income contingent loans is the risk-pooling feature (Rivlin Report, 1969), which reduces the risk for the individual and equalizes educational opportunity (Carnegie Commission, 1968), because repayment becomes less of a deterrent to matriculation (Carnegie Commission, 1968; Johnstone, 1972). Other advantages are that their use would emphasize student independence and responsibility (Carnegie Commission, 1968), that they would reduce financial restrictions on graduate job choice (Lamson et al., 1971), that colleges would take a greater interest in student earning power (Lamson et al., 1971), and that they would allow the option of forgiving part of a borrower's debt (Johnstone, 1972).

Most of the arguments against income contingent loans are "directed toward reliance on student loans *of any form* as a means of financing higher education" (Johnstone, 1972, p. 48). It has been suggested that such programs are antithetical to the nation's tradition of public support for higher education (Wharton, 1971). Such arguments typically come from the public higher education sector because of possible loss of broad public financial support through increasing reliance on the individual's payment of the cost of higher education (Johnstone, 1972).

In 1967 the Panel on Educational Innovation, the Director of the National Science Foundation, and the Special Assistant to the President for Science and Technology proposed the Educational Opportunity Bank (Zacharias Plan). This plan recommended the establishment of a federal educational opportunity bank that would make income contingent loans to students regardless of need. Repayment was to be over thirty years with no liability thereafter at one percent of future gross income for each $3,000 borrowed. The proposal was considered by the National Association of State Universities and Land-Grant Colleges and the American Association of State Colleges and Universities as "a pandora's box of ill-considered, obsolete, and contradictory ideas" (Wolk, 1968, p. 31). Since then the Carnegie Commission on Higher Education has proposed a similar program which it calls the National Student Loan Bank (Carnegie Commission, 1968, 1970).

Arguments against such loan banks are: (a) The start-up costs would be excessive. (b) There would be a liquidity problem in the debt accumulation, because such long-term debts are not the kind of assets with which a lending institution likes to get stuck (Lamson et al., 1971). (c) Society gains more than the individual from higher education, especially in terms of manpower and new knowledge, so society and not the individual should pay. (d) Low-income students might view such loans as a poor investment and, therefore, might not attend college (Wharton, 1971). However, two studies conducted on students' attitudes toward the desirability of income contingent loans suggest there is a potential market for them (Johnstone, Wackman, & Ward, 1972; Lamson et al., 1971).

ADMINISTRATION

A functionally autonomous office which reports directly to the chief student personnel services administrator is the most frequently recommended position for financial aid in the institution. One reason for such a position is that financial problems are personnel problems that are best addressed through a total student services program (Arbuckle, 1953). Other advantages of this placement of the aid office are that equitable functioning of the program is optimal; the dangers of affiliation with the admissions or the business office are avoided; the office can be truly student oriented; the position fits with the counseling function performed in financial aid; the aid officer can assume the role of student advocate or adversary of the business and admissions offices (Davis, 1968; Dickson, 1969; Hage, 1973; Stamatakos & Bekkering, 1972).

Research indicates that the financial aid office reports most frequently to the chief student personnel administrator. As cited in Stamatakos and Bekkering, 49 percent of the full-time aid offices reported to a dean, usually the dean of students, and 73 percent of the part-time and 16 percent of the full-time officers reported directly to the president. Rauh's (1972) survey of twenty-four private colleges showed that one fourth of the aid offices reported to the dean of students, and the remaining were fairly evenly divided between admissions, the business office, the president, and an academic officer or provost. In surveying 131 institutions with enrollments of 10,000 or more Casazza (1971) found that 79 percent of the aid offices were located in the student personnel division of their institution. He also found that 43 percent of the aid directors reported to the vice-president, 4 percent to the president, and 41 percent had two administrators between themselves and the president.

Centralization

It is generally agreed that the student financial aid services on campus should be centralized within one office (Adams &

Stephens, 1970; Allen, 1967; Arbuckle, 1953; Babbidge, 1960; Hage, 1973; Lavery, 1966; Moon, 1966; Mueller, 1961; Risty, 1949; Van Dusen & O'Hearne, 1973). During the 1960's the rise of federal financial aid programming, the need principle, and the practice of packaging greatly increased the complexity of aid administration (Allen, 1967; Henry, 1963). Better coordination through centralization is the most frequently recommended strategy for meeting this complexity (Adams & Stephens, 1970; Allen, 1967; Moon, 1966; Mueller, 1961; Van Dusen & O'Hearne, 1973). Centralization provides efficiency, uniformity, equity, standardization, and verification (Mueller, 1961). Also, aid opportunities are easier for students to find and explore; procedures are simplified, there is less paperwork, less overrewarding, and, thereby, funds are used more efficiently; coordination among the diverse types and procedures of aid is facilitated; and data is more readily available because records are consolidated (Van Dusen & O'Hearne, 1973).

Information Processing

The huge increases of aid applications that resulted from the availability of federal monies in the late 1950's and early 1960's led to rapid advances in the application of automation to the aid office (Jepsen, Matejka, & Hulet, 1972). The major reason computers and information processing systems have been so well received is their unique capabilities in the storing and sorting of data (Bellia, 1973; King & Wedemeyer, 1974), such as correlations of student characteristics in relation to aid receipt, projection of funds, and generation of statistical bases for proposals. Computers can match funds with student characteristics, make awards, notify recipients, process checks (Henry, 1969), and follow-up on loan repayment (Miller, 1975). The net results are increased speed and accuracy in routine decision making which, in turn, save time and reduce costs (Jepsen et al., 1972; King & Wedemeyer, 1974; L. K. Miller, 1975; North, 1975; Wootton, 1975).

Some people fear that increased automation of the aid office will lead to a less personal and humanistic approach to financial' aid (Ryan, 1967). However, computerization has allowed more personalization (Henry, 1969; Jepsen et al., 1972) because aid personnel are relieved of routine matters; are freed to spend more time in personal contact with students (Henry, 1969; Jacoby, 1967; Jepsen et al., 1972; King & Wedemeyer, 1974); and can spend more time in staff development, program planning, and evaluation (Jepsen et al., 1972); King & Wedemeyer, 1974).

Management of Loans

The management of loans includes accounting, record keeping, collection, and reporting to the appropriate federal or state agency (Maynard, 1974). It is because of the second area — collection — that loan management is the most complex administrative problem in financial aid work (Babbidge, 1960). The collection process is complicated by several unique features of educational loans: (a) The length of time involved is much longer than for most other personal loans. (b) Cancellations and deferments are possible with some federal programs. (c) The borrower generally does not live where the institution is located. (d) Since educational loans are one-shot affairs, student borrowers do not worry as much about their credit records. (e) Colleges and universities are new to this problem (Maynard, 1974).

Higher education institutions also base their loans more on faith than on past borrowing records, which violates sound lending principles in that the borrower may not be of the age of majority, usually does not have a credit record, has no income or employment, and is unknown in the community (Maynard, 1974; Spencer, 1974). In addition, the more disadvantaged the background of the borrower the larger the loan. Thus, there is little resemblance between a financial aid office and a commercial lending institution.

NEED AS AN AID CRITERION

The concept of financial need as the criterion for awarding aid only recently has become a part of the definition of financial aid, but the need basis for awarding aid is not a recent phenomenon. What is recent is the relative emphasis placed on it. In fact, it was not until the 1950's "that the concept of financial need was defined, formalized, and evaluated as a criterion for receiving financial aid" (Orwig, 1971b, p. 2). It was then that a few colleges in the Northeast developed a cooperative arrangement whereby the amount of aid offered to students for recruitment purposes was limited. This arrangement later developed into need analysis in an effort to minimize competition (Orwig, 1971b).

Need has not always been so heavily relied on in the granting of aid. For example, Wrenn (1951) said that aid should be distributed "in terms of academic promise, integrity, and need" (pp. 367-368, italics omitted) and West (1963) concluded that "there is almost universal agreement that the first consideration must be the ability of the student" (p. 111). The emphasis on *talent* probably reached its peak in the 1950's when the country was trying to outdistance the rest of the world in the educational/technological race. Of course, graduate fellowships are still awarded on the basis of talent (Panel on Student, 1971).

The increase in the use of the need criterion, which closely paralleled the rise of the college student personnel point of view (Risty, 1949), decreased the unequal distribution of aid monies to those from higher socioeconomic backgrounds (Nash, 1969). The need criterion recognizes that it is not reasonable to expect needy students to work their way through college because the cost of attending college makes it very hard to earn enough while in college and higher academic standards require more study time and leave less time for work (West, 1963). So it is that today's institutional financial aid programs almost universally use the need basis for granting aid (Panel on Student, 1971), and the federal programs do so as well (Orwig, 1971b). (See the first principle of the College Scholarship Service Assembly's Statement of Principles at the end of this chapter.)

The use of need in awarding aid is not without its difficulties (Green, 1962; Henry, 1975). Actual costs must be made known to the student and a realistic expense budget must be devised for each student within the context of the particular college.

Data gathering for need analysis is difficult. For efficiency, need analysis must be standardized, yet exceptional cases and specific problems, such as married, graduate, and international students, must be recognized. Financial information on applications must be verified in some way and the level of parental support that is reasonable to expect must be determined.

Need Criterion Research

Studies of financial aid recipients suggest that the need basis is not operating exclusively in the determination of aid awards. Carpenter (1971), who questioned 500 aid recipients, 500 rejected aid applicants, and 471 students who never applied for aid at the University of Texas, found that the lower the student's income the greater the likelihood of receiving aid. And a survey of over 19,000 aid applicants in ten northeastern states indicated that lower-class applicants, as defined by occupation, income, and source of income, had a better chance of getting aid and getting larger amounts than upper-class applicants. However, upper-class applicants were more likely (45% as opposed to 26%) to get aid in the form of grants. Thus, while the need basis was working because the lower-class applicants got more aid in each category, the use of admissions tests as the packaging criteria resulted in the greater proportion of grants going to the less needy (Schlekat, 1968).

The Panel of Student Financial Need Analysis (1971) found that at eighty-six institutions the average amount of financial aid received correlated positively with parental assets and that high ability students from wealthier families got a disproportionate amount of grants. Apparently ability, and not need, was the best predictor of the amount of grant component of the package from those colleges. Similarly, Seymour, Zimmerman, and Donato (1972) found a slight positive relationship between academic ability and amount of financial aid received for 1,781 students at one midwest institution. However, Ferrin (1971) found from 154 financial aid officers at colleges in Arkansas, New Mexico, Oklahoma, and Texas that grants tended to go to those with greater need, while loans and work opportunities were taken by those from higher socioeconomic backgrounds.

Need Analysis

Need analysis is the process whereby the student's financial need is measured. The process includes cost analysis or determining the costs faced by the student upon college attendance, measuring the student's ability or assets and resources to meet those costs, and computing the difference between costs and resources (Babbidge, 1960; Orwig & Jones, 1970).

Analyzing student need may be done by the school itself if it is small and has few aid applicants, but larger institutions usually find it to their advantage to use an outside need analysis agency (Van Dusen & O'Hearne, 1973). The disadvantages of internal need analysis at larger schools are that it is too time consuming and expensive; it is administratively inconvenient; and students and their parents, to whom need analysis and its findings are hard to explain, will more readily accede to the judgement of an outside agency which several institutions use (Van Dusen & O'Hearne, 1973). In general, then, the use of a separate agency for need analysis frees staff to work on special problem situations.

There are presently two need analysis agencies: the College Scholarship Service (CSS) and the American College Testing (ACT) Program's need analysis service. The ACT service was developed in 1967 and, although not as widely used as CSS, it has a sizable share of the market (Orwig, 1971b). CSS was created in 1954, and its growth since then has been practically synonymous with the emergence of need analysis and the philosophy of need (Moon, 1963).

CSS serves principally as a "clearinghouse for family financial information" (Moon, 1959, p. 343). Member schools have aid applicants' parents submit a Parents' Confidential Statement which is a simplified family financial statement. CSS then computes the applicant's need and sends the information to colleges where the student has applied for financial assistance. The particular financial aid office then uses this information in making its decisions on the application (West, 1963).

Analyzing the family's financial situation involves determining the amount of income necessary for the family to maintain a given standard of living and determining how much the family can contribute from any remaining income (Orwig, 1971b).

Need Analysis Systems Criticisms

Need analysis systems have been criticized for being sophisticated statistical devices which detract from the personalistic approach to awarding aid (Ryan, 1967); for not adequately reflecting minority students' needs, especially in their inappropriate application of white, middle-class financial criteria to the situations of lower income minorities (McClellan, 1970; Saurman, 1972); for the Parents' Confidential Statement being too complicated and remote for many minority parents with very limited resources (McClellan, 1970); for the CSS's asset treatment being too complicated and too sophisticated (Jones, 1973); and for the CSS's analysis demanding too much financial sacrifice from parents, especially middle-class parents (Schaefer, 1973). Also the existence of three need analysis systems (CSS, ACT, and the federal system for BEOG) creates award coordination problems (Marmaduke, 1974).

Parental Contribution Problems

The broadest problem with respect to parental financial contributions to their children's higher education concerns what they can reasonably be expected to contribute or "to what extent should families be asked to sacrifice to pay for college" (Orwig, 1971b, p. 9)? (See principle four of the CSS Statement of Principles at the end of this chapter.) Further compounding the contribution problem is the recent reluctance, and, in some cases, outright refusal of middle income parents to pay the costs of their children's education (Schaefer, 1973).

Another problem with respect to parental contribution is verification of parents' estimates of their income. Sharon and Horch (1972) found from 39,000 Parents' Confidential Statements that lower income families tend to overestimate their future year's income, while higher income families tend to underestimate the same. For example, families in the $10,000 to $14,999 income range had, on the average, an underestimation of about $200 or 2 percent of their actual income. Cunningham's (1972) findings were similar except that the average underestimation was 10.8 percent.

Collins (1973) studied 1,202 applications for financial aid and compared parents' estimates of their next year's income with their Federal Tax Return. The total difference between those figures was $1.7 million and the average underestimation was $1,490. By income range, his results were: 0 to $5,999 — average overestimation of $280; $6,000 to $8,999 — average overestimation of $26; $9,000 to $11,999 — average underestimation of $1,030; $12,000 to $17,999 — average underestimation of $2,114.

Unfortunately, verification of parents' financial information is difficult (Babbidge, 1960) in that the only apparent options open to the aid office are requiring copies of income tax returns, using credit agencies, or conducting their own investigations. Requiring income tax returns is probably the simplest and most accurate of the options, although not without problems because of different filing dates and time periods that do not coincide (Orwig, 1971b; Rutter & Wickstrom, 1976).

Nontraditional Student Difficulties

The financial need of nontraditional students such as self-supporting or independent students poses special problems because of the difficulty in determining the appropriate degree of financial independence from their parents and making fair allotments in comparison to similar traditional students. These nontraditional students include returning veterans, working students who have established their own residences, orphans or wards of the state, and those who refuse parental help or whose parents refuse to give help (Sidar, 1973). Even using the federal aid programs' rather stringent guidelines on who is an independent student (D. Moore, 1973), the number of self-supporting students in college today is surprising. At 276 of the institutions in the CSS's Western Region, 37 percent of the students at public colleges and 20 percent at private colleges qualified as self-supporting (Hensley, 1974). A recent survey of sixty-four Michigan colleges and universities showed that some 16 percent of the overall pool of aid applicants were independent or self-supporting (Research Committee, 1976).

Other nontraditional students, such as married students, have unique problems in that they tend to be under greater financial stress, their resources tend to be greater, their budgets are bigger, the range of their earning capabilities is wider, and there is often uncertainty regarding the employment of the student's spouse (Sauber, 1971). Because of these variations, there is more likelihood of error in computing married students' financial need. Also, officers and governmental agencies may cut married students' budgets to unrealistic levels to insure that they do not receive undue preference (Horch, 1973).

PROGRAMS

Financial aid funds come from private donations, public appropriations, and reductions offered by the institutions themselves (Nash, 1968b). While federal support has been increasing in recent years, state support for higher education has been falling proportionately (Carnegie Commission, 1968) and private philanthropy has been on the decline (Rauh, 1972). Van Dusen and O'Hearne (1973) estimate that the total amount of funds available for financial aid in the 1973 to 1974 academic year was in excess of $4 billion. If commercial loans to students are also considered as a source of funds, then financial aid resources could be considered unlimited, provided students who need loans have adequate credit ratings (West, 1963). Current aid policies and practices have been criticized for being chaotic (Owen, 1970) and frequently overlooking local community funding sources, such as merchants, service clubs, philanthropic societies, and private citizens (Allen, 1967).

Federal Programs

Zelenak (1973) identified five commonalities between the

major federal programs: (a) The student must be a citizen or national of the United States. (b) The student must be a high school graduate or the equivalent. (c) Loan obligations are cancelled in the event of death or permanent and total disability. (d) Discrimination is prohibited. (e) The student must demonstrate financial need, except for the G. I. Bill. Relative need, which is computed as the difference between the cost and the person's ability to cover the cost, is used by all but one of the programs. The exception is the Supplementary Educational Opportunity Grant, which uses absolute need, based on the amount of parental or personal contribution without regard to the cost (Orwig, 1971b).

G. I. Bill

This program provides aid to veterans and needs little comment except that it has done little for the education of women (Morse, 1964); it was used very little in the 1960's by discharged Vietnam veterans in comparison to previous war veterans (Steif, 1969); and yet it has been funded at unprecedented levels for the Vietnam veterans.

National Direct Student Loan Program (NDSL)

Initially titled the National Defense Student Loan Program until the Education Amendments of 1972 (PL 92-318) changed it, this program was designed to encourage students into occupational groups (science and teaching) with national labor shortages. Undergraduates may borrow up to $1,000 per year to a total of $5,000; graduates and professional students may borrow up to $2,500 per year and no more than $10,000 throughout their undergraduate and graduate years. Repayment is not expected until nine months after the student's studies are terminated, with deferments available for military and some volunteer governmental service. The partial or complete loan forgiveness for teaching service (Trimble, 1969) has been attacked as no longer necessary, particularly when discontinuing it would free funds for middle income students (Pernal, 1972).

College Work-Study Program (CW-S)

This program gives annual grants to participating colleges to provide employment opportunities to needy students by covering 80 percent of students' salaries, with the other 20 percent provided by the employer, usually the institution (Apostal & Doherty, 1972). The program "is based on the principle that the participants ... achieve a more enriched education than they would have acquired had they not experienced both physical and mental work in receiving their degrees" (Adams & Stephens, 1970, p. 40). To be eligible, students must be enrolled at least half-time in a college or university, a proprietary institution, or an area vocational school (Zelenak, 1973). Originally, students were limited to an average of fifteen hours per week during the school year, but in 1973 that restriction was removed, though limits on the number of hours may still be set by the institution (Zelenak, 1973). The Carnegie Commission (1968, 1970) has recommended that funding of this program be increased substantially.

Guaranteed Student Loan Program (GSL)

This title refers to all federal, state, and private nonprofit insured loan programs under the Higher Education Act of 1965. The Federal Insured Student Loan Program (FISL) is the federal portion of the GSL which was established by the 1972 Amendments (Van Dusen & O'Hearne, 1973; Zelenak, 1973). The GSL was designed to aid the "disadvantaged middle class" (Hartline, 1972; Henry, 1969). Under it, any student enrolled at an eligible institution may borrow up to $2,500 per year and an aggregate of $7,500 ($10,000 for graduate students) from an eligible lending institution, including one of a variety of commercial lending establishments (Zelenak, 1973). The GSL has been used mostly by students with gross incomes over $7,500, while the NDSL has been used primarily by those with incomes under that figure (Brugel & Hofmann, 1974). A repayment schedule of five to ten years begins shortly after the borrower leaves school, with deferments available to military, Peace

Corps, and VISTA personnel (Trimble, 1969).

The 1972 Amendments sought to remedy several problems with the GSL. To prevent students from borrowing money for noneducational purposes, a notarized statement that the funds would only be used for education was required. The maximum gross income level of $15,000 was eliminated so that those with unusual expenses and incomes over that level could qualify. The use of need analysis for the program was established (Brugel & Hofmann, 1974) in response to the unanticipated side effect of unnecessary borrowing under the original program (Marshall, 1968).

Another problem with the GSL has been the increasing rate of defaults on loan payments. In 1965 the default rate on loans guaranteed by United Student Aid Funds, Inc., a nation-wide, nonprofit agency which guarantees student bank loans, was 2.5 percent, but by 1973 it had risen to 5 percent. The default rate on federally insured loans was 4 percent in 1973 with one region reporting 13.6 percent. State agencies have reported similar increases on default rates (Mathis, 1973). Finally, despite the fact that the GSL represents the most significant growth in financial aid programs — since 1965 it has made $3 1/3 billion available to 3 million students and in 1972 alone it guaranteed approximately $1 billion — (Wedemeyer, 1972), the FISL has been criticized for rejecting a larger number of qualified applicants (Mayes, 1973).

Supplementary Educational Opportunity Grant Program (SEOG)

Originally titled Educational Opportunity Grants (EOG), this program is designed to provide outright grants to exceptionally needy students who otherwise would be unable to attend an institution of higher education (Zelenak, 1973). These grants generally range from $200 to $1,000 per year with a one-year ceiling of $1,500 and a five-year maximum of $5,000. The grant cannot amount to more than one half of the total aid given to the students. Additional eligibility criteria for this program are that the student must be a full-time undergraduate in good standing; show evidence of academic or creative promise, that is, be able to complete a course of study; and meet a rigorous need test (Trimble, 1969; Zelenak, 1973).

Basic Educational Opportunity Grant Program (BEOG)

This program provides grant assistance in the form of an entitlement, a concept that assures the student a certain amount for attending any institution regardless of cost once the basic eligibility requirements are met (Van Dusen & O'Hearne, 1973). A student applies through the American College Testing Program and submits his or her Family Contribution Analysis Report. The educational institution then determines the amount of the award, which may range from $200 to $1,400 minus the family contribution or one half the educational cost (Zelenak, 1973).

Since its inception the BEOG has had difficulty: Legislation protective of the traditional federal programs has kept it underfinanced (Hogan, 1973); because of its unique definition of an independent student, it has raised serious issues regarding the criteria for judging students' independence from their parents (Hogan, 1973); and in creating another program to coordinate, it has added to the managerial problems of financial aid officers (Marmaduke, 1974).

Programs for Particular Fields

There are five federal financial aid programs designed for students in particular fields of study. Four of them are supportive of health-care-related careers: Nursing Student Loan Program, Nursing Scholarship Program, Health Professions Student Loan Program, and the Health Professions Scholarship Program. The fifth is the Law Enforcement Education Program.

Future of Federal Involvement

The future of federal involvement in student financial aid is not clear. However, trends include the shift away from eligibility at the institutional level to the concept of entitlement (Wattenbarger, 1971); the increasing emphasis on student debt as the means for financing higher education (Hartline, 1972); and improved cooperation and coordination among the various federal, state, and institutional programs (Prentice, Hill, & Nelson, 1971).

What seems to be needed at the federal level is a comprehensive national policy of financing higher education, if not all forms of post-secondary education, rather than the current "piecemeal pattern of funding" (Austin, 1967, p. 513; Boyd, 1975; Hatch, 1969). Also, considerably more money is needed for the federal aid programs (Carnegie Commission, 1968, 1970), because in the past they have not had sufficient funds to help all who qualified (Sanders & Nelson, 1971). No matter what role the federal government decides to take in the future, it is hoped that the diversity of institutions, genuine access for all socioeconomic levels, and "improving higher education quality by providing more resources per student — more qualified faculty, better buildings and equipment" (Rivlin & Weiss, 1969, p. 548) will be retained.

Loans

Students prefer gifts, loans, and work in that order (Panel on Student, 1971), though loans have become increasingly popular as economic pressures have increased (Babbidge, 1960; German, 1970; Jacobsen, 1967). Loans are considered beneficial in that they teach responsibility to the student and hence are developmental; students have a better appreciation for their education when they must pay for it; money allocated for lending returns to benefit others; and a need test is built in since most people will not borrow more than they need.

However, loans have led to the "negative dowry theory," which has probably been overplayed and which holds that students finishing college with an obligation to repay a loan are not as desirable as marriage partners as those without that liability (German, 1970). Also, loans are often unacceptable to low income students who come from a culture "where borrowing is associated with exploitative merchants" (Panel on Student, 1971, p. 30).

Student Employment

In 1963, Henry wrote, "there is a lack of proper attention to the role of student employment as a source of student financial aid" (p. 91). He attributed the bias against student work to the then commonly held notions that work hurts academic performance, that it detracts from the student's extracurricular involvement, and that students should devote all their energies to school. Today, part-time work for the college student is seen by some as an important part of preparation for life (Adams, 1975; Adams & Stephens, 1970; Burson, 1975; Evans, 1975; Griffin & Lenz, 1975; Henry, 1963; Ramsay, 1975), an opportunity for self-help (Babbush, 1966; Burson, 1975; Ramsay, 1975), and valuable work experience (Babbush, 1966; Henry, 1963). The extent of the value of the experience is, of course, contingent upon the degree to which the work relates to the student's educational program and vocational interest (Arbuckle, 1953; Baker, 1970; Moon, 1966). It is also important to coordinate the type and amount of employment with the rest of the aid package (Babbidge, 1960).

Three trends in student employment have been identified by Adams and Stephens (1970): (a) The advent and continuation of year-round educational programs creates more on-campus work opportunities. (b) The College Work-Study Program provides for full-time work for qualified students in certain settings in the institution and in governmental agencies and nonprofit organizations. (c) More business and industry employers are hiring qualified students, usually juniors, for summer work.

However, student employment may work a hardship on students whose inexperience in middle-class verbal skills requires more study time. Also, despite the widespread conviction that the students' work should be relevant to their educational and vocational needs, all too often the only work available is relatively meaningless to the students in terms of their future plans. Yet if students' income needs and the institution's need for cheap manpower (Babbush, 1966; Henry, 1963) are to be met, mismatches are likely to occur. Unfortunately, research on student attitudes toward their work-study jobs indicates that they often feel their jobs are dull, tedious, and not well related to their future plans (Panel on Student, 1971).

Financial Aid Counseling

Financial aid counseling developed as a result of increasing individualization of aid programs (Gross, 1962). It is

a recognition of individual differences in assisting a student in orienting himself [herself] to the problem of financing his [her] education, particularly in the direction of independence and a high order of personal responsibility (Risty, 1949, p. 223).

As a function of the aid office, it may be viewed as a learning process for the client/applicant/recipient (Lavery, 1966) and is considered by some to be the most important task in financial aid (Bowman, 1975; Windham, 1972). Given increasing systemization of need analysis and the entire awarding process, the anticipated future role of financial aid personnel is general financial counseling (Johnstone, 1973), for which training should be obtained (Bowman, 1975; Fields, 1974; Lavery, 1966; Quesada-Fulgado, 1974).

Counseling within a financial aid context occurs in regard to student expenses, financial aid opportunities, and money management (Bowman, 1975; Fields, 1974; Gross, 1962; Moon, 1966; Risty, 1949; Van Dusen & O'Hearne, 1973). Related activities are teaching fiscal responsibility (Fields, 1974; Moon, 1966), guiding students in decision making with respect to money matters (Gross, 1962; Risty, 1949), and information dissemination to specific groups, such as potential students, new students including freshmen and transfers, aid applicants, aid recipients, aid donors, parents, and students leaving the institution (Van Dusen & O'Hearne, 1973).

Counseling also may be needed to help students and their

parents understand why costs are so high; help them understand why they must support themselves as much as possible; help them decide which self-support method is best for them; advise them regarding academic and personal adjustment as it relates to financial matters; help them appreciate the underlying rules, regulations, and standards of the aid office; help parents understand the importance of full disclosure in financial self-report forms; inform high school counselors of the rules; and insure that all of the office's operations are student-centered (Moon, 1966).

Counseling in a financial aid office is much like counseling in a campus counseling service in regard to confidentiality and relationship skills, particularly for students who find it hard to admit financial need (Fields, 1974) and for those who feel they are being treated impersonally (see Ryan, 1967).

> Financial counseling is not too different from counseling in related problems *as far as the student is concerned* because the student's own needs are interwoven. The knowledge of financial and job resources, of legal limitations, and of the means of appraising financial need makes the financial counselor's task, however, a highly specific one (Wrenn, 1951, pp. 381-382).

One problem in counseling in the financial aid office is the relative responsibility of the financial counselor to the institution and to the client. If the counselor's role is defined as a controller of institutional funds, the student's needs may not be met. If the counselor is primarily concerned with the student's needs, the institutional responsibility may be neglected. Gross (1962) suggests this solution to the dilemma:

> [The counselor must] conscientiously and explicitly ... associate himself [herself] and attempt to associate the student with both functions. The approach is one of *cooperative* decision-making (p. 149).

By sharing the evaluative role, the counselor presumably will get better information and the decision will be more acceptable to the student. Thus, both the counseling objective and the fiscal objective are served.

The presenting problem in financial aid counseling is almost always that the student does not have adequate funding to meet educational expenses. But as in other counselor settings, this presenting problem is sometimes complexly interrelated with other personal problems (Fields, 1974; Gross, 1962; Quesada-Fulgado, 1974), such as unrealistically high educational-vocational goals (Fields, 1974).

A third problem area in financial aid counseling has to do with the counseling of minority students from poverty backgrounds. Such students may arrive at school with no money at all (Saurman, 1972), have unrealistic perceptions of the campus (Harris, 1968), find that attending college means a break in once-strong family ties (Harris, 1968), and feel their position in college is precarious because they are dependent upon an apparently thin thread of financial aid (Harris, 1968). Also, the college frequently becomes a home for these students, with the result that they need a place to live and a source of income when the college is not in session (Saurman, 1972).

One of the major problems in this area is that minority students from poverty backgrounds frequently do not manage money in the conventional middle-class mold. As Harris (1968) has put it, "the culture of poverty is not the best place to acquire a willingness to delay gratification" (p. 25). He suggests that the financial aid officer must function as an educator, teaching the value of budgeting in the middle-class way. On the other hand, Saurman (1972) prefers the approach of budgeting for the different values and needs of the minority student. According to him, the average black student needs a budget between $300 and $400 more than the average white student because minorities are often charged exorbitant rental prices for housing near campus; they tend to live over their means when they get to college because of previous lack of material things; and their desire for fashionable clothing and automobiles is a rationalization or compensation for "all the wrong doing that was befallen their race" (p. 25). He concludes that a white budget is often simply unrealistic within the black culture.

The counseling of minority students not only expanded the duties of aid personnel in terms of numbers of students, but also with respect to the investment of time and effort required to properly counsel them (Harris, 1968). Many financial aid officers were "like the suburban commuter who flashes through the ghetto on the freeway" (Baker, 1970, p. 150) as they lacked the experiential base necessary to relate to poor students' problems. Baker suggests listening and learning from these students while Klingelhofer (1971) suggests communicating in a straight-forward and comprehensible manner, taking into account the environmental pressures on them, and trying to understand, not reject, the difference in their lifestyle.

Bellia (1971) studied the perceptions of 81 black and 133 white counselees' rapport with the all-white financial aid counseling staff at one college in New York. Generally, the white students had more positive reaction toward the counselors than the blacks. The black counselees felt less accepted as individuals; felt more like they were being treated as "cases"; were less likely to trust and be confident in the counselor; were more likely to report frustration in dealing with the counselor; and were much more likely to feel insecure in the counseling relationship. On the average, the black students were 14 percent less positive about their financial aid counseling experience than were the whites.

Graduate Financial Aid

Financial aid for graduate students is different from aid to undergraduates primarily because the service typically is performed at the departmental level or, in the case of professional schools, at the college level. That most graduate aid is administered in this manner has led to the criticism that the service is uncoordinated and that the standards lack uniformity (Mueller, 1961). Graduate aid emphasizes high academic performance as the primary criterion for awards, though there has been some movement in the direction of including need (Moon, 1963; Panel on Student, 1971). Sources of graduate aid are also unique in that many are specialized support from the federal government (Moon, 1963). Finally, the nature of graduate assistantships are different in that they can rarely be classified as "employment," for [they] are given on the basis of promise and ability as well as need, and always have the nature of an internship. Often they do not require a full quota of work in exchange for the subsidy, but, on the other hand, they may exploit the students' skills without adequate compensation (Mueller, 1961, p. 475).

Community College Financial Aid

G. S. Miller (1971) believes that "community colleges have historically avoided providing financial aid services" (p. 24), because the myth of "cost free" somehow became associated with the idea of "tuition free" (see also Murphy, 1966; Russo, 1976).

However, a 1969 survey of 308 regionally accredited two-year colleges (Puryear, 1974) revealed that 92 percent of the respondents had full aid programs, including scholarships, grants, and loans. Further, 82 percent of them had one or more administrators devoting ten or more hours per week to financial aid (see Junior College Services chapter).

PERSONNEL

Characteristics

Although there is a wide range of ages among financial aid officers, the average officer is in the late 30's or early 40's (Hinko, 1971; Nash, 1968a; Puryear, 1974). In a recent national survey of over 1,850 aid officers (Bushaw, 1974), 22 percent were between thirty-five and forty and 14 percent between forty-one and forty-five. Over 80 percent of the officers were married and over 75 percent were men (Bushaw, Hinko; Puryear). Bushaw found that 90 percent were white, 7 percent were black, 2 percent were of Spanish heritage, .5 percent were American Indians, and .4 percent were Oriental.

Education

Most aid administrators have at least a Master's degree. In

Bushaw's survey of all forms of post-secondary schools, he found 28 percent had a Bachelor's degree, 47 percent had a Master's degree, 11 percent had a degree between a Master's and Ph.D., and 4 percent had a doctorate. Nash's study of four-year institutions found 66 percent with Master's and 17 percent with doctorates. At two-year colleges Hinko found 63 percent had a Master's or more (75% of them in Guidance and Counseling and 11% in School Administration) and Puryear more recently found 89 percent with Master's or more (70% in education) and 9 percent with doctorates. Such a high percentage of Master's degree holders in two-year colleges may be the result of smaller staffs; for example, Hinko's sample included 82 percent one-person offices.

In-service training in the operational aspects of the financial aid office, as well as a broad background in higher education, psychology, counseling, educational psychology, measurement, and research method and design, is frequently called for (Delaney, Hylander, Karp, & Lange, 1974; Evans, 1975; Johnson, 1972; Keene, Adams, & King, 1975; G. S. Miller, 1971; S. B. Moore, 1971; Smith, 1964). D. R. Moore (1975) recommends a competency-based certification approach as a means of insuring well-qualified personnel in the field.

Career Patterns

The typical financial aid officer has been in financial aid for three to four years and in some colleges in an administrative position for a few years longer. In two-year colleges the average length of employment in financial aid was found to be two years by Hinko and 3.3 years by Puryear. Willingham's (1970) survey of 122 western institutions found that in the community colleges 69 percent of the aid officers had been in financial aid less than three years and 31 percent less than one year. In four-year colleges Willingham and Nash found the average to be approximately three years. Bushaw's findings were similar: less than one year, 13 percent; one to two years, 18 percent; three to four years, 25 percent; five to seven years, 25 percent;

eight to ten years, 12 percent; and over 11 years, 6 percent. With respect to the total number of years in higher education administration, Puryear found the average to be 6.6 years in two-year colleges and Nash found it to be eight years in four-year colleges.

Professional Activities

Willingham found that 25 percent of the aid officers did not attend meetings of their regional associations; 33 percent participated in their aid association in some way; and 40 percent did not read the two major journals in financial aid. However, four years later, almost 80 percent of Bushaw's respondents reported they would attend state aid association meetings to keep current; 54 percent would attend regional meetings; and about 25 percent would go to the national meeting. Also 76 percent reported that they read "Financial Aid Newsletters" and 49 percent said they read the *Journal of Student Financial Aid*. With respect to membership in aid associations, 92 percent reported they belonged to their state financial aid association and 76 percent belonged to their regional association.

RESEARCH ON AID RECIPIENTS

Academic Achievement

Research in financial aid has been devoted to examining the academic achievement of aid recipients more than any other topic. Scholarships or grants do not appear to influence academic achievement. A study of forty-two matched pairs of freshmen recipients and nonrecipients of State of Kansas Scholarships from 1963 to 1964, forty-eight matched pairs in 1964 to 1965, and forty-five from 1965 to 1966, found that the scholarship recipients got higher grade point averages in all years but that the difference was significant only in 1965 to 1966 (Bergen, Upham, & Bergen, 1970; see also Elton & Rose, 1967). No significant differences in grade point average were found for

2,801 freshmen recipients at Oregon State University (Fields & LeMay, 1973) and for 233 Educational Opportunity Grant freshmen at the University of Missouri, Columbia (Rhodes & Caple, 1969). Similarly, no significant difference in grades was found for thirty-two matched pairs of freshmen EOG recipients at a two-year community college in the late sixties (Immenhausen, 1975).

Higher academic achievement may be related to loan repayment. Bergen, Bergen, and Miller (1972) studied 1,374 National Defense Student Loan borrowers at Kansas State University who had established at least an eighteen-month repayment pattern. They found that the higher the grades of student borrowers, the less likely they are to be delinquent with repayments. However, Harrington (1964) could find no significant relationship between grades and loan repayment for twenty-five students at Ohio University. A related finding is that students from higher socioeconomic backgrounds are more likely to meet their loan obligations (Pattillo & Wiant, 1972).

The single most researched subject in financial aid is the impact of part-time work on students' academic achievement. Most studies indicate that part-time work, usually defined as something less than twenty hours per week, does not diminish academic achievement (Anderson, 1966; Apostal & Doherty, 1972; Augsburger, 1974; Barnes & Keene, 1974; Dickinson & Newbegin, 1959; Gaston, 1973; Henry, 1967; Kaiser & Bergen, 1968; Trueblood, 1957). One study not in agreement with the above had mixed results (Hay & Lindsay, 1969); another study found that students working less than twenty hours per week achieved significantly higher grades than nonworking students (Augsburger, 1974). In a review of the literature in this area, Nash (1969) concluded that working does not hurt students' academic performance unless they are already academically weak or they work excessive amounts.

Attitudes about Work

To determine students' feelings about work, Brown (1962) surveyed 653 graduate students (73% fellowships, 23% teaching assistantships, and 22% research assistantships) at an Ivy League university. The students identified several income, educational, and occupational advantages of their work and 55 percent said it was more helpful than an equivalent amount of study time. Most of the dissatisfactions arose from assignment problems and other administrative difficulties, especially the nature of the work (41%) and mismatch of interests (31%). Carpenter (1971) found that 80 percent of the aid recipients said that the aid they received positively affected their lives, 17 percent reported it to be neutral and only 3 percent described it in negative terms (most of these were dissatisfied with the amount).

Matriculation

Financial aid seems to increase a student's likelihood of matriculation. Crawford (1966) found a highly significant difference in the percentage of National Merit Finalists who enrolled and got aid (98%) and those who did not receive assistance (76%). Similarly, Fields and LeMay (1973) found matriculation rates of 45 percent and 55 percent for nonrecipients of aid in the two years studied as compared to 90 percent and 76 percent for aid recipients.

Fenske and Boyd (1971) examined the effect of receiving a grant on students' choice of school. From 757 scholarship recipients and 630 grant recipients in Illinois, they found that 25 percent of the sample reported they would have attended a different college had they not received aid. Of those, 82 percent said they would have gone to a public institution instead of a private one. However, Kimball (1968) found in his survey of 367 recipients and 148 nonrecipients of Citizens Scholarships (ranging from $100 to $500) in 1965 throughout New Hampshire that less than one third of the recipients reported that receipt of a larger scholarship would have made any difference in their educational plans.

Persistence

The data regarding the impact of gift aid on student persistence is contradictory. Crawford (1966) studied 1,545 National Merit Finalists from 1959 to 1961 and found that 17 percent of the aid recipients withdrew from school compared with 34 percent of the nonrecipients. Similarly, Rhodes and Caple (1969) found that 89 percent of the Educational Opportunity Grant students persisted as opposed to the 75 percent freshmen average. Bergen, Upham, and Bergen (1970) also found that scholarship recipients persisted longer, but their results were not statistically significant. In contrast, Fields and LeMay (1973) and Selby (1973), who studied thirty matched pairs of freshmen in 1968 at the University of Missouri, Columbia, found no significant relationship between financial aid and persistence.

Student Expenses

Student expenditure patterns were examined by Jepsen, Maxey, and Henry (1973). They surveyed a large stratified random sample of upper-class students selected from the thousands who had the ACT need analysis done and their findings are based on unadjusted 1971 dollar figures. They found that students living with parents or relatives reported expenses ranging from $700 to $900 less than other residential groups; that the common rule of thumb used by aid officers of adding $400 to $500 miscellaneous expenses to tuition, fees, room, and board expenses was supported; and that students overestimated by approximately $250 the amount of money they could save over the summer. A separate but related finding was that across all races an average of 10 percent of students contribute to their family's income and the percentages tend to be much higher for Chicanos and blacks.

Stewart (1975) studied 280 freshmen in the fall of 1971 at Ohio State University. Comparing black students and white students on total educational costs for the academic year, he found that black students reported their expenses to be about 18 percent higher than the white students reported. The groups reported similar costs for tuition, fees, books, and supplies, but their food, housing, clothing, and recreational expenses were substantially different.

RELATIONSHIPS TO OTHER SERVICES

The administrative relationship of financial aid to admissions is probably the most significant (Van Dusen & O'Hearne, 1973). Both offices are concerned with the same students and often an individual's decision about whether or not to attend a particular institution is contingent upon the availability of aid (DeJarnett, 1975; North, 1975; Sheffield & Meskill, 1973; Van Dusen & O'Hearne, 1973). According to Nash and Lazarfield's 1968 study (in Stamatakos & Bekkering, 1972) of 849 four-year institutions of higher education, 80 percent of the aid offices had no formal administrative relationship with the admissions office and 69 percent of the aid offices were administratively separate from admissions, but 70 percent reported fairly close or close coordination of functions. As evidence of this, almost all financial aid advisory committees included someone from the admissions staff; however, only 30 percent of the financial aid directors served on admissions committees.

The relationship of the aid office to the business office is "another area of mutual administrative dependency" (Van Dusen & O'Hearne, 1973, p. 41). Because both offices deal with money and have overlapping accounting and reporting requirements, a close cooperative arrangement is required (DeJarnett, 1975; North, 1975; Stamatakos & Bekkering, 1972; Van Dusen & O'Hearne, 1973). This need for coordination is especially acute concerning student loans since most financial aid officers do not get involved in collection and repayment (Newell, 1970; Van Dusen & O'Hearne, 1973) and it is generally agreed that collection is best left to the business office (Hage, 1973; Van Dusen & O'Hearne, 1973; cf. Swift, 1976).

STATEMENT OF PRINCIPLES

The following "Statement of Principles" was adopted in

1961 by the College Scholarship Service Assembly of the College Entrance Examination Board. The more than 1,600 members of the Assembly including post-secondary institutions, secondary schools, and agencies support the statement.

1. The purpose of any financial aid program — institutional, governmental, or private — should be to provide monetary assistance to students who can benefit from further education but who cannot do so without such assistance. The primary purpose of a collegiate financial aid program should be to provide financial assistance to accepted students who, without such aid, would be unable to attend that college.

2. Each college has an obligation to assist in realizing the national goal of equality of educational opportunity. The college, therefore, should work with schools, community groups, and other educational institutions in support of this goal.

3. The college should publish budgets that state total student expenses realistically including, where applicable, maintenance at home, commuting expenses, personal expenses, and necessary travel.

4. Parents are expected to contribute according to their means, taking into account their income, assets, number of dependents, and other relevant information. Students themselves are expected to contribute from their own assets and earnings, including appropriate borrowing against future earnings.

5. Financial aid should be offered only after determination that the resources of the family are insufficient to meet the student's educational expenses. The amount of aid offered should not exceed the amount needed to meet the difference between the student's total educational expenses and the family's resources.

6. The amount and type of self-help expected from students should be related to the circumstances of the individual. In the assignment of funds to those students designated to receive financial aid, the largest amounts of total grant assistance should go to students with the least ability to

pay.

7. The college should review its financial assistance awards annually and adjust them, if necessary, to reflect changes in the financial needs of students and the expenses of attending the institution. The college has an obligation to inform students and parents of the financial aid renewal policies for enrolled students at the time of the initial offer of financial assistance.

8. Because the amount of financial assistance awarded reflects the economic circumstances of the student and his [her] family, the college should refrain from any public announcement of the amount of aid offered, and encourage the student, his [her] secondary school, and others to respect the confidentiality of this information.

9. All documents, correspondence, and conversations between and among the aid applicant, his [her] family, and financial aid officers are confidential and entitled to the protection ordinarily arising from a counseling relationship.

10. Concern for the student should be paramount. Financial aid should be administered in such a manner that other interests, important though they may be, are subordinate to the needs of the student. (Reprinted with permission of the College Entrance Examination Board, New York.)

REFERENCES

Adams, F. C. Administering the office of student work and financial assistance. In R. Keene, F. C. Adams, & J. E. King (Eds.), *Money, marbles, or chalk: Student financial support in higher education.* Carbondale: Southern Illinois University Press, 1975.

Adams, F. C., & Stephens, C. W. *College and university student work programs: Implications and implementations.* Carbondale: Southern Illinois University Press, 1970.

Allen, D. J. Financial aid updated. *Journal of the National Association for Women Deans, Administrators, and Counselors,* 1967, *30,* 57-62.

Anderson, B. D. The academic load of the employed student. *Journal of College Student Personnel,* 1966, *7,* 23-26.

Apostal, R. A., & Doherty, C. P. Effects of positive and routine job assignments on academic performance. *Journal of College Student*

Personnel, 1972, *13,* 270-272.

Arbuckle, D. S. *Student personnel services in higher education.* New York: McGraw-Hill, 1953.

Augsburger, J. D. An analysis of academic performance of working and nonworking students on academic probation at Northern Illinois University. *Journal of Student Financial Aid,* 1974, *4*(2), 30-39.

Austin, C. G. On financing higher education. *Journal of Higher Education,* 1967, *38,* 511-513.

Babbidge, H. D. *Student financial aid: Manual for colleges and universities.* Washington, D. C.: American College Personnel Association, 1960. (Student Personnel Monograph Series, No. 1)

Babbush, H. E. The work-study program in action. *Journal of College Student Personnel,* 1966, *7,* 271-274.

Baker, W. The financial aid office and minority students. In R. A. Altman & P. O. Snyder (Eds.), *The minority student on the campus: Expectations and possibilities.* Boulder, Colo.: Western Interstate Commission for Higher Education, 1970.

Barnes, J. D., & Keene, R. A comparison of the initial academic achievement of freshman award winners who work and those who do not work. *Journal of Student Financial Aid,* 1974, *4*(3), 25-29.

Bellia, A. J. Variations in the response of black and white students in their relationship with the financial aid counselor. *Journal of Student Financial Aid,* 1971, *1*(2), 41-46.

Bellia, A. J. Computerized student financial aid reporting: How it works at a small private college. *Journal of Student Financial Aid,* 1973, *3*(1), 39-44.

Bergen, G. R., Upham, J. A., & Bergen, M. B. Do scholarships affect academic achievement? *Journal of College Student Personnel,* 1970, *11,* 383-384.

Bergen, M. B., Bergen, G. R., & Miller, D. G. Do GPA and loan size affect' NDSL repayments? *Journal of College Student Personnel,* 1972, *13,* 65-67.

Bingham, R. G. Financial aid packaging: Student-serving or institution-serving? *National Association of College Admissions Counselors Journal,* 1970, *15*(2), 23-25.

Bowen, H. R. Finance and the aims of American higher education. In M. D. Orwig (Ed.), *Financing higher education: Alternatives for the federal government.* Iowa City, Iowa: American College Testing Program, 1971.

Bowman, A. E. The financial aid counselor — a true educator. In R. Keene, F. C. Adams, & J. E. King (Eds.), *Money, marbles, or chalk: Student financial support in higher education.* Carbondale: Southern Illinois University Press, 1975.

Boyd, J. D. State programs of financial aid. In R. Keene, F. C. Adams, & J. E. King (Eds.), *Money, marbles, or chalk: Student financial support in higher education.* Carbondale: Southern Illinois University Press, 1975.

Brown, D. G. A student evaluation of research assistantships. *Journal of Higher Education,* 1962, *33,* 436-442.

Brugel, J., & Hofmann, G. The revised Guaranteed Student Loan Program: An impact analysis. *Journal of Student Financial Aid,* 1974, *4*(1), 11-18.

Burns, W. J. The partnership between financial counseling and NDEA loans. *Journal of College Student Personnel,* 1963, *4,* 240-242; 245.

Burson, R. F. Student employment and the off-campus employer. In R. Keene, F. C. Adams, & J. E. King (Eds.), *Money, marbles, or chalk: Student financial support in higher education.* Carbondale: Southern Illinois University Press, 1975.

Bushaw, W. J. *Survey of financial aid administrators.* Unpublished manuscript commissioned by the National Association of Student Financial Aid Administrators, University of Iowa, 1974.

Caldwell, O. J. American higher education and the federal government. In R. Keene, F. C. Adams, & J. E. King (Eds.), *Money, marbles, or chalk: Student financial support in higher education.* Carbondale: Southern Illinois University Press, 1975.

Carnegie Commission on Higher Education. *Quality and equality: New levels of federal responsibility for higher education.* New York: McGraw-Hill, 1968.

Carnegie Commission on Higher Education. *Quality and equality: Revised recommendations.* New York: McGraw-Hill, 1970.

Carpenter, E. A study of needs and activities of financial aid recipients and non-recipients. *Journal of Student Financial Aid,* 1971, *1*(2), 8-17.

Casazza, C. L. Career patterns of financial aid directors. *Journal of Student Financial Aid,* 1971, *1*(2), 33-40.

Cohen, W. J. NDEA: An idea that grew. *American Education,* 1968, *4*(8), 2-3.

Collins, J. S. Verification of parental income estimates by means of federal tax returns — the experience at one institution. *Journal of Student Financial Aid,* 1973, *3*(3), 20-25.

Crawford, N. C. *Effects of offers of financial assistance on the college-going decisions of talented students with limited financial means.* Evanston, Ill.: National Merit Scholarship Corporation, 1966. (ERIC Document Reproduction Service No. ED 017 000)

Cunningham, P. J. Estimating parents' income in succeeding years — accuracy of present CSS system. *Journal of Student Financial Aid,* 1972, *2*(2), 8-12.

Davis, F. Two worlds of integrity. *National Association of College Admissions Counselors Journal,* 1968, *13*(2), 1-4; 30.

DeJarnett, R. P. The organization of student support programs in institutions of higher learning. In R. Keene, F. C. Adams, & J. E. King (Eds.), *Money, marbles, or chalk: Student financial support in higher education.* Carbondale: Southern Illinois University Press, 1975.

Delaney, F. H., Jr., Hylander, G. L., Karp, R., & Lange, R. J. A taxonomy of objectives for the training of financial aid administrators. *Journal of Student Financial Aid,* 1974, *4*(3), 5-12.

Dickinson, C., & Newbegin, B. Can work and college mix? *Personnel and Guidance Journal,* 1959, *38,* 314-317.

Dickson, D. R. Do you believe any of these 10 myths about financial aid? *College Board Review,* 1969, *73,* 14-18.

Doermann, H. Lack of money: A barrier to higher education. In *Barriers to higher education.* New York: College Entrance Examination Board, 1971.

Elton, C. F., & Rose, H. A. Personality characteristics of male scholarship recipients. *Journal of College Student Personnel,* 1967, *8,* 261-264.

Evans, W. A. Supervisors of student workers as teachers. In R. Keene, F. C. Adams, & J. E. King (Eds.), *Money, marbles, or chalk: Student financial support in higher education.* Carbondale: Southern Illinois University Press, 1975.

Feingold, S. N. *Scholarships, fellowships and loans* (Vol. III). Cambridge, Mass.: Bellman Publishing, 1955.

Fenske, R. H., & Boyd, J. D. The impact of state financial aid to students on choice of public or private college. *College and University,* 1971, *46,* 98-107.

Ferrin, R. I. *Student budgets and aid awarded in southwestern colleges* (Higher Education Surveys Report No. 5). Palo Alto, Calif.: College Entrance Examination Board, 1971.

Fields, C. R. Financial aid officer: Accountant or counselor? *Journal of Student Financial Aid,* 1974, *4*(2), 8-14.

Fields, C. R., & LeMay, M. L. Student financial aid: Effects on educational decisions and academic achievement. *Journal of College Student Personnel,* 1973, *14,* 425-429.

Gaston, M. A study of the effects of college-imposed work-study programs on grade point averages of selected students at Western Washington State College. *Journal of Student Financial Aid,* 1973, *3*(1), 19-26.

German, K. The financial drain on the average-income student. In *Financing equal opportunity in higher education.* New York: College Entrance Examination Board, 1970.

Green, R. K. Assessment of student financial needs: The rationale and purpose. *Journal of College Student Personnel,* 1962, *4,* 11-16.

Griffin, J. R., & Lenz, C. D. The on-campus student work program. In R. Keene, F. C. Adams, & J. E. King (Eds.), *Money, marbles, or chalk: Student financial support in higher education.* Carbondale: Southern Illinois University Press, 1975.

Gross, S. J. Financial counseling reconsidered. *Journal of College Student Personnel,* 1962, *3,* 146-154.

Gross, S. J. A critique of practice in the administration of financial aid. *Journal of College Student Personnel,* 1966, *7,* 78-85.

Hage, R. K. How well is your financial aid office being run? *College Board*

Review, 1973, *89*, 13-15; 24-25.

Hansen, W. L., & Weisbrod, B. A. A new approach to higher education finance. In M. D. Orwig (Ed.), *Financing higher education: Alternatives for the federal government.* Iowa City, Iowa: American College Testing Program, 1971.

Harrington, C. An evaluation of an emergency student loan program. *Journal of College Student Personnel*, 1964, *5*, 234-237.

Harris, J. W. New role for the student aid officer: "Resourceful uncle." *College Board Review*, 1968, *67*, 24-26.

Hartline, J. C. Student financial aid and the role of student loans. *College and University*, 1972, *47*, 106-117.

Hatch, W. T. Could this financial aid plan help end student unrest? *College Board Review*, 1969, *72*, 18-25.

Hay, J. E., & Lindsay, C. A. The working student: How does he achieve? *Journal of College Student Personnel*, 1969, *10*, 109-114.

Henry, J. B. Current issues in student financial aid. *Journal of College Student Personnel*, 1963, *5*, 89-92; 102.

Henry, J. B. Family financial power and college attendance. *Personnel and Guidance Journal*, 1965, *43*, 775-779.

Henry, J. B. Part-time employment and academic performance of freshmen. *Journal of College Student Personnel*, 1967, *8*, 257-260.

Henry, J. B. Trends in student financial aid. *Journal of College Student Personnel*, 1969, *10*, 227-231.

Henry, J. B. Student financial need analysis. In R. Keene, F. C. Adams, & J. E. King (Eds.), *Money, marbles, or chalk: Student financial support in higher education.* Carbondale: Southern Illinois University Press, 1975.

Hensley, M. R. The self-supporting student: Trends and implications. *Journal of Student Financial Aid*, 1974, *4*(2), 23-29.

Hinko, P. M. Financial aid officers and institutional programs. *Community and Junior College Journal*, 1971, *41*(7), 20-23.

Hogan, H. J. The basic educational opportunity grant program: Its impact upon the middle class. *Journal of Student Financial Aid*, 1973, *3*(2), 19-26.

Horch, D. H. Measuring the ability of undergraduate married students to contribute to educational costs. *Journal of Student Financial Aid*, 1973, *3*(3), 34-43.

Iffert, R. E. *Retention and withdrawal of college students.* (Bulletin No. 1). Washington, D. C.: Office of Education, 1958.

Immenhausen, R. L. Academic performance of Chicano educational opportunity grant recipients. *Journal of Student Financial Aid*, 1975, *5*(1), 50-56.

Ingraham, M. H., with the collaboration of King, F. P. *The outer fringe: Faculty benefits other than annuities and insurance.* Madison: University of Wisconsin Press, 1965.

Jacobsen, S. Financial aid for college students. In M. L. Farmer (Ed.), *Student personnel services for adults in higher education.* Metuchen, N. J.: Scarecrow Press, 1967.

Jacoby, D. L. Automating merged admissions and financial aid data. *College and University,* 1967, *42,* 496-498.

Jencks, C. Social stratification and higher education. In M. D. Orwig (Ed.), *Financing higher education: Alternatives for the federal government.* Iowa City, Iowa: American College Testing Program, 1971.

Jepsen, K. J., Matejka, L. E., & Hulet, R. E. Do more with less: "Computer packaging" — one possibility. *NASPA Journal,* 1972, *10,* 156-160.

Jepsen, K. J., Maxey, E. J., & Henry, J. B. Student expenditure patterns. *Journal of Student Financial Aid,* 1973, *3*(3), 3-9.

Johnson, B. G. Mini-internships — a method for professional improvement, orientation, and recruitment. *Journal of Student Financial Aid,* 1972, *2*(2), 19-22.

Johnstone, D. B. *New patterns for college lending: Income contingent loans.* New York: Columbia University Press, 1972.

Johnstone, D. B. Beyond need analysis. *College Board Review,* 1973, *87,* 12-16.

Johnstone, D. B., Wackman, D. B., & Ward, S. Student attitudes toward income contingent loans. *Journal of Student Financial Aid,* 1972, *2*(1), 11-27.

Jones, J. S. Some thoughts on the CSS treatment of family assets. *Journal of Student Financial Aid,* 1973, *3*(2), 4-11.

Kaiser, H. E., & Bergen, G. Shall college freshmen work? *Journal of College Student Personnel,* 1968, *9,* 384-385.

Kaufman, M. L. Federal aid to education, 1867-1971: Assumptions, needs, and behavioral objectives. *Journal of Education,* 1972, *154*(3), 25-31.

Keene, R., Adams, F. C., & King, J. E. New philosophy — new profession. In R. Keene, F. C. Adams, & J. E. King (Eds.), *Money, marbles, or chalk: Student financial support in higher education.* Carbondale: Southern Illinois University Press, 1975.

Kimball, R. B. Do scholarships help? *Personnel and Guidance Journal,* 1968, *46,* 782-785.

King, L. J., & Wedemeyer, D. J. Designing an information system for student financial aids. *Journal of Student Financial Aid,* 1974, *4*(1), 5-10.

Klingelhofer, E. L. Do race and economics decide who gets what? *Journal of Student Financial Aid,* 1971, *1*(1), 34-45.

Lamson, G., Johnson, M., & Lundeen, D. *Income contingent loans: Conceptual and applied framework for the small college.* Bloomington, Ind.: Midwest Association of Student Financial Aid Administrators, 1971.

Lavery, J. W. Financial aids: Everyone's business. *NASPA Journal,* 1966, *4,* 7-11.

Marmaduke, A. S. Who will pay for college? *Journal of Student Financial*

Aid, 1971, *1*(1), 22-27.

Marmaduke, A. S. The status of student financial aid: An observation. *Journal of Student Financial Aid*, 1974, *4*(2), 5-7.

Marshall, A. D. Some problems facing the guaranteed loan program. *Educational Record*, 1968, *49*, 311-315.

Mathis, J. H. Defaults: Lowering cloud over the guaranteed loan program. *Journal of Student Financial Aid*, 1973, *3*(1), 27-31.

Mayes, C. R. Revamp the Guaranteed Loan Program — and unlock the bank vault. *Journal of Student Financial Aid*, 1973, *3*(3), 10-19.

Maynard, A. P. Suggestions for improving student loan billing procedures and collection techniques. *Journal of Student Financial Aid*, 1974, *4*(2), 15-22.

McClellan, F. A black student's reaction to the present system of financial aid. In *Financing equal opportunity in higher education*. New York: College Entrance Examination Board, 1970.

McCormick, J. L. The role of the federal government in student financial aid — a history. *Journal of Student Financial Aid*, 1972, *2*(1), 47-56.

Meade, R. C. The development and significance of state scholarship programs. *Journal of Student Financial Aid*, 1972, *2*(1), 41-46.

Miller, G. S. The community college: Upstart on the financial aid scene. *Journal of Student Financial Aid*, 1971, *1*(2), 22-27.

Miller, L. K. Computer assisted financial aid disbursement and loan collection. *Journal of Student Financial Aid*, 1975, *5*(3), 27-34.

Moon, R. G. Care, cooperation, and coordination in student financial aid administration. *Educational Record*, 1959, *40*, 342-347.

Moon, R. G. *Student financial aid in the United States: Administration and resources*. Princeton, N. J.: College Entrance Examination Board, 1963.

Moon, R. G. Financial aids, present and future. *National Association of College Admissions Counselors Journal*, 1965, *10*(4), 22-24.

Moon, R. G. Student aid in a decade of decision. In G. J. Klopf (Ed.), *College student personnel work in the years ahead*. Washington, D. C.: American Personnel and Guidance Association, 1966. (Student Personnel Monograph Series, No. 7)

Moore, D. The independent student and the philosophy of financial aid officers. *Journal of Student Financial Aid*, 1973, *3*(2), 34-37.

Moore, D. R. Certification of financial aid professionals. *Journal of Student Financial Aid*, 1975, *5*(3), 15-20.

Moore, S. B. Suggested courses for the preparation of financial aid administrators. *Journal of College Student Personnel*, 1971, *12*, 143-146.

Morison, S. E. *The founding of Harvard College*. Cambridge, Mass.: Harvard University Press, 1935.

Morrison, R. J. The negative income tax and the private institution. *Educational Record*, 1970, *51*, 379-385.

Morse, J. F. Our groaning financial aid structure. *College Board Review*,

1964, *53*, 22-26.

Mueller, K. H. *Student personnel work in higher education.* Boston: Houghton Mifflin, 1961.

Murphy, J. T. A search for a more dynamic financial aid program in our community colleges. *NASPA Journal,* 1966, *4*, 11-13.

Nash, G. The current status of financial aid administration. *National Association of College Admissions Counselors Journal,* 1968, *13*(2), 5-8. (a)

Nash, G. The history and growth of student financial aid. *National Association of College Admissions Counselors Journal,* 1968, *13*(3), 11-17; 20. (b)

Nash, G. A review of financial aid research. *National Association of College Admissions Counselors Journal,* 1969, *14*(1), 20-28.

Newell, B. W. Enter now and pay later. *Educational Record,* 1970, *51*, 57-59.

North, W. M. The role of the aid officer in the institution. In R. Keene, F. C. Adams, & J. E. King (Eds.), *Money, marbles, or chalk: Student financial support in higher education.* Carbondale: Southern Illinois University Press, 1975.

O'Hearne, J. J. Financial aid may help most by helping fewer students. *College and University Business,* 1970, *49*(2), 37-39.

O'Hearne, J. J. Financial aid office management. *Journal of Student Financial Aid,* 1973, *3*(2), 27-33.

Orwig, M. D. Alternatives for the federal government. In M. D. Orwig (Ed.), *Financing higher education: Alternatives for the federal government.* Iowa City, Iowa: American College Testing Program, 1971. (a)

Orwig, M. D. *Toward more equitable distribution of college student aid funds: Problems in assessing student financial need* (Research Report No. 43). Iowa City, Iowa: American College Testing Program, 1971. (b)

Orwig, M. D., & Jones, P. K. *Can financial need analysis be simplified?* (Research Report No. 33). Iowa City, Iowa: American College Testing Program, 1970.

Owen, J. D. *Toward a more consistent, socially relevant college scholarships policy.* Baltimore, Md.: Center for the Study of Social Organization of Schools, Johns Hopkins University, 1970. (ERIC Document Reproduction Service No. ED 036 280)

Panel on Financing Low-Income and Minority Students in Higher Education, College Entrance Examination Board. *Toward equal opportunity for higher education.* New York: Author, 1973.

Panel on Student Financial Need Analysis, College Entrance Examination Board. *New approaches to student financial aid.* New York: Author, 1971.

Pattillo, L. B., & Wiant, H. V. Which students do not repay college loans? *Journal of Student Financial Aid,* 1972, *2*(2), 32-35.

Pernal, M. State colleges and the middle income student: A dilemma for the financial aid officer. *College and University,* 1972, *48*, 84-86.

Prentice, J. T., Hill, W., & Nelson, J. Financial aid — direction for the 70's. *College and University*, 1971, *46*, 569-582.

Puryear, J. B. Two-year college financial aid officers. *Journal of College Student Personnel*, 1974, *15*, 12-16.

Quesada-Fulgado, C. The role of counseling in financial aid. *Journal of Student Financial Aid*, 1974, *4*(1), 19-24.

Ramsay, W. R. Students as manpower. In R. Keene, F. C. Adams, & J. E. King (Eds.), *Money, marbles, or chalk: Student financial support in higher education.* Carbondale: Southern Illinois University Press, 1975.

Rauh, M. A. *Student financial aid at private colleges.* Ann Arbor, Mich.: The Great Lakes Colleges Association, 1972.

Research Committee of the Michigan Student Financial Aid Association. Independent student policies and practices in Michigan. *Journal of Student Financial Aid*, 1976, *6*(1), 3-10.

Rhodes, L. L., & Caple, R. B. Academic aptitude and achievement of educational opportunity grant students. *Journal of College Student Personnel*, 1969, *10*, 387-390.

Risty, G. B. Financial counseling. In E. G. Williamson (Ed.), *Trends in student personnel work.* Minneapolis: University of Minnesota Press, 1949.

Rivlin, A. M. *The role of the federal government in financing higher education.* Washington, D. C.: Brookings Institution, 1961.

Rivlin, A. M., & Weiss, J. H. Social goals and federal support of higher education — the implications of various strategies. In *The economics and financing of higher education in the United States* (A compendium of papers submitted to the Joint Economic Committee, Congress of the United States). Washington, D. C.: U. S. Government Printing Office, 1969.

Rivlin Report, *Toward a long-range plan for federal financial support for higher education.* Washington, D. C.: United States Department of Health, Education, and Welfare, 1969. (ERIC Document Reproduction Service No. ED 038 102)

Roose, K. D. Aid to students — or to institutions? *Educational Record*, 1970, *51*, 356-367.

Rothschild, J. The NDEA decade. *American Education*, 1968, *4*(8), 4-11.

Rudolph, F. *The American college and university.* New York: Vintage Books, 1962. (a)

Rudolph, F. The origins of student aid in the United States. In *Student financial aid and national purpose.* New York: College Entrance Examination Board, 1962. (b)

Russo, J. A. Community college student aid: A hard look from within. *Journal of Student Financial Aid*, 1976, *6*(1), 20-27.

Rutter, T. M., & Wickstrom, N. The use of income tax returns in the need analysis procedure. *Journal of Student Financial Aid*, 1976, *6*(1), 15-19.

Ryan D. W. Let's not award financial aid "by the numbers!" *College Board Review*, 1967, *62*, 18-19.

Sanders, E., & Nelson, J. Financing of undergraduates, 1969-1970. *College Student Personnel Abstracts*, 1971, *6*, 456. (Abstract)

Sauber, S. R. Money and marriage in college. *College and University*, 1971, *46*, 245-250.

Saurman, F. S. Minority students: Are we giving them adequate support? *Journal of Student Financial Aid*, 1972, *2*(3), 23-31.

Schaefer, W. P. College costs vs. middle incomes — a proposal. *Journal of Student Financial Aid*, 1973, *3*(2), 38-48.

Schlekat, G. A. Do financial aid programs have a social conscience? *College Board Review*, 1968, *69*, 15-20.

Selby, J. E. Relationships existing among race, student financial aid, and persistence in college. *Journal of College Student Personnel*, 1973, *14*, 38-40.

Seymour, W. R., Zimmerman, S. A., & Donato, D. J. Financial aid: What influences who gets it? *Journal of Student Financial Aid*, 1972, *2*(3), 10-17.

Sharon, A. T., & Horch, D. H. Accuracy in estimating parents' contribution to students' college expenses. *Journal of College Student Personnel*, 1972, *13*, 448-451.

Sheffield, W., & Meskill, V. P. First aid for recruiting — financial aid. *National Association of College Admissions Counselors Journal*, 1973, *18*(3), 13-15.

Sidar, A. G. Where small-college financial aid programs go wrong. *College Board Review*, 1966, *61*, 23-26.

Sidar, A. G. What makes a self-supporting student? *College Board Review*, 1973, *87*, 16-17; 28.

Smith, R. E. The training of financial aid administrators. *Journal of College Student Personnel*, 1964, *6*, 90-94.

Spencer, L. E. Risk measurement for short term loans. *Journal of Student Financial Aid*, 1974, *4*(3), 30-35.

Stamatakos, L. C., & Bekkering, J. R. Financial aid: Whom should it serve? *Journal of College Student Personnel*, 1972, *13*, 61-64.

Steif, W. GI bill failing to attract Vietvets. *College and University Business*, 1969, *47*(3), 63-65.

Stewart, M. A. Financial aid recipients: An appraisal by race. *Journal of College Student Personnel*, 1975, *16*, 238-243.

Swift, J. S., Jr. Collecting National Defense/Direct Student Loans: Is it a financial aid office responsibility? *Journal of Student Financial Aid*, 1976, *6*(1), 28-32.

Thackery, R. I. Aid to students — *and* to institutions: A rejoinder to Kenneth D. Roose. *Educational Record*, 1971, *52*, 23-30.

Tombaugh, R. L. Direct or indirect student aid? *Journal of Student Financial Aid*, 1972, *2*(1), 28-34.

Trimble, V. Student financial aid: What, where, and how. *American Education*, 1969, *5*(2), 7-8.

Trueblood, D. L. Effects of employment on academic achievement. *Personnel and Guidance Journal*, 1957, *36*, 112-115.

Van Dusen, W. D. Toward a philosophy of financial aid programs. *NASPA Journal*, 1966, *4*, 3-7.

Van Dusen, W. D., & O'Hearne, J. J. *A design for a model college financial aid office*. New York: College Entrance Examination Board, 1973.

Walkup, L. J., & Hoyt, W. G. The institution as an agency of student support. In R. Keene, F. C. Adams, & J. E. King (Eds.), *Money, marbles, or chalk: Student financial support in higher education*. Carbondale: Southern Illinois University Press, 1975.

Wattenbarger, J. L. Student fees and public responsibility. In M. D. Orwig (Ed.), *Financing higher education: Alternatives for the federal government*. Iowa City, Iowa: American College Testing Program, 1971.

Wedemeyer, R. H. A review of the literature and research: Guaranteed student loan program. *Journal of Student Financial Aid*, 1972, *2*(3), 32-37.

West, E. D. *Financial aid to the undergraduate*. Washington, D. C.: American Council on Education, 1963.

Wharton, C. R. Study now, pay later: Threat to a great commitment. *Chronicle of Higher Education*, 1971, *6*(11), 12.

Wilbanks, J. J. Tuition remission and the faculty child. *American Association of University Professors*, 1972, *58*, 419-422.

Willingham, W. W. *Professional development of financial aid officers*. Palo Alto: College Entrance Examination Board, 1970. (ERIC Document Reproduction Service No. ED 051 757)

Windham, D. M. Tuition, the capital market, and the allocation of subsidies to college students. *School Review*, 1972, *80*, 603-618.

Winter, R. An analysis of the effects of tuition and financial aid policies. In R. G. Cope (Ed.), *Tomorrow's imperatives today*. Vancouver, B. C.: Association for Institutional Research, 1973.

Wolk, R. A. *Alternative methods of federal funding for higher education*. Berkeley, Calif.: Carnegie Commission on the Future of Higher Education, 1968.

Wootton, R. T. Business management and data systems for financial aid offices. In R. Keene, F. C. Adams, & J. E. King (Eds.), *Money, marbles, or chalk: Student financial support in higher education*. Carbondale: Southern Illinois University Press, 1975.

Wrenn, C. G. *Student personnel work in college*. New York: Ronald Press, 1951.

Young, H. E. New federal support to institutions and students: What emphasis? *Liberal Education*, 1970, *56*, 305-308.

Zelenak, B. M. *Student financial aid handbook*. Unpublished manuscript, University of Iowa, 1973.

CHAPTER 3

ORIENTATION

MICHAEL DANNELLS AND GEORGE D. KUH

HISTORY

ORIENTATION began with the informal efforts of upperclassmen and faculty to welcome freshmen to campus. The first formal orientation program was introduced in 1888 when Boston University provided a course to acquaint new students with college life (Drake, 1966b; Mueller, 1961). By 1925, over twenty-five colleges had such courses (Drake, 1966b) with some institutions, such as Reed College in 1911, offering them for academic credit (Mueller, 1961). Ranging in duration from two weeks to a full academic year, orientation courses typically sought to impart study and library skills along with information about the school's purpose and campus activities (Brubacher & Rudy, 1968).

Freshman Week, an orientation program first used in 1923 by the University of Maine (Black, 1964; Drake, 1966b), had goals similar to those of the orientation course, but programming was concentrated in the week immediately preceding the fall semester (Brubacher & Rudy, 1968).

The number of orientation courses and freshman week programs greatly increased during the second and third decades of the Twentieth Century. Whether their increased popularity was due to a natural extension of the counseling or student personnel movement which appeared about 1918 (Brubacher & Rudy, 1968), or to a "great concern over excessive dropouts" (Grier, 1966, p. 37) is unclear.

During the 1930's the number of orientation courses was reduced considerably because faculty objected to the courses' emphasis on life adjustment which was often considered to be antithetical to the liberating experience associated with general education (Caple, 1964). Precollege or summer clinics, first instituted by Michigan State University in 1949 (Drake, 1966b), took the place of formal courses (Butts, 1971), and by the mid-1960's, freshman week and/or summer clinics were the preferred orientation format(s). Orientation courses were practically nonexistent during this time, although renewed interest in them has been noted in recent years (Cantor, 1974; Ehrlich, 1969; Felker, 1973; O'Banion, 1969; Snider, 1970).

DEFINITION

Defining orientation is difficult at best because the goals, techniques, and participants in the process vary from institution to institution (Butts, 1971; Cantor, 1974). Traditionally, orientation has implied a series of "mass meetings where college authorities and selected members of the student body impart rules, regulations, and general information to the new student" (Snider, 1970, p. 138). From this perspective, orientation can be considered the final stage of the admissions process (Mueller, 1961).

In its purest sense, orientation attempts to provide a balanced introduction to the constraints imposed by, and the opportunities available in, the collegiate environment as well as to enable students to more clearly define their educational purpose (Wrenn, 1951). In order to insure that students periodically reassess their own goals and personal development (Black, 1964), the definition of orientation should, perhaps, be expanded to suggest a process which continues during the entire college experience ("Can we meet," 1976; Cantor, 1974; Gohn, 1975; Wrenn, 1951).

Purpose and Philosophy

The major purpose of orientation is to articulate to new students that the college experience is most appropriately one of self-direction and intellectual stimulation (Morstain, 1972; Wrenn, 1951). Orientation "should contribute to the student's understanding of the relevance of higher education to his [her] life and problems" (Shaffer, 1962, p. 274). In philosophical terms, orientation can be thought of as either microcosmic or macrocosmic in scope and depth of purpose. Microcosmic programs are primarily concerned with the students' immediate relationship with the institution (Wigent, 1971), and macrocosmic programs attempt to help the new student come to understand the mission and purpose of higher education.

Regardless of purpose or philosophy chosen, most orientation directors agree that orientation should not do things for students. Rather, it should provide opportunities for students to do things for themselves (Black, 1964).

Implicit in most orientation programs is the notion that it is important to get the college experience off to a good start (Breckenridge, 1967; Mueller, 1961). This emphasis is supported by the law of primacy in social influence and persuasion which suggests that the side of an issue presented first is more effective and influential than the side presented subsequently. Therefore "orientation should be concerned with the purposeful exploitation of primacy in order to influence students to adopt new intellectual values and interests" (Williamson & Biggs, 1975, p. 184).

Goals and Objectives

Most orientation goals can be separated into those designed to disseminate information (Wigent, 1971) and those designed to help the student adjust to the college (McCann, 1967). Thus a general goal for most programs is to narrow the gap between the institution's and the students' expectations and needs (Li, 1962). Of course, most goals meet both groups of needs and fall into either group only in the degree to which they are emphasized.

Goals designed to inform include: completing enrollment procedures in a humane way (Butts, 1971); identifying the resources of the institution, such as study skills, career planning, and counseling services (Butts, 1971; Erickson, 1969; McCann, 1971); and disseminating other rules and regulations of the college community (Butts, 1971)1 Goals designed for student adjustment include: minimizing anxiety (Erickson, 1969; Wigent, 1971), which increases the student's receptivity to the new experiences (McCann, 1967); introducing students to new people and maximizing their interaction (Erickson, 1969) through community and relationship-building opportunities, such as residence hall orientation, social mixers, and Big Brother-Sister programs (Butts, 1971); creating a favorable disposition toward learning by emphasizing the uniqueness of the students and enhancing positive feelings about chances for success (Erickson, 1969).

To achieve any of these goals, administrative, faculty, and student support is necessary. Evaluated from a social persuasion perspective, it is important that these various constituencies not communicate conflicting messages (Williamson & Biggs, 1975). For example, students may emphasize the social aspects of college life while faculty tend to focus on the academic demands. Participation by all three groups and perhaps townspeople and parents in determining goals can increase their commitment to orientation and result in increased effectiveness of programming (Fitzgerald & Busch, 1963; Menning, 1975).

Needs of New Students

For many years orientation programs were more adequately meeting a number of administrative needs than attempting to discover and meet the needs of incoming students (Wigent, 1971). The earliest orientation programs operated under the assumption that the needs of new students were so obvious that everyone knew what these needs were: general information relevant to the academic and social environment which would, by itself, reduce anxiety (Drake, 1966b; Keil, 1966; Wigent, 1971). According to Van Eaton (1972), 90 percent of 200 institutions which offered orientation programs afforded students input in the development of the programs. Unfortunately, this information usually comes after the fact and from students who have been successful in coping with their new environment.

In order to determine the needs of new students prior to orientation, 100 high school seniors admitted to the 1958 freshman class at Purdue were sent a questionnaire listing ten areas considered to be relevant orientation topics (Tautfest, 1961). The following are the ranked order of reported needs: academic responsibility and study habits, academic program planning, familiarization with the campus, financial planning, extracurricular activities (student organizations, intramurals), social adjustment, special and remedial services, problems related to living away from home, purpose and value of education, and community facilities.

The belief that orientation programs should place less emphasis on social activities and more on academic-intellectual concerns (Keil, 1966; Li, 1962) is supported by these students' expressed desires. Probably different needs would be reported by students at other colleges. A systems approach (Spivack, 1973) may assist in conceptualizing the necessary steps in periodic needs-assessment and evaluation of orientation (Black, 1964).

ADMINISTRATION

The responsibility for orientation at four-year institutions is usually coordinated by the dean of students' office while at community colleges programming is most often (48%) provided by the counseling service (Van Eaton, 1972). In larger institutions, the orientation function is often afforded a separate office usually located in the Division of Student Affairs administrative structure.

Funding

Financial support for orientation is available from a variety of sources. A large portion of a typical budget, particularly professional and secretarial salaries and general supplies is provided by the institution's general fund. Other direct institutional support takes the form of assistance from academic departments or the use of college facilities. Other possible sources of funds may come from student government or from fees assessed to those who attend orientation. Also, scholarships or gift aid may be secured to enable students to take advantage of orientation who otherwise would be unable to attend (Butts, 1971).

Grant monies from public agencies and private foundations are perhaps the most sought after type of support but are the most difficult to obtain. Barr and Matthews (1975) offer some suggestions as to possible sources of extra-institutional support and outline the process through which such assistance can be secured.

Budget development and cost accounting procedures for an efficiently managed orientation program are beyond the scope of this chapter. Assistance should be requested from the budget officer of the academic or administrative unit through which orientation is administered.

PROGRAMS

Orientation programs can be categorized into calendar programs, classified by the times of the year they are offered and programs for special groups, classified by the clientele they serve.

Calendar Programs

Summer

Summer programs typically consist of a series of one to three day identical programs repeated on campus at various times throughout the summer (Forrest & Knapp, 1966). Summer orientation clinics, often referred to as precollege orientation, have become increasingly popular during the past few years ("Freshmen Get New Kinds," 1971). For example, in 1966 only 14 percent of 110 colleges offered precollege orientation (Drake, 1966a). But by 1972 about half of the community colleges, 43 percent of colleges and universities with enrollments of less than 10,000, and 84 percent of larger institutions utilized summer clinics (Van Eaton, 1972). One variation of the precollege clinic is the summer camp. These programs are held off-campus and are limited to a relatively small number of students. However, they tend to be costly, and as a result, have decreased in popularity (Williamson & Biggs, 1975).

Summer orientation can (Gohn, 1975) avoid interruption by interests and priorities which prevail during the school year; provide more personal attention because of the smaller number of students (100-400) in attendance; devote more time to the precollege anxieties of parents and students prior to classes; and serve as an additional recruitment effort for students undecided between one or more institutions (Bakas, 1975). However, summer programs are relatively expensive, require extra effort on the part of staff, faculty, administration, and student paraprofessionals, and require duplication in the fall for students who do not attend (Gohn, 1975; Grier, 1966).

Fall and Winter

Fall orientation programs have been the traditional method of orienting new students (Gohn, 1975). These programs are held the week preceding fall registration, average five days in length (Drake, 1966a), and tend to be somewhat less concerned with academic planning as they emphasize social, relationship-building activities (Cantor, 1974).

Summer and fall orientation programs can serve to compliment one another (Cantor, 1974) by providing small group interaction and academic planning in the summer, and social and cultural activities in the fall. Winter programs are similar in content to fall programs and serve to provide brief orientation for those students who enter at mid-year. The advantages and disadvantages of fall and winter orientation are the converse of summer programs.

Continuous

Ongoing or continuous orientation refers to programs which continue beyond the first few days new students are on campus.

The philosophical base of this approach is developmental in nature as students are perceived as continually growing and, therefore, in need of further orientation to new and unique experiences in college (White, 1972).

Ongoing orientation typically provides programs for particular interest groups, such as adults returning to post-secondary education. Some are specifically designed to continue over a semester or year, such as racism and sexism workshops. Gohn (1975) offers a number of ongoing programming suggestions and identifies relevant factors in choosing programming options: type of student body, such as scholastic ability and socioeconomic background; campus size, location, and facilities; advising and registration procedures; availability of staff, faculty, and student paraprofessionals; academic calendar; costs; and other planned institutional programs.

Special Groups

The rationale for developing programs for special student groups is essentially the same in each case: Orientation programs for groups of students with unique characteristics and needs provide information and assistance to optimize their personal development throughout college (Butts, 1971; Cantor, 1974; Goodale & Sandeen, 1971; Knoell & Medsker, 1965). Students who are members of specialized groups should be involved in planning the orientation programs for their group.

Freshmen

Traditionally, orientation has been considered an effort to smoothly facilitate new students' transition from high school to college. Freshmen programs should not coddle (Eddy, 1959) but should attempt to create conditions under which development can occur (Williamson & Biggs, 1975).

> If the first few weeks of college constitute a kind of developmental crisis which can result in a spurt of development, then the college would be well advised to arrange for their students an educational program embracing a series of such crises

(Sanford, 1962, p. 280).

Most freshman programs employ some variant of friendship orientation and emphasize the dual crises of identity and intimacy, two concerns which have some theoretical validity (Committee on the Student in Higher Education, 1968; Erickson, 1969) and are of interest to students (Chandler, 1972; Witkin, 1971).

Transfer

Transfer students tend to be highly critical of orientation programs (Butts, 1971; Sandeen & Goodale, 1972). Over half of 624 colleges did not provide specific transfer orientation programs, and of those that did, only 22 percent used former transfer students in the planning and delivery of programs (Sandeen & Goodale, 1972). The problem has its roots in the notion that the expectations of freshmen and transfers are similar (Knoell & Medsker, 1965; see Buckley, 1971). Most of the evidence, however, seems to suggest the opposite.

Transfer students differ from freshmen in that they tend to: be less independent, reflective, tolerant, and self-confident; more practical or conventional; perform less well academically; be from lower socioeconomic background; work more while enrolled in college; encounter financial difficulties to a greater degree; offer different reasons for attending college; be less interested in extracurricular activities (Goodale & Sandeen, 1971).

In addition, transfer students from different kinds of institutions may be dissimilar; for example, community college transfers and those from four-year institutions differ on the amount of credit transferred and on housing preferences (Worley & Conrad, 1973).

Culturally Distinct

Culturally distinct students (blacks, Chicanos, native Americans, etc.) have needs which differ from other campus student groups (Canizales, 1971; Gohn, 1975; Goodson, 1972; Harrold, 1970), but they may share personal and social problems (Smith,

1964). The issue of greatest controversy seems to be whether to separate the culturally distinct from other new students during orientation. However, separate programs may only serve to augment the distance in understanding and appreciation of cultural differences (Cantor, 1974). A reasonable solution seems to be a balance between the two, with some joint sessions and some specifically designed for the culturally distinct.

Adult

Some of the more obvious ways in which adult students are dissimilar from traditional undergraduates are: the tension resulting from possible role (family, work, student) conflict; the possible resentment or jealousy of a spouse; guilt feelings arising from neglect of spouse and family and related problems, such as child care; lack of study skills (Peavey, 1968); perceived or real lack of acceptance by other students; lack of appropriate university services to assist older students (DeWolf & Lunneborg, 1972; Gohn, 1975; Peavey, 1968). With the increasing numbers of older students returning to post-secondary education, these differences must be acknowledged with appropriate programming.

Foreign

Foreign students' most unique problems are associated with culture shock (Cantor, 1974). Foreign students not only must acclimate themselves to a particular institution but also to the culture which sustains it. Orientation staff have an obligation to support the concept of cultural relativity: "Respect the foreign student's sensitivity and pride in his [her] own culture" while at the same time assisting to "develop the ability to function comfortably and effectively in the host culture" (National Association for Foreign Student Affairs, 1964, p. 2).

Parents

For the most part, orientation programs acknowledge parents

for public relations purposes only (Butts, 1971; Cantor, 1974; Stamatakos, 1963). Since parents seem appreciative of programs specifically designed for them (Miller & Ivey, 1967; Winkworth, Brown & Braskamp, 1973), perhaps more should be attempted, particularly in the area of modifying the prevalent parental attitude that college is primarily vocational training (McCann, 1967). In addition, parent orientation could serve to: challenge stereotypes about the institution; develop awareness about new value systems and ideas to which their offspring will be exposed; introduce parents to faculty and staff; explain costs; describe changes they may expect in their son or daughter; increase parent-institution and student-parent understandings; and develop a feeling of trust between parents, students, and the institution (Gohn, 1975).

Programs have been developed to help students and their parents clarify their often divergent expectations of each other (Dorris & Williams, 1974), and to roleplay "student-parent conflicts [which] ... could well provide the most supportive bridge between different value systems" (Celio, 1973, p. 219). "If one is committed to the position that the progress of students is inextricably tied to parental attitudes and values, then the institution must do all that it can to make parents effective participants in the process" (Gohn, 1975, p. 32).

Community College Orientation

For the most part, orientation programs at community colleges have much in common with programs at other institutions. However, because of the diverse nature and sociodemographic characteristics of their students, community college orientation often includes a broader range of activities than four-year schools typically provide (Blocker, Plummer, & Richardson, 1965; Butts, 1971; Del Prete & Waterhouse, 1973; Sohn, 1975). In contrast to the social relationship programming characteristic of four-year residential colleges, the community college emphasizes counseling and academic placement (Butts, 1971, see Junior College Services chapter).

Others

As the demographic characteristics of persons pursuing post-secondary education increase in heterogeneity, it is imperative that orientation staff periodically assess the unique orientation needs of the various student groups on their respective campuses. Special groups which are likely to benefit from specific programming efforts are veterans, married students, part-time students, physically handicapped students, commuters (see Scheuer, 1967), residence hall boarders, and graduate students.

PERSONNEL

Professional

Van Eaton's (1972) survey of orientation directors divided institutions into community colleges, four-year colleges with less than 10,000 students, and four-year colleges with 10,000 or more students. Most orientation directors held Master's degrees although 24 percent of the directors at smaller four-year schools, 20 percent at large four-year institutions, and 11 percent at community colleges had doctorates. The average number of years of experience for directors was about five with several having as many as twenty-five years.

In the late 1940's, professional orientation personnel began meeting at an annual national conference to exchange programming innovations in hopes of increasing the effectiveness of orientation. In 1973, the National Orientation Director's Association (NODA) was formed. In addition to the annual NODA Handbook and the American Personnel and Guidance publications, the *National Orientation Bulletin* is the medium through which the profession communicates events and programs of interest.

Paraprofessional

Most paraprofessionals in orientation tend to be upperclass

(sophomore-senior) students and, for the most part, the literature is supportive of these student orientation assistants provided they have been well trained (Banta, 1969; Barr, 1975; Cantor, 1974; Delworth, Sherwood, & Casaburri, 1974; Foxley, 1969; Trotter, 1975; Wigent, 1971; Williamson & Biggs, 1975; Wrenn, 1951).

Rationale

Students are used in orientation programs because: They are energetic; their participation will sensitize the university to student needs; their perceptions of the campus environment are often fresh and stimulating (Delworth et al., 1974; Mueller, 1961; Trotter, 1975); and they are closer to the experience of the freshman and can provide more accurate information and empathy (Mueller, 1961). Perhaps most important is the consensus among orientation directors that new "students learn more from fellow students than from other sources" (Trotter, 1975, p. 36).

Function and Role

The use of students increases staff size considerably with minimal financial strain on the orientation budget and can serve to personalize the orientation process as more small group experiences can be provided. The major functions of student orientation paraprofessionals are campus resource, group facilitation, and public relations (Delworth et al., 1974). As campus resource persons, student orientation advisors can offer accurate information and perceptions about the social and academic dimensions of the institution. As group facilitators, students may be utilized to lead campus tours and moderate group discussions which facilitate socialization and personal and environmental insight. However, it is evident that limiting paraprofessionals to introducing new students to an institution's social activities is inadequate to accomplish the goals of most orientation programs (Delworth et al., 1974; Foxley, 1969). As a public relations liaison, students may provide parents with accurate accounts of college life from the students' perspective and enlighten them concerning the problems their offspring are likely to encounter.

Certainly there are limitations to what student paraprofessionals can do. They may go "beyond their scope of experience and expertise" (Delworth et al., 1974, p. 36) when advising new students and parents and may attempt to offer resolutions to problems which should be referred to professional staff. However, a well-designed and comprehensive selection and training program can minimize these problems.

Selection

Composition of the selection committee is an important consideration. Certainly both sexes should be represented. In addition to orientation staff persons, the committee should include representatives from the faculty, administration, and students, preferably some of whom are former orientation paraprofessionals. The first task of the committee is to adopt or revise selection criteria. Specific selection criteria may vary by institution but assessment of the candidate's leadership experience, knowledge of the institution, interpersonal skills, and academic ability seem appropriate (Delworth et al., 1974). Those seeking prestige rather than an outlet for altruism may be less effective staff members (Snider, 1970).

The selection process is time-consuming but critical to building a competent, enthusiastic staff (Trotter, 1975). The selection criterion receiving greatest emphasis is the prospective paraprofessional's style of interaction when meeting with the selection committee. The advantages of group versus individual selection interviews have been discussed at length with apparent preference for the former:

> The results of studies comparing the efficacy of the two methods have shown that they are equally valid (Banta, 1969). The use of the leaderless group discussion or group interview technique, however, does offer some practical advantages. First, the time spent reviewing applicants is reduced. Second, the group discussion setting involves the applicants in an

actual situation in dealing with people and would seem to be a valid predictor of future performance .... Banta (1969) also found that group discussions are more likely to retain the attention and interest of the raters and express more aspects of the candidate's personality. A group situation also allows the student to demonstrate his [her] interpersonal skills in front of the selection committee (Delworth et al., 1974, pp. 37-38).

Training

The most appropriate content for the preservice training of student paraprofessionals eludes consensus. Among the general areas of expertise are: knowledge of the institution and its resources (some of this can be provided by various academic and student service offices); interpersonal and group skills acquired through group participation and outside reading in group dynamics and human relations; special skills (audiovisual or public speaking) acquired with the assistance of professionals in their respective areas (Banta, 1969; Cantor, 1974; Delworth et al., 1974; Trotter, 1975).

The method of acknowledging the participation of paraprofessionals should be determined and agreed to by the students prior to training. Four common forms of recognition are direct financial compensation (salary), indirect financial compensation (room and board), academic credit, and certification in leadership training (Delworth et al., 1974; Trotter, 1975).

RESEARCH

Evaluation

In order to determine the effectiveness of program design and staff performance, systematic evaluation of orientation programs is essential (Cantor, 1974). Comprehensive evaluation must, by definition, ask several questions: What are the students' orientation needs? How can these needs be clearly determined? How, and to what extent, are or can these needs be met (Nelson, 1970, see also Breckenridge, 1967; Butts, 1971; Drake,

1966b; Kopecek, 1971; Pappas, 1967a; Patty, 1966)?

In a study of orientation practices, Van Eaton (1972) found that only a third of the institutions surveyed conducted research concerning their programs. Most orientation research is evaluative in nature and findings are frequently contradictory. Because many studies evaluate orientation innovations at particular institutions and usually exhibit methodological problems, the results often cannot be generalized to other programs.

Academic Success

Much of the research in orientation attempts to measure the impact of programming on participants' academic achievement. With some exceptions, most studies have found that orientation programs do not affect academic performance. Between those who attend orientation and those who do not, few differences have been found in regard to grades, attrition, and stability of college major (Cole & Ivey, 1967; Gerber, 1970; Griffin & Donnan, 1970; Jesseph, 1966; Rothman & Leonard, 1967; Weigel & Smith, 1972). However, Chandler (1972) found that 738 attenders at a two-day camp with small group format got better grades and were less likely to drop out than were 754 nonattenders; and Rising (1967) found up to 50 percent lower attrition rate among freshmen engineering students who attended an intensely academic two-week program. Whether orientation increased the attenders performance or whether they differed from nonattenders on other dimensions (e.g. motivation) is not known.

Attitudes

Several investigations have sought to assess attitudinal changes resulting from orientation programs. Two studies (Donk & Hinkle, 1971; Rothman & Leonard, 1967) found no significant attitude changes based on pre- and post-orientation measures. Another (Herron, 1974) found little relationship between orientation attendance and students' feelings of alienation.

Yet some orientation programs have been found to affect students' attitudes in the following ways: more realistic expectations of academic demands (Cole & Ivey, 1967) and the environment in general resulting in greater satisfaction and better adjustment (Robinson, 1970); a general increase in positive feelings toward college life and learning (Reiter, 1964); greater interest in the extracurriculum (Chandler, 1972); and a clearer understanding of the student role and its responsibilities (Rising, 1967). Finally, an orientation program considered too "fun-and-games" in its approach influenced students to view their college environment as less orderly, less academic, and providing less opportunity for personal expansion and enrichment (Foxley, 1969).

Information Dissemination

For the most part, research regarding the effectiveness of information dissemination has compared different presentation methods. From the results of two studies (Forrer, 1974; Winkworth, Brown, & Braskamp, 1973), it is not clear whether parents gain more factual knowledge about the college environment from mailings or from on-campus presentations. With respect to getting information to students, mailings that repeat information presented in other ways are of questionable value (Weigel & Smith, 1972), formal classroom presentations seem preferable to less structured group experiences for teaching campus rules and regulations (Gerber, 1970), and lectures are preferred over programmed instruction techniques (Packard, 1967, 1968).

Program Content

Comparing student satisfaction with various types of orientation programs has provided some interesting findings. In the early 1960's Ivey (1963) found that students had an overwhelming preference for information-giving and social, as opposed to academic and intellectual, orientation activities. Later Volkwein and Searles (1965) reported an increasing interest in presentations emphasizing academic concerns. In 1966 Gibbs (1968) found that, in general, academic programs were better received than were social events. Some other findings about program popularity include students' preference for small group experiences as opposed to large assemblies (Miller & Ivey, 1967; Pappas, 1967b); students' perception of information dissemination as the most important function of orientation (Miller & Ivey, 1967); and students' unfavorable reactions to a required orientation course (Gerber, 1970).

Conclusion

Considering the amount of financial resources committed annually, the lack of rigorous research and evaluation concerning orientation programs is somewhat surprising (Butts, 1971; Kopecek, 1971; Pappas, 1967a; Patty, 1966). Extremely rare is research which supports commonly held beliefs about new student characteristics and needs as well as the extent to which orientation meets these needs (Breckenridge, 1967; Drake, 1966b). As the proportion of "traditional students" seeking higher education continues to shrink, the presumptions about the orientation needs of new students need to be carefully reexamined.

REFERENCES

Bakas, J. Orientation and student recruitment. In A. G. Matthews (Ed.), *Handbook for orientation directors.* Iowa City, Iowa: National Orientation Directors Association, 1975.

Banta, T. Selecting student orientation assistants: A comparison of approaches. *Journal of College Student Personnel*, 1969, *10*, 240-243.

Barr, M. J. Student input. In A. G. Matthews (Ed.), *Handbook for orientation directors.* Iowa City, Iowa: National Orientation Directors Association, 1975.

Barr, M. J., & Matthews, A. G. Funding and budget. In A. G. Matthews (Ed.), *Handbook for orientation directors.* Iowa City, Iowa: National Orientation Directors Association, 1975.

Black, B. R. Student needs and orientation directors' aspirations. *Journal of College Student Personnel*, 1964, *6*, 102-108.

Blocker, C. E., Plummer, R. H., & Richardson, R. C. *The two year college: A social synthesis.* Englewood Cliffs, N. J.: Prentice-Hall, 1965.

Breckenridge, J. W. New student testing and orientation. *NASPA Journal,* 1967, *5,* 210-212.

Brubacher, J. S., & Rudy, W. *Higher education in transition.* New York: Harper & Row, 1968.

Buckley, H. D. A comparison of freshman and transfer expectations. *Journal of College Student Personnel,* 1971, *12,* 186-188.

Butts, T. A. *Personnel services review: New practices in student orientation.* Ann Arbor: University of Michigan, 1971. (ERIC Document Reproduction Service No. ED 057 416)

Can we meet the challenge of orientation? *National Orientation Bulletin,* 1976, *6*(1), 1; 3.

Canizales, F. Orientation and counseling services for minority students. In R. A. Altman & P. O. Snyder (Eds.), *The minority student on the campus: Expectations and possibilities.* Boulder, Colo.: Western Interstate Commission for Higher Education, 1971.

Cantor, S. J. *Issues in orientation: Programs and goals.* Unpublished manuscript, University of Iowa, 1974.

Caple, R. B. A rationale for the orientation course. *Journal of College Student Personnel,* 1964, *6,* 42-46.

Celio, D. L. After innovation: Perspective on a parent orientation program. *Journal of College Student Personnel,* 1973, *14,* 216-219.

Chandler, E. M. Freshman orientation — is it worthwhile? *NASPA Journal,* 1972, *10,* 55-61.

Cole, C. W., & Ivey, A. E. Differences between students attending and not attending a precollege orientation. *Journal of College Student Personnel,* 1967, *8,* 16-21.

Committee on the Student in Higher Education. *The student in higher education.* New Haven, Conn.: Hazen Foundation, 1968.

Del Prete, R. P., & Waterhouse, P. G. Human development orientation module. *NASPA Journal,* 1973, *10,* 238-242.

Delworth, U., Sherwood, G., & Casaburri, N. *Student paraprofessionals: A working model for higher education.* Washington, D. C.: American College Personnel Association, 1974. (Student Personnel Monograph Series, No. 17)

DeWolf, V., & Lunneborg, P. W. *Descriptive information on over-35 undergraduate students* (Project No. 139). Seattle: University of Washington, Bureau of Testing, 1972.

Donk, L. J., & Hinkle, J. E. Pre-college orientation and longitudinal changes in student attitudes. *NASPA Journal,* 1971, *8,* 264-269.

Dorris, J. F., & Williams, C. Parents-students: Split heirs. *Journal of College Student Personnel,* 1974, *15,* 49-52.

Drake, R. W. *Freshman orientation in the United States colleges and universities.* Fort Collins: Colorado State University, 1966. (ERIC

Document Reproduction Service No. ED 030 923) (a).

Drake, R. W. *Review of the literature for freshman orientation practices in the United States.* Fort Collins: Colorado State University, 1966. (ERIC Document Reproduction Service No. ED 030 920) (b)

Eddy, E. D., Jr. *The college influence on student character.* Washington, D.C.: American Council on Education, 1959.

Ehrlich, R. S. A new approach in orienting students. *Improving College and University Teaching,* 1969, *17,* 206-207.

Erickson, F. M. *Orientation — a continuing dilemma.* Paper presented at the National Orientation Conference, Salt Lake City, March, 1969.

Felker, K. R. GROW: An experience for college freshmen. *Personnel and Guidance Journal,* 1973, *51,* 558-561.

Fitzgerald, L. E., & Busch, S. A. Orientation programs: Foundation and framework. *College and University,* 1963, *38,* 270-275.

Forrer, S. E. Dissemination systems in university orientation: An experimental comparison. *Journal of College Student Personnel,* 1974, *15,* 394-399.

Forrest, D. V., & Knapp, R. H. Summer college orientation programs. *Journal of College Student Personnel,* 1966, *7,* 47-49.

Foxley, C. H. Orientation or dis-orientation? *Personnel and Guidance Journal,* 1969, *48,* 218-221.

Freshmen get new kinds of transitional help. *College Management,* 1971, *6*(5), 6-8; 10-11.

Gerber, S. K. Four approaches to freshman orientation. *Improving College and University Teaching,* 1970, *18,* 57-60.

Gibbs, A. Student evaluation of orientation. *Journal of College Student Personnel,* 1968, *9,* 158-160.

Gohn, L. A. Program development. In A. G. Matthews (Ed.), *Handbook for orientation directors.* Iowa City, Iowa: National Orientation Directors Association, 1975.

Goodale, T., & Sandeen, A. The transfer student: A research report. *NASPA Journal,* 1971, *8,* 248-263.

Goodson, W. D. *The effect of a five week pre-college orientation program for Indian students.* Paper presented at the meeting of the American Personnel and Guidance Association, Chicago, March, 1972.

Grier, D. J. Orientation — tradition or reality? *NASPA Journal,* 1966, *3,* 37-41.

Griffin, M. H., & Donnan, H. Effect of a summer pre-college counseling program. *Journal of College Student Personnel,* 1970, *11,* 71-72.

Harrold, R. D. College orientation and the black student. *Journal of College Student Personnel,* 1970, *11,* 251-255.

Herron, D. G. Orientation effects on student alienation. *Journal of the National Association for Women Deans, Administrators, and Counselors,* 1974, *37,* 107-111.

Ivey, A. E. A three year evaluation of a college freshman week program.

Journal of College Student Personnel, 1963, *5*, 113-118.

Jesseph, J. R. Pre-college orientation conferences and subsequent behavior of freshmen. *Journal of College Student Personnel*, 1966, *7*, 289-294.

Keil, E. C. College orientation: A disciplinary approach. *Liberal Education*, 1966, *52*, 172-180.

Knoell, D. M., & Medsker, L. L. *From junior to senior college: A national study of the transfer student*. Washington, D. C.: American Council on Education, 1965.

Kopecek, R. J. Freshman orientation programs: A comparison. *Journal of College Student Personnel*, 1971, *12*, 54-57.

Li, P. Freshman orientation and the goals of general education. *Journal of College Student Personnel*, 1962, *3*, 130-135.

McCann, C. J. Trends in orienting college students. *Journal of the National Association for Women Deans, Administrators, and Counselors*, 1967, *30*, 85-90.

Menning, A. Policy. In A. G. Matthews (Ed.), *Handbook for orientation directors*. Iowa City, Iowa: National Orientation Directors Association, 1975.

Miller, C. D., & Ivey, A. E. Student response to three types of orientation programs. *Personnel and Guidance Journal*, 1967, *45*, 1025-1029.

Morstain, B. The importance of student interaction in the freshman year: Some bases of an experimental living-learning program. *NASPA Journal*, 1972, *9*, 283-287.

Mueller, K. H. *Student personnel work in higher education*. Boston: Houghton Mifflin, 1961.

National Association for Foreign Student Affairs. *Initial orientation of foreign students*. Cleveland, Ohio: Author, 1964. (ERIC Document Reproduction Service No. ED 024 964)

Nelson, D. E. *Orienting students to an individualized educational system of the 1970's*. Washington, D. C.: American Personnel and Guidance Association, 1970.

O'Banion, T. Experiment in orientation of junior college students. *Journal of College Student Personnel*, 1969, *10*, 12-15.

Packard, R. E. *The use of programmed materials in a freshman orientation program*. Minneapolis: University of Minnesota, 1967. (ERIC Document Reproduction Service No. ED 019 938)

Packard, R. E. Programmed-instruction technique in new student orientation. *Journal of College Student Personnel*, 1968, *9*, 246-252.

Pappas, J. G. Effects of three approaches to college orientation on academic achievement. *Journal of College Student Personnel*, 1967, *8*, 195-198. (a)

Pappas, J. G. Student reactions to a small-group orientation approach. *College and University*, 1967, *43*, 84-89. (b)

Patty, A. H. Freshman orientation: A continuing concern. *Improving College and University Teaching*, 1966, *14*, 184-188.

Peavey, R. V. Mental health crisis of university students. *Canada's Mental Health,* 1968, *16,* 15-17.

Reiter, H. M. The effect of orientation through small-group discussion on modification of certain attitudes. *Journal of Educational Research,* 1964, *58,* 65-68.

Rising, E. J. *The effects of a pre-freshman orientation program on academic progress.* Amherst: University of Massachusetts, 1967. (ERIC Document Reproduction Service No. ED 022 413)

Robinson, J. D. Effects of summer orientation on the adjustment of freshmen. *Journal of the National Association for Women Deans, Administrators, and Counselors,* 1970, *33,* 134-138.

Rothman, L. K., & Leonard, D. G. Effectiveness of freshman orientation. *Journal of College Student Personnel,* 1967, *8,* 300-304.

Sandeen, A., & Goodale, T. Student personnel programs and the transfer students. *NASPA Journal,* 1972, *9,* 179-200.

Sanford, N. Developmental status of the freshman. In N. Sanford (Ed.), *The American college.* New York: Wiley, 1962.

Scheuer, L. M. A new orientation program for a commuter campus. *Journal of the National Association for Women Deans, Administrators, and Counselors,* 1967, *30,* 162-164.

Shaffer, R. H. A new look at orientation. *College and University,* 1962, *37,* 272-279.

Smith, P. M. Some implications for freshmen orientation activities with Negro college students. *Journal of College Student Personnel,* 1964, *5,* 176-179.

Snider, P. A. A student comes to us. *Journal of the National Association for Women Deans, Administrators, and Counselors,* 1970, *33,* 138-141.

Sohn, M. Community college orientation. In A. G. Matthews (Ed.), *Handbook for orientation directors.* Iowa City, Iowa: National Orientation Directors Association, 1975.

Spivack, L. M. A systems approach for humanizing a college orientation program. *Journal of College Student Personnel,* 1973, *14,* 273-276.

Stamatakos, L. C. An orientation week reception — vehicle for improved public relations. *Journal of College Student Personnel,* 1963, *5,* 32-34.

Tautfest, P. B. An evaluation technique for orientation programs. *Journal of College Student Personnel,* 1961, *3,* 25-28.

Trotter, M. Selection and training of student paraprofessionals who serve as orientation leaders. In A. G. Matthews (Ed.), *Handbook for orientation directors.* Iowa City, Iowa: National Orientation Directors Association, 1975.

Van Eaton, E. N. National study of trends in orientation. *The National Orientation Bulletin,* 1972, *2*(4), 3.

Volkwein, J. F., & Searles, A. Evaluation of three-day new student orientation. *Journal of College Student Personnel,* 1965, *6,* 293-294.

Weigel, R. G., & Smith, T. T. The effects of pre-orientation information dissemination on academic choices and performance. *Journal of College Student Personnel,* 1972, *13,* 452-455.

White, B. C. Principles of learning theory may aid orientation. *National Orientation Bulletin,* 1972, *2*(3), 2.

Wigent, P. A. A student-directed orientation program. *Journal of College Student Personnel,* 1971, *12,* 370.

Williamson, E. G., & Biggs, D. A. *Student personnel work: A program of developmental relationships.* New York: Wiley, 1975.

Winkworth, J. M., Brown, R. D., & Braskamp, L. A. Intervention programs designed to improve communication between parents and students. *Journal of College Student Personnel,* 1973, *14,* 206-215.

Witkin, M. H. A human relations experiment in a student orientation program. *Journal of College Student Personnel,* 1971, *12,* 372.

Worley, B., & Conrad, R. Orientation and activities for transfer students: Are freshmen models appropriate? *NASPA Journal,* 1973, *10,* 333-338.

Wrenn, C. G. *Student personnel work in college.* New York: Ronald Press, 1951.

CHAPTER 4

HOUSING

Lynette Daniels Schneider

HISTORY

THE earliest form of student housing was the traditional dormitory of the colonial private colleges. Set in the countryside and generally isolated from local towns, colleges had to provide students with facilities for such basic physical needs as eating and sleeping. They also tried to implement the English residential college concept of a community of scholars settled in a close-knit intellectual environment, but the idea failed to take hold. Run by nonprofessionals and restricted to single students of the same sex, such dormitories developed individual reputations and strong traditions.

By World War I the demand for and construction of these smaller traditional units began to ebb. Sharp increases in student enrollment led to two innovations in housing after World War I. Apartment style housing was constructed to handle the large influx of married students, many entering on the G. I. Bill. At the same time thousands of single undergraduate students entering public colleges were housed in new residential halls. By the 1950's and 1960's these large units, standardized in appearance, managed by professionals, and organized to provide service and control students, had become the dominant mode of housing.

In recent years a new trend in living-learning units and experimental colleges has brought student housing full circle back to the traditional small college concept (Useem, 1966). As colleges increased in number and size, most colleges accepted the responsibility for providing student housing, but controversy still rages over purposes, personnel, and appropriate facilities. Today, approximately 63 percent of all colleges in the

125

United States have college-owned facilities (Binning, 1969) open for student occupancy.

RATIONALE

Although it has been taken for granted that colleges provide housing for students, housing, per se, has not been an integral part of the educational process. Yet, colleges and universities remain in the housing business for a variety of reasons.

Behavior Control

Colleges in the United States historically have viewed student housing as a means to provide the basic physical necessities and to control student behavior (Useem, 1966). The right to establish rules and regulations circumscribing student conduct stems from the traditional view of housing as an appropriate area in which the college may act *in loco parentis* (Beder & Rickard, 1971). That policy is still operational in many student residences today (Mueller, 1961).

Rules and regulations construed by students as behavior control take various forms, such as hours for freshmen and women and regulations against visitation by members of the opposite sex. Despite student discontent with such regulations (Tautfest & Young, 1969) and the fact that attempts to use residence halls as a means to control behavior have always failed (Williamson, 1958), this rationale continues to hold weight with many state legislators and business managers who view housing as a means to strengthen the educational system and protect public investments (Eberle & Muston, 1969). Many parents also feel more secure with such rules because the rules are perceived as protecting their offspring from misbehavior. The need and desire of students for some regulations also should not be ruled out.

Majority rights legislation (Young, 1973) called into question many of these regulations which were based on the consideration that most undergraduates were minors. Majority rights legislation suggests that disciplinary systems need to be restructured (see Discipline chapter), and that in regard to housing, the college could have landlord rights and be concerned with such problems as theft, vandalism, and public health. However, social regulations might be developed by students themselves after the pattern of civil law (Beder & Rickard, 1971) with local, state, and federal laws being handled by the appropriate non-college authorities.

Student Development

Housing can also be considered one subsystem of the larger educational organization which supports the achievement of the total system's goals, namely the goals of higher education (Riker, 1956).

Housing should be planned and organized to support the instructional and educational programs of the college (Clarq, 1970; Fairchild, 1961, 1963; Williamson, 1958). The purpose of such educational programs may be to further the intellectual development of students (Murphy, 1969), to provide educational encouragement in an informal environment conducive to learning (Ferber, 1962), to develop a rapport between faculty and student (Nudd & Stier, 1969), and to enable students to learn and grow as human beings (Riker, 1965).

Housing programs designed to achieve the educational objectives of a college are broad in purpose, such as to facilitate student growth and development (Brown, 1972). Basically, adherence to a concept of student development means provision for the physical accommodations critical to the physical and educational well-being of students (Stoner & Yokie, 1969), such as protecting students' health and safety. But residence halls are also student life centers for recreation and relaxation (Williamson, 1958), and their programs can go beyond basic needs.

Goals for Student Development

Implementing the concept of student development in housing primarily requires programs that enhance the individual development of the student (Brown, 1969). Major goals for student development in housing are to foster social-personal value systems, receptivity and sensitivity to cultural experience, and general intellectual development (Brown, 1969). DeCoster & Mable (1974a) add the goals of self-actualization and self-identification.

There are other more specific objectives for student development programs. Residence halls can facilitate adjustment to college life for the new student (Butler, 1964), and when the halls are situated close to the center of campus, they can provide greater opportunity for the student to become involved in on-campus activities (Cedar, 1967). Housing programs can effectively assist the less experienced student in his or her personal growth and development (Tautfest & Young, 1969). Being in contact with students different from oneself allows the student the opportunity to develop a sense of self-integrity (Chickering, 1967) and personal autonomy and identity (Eberle & Muston, 1969), whereby personal values and congruent behavior are established. Residence halls can provide solitude and privacy for individual thought and reflection (Stoner & Yokie, 1969), as well as provide students with valuable experience in group living (Riker, 1956). Group living can foster a sense of community (White, 1969) whereby the living unit acquires the characteristics of a reference group (Chickering, 1967). Group living also can facilitate an understanding of self-discipline and leadership (Stoner & Yokie, 1969).

Policies and Practices

Mueller (1961) proposes that the policies and practices designed to enhance student development can be organized into three basic patterns. Under the leadership or group dynamics pattern, students are viewed as individuals within a miniature community. Wise (1958) called this the managerial attitude whereby staff attitudes become dominant and cooperation is emphasized. The danger is that students will become over-adjusted to the established community (college life) and unable to successfully function in the outside world (Mueller, 1961).

The second pattern is defined as the counseling service (Mueller, 1961) or psychological services attitude (Wise, 1958).

In this case the emphasis is on the individual, rather than the group. The danger is that individual counseling becomes the primary means for student growth and learning, thus limiting the kinds of learning available to students in their living unit. The third pattern is concerned with the social and personal development attitude in which living units become the focus for training in social skills (Mueller, 1961) and self-government (Wise, 1958).

A comprehensive discussion of the philosophies, practices, and problems involved in the implementation of student development in residence halls is available in DeCoster & Mable (1974b).

ADMINISTRATION

Students and Housing Choice

Parietal Rules

On most campuses today students have two or more options for housing including fraternities and sororities, large residence halls, coed living dorms, off-campus apartments, or small houses. However, some students, usually freshmen and sophomores, are required by parietal rules to reside in college owned and operated residence halls. These parietal rules may result from a desire to keep the units financially solvent or to carry out *in loco parentis* responsibilities.

The legality of such rules has been tested in the courts. In *Mollere v. Southeastern Louisiana College* (1969) a Federal District Court found that parietal rules unequally applied among the student population were invalid when the only reason given for the requirement was to fill vacancies and thereby raise sufficient revenues to meet financial obligations on the construction of the housing units. But, when a college can show proof that mandatory on-campus living can provide educational benefits to students, the courts have allowed such rules to stand (*Pratz et al. v. Louisiana Polytechnic Institute,* 1970).

Choice of Housing

For most students the question of where to live is a matter between student and parents. In choosing among the alternative housing situations available, cost has usually been considered a major factor, but there is evidence indicating that this is not the case (Alfert, 1968). Titus (1972) found that students were concerned with quietness and privacy as well as facilities for study in their living quarters; but they do not choose a specific housing alternative on the basis of academic aptitude, achievement, or progress (Tautfest & Townsend, 1968). Convenience in the living quarters and within the college community also are important factors (Titus, 1972). But the primary consideration among students in choosing a housing situation is the opportunity for a wide range of freedom and the establishment of their own systems of control (Titus, 1972).

Personality and Choice

If the parameters mentioned above were the sole determinants of an acceptable housing arrangement, one unit could be designed to satisfy the whole student population. But, since students within most colleges differ considerably on several variables (McConnell & Heist, 1962), their decisions regarding choice of housing may be related to such factors as personality (Yonge & Regan, 1970). In a study at the University of California at Davis, Yonge and Regan (1970) found that intellectually oriented males tended to live in large houses while collegiate men tended to live in fraternities. Esthetically oriented women tended to live in small houses. Alfert (1968), in a study at the University of California at Berkeley, concluded that housing choice was related to the developmental stage of the student. With maturity, students move from living with their parents toward the greater independence of an off-campus apartment (see also Montgomery, McLaughlin, Fawcett, Pedigo, & Ward, 1975). The college residence hall, then, is a compromise between parental supervision and full independence from supervision.

Personality Differences

The type of student attracted to particular residential units will vary (Dollar, 1966). The concentration of similar students will contribute to the overall characteristics of the living unit as well as influence the student's differential perceptions of the characteristics of the college environment (Baker, 1966). For example, students in fraternities and sororities tend to value social activity and see themselves as popular and sociable. Students in off-campus rooms, on the other hand, tend to be disinterested in social activity and influence (Baird, 1969). Students living at home are less involved in social activity related to college life (Ryan, 1970). Residents of large residence halls as compared to those in smaller halls become less involved in group formation and interpersonal relations (Sinnett, Sachson, & Eddy, 1972). Despite these apparent differences, students in the various housing alternatives do not describe themselves differently, at least with regard to abilities, conservatism, perseverance, and sense of humor (Baird, 1969).

Student Satisfaction

Student satisfaction with any one type of housing is relative to the particular campus and student. For instance, one study indicated students in on-campus housing were more satisfied with college life (Baird, 1969) while another indicated that residential students were the most displeased with their living arrangements (Ryan, 1970). The best indicator of student overall satisfaction with his or her housing is the image or impression the student has of the residential unit as a whole, rather than any of its individual parts (Davis, 1971). Generally, large residence halls are negatively viewed as the institutionalization and regimentation of college life (Davis, 1971). But, on any one campus, units may be rated favorable on some variables, while other units may be rated unfavorable on the same variables (Sommer, 1968).

Housing Facilities

The frequent appearance of large institutional residence halls on college campuses might suggest that high-rise, standardized residence halls are ideal by virtue of their wide acceptance. Gores (1963) and others suggest colleges avoid this model if they are concerned with students as individuals. Yet, colleges faced with the task of providing housing for students find there are architectural limits for large numbers of students and financial constraints.

Variables in Planning

An ideal plan for a residence hall is one designed for a specific situation in which careful study and planning has delineated all relevant variables and considered the advice of appropriate experts. The purposes and goals of a residence unit should be understood and agreed upon by all those concerned (Barak, 1973). Students should be surveyed to ascertain their complaints about present housing facilities and desires for future housing. Construction considerations include land usage (Crane, 1962), site requirements, geographical locations, facilities and services provided, operational factors, and the sociological implications (*High Rise or Low Rise*, 1964).

Student Satisfaction

Student satisfaction is of prime importance in the consideration of building plans despite a report arguing that at least at one college, student satisfaction was best determined by the living unit type, rather than any particular architectural variable (University of California at San Diego, 1971). In several surveys students have reported their concern for privacy and freedom (Shay, 1969), a sense of community (Geddes, 1965), and an atmosphere that is comfortable as a home-away-from-home and conducive to study (Christo, 1965).

Grant (1974) argues that in order to humanize the residence hall environment, students must live in an environment with polar characteristics: stimulation v. security; freedom v. order. If each individual is provided full control of a small piece of territory and has membership in a small group with a territory (central lounge) of its own, then the individual can maximize his ability to structure his environment to satisfy his own human needs and, at the same time, foster his own human development.

The Ideal Housing Unit

In order for residential units to be constructed so that the physical design may contribute to the achievement of the particular goals chosen at any one time, the building features must be adaptable (Riker & Lopez, 1961). For instance, residential units could be designed so that walls are moveable and furniture is not attached to the wall, thus allowing for student individuality in living space. Also, designers could experiment with different building materials and methods (Riker & Lopez, 1961) so that students may, for example, have walls upon which they are allowed to hang, paste, and paint without reproach. Housing can provide students with options from single rooms to self-contained apartments (Robb, 1970) or plug-in kitchen units ("Award Winning Dorms," 1965). The ideal residential unit for a college would be one that is capable of growth and change (Robb, 1970). Yet, the ideal situation for a campus can never be ideal for each and every student it is designed to serve, because the student population is so diverse. Therefore, colleges should seek to provide students with a variety of housing options from which each may choose (Greenleaf, 1972).

Financial Limitations

It is axiomatic that cost must determine to some extent the structure of residential units. In 1969-1970 the average projected expenditure for student housing at a public university was $1,036,000 (Binning, 1969). The Federal Housing and Home Finance Agency, which encourages low cost housing, provides a large portion of these funds and, in so doing, encourages the construction of such low cost, unsatisfactory structures as built-in furniture ("Financing Residence Halls," 1965). Presently, the most popular means of fund raising is through the sale of revenue bonds ("Financing Residence Halls," 1965).

Increasing costs and numbers of students have forced college officials to seek more economical alternatives. Prefabricated structures, either units or component systems, are a possible alternative (Gores, 1963). More often, colleges contract with private companies to build student housing. The units are financed by individuals, savings and loan associations, and corporations specializing in the construction of student housing (Landrith, 1967). While the private developers maintain ownership, the college often maintains a degree of supervision over the students ("Financing Residence Halls," 1965). Although privately owned residential units have a higher cost per student, they are designed with the student in mind. Private units can be secured in less time than is possible with college operated dorms and the units are constructed and operated without cost to the college (Landrith, 1967). If cost forces more colleges to rely on privately owned housing, the concept of living-learning centers for student housing may not survive.

Housing for the Future

Expansion of student housing in recent decades came on the heels of a large increase in student enrollments. But future years will see a leveling off of students attending traditional four-year liberal arts colleges (Kerr, 1972). Any increase in enrollments will most likely be due to expansion of open colleges, credit by exam, and off-campus educational programs (Kerr, 1972). These factors, along with the effect of majority rights legislation on parietal rules, will lead to decreased demand for student housing and subsequent cuts in residence halls construction (Greenleaf, 1969). Freshmen and sophomores will be the primary occupants as older students depart (Greenleaf, 1969).

As costs rise and occupancy declines, residence halls will be held accountable for their expenditures, administration, and services. Evaluation will be the main tool to demonstrate accountability (Stimpson & Simon, 1974). Still, the residential units remaining will have to do more to attract students. Colleges will be forced to provide a variety of facilities and greater flexibility in planning (Sommer, 1968). Residence administrators will have to show greater concern for the individual (Riker, 1965) and establish fewer rules for controlling behavior (Greenleaf, 1969). Residence hall programs will be designed to orient students to college, to provide learning experiences, and to integrate residence life into the academic community (Greenleaf, 1969; Riker, 1965). The staff will be more concerned with student development than discipline (Greenleaf, 1969) and group living will be viewed as part of the curriculum (Riker, 1965). The future of college residence halls, then, depends on a commitment to the philosophy that learning is a total process (DeCoster & Mable, 1974a; see Fitzgerald, 1974).

PROGRAMS

Coed Living

Coed housing is a relatively new phenomenon on the American campus, having first appeared in the 1950's (Imes, 1966). Coed living provides for programs and the use of facilities for learning and changing by students of both sexes who work and learn together in the changing process of human relationships (Allen, Collins, Gee, & Nudd, 1964).

Several approaches to coed living have been developed. Dorms constructed to handle the yearly fluctuation of the male/female ratio can handle either men or women or both, but may not be viewed as coed living. On the other hand, a college can build coed houses almost totally and consider the coed living experience as an integral part of the educational process. In between the extremes colleges can construct single sex units with coed use of public areas or place men and women on alternate floors. The sexes can live on divided floors or in alternate rooms on the same floor or in single sex separate wings with common lounge facilities (Imes, 1966).

There are several advantages to coed living, one of which is a more effective use of space. Coed living can also be an important factor in student development (Duncan, 1974); assures a more natural setting and climate of association and contact for young men and women (Brown, Winkworth & Braskamp, 1973); may lead to positive changes in the understanding of love and heterosexual adjustment (Duncan, 1974); modifies social behaviors such as dress and conduct to more closely approximate acceptable societal standards (Imes, 1966); facilitates more creative cultural, educational, and social programs since the variety of ideas from students is usually broader in scope than when dealing with a single sex population (Imes, 1966); and may facilitate self-actualization (Schroeder & LeMay, 1973).

Although self-selection tends to place students in coed living units who are more mature and flexible in the application of their values and who possess a greater capacity to develop meaningful interpersonal relationships, coed living has been shown to have a positive effect on the development of healthier and more mature relationships (Schroeder & LeMay, 1973). Students say they have a strong feeling of belonging in their coed living situation (Corbett & Sommer, 1972). The atmosphere is friendly and it is easy to meet people (Brown, Winkworth, & Braskamp, 1973). Coed halls are marked by casualness and the development of strong brother-sister relationships. Brown, Winkworth, and Braskamp (1973) found no evidence to indicate an increase in overt sexual behavior despite the more relaxed atmosphere, but Katz (1974) reports that a study at Stanford and four other universities found greatly expanded sexual activity among women students.

Few serious problems have appeared that can be traced to the establishment of coed housing. Counseling services do not report an increase in clients from coed living units, nor is there other evidence to prove that the living arrangements have placed undue sexual pressure on the students (Locher, 1972). Vestiges of the double standard remain in the leadership positions of student government, but the imbalance can be remedied easily (Imes, 1966). Katz (1974) did find that supports provided by tradition and social norms were weakened by the coed living arrangement, leading to some increase in anxiety among the participating students. Problems of this nature and the overall unique nature of the coed living arrangement require that special attention be paid to the areas of programming and staffing (Brown, Winkworth, & Braskamp, 1973).

Living-Learning

Programs designed to supplement the educational objectives of the college often conform to the living-learning center model (Riker, 1965). The concept of fusing living and learning (Brunson, 1963) is the modern version of the English idea of welding the academic and residential life into a meaningful whole (Nudd & Stier, 1969). According to Riker (1965), the assumptions which underlie the rationale for student housing as living-learning centers are that the environment, both physical and social, influences behavior; enrichment of the environment enhances intellectual activity; and learning is a total process — the student must be ready to learn.

Implementing a program for living-learning units often necessitates redesigning programs or facilities in the already existing large residence halls. Basic considerations in planning an educational program for a college residence hall include the need for student involvement in program planning, especially through the structure of student government; the extension of the program over a period of time; the utilization of the widest variety of educational techniques in the programs; the need for consultation with resource experts in the planning stage; and the participation by students in the teaching portions of the program (Stark, 1964b). Effective programs demand the support and participation of students, faculty, and skilled staff personnel (Greenleaf, 1969).

A major goal of educational programs designed for large residence halls is to encourage scholarship. This requires an atmosphere conducive to the development of good study habits (Hood, 1962), the effective use of libraries, organized tutoring programs (Association of College and University Housing Officers, 1963), seminars (Clarq, 1970), and Free University type classes in which students serve as instructors for courses in which they have expertise (Adams, 1974). To insure these efforts are effective, residence halls need small libraries with standard reference works, copies of materials assigned to students, magazines, journals, and space for teaching and technical aids. Faculty participation is a necessary supplement to these efforts (Clarq, 1970) and space for counselors to offer vocational and personal counseling within the living situation is important (Centra, 1968).

The flexibility of the living-learning model suggests educational programs which can be adopted to several environmental situations in large residence halls (Hubbell & Sherwood, 1973): (a) specialty or thematic houses where programs are designed around a theme such as "Self in Society," (see also Morstain, 1972; Stanford University, 1968); (b) academic floors or houses where the common bond is a specified area of learning; (c) environmental choice areas where information cards filled out by each student are used to match student needs and desired environments; (d) limited staff or no-staff halls; (e) special interests (nonacademic) floors where the common bond may be some form of extracurricular activity; (f) coed dorms where the living environment is more natural; and (g) residential or experimental colleges that emulate the old style community of scholars.

Research

Environmental press is a major variable in the success of educational programs in student housing. Student occupants will, to a large extent, determine the environmental press (Snead & Caple, 1971) and student residents will be most influenced by those in greatest proximity to them (Menne & Sinnett, 1971). For a detailed consideration of the research regarding the impact of residence halls on students, see Williams and Reilley (1972).

Student Groups

There is some evidence that arrangement of student residents into homogeneous groups on a number of variables has a positive effect (Snead & Caple, 1971). If a majority of students on a residence hall floor share common majors and interests, then proximity will influence friendship patterns and those in the minority group will be adversely affected (Brown, 1968). Yet, roommates matched by major, as well as by age and size of high school, show no effects (Volkwein, 1966). In a study to determine the effects of a program of intellectual discussions, Brown (1968) found a differential effect on science and humanities students, stimulating them to pursue activities in areas in which they were already interested.

Studies grouping students with members of their class have mixed results. Dunn and Rickard (1971) found that the presence of upper-class women in a female dorm served as an appropriate role model in an environment of peer group assistance. On the other hand, Chesin (1969) found that freshmen males became more mature and less stereotypic in attitudes and beliefs and less traditional in their system of values, regardless of contact with upperclassmen.

The greatest attention has been given the effect of homogeneous and diverse grouping on academic achievement, perhaps because grade point average is easily measured and assumed to be an accurate measure of educational growth. Several studies found that grouping students with common courses and interest would positively affect their achievement (Crew & Giblette, 1965; Taylor & Hanson, 1971). When grouped together, high ability students had better academic success and perceived their living arrangements as more desirable (DeCoster, 1968) than when randomly assigned to residence halls. DeCoster (1968) found that high ability women were more influenced by homogeneous assignment than were high ability men, which suggests the possibility of significant sex differences in the learning process. Yet Taylor and Hanson (1971) discovered that high ability students did as well as predicted or better regardless of their living arrangement. Among diverse groups in various living arrangements on and off campus (Prusok & Walsh, 1964) and in on-campus residence halls with different policy options (Whitney, Perrin, Casse, &

Albertus, 1973), there were no differential effects on academic achievement.

Other study results argue against the conclusion that homogeneous groups have a positive effect on academic achievement. While Snead and Caple (1971) found that students divided into groups by Holland's (1966) six personality types did show a positive effect on academic achievement, Caple (1970) found no such effect. Housing students according to major does not influence first semester college achievement (Elton & Bate, 1966). The elimination of closing hours in residential units had no differential effect on grades (Sims & Suddeck, 1972). Nor were there differences in grades among pledge class students inducted into "good," "mediocre," and "poor" scholarship programs (Prusok & Walsh, 1964).

Student Satisfaction

On the whole student reaction to living-learning units in residence halls has been favorable. In a comparison of large living-learning units and conventional style residence halls, students perceived the living-learning units to be as friendly and group oriented as the conventional halls despite their size (Centra, 1968). Students in this study did not, however, perceive differences on an intellectual and conforming dimension. At Michigan State University 95 percent of the students surveyed said they would recommend living-learning units to new freshmen. Although a majority of the students felt that study conditions in the living-learning complex were superior to those in other residential units, they did not perceive a difference in the level of competence among students or in the emphasis on study (Olson, 1964b). At the University of Vermont students rated the new living-learning center "better" in terms of living accommodations, intellectual atmosphere, educational opportunities, and extracurricular activities (Magnarella, 1975).

Asked what they liked best about the living-learning units, students at Michigan State University mentioned the convenience of classes (Olson, 1964b). The Stephens College House Plan provided for four core courses to be taught in the house.

The students were enthusiastic and the administration felt that this action, as well as other aspects of the program, heightened the effectiveness of the total college experience (Leyden, 1962).

Experimental Colleges

The appearance of experimental colleges marks the revival of the English community of scholars or residential colleges (Brown, 1972). Growing numbers of students, the institutionalized nature of many campus housing complexes, and the lack of individual attention given to students contributed to the rise of the small-college concept in which a close-knit group exerts a considerable influence on students and provides a strong intellectual environment (Greenleaf, 1965). The viability of the residential college concept is based on the assumptions that the psychosocial and cognitive development of students interact with each other; different college environment presses have a different impact on college students; and peer group influence plays an important role (Brown, 1972).

The residential living program, as well as all living-learning models, is designed to support the broad objectives of higher education (Greenleaf, 1965). It can provide informal stimulation for the individual, continuous learning, an academic climate enhanced by student/faculty interaction (Shaffer & Ferber, 1965), and the integration of all educational experiences, including the development of a student's identity (Andrews, 1967). Residential living is a community concept with a unified purpose that can offer maximum use of all its intellectual resources (Shaffer & Ferber, 1965). The residential college challenges the student to meet responsibilities for learning while providing the most supportive environment available to enhance that learning (Greenleaf, 1965).

Where colleges have implemented the residential college concept, results generally have been favorable. At Nebraska Centennial College faculty and students became more interested in each other and a strong sense of community was achieved (Brown, 1972). While the faculty enjoyed the closer personal contact with students, they had less time to pursue professional and family interests which led to some discontent. Both at Nebraska and at Harvard good informal social relations within and between the sexes developed (Brown, 1972; Jencks & Reisman, 1962). Although Jencks and Reisman (1962) found that the Harvard House System had not totally rid students of the assumption that ideas belong in the classroom or library, it had done a great deal to preserve intellectual and humane qualities in the academic community. At Michigan State University a comparison of graduating seniors housed in the residential colleges with other seniors showed that the residential students responded more favorably to questions associated with intellectual growth and stimulation and personal adjustment and well-being (Nosow, 1975).

PERSONNEL

Residence Counselor or Assistant

The residence counselor or advisor has long been a part of student housing. Once considered the strong-arm disciplinarian, the advisor has become more of a friend and counselor. As student housing moves further toward embracing a living-learning concept, counseling and teaching may emerge as the basis for professional training of residence counselors. Yet, the contemporary residence counselor finds that the newer role conflicts with pressures to maintain a disciplinarian posture.

Residence counselors, in the form of faculty members, first appeared in student residences as *in loco parentis* substitutes. Over the years faculty members disappeared, but the counselors replacing them were still perceived as a "Mom," "Big Brother," housekeeper, or other overseer for the college (Hardee, 1965). The residence counselor also functioned as an administrator when housing units became large and some organization was required if only to achieve communication between students and housing personnel (Beder & Richard, 1971).

In recent years emphasis has shifted away from the disciplinarian role to a counseling philosophy in which counselors function to advise and help students with their adjustment to college and personal problems (Nair & Sanders, 1969; Schroeder, Hill, Gormally, & Anthony, 1973). In their place student governments and judicial bodies perform regulation and policy-making functions. In some colleges where living-learning housing units have already been established, residence counselors are expected to be intellectual leaders (Keniston, 1965) or a new breed of teacher (Stark, 1960) who may have some academic training and might be asked to teach.

The modern residence counselor is expected to provide dynamic leadership and not merely react to the environment (Butler, 1964). According to DeCoster and Mable (1974a), counselors should act as "catalysts, consultants, and resources" within the residence hall to facilitate learning experiences in which student responsibility is recognized and encouraged. In a similar vein Brown (1974) suggests that the student personnel workers responsible for residence halls should be social engineers or behavioral scientists. The counselor must be empathic and warm (Wyrick & Mitchell, 1971), motivated to help and understand people (Spurrier & Collins, 1973), sensitive, friendly, and extroverted (Wotruba, 1969), able to guide students, and promote social interaction and adjustment (Schroeder et al., 1973).

One consideration in the selection of residence hall assistants should be the characteristics of the students the assistant is responsible for. Thus, if a residence hall has a minority student population or has a student population selected for their interest in music or art, then the selection of an assistant for each of these halls might be guided by this knowledge and reflect the student population (Greenleaf, 1974).

Complex functions demand professional training. Some colleges screen their residence counselor applicants with personality tests, interest inventories, and leadership questionnaires (Wotruba, 1969). Training programs, averaging several days to a week, which include lectures and discussion groups might stress job duties (Biggs, 1971), training to initiate creative projects (Brown, Brown, Canon, Scott & Winkworth, 1969), and development of professional attitudes and techniques to enhance students' personal and social adjustment (Biggs, 1971).

More recent programs have provided human relations training (Schroeder et al., 1973), engaged applicants in sociodrama or role playing (Nair & Sanders, 1969) and simulation exercises (Newton, 1974); provided in-service training which stressed counseling skills, student development (Powell, 1974), and evaluation research (Spurrier & Collins, 1973); and offered experiential training programs in the wilderness which emphasize challenge and response theories (Schroeder, 1976).

In recent years residence counseling has drawn the attention of many student personnel workers. A thorough review of the literature in this area is available (Stark, 1964a).

Faculty Participation

Faculty participation is essential to the total success of any living-learning housing center. Faculty involvement may be as brief as a weekly dinner hour visit with students (Clarq, 1970). Greater faculty commitment may involve housing faculty offices within the residential unit (Centra, 1968) or providing living quarters for faculty members among those provided for the students (Clarq, 1970). However, faculty are not always agreeable to this commitment.

Borland (1971) notes that in explaining the lack of faculty participation, it is often said that faculty lack the interest and concern for students outside the classroom; yet in some cases where faculty have expressed interest, their subsequent involvement in a program has led to disillusionment and loss of interest. Disinterest among the faculty may be due to the institution itself, which, through its demands for research and publication, puts too much pressure on faculty to allow them time for interaction with students, especially undergraduates (Murphy, 1969). This pressure could be alleviated if institutions gave recognition for faculty participation in some tangible form (Murphy, 1969), as additional salary drawn from the residential program's budget (Borland, 1971).

It is also said that faculty are more concerned with contact with their colleagues than with students (Borland, 1971). Therefore, living in close proximity to student housing would hamper departmental contact and time with faculty. On the other hand, Olson (1964a) has shown that programs can be devised in which the majority of the faculty will have sufficient communication and interaction with their colleagues. A survey of faculty in the program at Michigan State University showed that faculty were receptive to the idea of holding classes and locating offices in residence halls because they believed it would enhance faculty/student interaction (Olson, 1964a). At the University of Nebraska a cooperative effort by one student and one professor to establish a living-learning unit in a residence hall proved successful (Brown, Knoll, Donaldson, & Ensz, 1975).

A final concern is that large faculty turnover in these programs can be interpreted as failure of the program (Borland, 1971). Borland (1971), however, suggests that a successful program has no need to trap faculty in permanent commitments to obtain their participation. If commitment to a program is flexible, a program can establish a pool of motivated faculty who may be more easily induced to participate. It is apparent that if student housing administrators wish to instigate living-learning programs with the commitment of faculty members, they should not prejudge the willingness of faculty to participate nor ignore the obstacles to successful participation. Many difficulties can be avoided if faculty are consulted in the planning stages of the program.

REFERENCES

Adams, D. V. Residential learning opportunities. In D. A. DeCoster & P. Mable (Eds.), *Student development and education in college residence halls*. Washington, D. C.: American College Personnel Association, 1974.

Alfert, E. Developmental stage and choice of residence in college. *Journal of College Student Personnel*, 1968, *9*, 90-93.

Allen, J. G., Collins, B. B., Gee, C. Y., & Nudd, T. R. Coeducational residence halls. *Journal of College Student Personnel*, 1964, *6*, 82-87.

Andrews, E. E. *The residential college student: A study in identity crisis.* Washington, D. C.: 44th Annual Meeting of the American Orthopsychiatric Association, March, 1967. (ERIC Document Reproduction Service No. ED 015 489)

Association of College & University Housing Officers. *Proceedings of the 15th annual conference.* Los Angeles, Association of College and University Housing Officers, August 4-8, 1963. (ERIC Document Reproduction Service No. ED 035 169)

Award-winning dorms break tradition. *American School and University,* 1965, *37*(7), 34-35.

Baird, L. L. The effects of college residence groups on students' self-concepts, goals, and achievements. *Personnel and Guidance Journal,* 1969, *47,* 1015-1021.

Baker, S. R. The relationship between student residence and perception of environmental press. *Journal of College Student Personnel,* 1966, *7,* 222-224.

Barak, R. J. A systems approach to residence hall planning. *NASPA Journal,* 1973, *10,* 255-258.

Beder, H. W., & Rickard, S. T. Residence hall regulations and staff roles: A substitute model *in loco parentis. NASPA Journal,* 1971, *9,* 57-61.

Biggs, D. A. Selecting residence counselors — job viewpoints and interpersonal attitudes. *Journal of College Student Personnel,* 1971, *12,* 111-115.

Binning, D. W. 1969-1970 college operating practices analysis. *College and University Business,* 1969, *47*(5), 47-62.

Borland, D. T. Faculty participation in university residence hall classes. *NASPA Journal,* 1971, *9,* 62-70.

Brown, R. D. Manipulation of the environmental press in a college residence hall. *Personnel and Guidance Journal,* 1968, *46,* 555-560.

Brown, R. D. Resident adviser programming. *NASPA Journal,* 1969, *7,* 86-90.

Brown, R. D. Student development in an experimental college or I may have seen a unicorn. *Journal of College Student Personnel,* 1972, *13,* 196-201.

Brown, R. D. Student development and residence education. In D. A. DeCoster & P. Mable (Eds.), *Student development and education in college residence halls.* Washington, D. C.: American College Personnel Association, 1974.

Brown, R. D., Brown, R., Canon, H., Scott, R., & Winkworth, J. *Residence hall programming for student development: A working model.* Las Vegas, Nevada: Annual Convention of the American Personnel and Guidance Association, March 30-April 3, 1969. (ERIC Document Reproduction Service No. ED 033 400)

Brown, R. D., Knoll, R. E. Donaldson, C., & Ensz, G. Making a living-learning unit work: One student, one professor and an idea. *Journal of College Student Personnel,* 1975, *16,* 24-29.

Brown, R. D., Winkworth, J., & Braskamp, L. Student development in a coed residence hall: Promiscuity, prophylactic, or panacea. *Journal of College Student Personnel,* 1973, *14,* 98-104.

Brunson, M. A. Residence halls as centers of learning. *Journal of the National Association of Women Deans and Counselors*, 1963, *27*, 32-36.

Butler, W. R. Individual growth in the residence hall program. *Journal of College Student Personnel*, 1964, *6*, 12-17.

Caple, R. *Group cohesiveness and academic achievement as related to residence hall students assigned according to Holland's theory of vocational choice.* Columbia: Missouri University, College of Education, 1970. (ERIC Document Reproduction Service No. ED 045 032)

Cedar, T. *Student housing survey, Fall, 1966.* Detroit, Mich.: Wayne State University, March, 1967. (ERIC Document Reproduction Service No. ED 037 906)

Centra, J. A. Student perceptions of residence hall environments: Living-learning vs. conventional units. *Journal of College Student Personnel*, 1968, *9*, 266-272.

Chesin, S. E. Effects of differential housing on attitudes and values. *College Student Journal*, 1969, *3*(3), 62-65.

Chickering, A. W. College residences and student development. *Educational Record*, 1967, *48*, 179-186.

Christo, V. Interior design of dormitories. *American School and University*, 1965, *37*(7), 39-40.

Clarq, J. R. The educational impact of residence halls. *Improving College and University Teaching*, 1970, *18*(1), 44-45.

Corbett, J., & Sommer, R. Anatomy of a coed residence hall. *Journal of College Student Personnel*, 1972, *13*, 215-217.

Crane, W. J. Practices and problems in residence hall planning. *Personnel and Guidance Journal*, 1962, *40*, 448-452.

Crew, J. L., & Giblette, J. F. Academic performance of freshmen males as a function of residence hall housing. *Journal of College Student Personnel*, 1965, *6*, 167-170.

Davis, G. How students rate dorms. *American School and University*, 1971, *44*(4), 8-11.

DeCoster, D. A. Effects of homogeneous housing assignments for high ability students. *Journal of College Student Personnel*, 1968, *9*, 75-78.

DeCoster, D. A., & Mable, P. Resident education: Purpose and process. In D. A. DeCoster & P. Mable (Eds.), *Student development and education in college residence halls.* Washington, D. C.: American College Personnel Association, 1974. (a)

DeCoster, D. A., & Mable, P. *Student development and education in college residence halls.* Washington, D. C.: American College Personnel Association, 1974. (b)

Dollar, R. J. Student characteristics and choice of housing. *Journal of College Student Personnel*, 1966, *7*, 147-150.

Duncan, J. P. Emphasis on the education in coeducational living. In D. A. DeCoster & P. Mable (Eds.), *Student development and education in college residence halls.* Washington, D. C.: American College Personnel Association, 1974.

Dunn, G., & Rickard, S. T. A survey of student responses to twenty-four hour parietals. *Journal of College Student Personnel,* 1971, *12,* 329-331.

Eberle, A. W., & Muston, R. A. The role of the chief student personnel administrator and the residence hall: Locus of conflict. *NASPA Journal,* 1969, *7,* 91-96.

Elton, C. F., & Bate, W. S. The effect of housing policy on GPA. *Journal of College Student Personnel,* 1966, *7,* 73-77.

Fairchild, E. Current problems and programs in residence halls. *Journal of the National Association of Women Deans and Counselors,* 1961, *24,* 144-149.

Fairchild, E. Evaluating residence halls through trifocals. *Journal of College Student Personnel,* 1963, *4,* 171-176.

Ferber, D. A. Academic influences in student housing. *Journal of College Student Personnel,* 1962, *4,* 2-10.

Financing residence halls. *American School and University,* 1965, *37*(7), 36-38.

Fitzgerald, L. E. The future for college residence halls. In D. A. DeCoster & P. Mable (Eds.), *Student development and education in college residence halls.* Washington, D. C.: American College Personnel Association, 1974.

Geddes, R. L. Residence halls: Their planning, financing, and operation. *American School and University,* 1965, *37*(7), 31-33.

Gores, H. B. *Facilities for the future.* 49th Annual Meeting of the Association of American Colleges, March, 1963. (ERIC Document Reproduction Service No. ED 031 900)

Grant, W. H. Humanizing the residence hall environment. In D. A. DeCoster & P. Mable (Eds.), *Student development and education in college residence halls.* Washington, D. C.: American College Personnel Association, 1974.

Greenleaf, E. A. The residence community. In H. Lane & J. H. Taylor, *Research conference on social science methods and student residences.* Ann Arbor: University of Michigan, Center for Research on Language and Language Behavior, 1965. (ERIC Document Reproduction Service No. ED 010 266)

Greenleaf, E. A. Residence halls 1970's. *NASPA Journal,* 1969, *7,* 65-71.

Greenleaf, E. A. Needed policy changes in residence hall administration. *Journal of the National Association of Women Deans and Counselors,* 1972, *35,* 139-144.

Greenleaf, E. A. The role of student staff members. In D. A. DeCoster & P. Mable (Eds.), *Student development and education in college residence halls.* Washington, D. C.: American College Personnel Association, 1974.

Hardee, M. D. The residence hall: A locus for learning. In H. Lane & J. H. Taylor, *Research conference on social science methods and stude residences.* Ann Arbor: University of Michigan, Center for Research on Language and Language Behavior, 1965. (ERIC Document Reproduction Service No. ED 010 266)

High rise or low rise: A study of decision factors in residence hall planning. Madison, Wis.: University Facilities Research Center, 1964. (ERIC Document Reproduction Service No. ED 017 119)

Holland, J. L. *The psychology of vocational choice.* Waltham, Mass.: Blaisdell, 1966.

Hood, A. B. An experiment utilizing residence counselors to teach educational skills. *Journal of College Student Personnel,* 1962, *4,* 35-40.

Hubbell, R. N., & Sherwood, G. P. A model for developing new residence hall environments. *NASPA Journal,* 1973, *10,* 243-254.

Imes, S. *A look at coed housing in institutions of higher learning in the United States.* New York: Syracuse University, School of Education, 1966. (ERIC Document Reproduction Service No. ED 034 255)

Jencks, C. S., & Riesman, D. Patterns of residential education: A case study of Harvard. In N. Sanford (Ed.), *The American College.* New York: John Wiley, 1962.

Katz, J. Coeducational living: Effects upon male-female relationships. In D. A. DeCoster & P. Mable (Eds.), *Student development and education in college residence halls.* Washington, D. C.: American College Personnel Association, 1974.

Keniston, K. The residence house: Research roadblocks and prospects. In H. Lane & J. H. Taylor *Research conference on social science methods and student residences.* Ann Arbor: University of Michigan, Center for Research on Language and Language Behavior, 1965. (ERIC Document Reproduction Service No. ED 010 266)

Kerr, C. Policy concerns for the future. In D. W. Vermilye (Ed.), *The expanded campus.* San Francisco: Jossey-Bass, 1972.

Landrith, H. F. Private dormitories profit colleges' investors. *American School and University,* 1967, *40*(1), 37-38.

Leyden, R. C. The Stephens College house plan. *Journal of the National Association of Women Deans and Counselors,* 1962, *25,* 74-80.

Locher, N. W. Administrative attitudes toward coed housing at 16 small colleges. *Journal of College Student Personnel,* 1972, *13,* 395-401.

Magnarella, P. J. The University of Vermont's living-learning center: A first year appraisal. *Journal of College Student Personnel,* 1975, *16,* 300-305.

McConnell, T. R., & Heist, P. The diverse college student population. In N. Sanford (Ed.), *The American college.* New York: John Wiley, 1962.

Menne, J. M. C., & Sinnett, E. R. Proximity and social interaction in residence halls. *Journal of College Student Personnel,* 1971, *12,* 26-31.

Mollere v. Southeastern Louisiana College, 304 F. Supp. 826 (1969).

Montgomery, J. R., McLaughlin, G. W., Fawcett, L. R., Pedigo, E. A., & Ward, S. S. The impact of different residence hall environments upon student attitudes. *Journal of College Student Personnel,* 1975, *16,* 389-394.

Morstain, B. The importance of student interaction in the freshmen year: Some bases of an experimental living-learning program. *NASPA Journal,* 1972, *9,* 283-287.

Mueller, K. *Student personnel work in higher education.* Boston: Houghton Mifflin, 1961.

Murphy, R. O. Developing educational meaning for residence halls. *NASPA Journal,* 1969, *7,* 61-64.

Nair, D. A., & Sanders, O. L. Sociodrama in the selection and training of male student residence hall advisers. *NASPA Journal,* 1969, *7,* 81-85.

Newton, F. B. The effect of systematic communication skills training on residence hall paraprofessionals. *Journal of College Student Personnel,* 1974, *15,* 366-369.

Nosow, S. An attitudinal comparison of residential college seniors with other seniors. *Journal of College Student Personnel,* 1975, *16,* 17-23.

Nudd, T. R., & Stier, D. A. Do you really want classes taught in your residence hall? *NASPA Journal,* 1969, *7,* 101-103.

Olson, L. A. Living-learning units as seen by the faculty. *Journal of Higher Education,* 1964, *35,* 83-87. (a)

Olson, L. A. Students' reactions to living-learning residence halls. *Journal of College Student Personnel,* 1964, *6,* 29-31. (b)

Powell, J. R. Inservice education for student staff. In D. A. DeCoster & P. Mable (Eds.), *Student development and education in college residence halls.* Washington, D. C.: American College Personnel Association, 1974.

Pratz v. Louisiana Polytechnic Institute, 316 F. Supp. 872 (1970).

Prusok, R. E., & Walsh, W. B. College students' residence and academic achievement. *Journal of College Student Personnel,* 1964, *5,* 181-184.

Riker, H. C. *Planning functional college housing.* New York: Teachers College, Columbia University, 1956.

Riker, H. C. The emerging role of student residences. In H. Lane & J. H. Taylor, *Research conference on social science methods and student residences.* Ann Arbor: University of Michigan, Center for Research on Language and Language Behavior, 1965. (ERIC Document Reproduction Service No. ED 010 266)

Riker, H. C., & Lopez, F. G. *College students live here: A study of college housing.* New York: Educational Facilities Laboratory, 1961. (ERIC Document Reproduction Service No. ED 031 071)

Robb, G. *Radical new programs for university living.* Chicago: "Neocon II" Conference, June 18, 1970. (ERIC Document Reproduction Service No. ED 044 778)

Ryan, J. T. College freshmen and living arrangements. *NASPA Journal,* 1970, *8,* 127-130.

Schroeder, C. C. Adventure training for resident assistants. *Journal of College*

Student Personnel, 1976, *17,* 11-15.

Schroeder, C. C., & LeMay, M. L. The impact of coed residence halls on self-actualization. *Journal of College Student Personnel,* 1973, *14,* 105-110.

Schroeder, K., Hill, C. E., Gormally, J., & Anthony, W. A. Systematic human relations training for residence assistants. *Journal of College Student Personnel,* 1973, *14,* 313-316.

Shaffer, R. H., & Ferber, D. A. Residential college concept: Campus organizational patterns for quality with quantity. *Bulletin of the School of Education* (Indiana University), 1965, *41*(3). (ERIC Document Reproduction Service No. ED 037 925)

Shay, J. E., Jr. Freedom and privacy in student residences. *NASPA Journal,* 1969, *7,* 76-80.

Sims, O. S., Jr., & Suddeck, D. E. Effect of residence hall closing hours on grade averages of freshmen women. *Journal of the National Association of Women Deans and Counselors,* 1972, *35,* 178-179.

Sinnett, E. R., Sachson, A. D., & Eddy, G. The influence of living units on the behavior of college students. *Journal of College Student Personnel,* 1972, *13,* 209-214.

Snead, R. F., & Caple, R. B. Some effects of the environmental press in university housing. *Journal of College Student Personnel,* 1971, *12,* 189-192.

Sommer, R. Student reactions to four types of residence halls. *Journal of College Student Personnel,* 1968, *9,* 232-237.

Spurrier, J. L., & Collins, P. C. Developing a residence assistant training program. *NASPA Journal,* 1973, *10,* 259-262.

Stanford University. University residences and campus life: The study of education at Stanford. *Report to the University.* Palo Alto, Calif.: Stanford University, November, 1968. (ERIC Document Reproduction Service No. ED 032 846)

Stark, M. Residence living and education. *Journal of Higher Education,* 1960, *31,* 161-162.

Stark, M. *An annotated bibliography on residence counseling.* Ann Arbor, Mich.: Association of College and University Housing Officers, 1964. (a)

Stark, M. Human relations activities as an educational program in a college residence hall. *Journal of College Student Personnel,* 1964, *6,* 18-20. (b)

Stimpson, R., & Simon, L. A. K. Accountability for the residence program. In D. A. DeCoster & P. Mable (Eds.), *Student development and education in college residence halls.* Washington, D. C.: American College Personnel Association, 1974.

Stoner, K. L., & Yokie, J. A. Residence halls and the future. *NASPA Journal,* 1969, *7,* 72-75.

Tautfest, P. B., & Townsend, D. Housing selected by senior women and academic aptitude, achievement, and progress. *Journal of College*

Student Personnel, 1968, *9,* 94-96.

Tautfest, P. B., & Young, G. C. *Student-parent attitudes toward certain regulations and the entering student's preparation for self-regulation.* Madison: University of Wisconsin, October, 1969. (ERIC Document Reproduction Service No. ED 036 826)

Taylor, R. G., & Hanson, G. R. Environmental impact on achievement and study habits. *Journal of College Student Personnel,* 1971, *12,* 445-454.

Titus, C. R. Students express their housing needs and preferences. *Journal of College Student Personnel,* 1972, *13,* 202-204.

University of California, San Diego. *Final report: Architectural determinants of student satisfaction in college residence halls.* San Diego: Author, January, 1971. (ERIC Document Reproduction Service No. ED 049 721)

Useem, R. H. A sociologist views learning in college residence halls. *Journal of the National Association of Women Deans and Counselors,* 1966, *29,* 116-122.

Volkwein, J. F. Freshmen roommates: Random vs. matched pairs. *Journal of College Student Personnel,* 1966, *7,* 145-147.

White, J. E. Style of life and student personnel policy in college residence halls. *Journal of the National Association of Women Deans and Counselors,* 1969, *32,* 123-125.

Whitney, D. R., Perrin, D. W., Casse, R. M., Jr., & Albertus, A. D. Effects of residence hall policies on academic achievement. *Journal of College Student Personnel,* 1973, *14,* 333-337.

Williams, D. E., & Reilley, R. R. The impact of residence halls on students. *Journal of College Student Personnel,* 1972, *13,* 402-410.

Williamson, E. G. Students' residences: Shelter or education? *Personnel and Guidance Journal,* 1958, *36,* 392-398.

Wise, W. M. Residence halls and higher learning. *Personnel and Guidance Journal,* 1958, *36,* 398-401.

Wotruba, R. T. Can residence hall staff be selected scientifically? *NASPA Journal,* 1969, *7,* 107-111.

Wyrick, T. J., & Mitchell, K. M. Relationship between residence assistants' empathy and warmth and their effectiveness. *Journal of College Student Personnel,* 1971, *12,* 36-40.

Yonge, G., & Regan, M. *Personality characteristics and student housing.* Berkeley: University of California at Berkeley, Center for Research and Development in Higher Education, 1970. (ERIC Document Reproduction Service No. ED 037 189)

Young, D. P. *Ramifications of the age of majority.* Washington, D. C.: Council of Student Personnel Associations in Higher Education, 1973.

CHAPTER 5

STUDENT ACTIVITIES

MARLIN R. SCHMIDT AND BETTY BLASKA

HISTORY

ORGANIZED student activities in the form of religious activities dominated student life in the colonial college. The development of moral character was an educational aim, and all colleges prescribed regular prayer, compulsory chapel, and theological studies. In the early Nineteenth Century, student activities reflected the fervent religious revival that occurred on the campuses, and numerous Christian associations were formed. As a result of the rigid discipline enforced by college faculties to insure that every student exhibited appropriate moral conduct, student life during this period was dominated by riots and rebellions against the multitude of rules and regulations. The establishment of literary societies, which functioned like debating clubs, allowed students to express their views at least on political issues.

Following the Civil War a vacuum was created in the social life of the campus. American college professors, returning from study abroad at German universities where the academic emphasis was on research and scholarship, were not interested in regulating and supervising student life but in developing careers as researchers and scholars. Under the Germanic influence, students were seen as adults who needed rigorous disciplining of the mind in the classroom but little or no regulation out of class.

In order to fill the social vacuum, students developed what has been referred to as the second curriculum (Bloland, 1971). Student interest became directed almost entirely upon football and fraternities. In 1865 there were only twenty-five national fraternities, but by the middle of the Twentieth Century,

seventy-seven national fraternities and forty-five national sororities existed. Even more impressive is the amount of property
these organizations held in custody. As early as 1927, the total
amount was estimated at $63,582,705 (Brubacher & Rudy, 1968).
Fun and frolic so dominated students' lives that many an undergraduate was admonished not to let studies interfere with
his or her education (Brubacher & Rudy, 1968) and Woodrow
Wilson (1909) was led to remark, "The side shows are so numerous, in diversity — so important, if you will — they have
swallowed up the circus" (Bloland, 1971, p. 2).

By World War I, educators were concerned that the extra
curriculum was working at cross-purposes to the central intellectual concerns of the colleges. Since it was impossible to
abolish the extracurriculum, every effort was directed at reinte-
grating the curriculum and extracurriculum within the objectives of higher education. The student personnel movement
represented an effort to restore a unified life to the American
college by conceiving of the student as a total personality who
learns both in and out of the classroom and whose intellectual
development is affected by his or her personal development. By
linking student activities to the basic purposes of higher education, the total development of the student could be accomplished. Student personnel specialists supported by faculty and
administration set about the process of reintegration.

Numerous programs were developed in the continuing effort
to integrate the two curricula. Residence halls became living-
learning centers. Student government participated in the maintenance of discipline, developed the honor system, and
supervised dormitory regulations. Student-faculty committees
revised curriculum and, in some cases, evaluated courses and
professors. Special interest groups sponsored debates and fo-
rums on intellectually relevant and controversial topics. Faculty advisors began to lend their expertise to committees, clubs,
and societies. Activities directors taught self-management and
leadership skills in the dormitories and Greek-letter organizations. Students practiced their educational skills by teaching
ghetto children.

DEFINITION

Philosophy

Three forces influenced the formation and philosophy of student activities. The family, traditionally responsible for the education, religious instruction, and recreation of its members, lost these functions to the "family life movement" composed of social workers, psychiatrists, faculty, and student personnel workers. Changes in the occupational structure such as capitalism, division of labor, bureaucracies, and specialization gave rise to a specialized body of personnel catering to students' noncurricular life. A change in cultural values, which led to the replacement of the Protestant Ethic with the Social Ethic, resulted in a belief in the group as a source of creativity, a belief in belongingness, and a belief in the application of science to achieve belongingness. Increasing secularism and the rise of the helping professions weakened the individual's reliance on self and furthered dependence on others. The spread of leisure time values prompted a multiplicity of group activities, including student activities at the college (Stroup, 1964).

These changes, especially the development of the Social Ethic, led to the conception of education as a social institution and were crucial to the development of student activities. Student activities are intended to fulfill students' nonintellectual needs and are based on the importance of both intellectual and sociopersonal principles, as well as the belief that the curriculum and extracurriculum are parallel tracks of interest.

Viewing education as a social institution has the effect of placing student activities in the center of university life as an integral and essential part of the educational process. Stroup (1964) says of student activities:

> They exist in order that the basic purpose of the institution be fulfilled. In part the student personnel worker performs specialized responsibilities which other university personnel could not accomplish as effectively. In part, however, his [her] functions are also the responsibility of practically every-

> one else within the university, since much of what he [she]
> attempts is by definition also within the province of others
> .... The student activities program secures its rationale only
> as it supports the chosen goals of the university in the details
> and general organization of its activities. Theoretically, there
> can never be a division between the student activities program
> and the rest of the university, between the curriculum and the
> noncurriculum (pp. 52-53).

Thus student activities share the college's aims to impart, discover, apply, and integrate knowledge, as well as to develop the whole student (Pokorny, 1967).

Williamson (1961) sees as central to the educational process the well-rounded development of the individual student. Although he places reason at the heart of education, he qualifies this aim as "reason fully integrated with a social ethic and a healthy personality" (p. 427). Similarly, Taylor (1949) considers a college education as one in which the intellectual and scholastic are married to the social, artistic, and physical:

> We must make the life of the college student an immersion in
> a total environment of learning, where the companionship of
> the scholar, the athlete, the wit and the artist are sought
> naturally and eagerly at various times and according to various
> needs (pp. 38-39).

From this view, higher education means student involvement in the entire college life (Taylor, 1950) and student activities are a crucial part of higher education (Hand, 1938; Strang, 1941) because they perform a function which classroom subjects cannot.

An additional feature of student activities is the cultivation of good citizenship traits and democratic values. The goals of student activities include both individual growth and social responsibility (Stroup, 1964).

> Student activities respects the requirements of democratic social living. Individual personal expression is freedom; social
> responsibility is order. Freedom and order in creative tension
> is a fundamentally accepted tenet in professional student activities (Stroup, 1964, p. 8).

Writing in the riot-dominated era of the 1960's, Stark (1967) says the old progressive philosophy of student activities is being replaced by the concept of social reconstruction. The progressive philosophy was characterized by Dewey's pragmatism and the American Council on Education's objective of adaptability to changing social conditions. Social reconstructionism, however, emphasizes goal-seeking and supplants the student-centered emphasis of the progressive educationists with the community-centered emphasis in which learning takes place by study and action combined. The civil rights movement and the anti-war, anti-imperialist protest moved students from intellectual discussion of issues to personal involvement and direct action.

There are several challenges which Stark (1967) feels the social reconstruction philosophy poses to student personnel workers:

> How should we assist students in modifying our society so there will be an improvement in human relations? Furthermore, how do we help our students make crucial value judgments on the desirable direction of modifications of our society (pp. 84-85)?

With the decline in student activism and the calm of the mid-1970's on most campuses, it is not clear whether social reconstructionism will continue as a valid philosophy of student activities.

Functions

There are six broad, overlapping functions of student activities: (a) academic and intellectual functions, (b) social functions, (c) group functions, (d) full student development, including personal and moral, (e) leadership and democratic functions, and (f) campus and community life functions (Arbuckle, 1953; Bergstresser & Wells, 1954; Edwards, Artman, & Fisher, 1928; Frederick, 1959; Lloyd-Jones & Smith, 1938; McKown, 1952; Mueller, 1961; Strang, 1951a; Stroup, 1964). In addition, some writers speak of a safety-valve function (McKown, 1952; Mueller, 1961; Strang, 1951b).

Academic and Intellectual

Student activities reinforce classroom instruction and supplement academic learning. This is the oldest, best understood, and most widely accepted function of student activities (Frederick, 1959). Through planned activities and events, formal learning can be effectively applied in the immediate out-of-class environment. For example, a journalism student may write for the school newspaper, a music major may try out for the varsity singers. Music, orchestra, theatre, newspapers and other college publications, and departmental clubs are prominent examples of formal education extended outside of classroom walls. Such "course-related student activity provides enrichment, extension, variation, enlarged interest, and understanding of the work which is being carried on in a regular subject of study" (Frederick, 1959, p. 56). Student activities also enables students to integrate learning. Thus a student may decide to start an ecology newsletter and therefore capitalize on skills and knowledge attained in English, journalism, and science courses.

While formal academics and student activities may overlap, differences are apparent.

> Regular classroom work is dominantly individualistic, impersonal, and intellectual. It is tightly organized in logical sequence. Student activities, on the other hand, mix emotions, ideas, prejudices, and physical action. The work of the classroom is guided and directed by the teacher. Student activities are primarily student-directed and operated (Frederick, 1959, pp. 55-56).

Student activities add a dimension of independence requiring a single-minded thought, initiative, drive, and disciplined behavior.

Social

Student activities offer instruction in the specific skills of social interaction and promote a deeper understanding of social relations. They help students adjust to and find a place in their student world. Social competence can be learned both in the classroom and outside, though the greatest variety of contacts is afforded by student activities. To promote diversity and the growth of new relations, activities involving large groups and mixing many groups are encouraged.

Students' activities allow for an understanding of the social and cultural forces that exert pressures on the attitudes, values, and actions of individuals and groups in the college community. As Lloyd-Jones and Smith (1938, p. 97) say, "they are as valuable as laboratories for social living as are science laboratories for scientific discovery." Also, the most elementary social needs for companionship, comaraderie, and social good will are met by student activities.

Group

Student activities offer students an opportunity for group interaction. They teach students to learn to live in groups, to organize groups, to conduct meetings, to get along with people, to exercise cooperation, and to exchange ideas. They instill in students a sense of responsibility as a member of a group. In groups, students decrease the social distance between themselves and others; they develop a depth of insight and understanding of others and of themselves in relation to groups. Further, groups also satisfy students' needs for belongingness, security, and companionship.

Full Student Development

Student activities facilitate the successful achievement of key developmental tasks. By knowing the characteristics and background of the student body, their interests, physical attributes, and social backgrounds, activities can be planned to match students at their particular stages of development. Students are at different levels of social maturation, moral development, physical status, and intellectual growth and need correspondingly different inputs to effect overall growth.

Through self-expression students develop their personality;

student activities facilitate this process, thus encouraging self-discovery and self-realization. "Stuadudents find themselves in campus activities" (Strang, 1951a, p. 211). In addition to personality development, growth in morals and values takes place. Values are developed in two processes: first, through conceptualization, which can be learned in or out of the classroom; second, through application to specific situations, most effectively accomplished through the vehicle of student activities. Thus student activities aid students' total life adjustment. This is consonant with the view that education is designed to teach students how to adjust to life. "The assertion is often made by students that they get better training for later life from the activities than from the curriculum" (Edwards et al., 1928, p. 115).

Leadership and Democratic

"The major purpose of an education would appear to be to help develop the good citizen" (Arbuckle, 1953, p. 249). Student activities are designed for this function in that they prepare students for life in a democracy, assist them in learning the qualities of good citizenship, offer the possibility to develop good qualities of leadership and followership, help develop moral courage, and foster concern for law and order.

> Because of the inherent nature of formal classroom study the living of the democratic life is seriously restricted. This limitation a rich program of student activities can remove, for student activities by their very nature call for individual and group interaction in a natural setting (Frederick, 1959, p. 59).

To fulfill this function, student activities should adhere uncompromisingly to democratic principles, values, and standards and be open to everyone on the basis of interest, ability, skill, and achievement. Democratic procedures can help students resolve many problems related to adult authority if students and faculty tacklee e problems with mutual respect.

Student activities foster an understanding of the role and acquisition of the techniques of leadership in a democratic society. Students learn the appropriate role of a follower in a democratically organized group and learn to select leaders for qualities which will further group goals, such as setting goals, moving towards goals, and improving the quality of interaction. In leadership workshops, trainees can examine their own behavior and try out new behaviors appropriate to effective leadership.

Campus and Community Life

Student activities provide a means of uniting the campus and community by enabling friendly contacts and improved relations between students and faculty and encouraging interaction among the variety of peoples: foreign students, minority students, graduates, and undergraduates. The unification of the campus is strengthened with the sponsorship of activities that relate the individual and the group to the college as a whole. Since the college experience is to prepare students for effective participation in community living after college, student activities provide students the opportunity to identify with the college community and to have the experience of contributing meaningfully to the common good. Similarly, student activities create school spirit and improve morale, thus increasing student interest in and service to the college.

In student activities it is necessary to adapt to new opportunities and needs arising from shifts in the composition of the student population, economic conditions, and other factors of social change. Programs must be imaginative, creative, and experimental, for as composition and characteristics of the student body change, the activity program must be modified.

Safety-Valve

A safety-valve conception of the role of student activities appears in the literature. Mueller (1961) speaks of the therapeutic value of the profitable use of student's leisure time; Strang (1951b) notes that student activities channel creative energy into approprite outlets and McKown (1952) believes that student activities capitalize, for educational benefit, on fundamental student drives.

Shortcomings

Stroup (1964) sees three shortcomings of student activities: submergence in trivialities, vapid sentimentality in organization and implementation, and provincial conceptualization of its role in the college. The first is a result of overspecialization and professionalism and an overemphasis on objectivity. Emphasis is misplaced when such things as concern with proper attire and speech and teacup etiquette predominate. The second problem is the finishing school concept which considers student activities as preparation for a stylized and sophisticated lifestyle. Such an emphasis has been criticized for the "historically limited, sentimental conception of ... [student activities'] place in the modern university" (Stroup, 1964, p. 31).

Probably the chief shortcoming has been the lack of an adequate theory and rationale for the role of student activities in higher education. Its history has been "a compound of sentimental humanitarianism, naive 'consciousness of kind,' and religiously conceived group ebullitions ... [with] layers of professional responsibility [borrowed] from related disciplines" (Stroup, 1964, p. 33). In the swing away from impersonalism and the recapturing of the colonial period's concern for the whole student, personnel workers tended to reject intellectualism. Williamson (1961) argues fiercely for not divorcing the intellectual from the personal.

ADMINISTRATION

The student activities staff may be the largest unit in the dean of students office or may be under a director who is equal to all the other student personnel service directors who report to the vice-president. The student activities staff may include the director of the college union, there may be a single director for both, or student activities may be the programming staff of the union.

Program Reviews

Through systematic program reviews, the staff is kept alert and informed as to what is happening on the campus and student leaders and groups learn to evaluate their program objectives. Program reviews aid the students in developing more effective ways to reach goals, teach them the use of expertise in program development, and integrate the student organizations into the university community. Emphasis is placed upon the educative role of the activities leader, and a need to change the conflict-type relationship between individual student and institution which previously had existed. Basic strategies are developed to (a) encourage the apathetic student to participate; (b) maintain a democratic atmosphere with the freedom to participate and the right to dissent without inducing dependency or conformity to group norms; and (c) make democratic group decisions arrived at through consensus which protects the rights and humanity of each student and is consistent with the educational goals of the institution (Williamson, 1961).

PROGRAMS

Organized programs and spontaneous activities comprise the full repertoire of activities in which students engage. This section primarily considers student organizations and organized student activities since the spontaneous activities of college students are innumerable. A student organization is chartered and recognized by the institution, listed in a student activities handbook, and usually develops a program of events or objectives for a semester or year.

Student activity groups exhibit varied forms of leadership, patterns or organization, group programs and activities, sizes, and compositions of members. Some groups are quite homogeneous, while others are fairly heterogeneous. Some groups are participant, such as hiking clubs; others require an audience, such as marching bands. Groups may be institutionally led, requiring supervision and control by college personnel, or they may be managed by the student members. Student groups may be curricularly oriented, such as home economics clubs, or noncurricularly oriented, such as groups of bridge players (Stroup, 1964).

Fraternities and Sororities

Called a "continuation of adolescent fervor" (Arbuckle, 1953, p. 253), fraternities and sororities are an embodiment of youth culture. Emphasis is on having a good time with adult values repudiated and adult discipline rebelled against. As such, the fraternity acts as a "shock absorber" (Twaddle, 1965) to aid in the student's transition from high school to college by providing a unique environment which affords a special adaptation to and identification with the college.

Bloland (1971) says that the Greek-letter organizations "provide the organizational muscle that contributes greatly to successful campus activities while providing a small group, face-to-face, living situation" (p. 25). Their principal function is:

> the establishment and maintenance of friendships. They provide a home-away-from-home for students, a group to which they belong, a place where they are fairly sure to find sympathy and understanding, to find people who will accept and support them under any circumstances (Scott, 1965, pp. 90-91).

Greek members themselves see a variety of functions served by their organizations: a home-away-from-home, a place to learn leadership behaviors, an environment for close personal relationships, a milieu of scholastic achievement, a force for community service, and an orientation for freshmen to the university (Packwood, Casse, Lyerly, & Moklebust, 1972).

Undoubtedly fraternities and sororities serve many functions for many students as evidenced by their substantial holding power throughout the years. It is also questionable that any greater rationale is needed for their continued existence than the sheer joy of belonging. Nevertheless, many problems have been identified with the Greek system. One is the importance of fraternities becoming relevant to the total purposes of higher education (Anderson, 1965; Bloland, 1971). The anti-intellectuality, discrimination, and frequent delinquency of fraternities are particular causes for concern in this regard (Bloland, 1971). Fraternities might consider the contribution the broader spectrum of students on campus today, such as part-time, married, low income, and graduate students could bring to the fraternity experience (Salisch, 1965). Fraternities also need not mandate a four-year residency since the four-year college venture is no longer a universal phenomenon and many students graduate in three years or transfer to another college. Also, the collegiate appeal characteristic of fraternities is losing ground in favor of a concern in college for vocational preparation.

Other reforms called for are programs that are individualized, purposive, flexible, positive, intellectually oriented (McEwen, 1969) and that attract the interest of upperclassmen; less devotion to time wasting activities such as ritual processes, hazing, and meaningless social activities and more emphasis on quality performance, excellence, and study in depth (Butler, 1965); local autonomy of fraternities (Butler, 1965; McEwen, 1969) and direct involvement of students in formulating issues and establishing guidelines.

Pritchard and Buxton's (1972) study of fraternity members identified what they considered the two major difficulties: cultural implosiveness or socioeconomic inbreeding and the heavy emphasis on personality factors in rushing and pledging. Socioeconomic inbreeding occurs when members are recruited from narrow socioeconomic status backgrounds and from those whose fathers were also members. Through self-selection and selective recruitment fraternity houses maintain a high degree of homogeneity, evidenced by the fact that the majority of members major in only four fields: medicine, law, engineering, and business. Also, students rushing must seek out houses in which the rush chairman's personality matches their own.

Longino and Kart (1973) found that Greeks are more conservative politically and socially than independents or non-Greeks. They score lower on measures of social and religious liberalism and higher on measures of authoritarianism, ethno-centrism, and prejudice. The authors point out that the notion that fraternities are nonintellectual is common, yet "no systematic data supports the view that the Greek organizations play an alienating role within the total campus culture" (p. 122).

Kamens (1967) was also interested in the question of anti-intellectualism. He collected data from 16,665 students on ninety-nine campuses and concluded that (a) the number of fraternities and the membership in them exist in higher proportions at high quality institutions; (b) at high quality colleges, fraternity members are less likely to drop out than are nonmembers; (c) fraternities attract members whose grades are a little bit higher than the grades of the general student population; (d) the likelihood of drop-out is greater among fraternity members with good grades than with low grades; (e) as a measure of college success, emphasis on good grades is decreased by fraternities; and (f) fraternity membership has the greatest effect on the meaning of good grades at small colleges where grades largely determine one's self-definition as a student.

Regarding legitimate assistance with course work, fraternity members were more likely than nonmembers to join study groups, borrow course notes, and study old examinations (Stannard, 1967). As to illegitimate means, fraternity members engaged in more cheating, publicly and privately, than nonmembers, though disapproval of cheating was the same in both groups.

Another issue is student activism and individualism. Greeks have been characterized as reactionary, passive, interested in social programs only, conformist, and isolated. However, a study on one campus (Packwood et al., 1972) found that individualism defined as a "do your own thing" philosophy, was endorsed by 93 percent of 244 fraternity members and 90 percent of 322 sorority members. A majority of both groups felt that this recent change in philosophy had hindered the usual tradition, solidarity, and group activities more characteristic of Greek organizations in the past. Also, smaller, more individualized group activities were replacing the usual large group activities, and there was a greater tolerance and use of drugs.

In the same study, Greeks as individuals were likely to be involved in political issues. However, fraternity members were about equally divided for and against group activism, while sororities were more likely to avoid group involvement. They placed a strong value on participation in university government. Ninety-five percent of fraternity and sorority respondents felt they as individuals should take an active role in university governance. Only 60 percent felt they should do so in groups.

These changes are blurring the differences between Greeks and non-Greeks. This seems to be a desirable trend, as 78 percent of fraternity members and 91 percent of sorority members felt it was unimportant or even detrimental for them to have a clearly distinct identity. The authors note "they appear to be just as individualistic, active, involved, interested in drugs and in participating in governance and as antitraditional as the non-Greeks" (Packwood et al., 1972, p. 228).

A final issue is the purported decline in fraternity membership. Longino and Kart (1973) list three factors suggestive of a decline: a decreasing proportion of fraternity members, the loss of control of student government by fraternities, and the decreased uniqueness of fraternities as student personnel services have grown to meet the needs of the entire student body. Yet, there is no convincing evidence that a decline in fraternities is being evidenced on all campuses. In fact campuses filled with upwardly striving sons and daughters of the lower middle-class may find fraternity membership increasing.

Student Government

Four roles have been ascribed to student government: a laborabory for learning, a mouthpiece of the student body, a policy and decision-making group, and a liaison for faculty, administrators, and students. Student government provides students an opportunity to learn how to study a problem, assemble relevant data, and present a forceful argument in addition to influencing administrative policies and decisions and setting campus climate (Bloland, 1971). Thus student government offers personal and citizenship goals and develops personality and social leadership potential (Stroup, 1964). However, students are rejecting the role of student government as a laboratory, since so much of it is seen by them as meaningless and trivial, and are demanding active participation (Shaffer, 1970). In this respect, it is possible for student government to be one of two extremes. One is an essential and effective branch of college administration, a community government; the other is a pressure group or lobbying group, a mouthpiece of the student body where administration and student government are two distinct entities (Gallo, 1964).

Peterson (1964) suggests that there are five different administrative views of student government: (a) an attractive nuisance; (b) a pipeline to student opinion; (c) a device to manipulate and control student behavior; (d) an opportunity to train for citizenship; and (e) an opportunity for active participation in the ongoing life of the community of which students are members. This last attitude may not be the most widely accepted, but it offers the most potential for involving students honestly in student government. Williamson (1968) stresses the liaison role of student government. It effectively ties together the student body, faculty, and administration and allows students to present complaints, observations, and solutions.

Louis (1950) ascribes to student government responsibility for: (a) operation and control of all student organizations and student activities of the college campus, (b) carrying out all college functions and programs, (c) formation of policies regarding student life and student activities, and (d) increasing mutual understanding and cooperation among students, faculty members, and administrators.

The growth and complexity of colleges has posed problems for student government. There are difficulties in maintaining student solidarity, remaining representative of student interests, countering apathy, and maintaining real decision-making power (Gilmore & Scott, 1970). Some of the proposed options for dealing with these problems include forming a union with bargaining power, decentralizing into smaller units, aligning more closely with faculty, disappearing entirely, or excluding social programs and concentrating more on a representational role. It is this last option that Gilmore and Scott see as the most viable.

Forrest (1965) contends that apathy causes student government's ineffectiveness. Apathy results when administration and faculty only give students power in "Mickey Mouse" areas, manipulate student leaders, and are unwilling to serve as active and idea-producing sponsors of student organizations. Antes (1971) sees real student government as the solution to problems of student dissatisfaction, diversity of students, and complexity of university purposes and organization. However, poor communication among students, faculty, and administration is a strong deterrent to its effectiveness. The tendencies of faculty and administrators to doubt the ability of students and to place their own views above student views must be overcome. Adequate interaction and communication is essential with inclusion of students on some level in all policy matters. Stroup (1964) believes that students are often more skilled and more successful in regulating their affairs than are faculty.

It would appear that students take their role in student government seriously. Data from fifty-six officers of the Associated Students at California State University, Long Beach were collected by Carpenter (1972). Seventy percent did not consider their activity as a leisure-time pursuit. Instead, they emphasized the educational nature of student government or said they wished to be involved or to make changes. Seventy percent also considered their participation to relate to future plans. Rating student government involvement on polar opposite adjectives they chose these adjectives: free, active, complex, serious, successful, pleasurable, curricular, work-related, relevant, valuable, responsible, educational, happy, exciting, meaningful, and academic.

Essential to students' effective participation in student government is leadership training. There are three main forms leadership training can take: the clinic type, a "how to" approach where factual information and experiential advice are presented; the problem type or case-study method; and the practice type which utilizes behavioral science techniques to develop productive relationships in small, task-oriented groups. Leadership training varies according to the philosophy or theory on which it is based. Talley (1971) presents some assumptions upon which leadership training can rest. He believes that leader behaviors can be taught and learned, people will vary in their capacity to learn leadership behaviors, and people with leadership potential can be identified.

Political Action Groups

Political activities educate students and induct them into the world of politics. Two potential problems are that students may advocate stands unpopular to the administration or the community and campus political groups can be subject to the manipulation or exploitation by off-campus parties (Bloland. 1971). Another problem is that at public institutions the use of state tax dollars for partisan political purposes is usually not allowed (Bloland & Nowak, 1967).

Student Publications

Publications, such as newspapers, yearbooks, and literary magazines are common to most campuses. Wells and McCalister (1930) point out the benefits of student publications. School publications train interested students in good journalism and English usage, foster a desire for creative literature, furnish information about the school, report school news, and enable growth through purposeful activity. They serve the school by unifying it, by encouraging desirable activities, by influencing public opinion, by informing other schools, and by recording school history.

Bloland (1971) emphasizes the necessity for a publications program to be tied to the journalism department to train students working on publications. An advisor is needed to convey the notion of journalistic ethics, to differentiate freedom from license, to differentiate informing student readers from manipulating them, and to give students feedback before and after publication.

Religious Clubs

Traditionally, colleges have concerned themselves with the religious or at least moral development of their students. Eddy and Jones (1974) report that a majority of public colleges accept some responsibility for religious activities, though not enough to establish a separate student affairs position. Most institutions coordinate these programs between student affairs and religious groups: lectures and discussion groups, religiously inspired concerts, and religious counseling.

Religious centers of many faiths are common on most campuses. One study (Biggs & Frishe, 1968) found that the largest number of student users frequented the center for eating, studying, and socializing. A small number participated in the center's organized activities (see Religion chapter).

Intellectual Discussion Groups

Many student personnel workers, as well as educators, are concerned with furthering the intellectual development of students outside the classroom to better integrate the curriculum and the extracurriculum. They contend that encouraging more informal faculty-student interaction gives students a more meaningful educational experience.

Hallberg and Speckler (1970) suggest what they call the "college forum" to facilitate free discussion among students and faculty. Three formats are described: (a) a lecture series where communication is one-way and the audience is heterogeneous, (b) a speakers program where topic, speaker, and audience are defined, and (c) an open speakers platform where free and unrestricted discussion and debate are allowed. Faculty might be involved in an interdisciplinary approach to a single topic or be invited to speak on issues outside their fields. National and international professors might be invited to participate in a visiting professors series.

Providing for greater faculty-student contact in an informal atmosphere is a program initiated at the University of Minnesota (Vaughan, 1968). This is a retreat program where students, faculty, and student personnel staff spend a weekend together off campus. Informal, small group discussion centers are formed around a chosen theme, such as the goals of higher education or academic freedom, which is analyzed from a variety of disciplines and points of view. Begun in 1956 as an experiment, the retreat program has moved from sponsorship by faculty and student personnel staff to student organization and planning.

The "New Consciousness Series" at Northern Michigan University (Hefke, 1973) brought together students, faculty, student personnel, and community people to create a series of forty-five minute videotapes. These videotapes enabled student audiences to see and hear noted speakers such as Ralph Nader and Dick Gregory and discuss current topics such as birth control and Vietnam. Sites for presentation included classrooms, residence halls, and the university center.

Volunteer and Services Activities

Eberly (1968) recommends volunteer or service activities as a valuable activity in which college students can increase their knowledge of themselves and of the larger world. When matched with an appropriate task, students stretch their capabilities. A publication, "College Student Volunteers in State Mental Hospitals" (1968), reports that 7,700 students from 301 U. S. colleges participated in 114 state mental hospitals in forty states. For two to four hours a week, student volunteers engaged in recreation and conversation, tutoring, occupational therapy, and teaching art. The program was seen as beneficial by almost all of the hospitals.

Educational Participation in Communities (EPIC), a program at California State College at Los Angeles, was formed to organize community action programs and to recruit and train student volunteers for community service (Brass, 1967, 1969). After contacts are made with community leaders and agencies, students are carefully matched to a service that will maximize their educational and professional training. Objectives of the program are to aid in community development, to help make students' education practical and relevant, and to encourage the community's use of the educational and cultural resources of the college. A similar organization, The Clearinghouse, was developed at the University of Colorado (Yoder, 1966). Its efficiency, plus the stringent selection process, contributed to a low student attrition rate.

Organized by the National Student Association (NSA) was the Community Action Project (K. Duncan, 1968). Its purpose was to encourage colleges to give academic credit to students doing field work in lower- and middle-class communities. The Project was also instrumental in establishing training programs, courses, and evaluation seminars. A list of fifty-nine programs at forty-eight institutions, published by NSA included such programs as field work, tutoring, social work training, work-study, VISTA, and Peace Corps.

Examples of activities for which students have volunteered are a clean-up and repair day; cultural and ethnic programs and a special orientation for Indian and Chicano students; research on nuclear power plants with a 12-page publication urging public debate on the issue (R. D. Duncan, 1971); seminars conducted by upperclass English and speech majors to help freshmen progress through an independent study course; and tutoring educationally and culturally deprived children (Griggs, 1968).

Women

Women college students are not adequately represented in student leadership positions. Baine (1968) found that women occupy few elected positions of power. Of 187 institutions responding, eight presidents were women, forty-four vice-presidents, 147 secretaries and 26 treasurers. Baine endorses the concept of autonomous women's organizations as essential in meeting the particular needs of the college female. A women's organization serves the objectives of attending to the values relating to sex roles, gaining insight into sex-role problems, evaluating roles, and determining equality as well as providing competition with men's organizations. Dodson (1968) feels women need to contribute as women, and the problems of sex roles will be resolved only when women create means through which they can have autonomy to test their own strengths and validate their own roles.

One example of an institution that has made strides towards creating programs for women is the University of Idaho (Hipple & Hill, 1972). Students, faculty, and student personnel staff assessed women's needs, presented evidence to the president, faculty, and staff, and developed new programs with funding from student government. Occupational information especially designed for women was distributed and a periodical detailing women's educational and vocational opportunities was established. Consciousness-raising groups to help women find themselves were initiated. Courses such as "Women's Role in Society" and "Alternatives" helped women deal with career and life choices and problems. "The Women's Caucus" was formed to deal with women's issues, problems, and areas of discrimination.

PERSONNEL

The activities advisor is the professional who is responsible for providing administrative leadership and coordination of the student activities program. Although the advisor's main role is to deal with student groups, the advisor also fulfills the function of interpreting the needs of students to the faculty and administration on the college campus. Over the years, the activities advisor's functions have changed according to the changing demands of the students in their campus environment.

Strang (1951a) preceived the activities advisor as a leader who shared responsibility with inexperienced groups of students who needed technical expertise. The leader functioned as a guide to student groups, a consultant and resource, a strategist in developing programs, and a specialist in group dynamics. Administrative responsibilities included providing group experiences that meet the needs of all students, the development of new student groups, acquainting students with opportunities for participation in campus activities, improving the quality of events, and encouraging overall planning.

Williamson (1961) emphasized the active rather than passive stance for the activities leader who is responsible for administrative review of student organizational programs. The activities professional serves as an advisor when asked by students regarding their own voluntary activities, a joint partner in planning institutional activities, a consultant on student reactions to institutional programs, a leader in adopting new objectives, and a technical consultant. The integration of the supervisory and advisory role is exceedingly important in the Williamson model to lessen resistance to the concept of authority. The professional needs to clearly delineate to students when he is acting in a supervisory manner and when he is functioning as an advisor.

Bloland (1971) defines four major responsibilities of the professional worker: research, counseling, education, and supervision. The professional activities advisor should utilize and contribute to research findings in order to improve the services rendered. With counseling training and background, the activities professional can provide counseling assistance to student group members and leaders on personal problems that have little to do with organizational activities.

In broadly stated terms, the professional in student activities is an educator who works with organized student groups in roles such as advisor, consultant, leader, supervisor, and strategist. An understanding of group dynamics and group skills provides the tools of the trade (Mueller, 1961). The curriculum may be informal in the sense that the objective is to help the student organization gain its goals through dynamic active participation or formalized into a course structure in which students receive academic credit for learning how to manage their activities. The overall objective is to provide academic relevancy within an atmosphere where individual personal development can be obtained.

REFERENCES

Anderson, G. R. Fraternities — their problems today. *NASPA Journal*, 1965, *3*, 7-9.

Antes, R. Involving students in university governance. *NASPA Journal,* 1971, *9,* 48-56.

Arbuckle, D. S. *Student personnel services in higher education.* New York: McGraw-Hill, 1953.

Baine, E. V. Women holders of leadership positions on the coeducational campus. *Journal of the National Association of Women Deans and Counselors,* 1968, *37,* 39-40.

Bergstresser, J. L., & Wells, D. E. Life outside the classroom. In E. M. Lloyd-Jones & M. R. Smith (Eds.), *Student personnel work as deeper teaching.* New York: Harper, 1954.

Biggs, D. A., & Frishe, N. *The religious foundation and the university student* (Cooperative Research Report No. 1). Minneapolis: University of Minnesota, Office of Dean of Students, 1968.

Bloland, P. A. *Student group advising in higher education.* Washington, D. C.: American Personnel and Guidance Association, 1971. (Student Personnel Monograph Series, No. 8)

Bloland, P. A., & Nowak, D. B. *Free speech areas, an informal survey of institutional policies and practices.* Los Angeles: Office of the Dean of Students, University of Southern California, 1967.

Brass, R. V. *EPIC: Educational participation in communities.* Paper presented at the meeting of the Association of College Unions-International, Philadelphia, April, 1967.

Brass, R. V. College students turn to community action. *Journal of College Student Personnel,* 1969, *10,* 3-6.

Brubacher, J. S., & Rudy, W. *Higher education in transition: A history of American colleges and universities, 1936-1968.* New York: Harper & Row, 1968.

Butler, W. R. Fraternities — 2000 A.D. *NASPA Journal,* 1965, *3,* 3-7.

Carpenter, G. *College student government as a leisure pursuit.* Long Beach: California State University, Office of Student Activities, January, 1972. (Abstract)

College student volunteers in state mental hospitals (U. S. Public Health Service Publication No. 1752). Washington, D. C.: U. S. Government Printing Office, 1968.

Dodson, D. W. Is it desirable for women's organizations to maintain their autonomy? *Journal of the National Association of Women Deans and Counselors,* 1968, *32,* 40-45.

Duncan, K. *Community action curriculum compendium.* Washington, D. C.: The United States National Student Association, 1968. (Abstract)

Duncan, R. D. Part 1: The involved student cleans up the city; Part II: The involved student recruits minorities; Part III: The involved student provides a forum. *College Management,* 1971, *6,* 32-37. (Abstract)

Eberly, D. J. Service experience and educational growth. *Educational Record,* 1968, *49,* 197-205.

Eddy, J. P., & Jones, G. W. Campus religious personnel: Emergent or abortive. *NASPA Journal,* 1974, *12,* 100-106.

Edwards, R. H., Artman, J. M., & Fisher, G. M. *Undergraduates.* Garden City: Doubleday, Doran, 1928.

Forrest, A. Point of view — what about student government? *NASPA Journal,* 1965, *2,* 36-38.

Frederick, R. W. *The third curriculum: Student activities in American education.* New York: Appleton-Century-Crofts, 1959.

Gallo, G. M. Student government: A student view. *NASPA Journal,* 1964, *2,* 12-15.

Gilmore, R. P., & Scott, W. G. University government and student organization. *Journal of the Council of Associations of University Student Personnel Services,* 1970, *5,* 23-30.

Griggs, J. H. *Relevance in undergraduate education.* Paper presented at the meeting of the North Central Association of Colleges and Universities, Chicago, March, 1968.

Hallberg, E. C., & Speckler, D. E. College forum: Encumbered or unencumbered. *Bulletin of the Association of College Unions-International,* 1970, *38,* 8.

Hand, H. C. (Ed.). *Campus activities.* New York: McGraw-Hill, 1938.

Hefke, N. E. Integrating curricular and extracurricular programs. *Journal of College Student Personnel,* 1973, *14,* 278.

Hipple, J. L., & Hill, A. J. Women's programs — a plan for action. *NASPA Journal,* 1972, *10,* 124-131.

Kamens, D. H. *Fraternity membership and college dropout in different institutional settings.* Paper presented at the meeting of the American Sociological Association, San Francisco, August, 1967.

Lloyd-Jones, E. M., & Smith, M. R. *A student personnel program for higher education.* New York: McGraw-Hill, 1938.

Longino, C. F., Jr., & Kart, C. S. The college fraternity: An assessment of theory and research. *Journal of College Student Personnel,* 1973, *14,* 118-125.

Louis, B. *The role of student government in the student personnel program.* Paper presented at the Annual Convention of the American College Personnel Association, Atlantic City, Spring, 1950.

McEwen, M. New challenges for national sororities. *Journal of the National Association of Women Deans and Counselors,* 1969, *33,* 43-45.

McKown, H. C. *Extracurricular activities.* New York: Macmillan, 1952.

Mueller, K. H. *Student personnel work in higher education.* Boston: Houghton Mifflin, 1961.

Packwood, W. T., Casse, R. M., Jr., Lyerly, B. J., & Moklebust, J. Greek individualism and activism: A new identity? *Journal of College Student Personnel,* 1972, *13,* 224-228.

Peterson, M. Student government: An administrative view. *NASPA Journal,* 1964, *2,* 8-12.

Pokorny, G. The other university. *The Intercollegian,* 1967, *85,* 14-16.

Pritchard, K. W., & Buxton, T. H. The social fraternity system: Its increasing problems. *Journal of College Student Personnel,* 1972, *13,*

218-223.

Salisch, M. S. A postscript or a prologue (focus on fraternities). *NASPA Journal*, 1965, *3*, 13-16.

Scott, W. A. *Values and organizations*. Chicago: Rand McNally, 1965.

Shaffer, R. H. Student government: Sandbox or soapbox? In J. Foster & D. Long (Eds.), *Protest: Student activism in America*. New York: William Morrow, 1970.

Stannard, C. I. The college fraternity as an opportunity structure, *Abstracts of Proceedings of the American Sociological Association*, San Francisco, August, 1967.

Stark, M. Human relations programs: Social reconstruction through college extracurricular activities. *Journal of National Association of Women Deans and Counselors*, 1967, *30*, 82-85.

Strang, R. *Group activities in college and secondary school*. New York: Harper and Bros., 1941.

Strang, R. Education through guided group experiences. In C. G. Wrenn (Ed.) *Student personnel work in college*. New York: Ronald Press, 1951. (a)

Strang, R. Problems and procedures of student activities. In C. G. Wrenn (Ed.), *Student personnel work in college*. New York: Ronald Press, 1951. (b)

Stroup, H. *Toward a philosophy of organized student activities*. Minneapolis: University of Minnesota Press, 1964.

Talley, B. C. A pro-leadership vaccine: The North Carolina Fellows program. *NASPA Journal*, 1971, *9*, 71-76.

Taylor, H. The future of American education. *The American Scholar*, 1949, *18*(1), 33-40.

Taylor, H. *The individual student: Essays in teaching*. New York: Harper, 1950.

Twaddle, A. C. The college fraternity and the academic community. *NASPA Journal*, 1965, *3*, 9-13.

Vaughan, C. E. *The special dean's retreat program: A co-curricular program for higher education* (ODS Staff Papers No. 40). Minneapolis: University of Minnesota, Office of the Dean of Students, November, 1968.

Wells, G. C., & McCalister, W. H. *Student publications*. New York: A. S. Barnes, 1930.

Williamson, E. G. *Student personnel services in colleges and universities*. New York: McGraw-Hill, 1961.

Williamson, E. G. *Activities and functions of student government* (ODS Staff Papers No. 28). Minneapolis: University of Minnesota, Office of the Dean of Students, August, 1968.

Yoder, R. *Tutorial project case study*. U. S. National Student Association, December, 1966.

CHAPTER 6

UNION

William T. Packwood

HISTORY

THE college union began in 1815 at Cambridge University in England as a forum for debate (Butts, 1965). The first union building was erected at Oxford University in 1857. Harvard University established the first debating organization in the United States in 1832, and the first union building was Houston Hall constructed on the University of Pennsylvania campus in 1896 (Beaty, 1940; Stevens, 1969).

The evolution of the union has been characterized by several stages, the first four of which were identified by Humphreys (1946): The Debate Stage (1815-1894) was a reflection of the English unions; The Club Stage (1895-1918) saw expansion to include the social life of the debaters; The Campus Democracy Stage (1919-1929) sought to serve all members of the college community in memory of those who had served in the war; The Community Recreation Stage (1930-1945) found the union becoming much like a community recreation center (see Barth, 1961), trying to develop a community feeling, and beginning to recognize its educational mission on the campus and its role in students' leisure time.

Additional stages of development for the union have been identified by Stevens (1969): The Educational Stage (1946-1956), with the demand for additional facilities from the flood of returning veterans, saw the federal government providing low cost loans to aid in the construction of unions because they contributed to the educational mission of the college; The Personalization Stage (1957-1966) saw an emphasis on providing personalized experiences to combat the impersonalization of mass education; The Humanization Stage (1967-present) found

179

the union responding to the various movements of the day by bringing programs related to social issues to campus to allow students vicarious involvement in them. In the 1970's over 900 college unions exist in the United States and Canada and at least 335 in some sixty other countries (Butts, 1967).

DEFINITION

The union is designed to meet the leisure-time needs of all members of the college community (Butts, 1971). Its role as the social-cultural heart of the campus is given in the Statement of Purpose adopted by the Association of College Unions-International (ACU-I) at its 1956 Annual Conference (Reprinted by permission of the publisher. See also "Vote Approaching," 1971; "ACU-I: Priorities for Effectiveness," 1975).

1. The union is the community center of the college, for all the members of the college family — students, faculty, administration, alumni and guests. It is not just a building; it is also an organization and a program. Together they represent a well-considered plan for the community life of the college.
2. As the "living room" or the "hearthstone" of the college, the union provides for the services, conveniences, and amenities the members of the college family need in their daily life on the campus and for getting to know and understand one another through informal association outside the classroom.
3. The union is part of the educational program of the college. As the center of college community life, it serves as a laboratory of citizenship, training students in social responsibility and for leadership in our democracy. Through its various boards, committees, and staff, it provides a cultural, social, and recreational program, aiming to make free time activity a cooperative factor with study in education. In all its processes it encourages self-directed activity, giving maximum opportunity for self-realization and for growth in individual social competency and group effectiveness. Its goal is the development of persons as well

as intellects.

4. The union serves as a unifying force in the life of the college, cultivating enduring regard for and loyalty to the college.

The union provides a variety of facilities in fulfilling its role. It is a lounge, store, dining room, reading room, student organization headquarters, game room, art gallery, office building, workshop, forum, theater, party center, music room, public relations agency, post office, outing center, ticket bureau, conference headquarters, and office building. Unions provide over 130 facilities and the trend is toward greater rather than less diversity (Butts, 1971; Jenkins & McQueen, 1973).

At one extreme a union may provide no more than minimal service, such as a room in the basement of one of the campus buildings with tables and chairs where students can relax, eat and play pool. At the other extreme it is a separate building with a variety of food and recreational services; provides the art and music programming for the campus; has speakers and other programs related to current political and social issues; and has strong ties with various academic departments, coordinating its programs with their coursework, if not offering its own courses. Regardless of the size of the union or its program, it should represent a comprehensive, well-considered plan for meeting the wide range of needs and interests of its particular college population (Butts, 1971).

PURPOSE

The main purpose of the union is service or provision of the basic anemities of college life: a place to sit between classes, hang one's coat, get a bite to eat, find out what is happening on campus, make a phone call, take a nap, buy a book or supplies, park one's car, or hold a meeting. In other words it meets the daily needs of students and saves precious time. The union seeks to meet these needs but hopefully does not become merely a service station (Berry, 1962).

A second purpose is to provide recreational opportunities,

perceived as necessary diversions from work or study (Noffke, 1963). These include card playing, pool, table tennis, bowling, television, photography labs, music listening, reading areas, craft shops, and outing equipment for hiking, camping, climbing, and canoeing. Because of the limited financial incomes of the college population, these services as well as others are offered at minimal cost to help students lower the cost of going to college (Lancaster, 1950). Relationships with noncollege commercial businesses have to be established so that state funds which support union programs are not viewed as taking customers away from the private sector which pays taxes into those state funds.

The social purpose of the union is met indirectly through programs and recreational opportunities which provide places and occasions for students to get together and talk. For example, when students were interested, dances and training in social etiquette were provided by unions. It is primarily within its social function that the union meets its commitment to unite the campus. It is a common ground where members of various segments of the college can come together: The art major can discuss politics with the engineering student; the student can have coffee with the faculty member; the almunus can discuss the new art exhibit with the freshman; the student from the farm can compare life styles with one from the city or a foreign country.

These social activities are intended to overlap with the two other union purposes, cultural and educational. Unions contribute to the culture of the campus by providing various kinds of art exhibits, music, and film programs (see Cultural Affairs section). Education is provided directly through debates and lectures, but primarily indirectly and informally through students participating in programs: education by propinquity or taking the person from coke to art (Berry, 1969). Through its programs and exhibits the union can supplement and compliment classroom experiences.

The educational purpose of the union is considered its capstone. Tinney (1953) suggests that the development of the student is more important than the attainment of a level of efficiency of union programs. It is through participation in union activities that students obtain practice in leadership, social skills, management, budgeting, group dynamics, and the appreciation and use of freedom; develop personality; and apply techniques learned in the classroom, including research if desired (Noffke, 1963). Tinney (1955) found that seventy-one unions offered 530 experiences of which 8 percent were for credit, though McWhorter (1960) found that 80 percent of the unions he surveyed opposed classes being taught in the union. Arrangements for credit for union activities is a possibility particularly if the union is conceived as being a social science delivery system (see Berry, 1973).

The purposes of the union stem from the belief that the college is much more than an agency for providing academic instruction and that to further the intellectual and personal development of its constituencies, the college must provide a wholesome and stimulating social environment (Cowley, 1933; Jones, 1935). If the union becomes a "temple of the good life" (Harper, 1960, p. 8), it will convey the seven enduring values of life: economic, physical, recreational, social, intellectual, aesthetic, and spiritual (Harper, 1960), as well as cultivate taste and intelligence in using discretionary time (Butts, 1965). However, students need to determine their own programs, since the union cannot interpret taste and propriety, nor know what is best for students (Cameron, 1968).

The role of the union is not without contradictions (Lake, 1961). It is dedicated to educational and service objectives but is founded on the profit motive. It is a socialistic enterprise based on a compulsory fee structure. It uses undemocratic selective/ elective processes in the supposed training for democracy. It is a big business with an archaic organizational structure subject to empire builders and guided by a board of directors characterized by youthful inexperience and immaturity. It is an enterprise for service but is subsidized by the college and afforded monopolistic privileges on campus. It is a social education organization whose annual report does not deal with values but with body statistics and dollars and cents (see also Brugger, 1965).

ADMINISTRATION

There have been several major studies of union operations: Whiting in 1951, Hesser (1958, 1960), Bell (1963, 1964), Jenkins and McQueen (1973). The data from the latter study are used throughout this chapter because they are the most current, though not without severe limitations.

Most union directors report to the student affairs dean, though some report to the president or business manager (Jenkins & McQueen, 1973). This is an improvement over an earlier finding (Lyons, 1963) that 44 percent of the union directors reported to two college administrative officials, one of which was the business manager. As Hesser (1963) says, it is impossible to serve two masters: student services and business management. The preference is clearly for the union director to be a student personnel person (Lancaster, 1950) and an educator (Kohler, 1960).

Boards

In order to serve the entire college community, the union is organized as a representation of its constituents. At the top of that organization, most unions have a policy-making board composed of members appointed from the union staff, student government, faculty, union program board, general student body, and student affairs office. Sometimes alumni, the college business office, the college's governing board, and other college administrative offices such as president and vice-president are represented. Although it would be more democratic to elect members to the board and there is a slight trend to do so, appointments insure that those committed to and willing to work for the union are given that responsibility. However, this procedure lends itself to maintenance of the status quo.

Usually, the policy board reports to the union staff, president of the college, or student affairs dean. Reporting to the union staff dilutes the power of the board, leaving it with perhaps only token authority or an advisory function since the staff can overrule its decisions. The advantages are that the staff are more intimately involved in the union, more aware of the practical implications of decisions made about it, know what can and cannot be done, provide continuity, and, of course, may elect to follow the spirit of the board's decisions. Reporting to the president of the college provides greater authority to the board and may make it equal with other student services. Reporting to the student affairs dean is much the same as reporting to the president but allows for much better coordination among student services and programs.

The second major organizational unit is the program board, which is the major working body of the union. This board is composed of representatives from the union staff, the general student body, and the student chairman of program committees. Student government, faculty, or student affairs deans may also be represented. Members of the program board are usually appointed, with union staff serving in an exofficio capacity. The program board may be responsible to the policy-making board, student government, or union staff. It is usually chaired by a representative of the union policy board, just as the chairman of the policy board is most often the student representative of the union programming board or student government. Most unions do not compensate students serving on the program board. Those that do, pay the president of the board from $100 to $1,000 annually as some recognition of the extensive amount of time devoted.

Most unions have less than nine program committees, with each committee composed of one to ten students. Most committees derive from the following eight areas: (a) social, dance; (b) visual arts, exhibits; (c) publicity, public relations; (d) special events; (e) lecture, forum, debate; (f) film; (g) games, tournaments; and (h) performing arts. These committees reflect the trend in union programming from social to cultural activities.

According to Jenkins and McQueen (1973) there are trends toward combining the policy and program boards, giving more authority to the student body, and having the student members elected from the general student body. Student input into the union has always been high, not only because the majority of the users of the union are students, but also because it provides students with excellent training, increases student interest and support, and helps students feel responsible for financial success.

Butts (1949) also recommends giving students final authority in the union for the same reasons, as well as the fact that they have been successful at it, but Cobb (1967), who divides the union into three areas which are operations, programs, and administration, allows students final authority in the program area only.

There is substantial interest in removing the union from politics, thus making it separate from student government (Blumberg, 1955; "Student-Faculty," 1968). Jenkins and McQueen (1973) found that 61 percent of the unions operated independently of student government, with the practice more prevalent at larger institutions. The rationale for depoliticizing the union is that all energies in the union should be devoted to providing quality programs and services rather than to arousing political ferment, which can be damaging and devisive.

Regardless of organizational structure, those who determine policy are the real authority for what happens in the union. Jenkins and McQueen (1973) found that most policy decisions were made by two groups: the business office alone and a combination of the business office and union staff. Employee benefits and book store price policies were determined primarily by the business office. Reserve fund, wage levels, food price, purchasing procedures, repair and replacement, and operating surpluses were split between the two groups. General business matters were primarily determined by coordination. Profit goals were established primarily by coordination, secondarily by the union staff alone. Student fees were usually determined by the university governing board or the business office. Building use and program policies were determined by the union policy board, the union staff, or the two in coordination. In all money matters the business office with its accounting and economic expertise has predominant input; in regard to program, the union boards and staff have the greater authority.

This division of authority is confirmed by Brewer's (1963) finding that the primary role of the policy board, as viewed by administrators, students, and staff, is planning and implementing the union's social and cultural program and not personnel decisions. The dominant role of the business office, which may be a reflection of a concentrated effort to deal with financially difficult times, does appear to make the union college-managed and to put financial considerations over student personnel or service concerns. The primary check on such a monetary emphasis is in the area of determining the degree of profit, where the union seems to retain primary authority.

Name

Hesser (1960) found that only 43 percent of the buildings he surveyed were called unions; others were called center, 17 percent; memorial, 18 percent; and house or hall, 9 percent. The term, *union*, is preferred because it conveys the goal of unity among diverse groups of people which the building fosters; center implies only a place (Butts, 1965); memorial was added after the wars to honor those who had fought and died for their country.

Sometimes unions are put in an accounting or budgetary category called auxiliary enterprises, along with food facilities, infirmaries, bookstores, print shops, and laundries. This practice seems to date back to 1922 when there were very few unions and business officers did not know how else to categorize them (Butts, 1965). Such a categorization is inappropriate because the union should, at a minimum, be equal with other student services on campus.

Similarly, student union is not a recommended name, primarily because the union is not just for students (Blumberg, 1955). It is designed for all the other members of the college, faculty, administration, staff, alumni, as well as participants in conferences and institutes. Calling it a student union suggests that other are outsiders or guests (Jones, 1965); does not do justice to the tradition of effective cooperation by the constituents of the university (Siggelkow, 1969); mistakenly suggests to students that they are the only ones who contribute financially to the union and should therefore have sole control; and hampers efforts to inform faculty about the role of the union on campus (Noffke, 1963).

Building

The union is most readily conceived of as a building, a structure. Most unions were built after 1950 and most have additions or are planning them. The best data available shows that the median size of unions is 75,000 gross square feet with a median investment for construction alone of over two million dollars. The major source of funding at public institutions was revenue bonds or HUD, while large single gifts and college funds were the predominant source at private institutions (Jenkins & McQueen, 1973).

The union should be tailor-made for its institution (Butts, 1965). The building should be located close to the geographical center of campus (Schoenfeld, 1955) or where the highest pedestrian traffic count occurs (Christensen, 1970). It should be designed so that it is inviting, inspiring, and humane (Butts, 1965). Inside space should be designed so that it can be used for multiple purposes according to varying needs and peak periods of the day, such as a cafeteria that could also accommodate a concert, lecture, dance, or reception (Butts, 1965).

Because many unions are too small shortly after they are built (Butts, 1961; Loomis, 1968a), competition for space and time can be fierce. A master calendar is frequently maintained by union staff to prevent scheduling competition and to insure that space is available, though some programs are difficult to schedule far in advance. Additionally, student organizations and student services housed in the union may find they have no room to expand. Deciding whether a room that becomes available goes to the counseling service, student activities, the women's group, or student government can be a challenge of the first order.

Security

Security has always been a concern of the union, but was

particularly heightened during the 1960's by the campus demonstrations. The union is perhaps one of the most vulnerable (Carlson, Davis, & Wedell, 1969; "Student Disruptions," 1969) of the student services, given its interest in easy access for campus constituencies ("Union Use Policy," 1970). Security problems include vandalism, bomb threats, actual bombing or fire bombing, sit-ins, demonstrations, fire, program and guest disruptions, theft, burglary, and employee safety (Hinde, 1972). Solutions seem to revolve around a well-defined policy on use of the union and extensive steps taken and plans devised to prevent such occurrences.

Some unions have had to restrict access, using identification checks of current registration or their equivalent for admission. Despite the need for this kind of restriction, at the very least it defeats the union purpose of making everyone feel welcome.

Financial Operations

Almost all unions are expected to be self-supporting. However, most (77%) receive student fees, which are used for building amortization and/or operation expenses. Thirty percent of the private colleges do not charge fees. Students who pay fees pay between $20 and $60 per academic year. Seldom do other groups such as faculty and alumni pay fees. As with all educational programs, continued rising costs indicate that fees will continue to be increased (Jenkins & McQueen, 1973).

One of the major sources of income for unions is their food service. Jenkins and McQueen (1973) found that 77 percent of the food services were expected to be self-supporting and 55 percent were expected to contribute profits to the total union operation. Much the same is true for bookstores in that most (89%) are self-supporting and one-third contribute profits to the union. Other sources of revenue include guest rooms; twenty-three types of concessions including vending machines, juke boxes, telephones, pinball machines, copy machines, and barber shops; and sixteen other services such as games, general/

services/merchandise desk, hall rentals, recreation equipment rentals, movies, and programs.

Students have upon occasion objected to the fee payment. In response to these objections, some institutions, such as New York, went to a voluntary fee basis but found their program thrown into chaos (Loomis, 1968b) and returned to compulsory fees for the most part (Spelman, 1972).

Financially, the union is a circular trap. Its primary mission is to provide service, say food, at low cost to students. If the food prices are much lower than the nearby competing commercial food businesses, the businesses will complain that state dollars are being used to damage their business. For the union to maintain low food prices, given rising food costs, labor or salaries must be low. However, most of the employees of the union are students, who use their salary to attend school ("Pacific, Midwest Unions," 1973). If salaries increase, the union food prices increase, and students complain or go to the commercial businesses for their food. Complicating this is the union's interest in, as well as legal necessity of, paying minimum wages, and the trend for more and more university employees to form labor unions (Reynolds, 1972). In response to such a plight, as well as for other reasons, 40 percent of Jenkins and McQueen's unions have employed a contract caterer (Hesser, 1960, 1963).

PROGRAMS

In addition to being a building and an organization, the union is also a program (Berry, 1964). Determining which programs are needed by the college and presenting them successfully is a major responsibility of the union. The infinite variety of programs is suggested by Sturgell's (1973) *Whole Earth Catalogue of Union Programming* and is possibly a reflection of unions' better meeting the needs of their particular institutions. However, the diversity of programming may be the result of greater fragmentation in the university administration (Pride, 1959, 1960), as more people have more input into more things. This is a healthy result if thorough coverage and overall impact of the programs are not reduced and duplication does not occur.

Nevertheless, some commonality has always been present. Wolf (1958) identified the ten most frequently sponsored programs and Berry (1965), who updated Wolf's work, found the continued leadership of twenty activities which might be considered a Basic Union Program Core. These twenty activities can be combined under the headings of art, games, reading, get-acquainted functions, lectures, films, and orientation (see also Andrews, 1969; Ketter, 1972).

Recent changes in union programming have been an increase in the cultural, recreational, travel, and outdoors areas and a decrease in social, more informal, and intimate programs. Dees (1969) suggests week-long programming such as Black Awareness Week and BACU-I ("Block Programming," 1972) reports savings made by block programming, that is, programming for all institutions within one state.

In regard to expenditures for programs, most unions (92%) spend more than $3,000 per year on free programs and 67 percent more than $10,000, making a range of $1 to $50 annual programming expenditure for each full-time day student.

Evaluation

Several methods of evaluating union programs have been suggested: interviewing students at the union door using a short questionnaire (Fritz, 1960); mailing a questionnaire to all members of the student body to determine their preferences (Alexander, 1958); a combination interview and questionnaire (McKoane, 1960); and the Texas Union Evaluation Questionnaire. Erdahl (1959) identifies several advantages of using the student poll as a tool in programming: (a) It makes the student aware of the union; (b) indicates interest in the student; (c) causes the union committee to constantly evaluate what they are doing: (d) suggests new programs, (e) balances desires versus needs; (f) indicates directions of campus interest; (g) gives insight into program reception; (h) indicates traffic and use in each area in the union; (i) gives percentage of student body use; (j) provides information with which to answer charges and to make the annual report to the president; and (k) provides data for additions. A recommendation of the 1962 Wisconsin Summer Course (see also AuBuchon, 1972) was that such studies be done every three years.

Evaluation of each program with the students who had responsibility for it is good policy. However, the "program was a failure but we learned a lot" attitude, which is a fraud (Carlson, 1973), prevents real evaluation. Continual evaluation helps to encourage students who are intrinsically motivated and who will take the risks necessary to execute successful programs.

Other evaluative approaches are more indirect. Duncan (1962) and Minahan (1957) found that students active on union committees were more active in a leadership way in community participation after graduation than those who were nonactive. Maneks (1963) found that 90 percent of a random sample of companies that hired college students advise students to participate in activities, particularly those that build leadership. Most companies (79%) questioned about extracurricular activities, 86 percent thought extracurricular activities were an aid to success, and 82 percent looked for personality. Similarly, Mullins (1960) found that employers prefer students who have participated in activities if they are interested in the nontechnical, technical sales, and technical production fields, but not if they are interested in the technical research field.

PERSONNEL

Most unions (55%) at colleges with enrollments of less than 2,500 have only one professional staff member. Most institutions (64%) with enrollments over 10,000 have six or more staff positions (Jenkins & McQueen, 1973). Almost all unions have directors, though alternative plans such as management teams have been suggested (Casse & Burke, 1971; Crabb & Handy, 1972).

Most (58%) union directors regardless of size of institution are also directly responsible for non-union functions. At smaller institutions, Lyons (1963, 1964a, b) found that 67 percent of the union directors had more than one outside function, the most prevalent being student activities coordination, teaching, and counseling. Martin (1972) found that small college union directors considered their three major problems to be inadequate operating budgets, inadequate facilities, and having too many areas of responsibility (see also Swenson, 1973). Jenkins and McQueen's directors listed twenty-seven types of non-union responsibilities, the most prevalent of which were student activities coordination, organization advising, campus committee work, special events scheduling, master calendars, general student personnel work, and teaching.

Most (62%) union directors have M.A.'s and one third of them have faculty rank (Jenkins & McQueen, 1973). Kohler (1960) found that 40 percent of the directors he studied had tenure or similar job security. Kohler also found that 50 percent of the directors had written professionally or for publication. It has been recommended that union staff be faculty members so that students involved in the union can get credit for work in the field of community recreation ("Union Activities," 1940).

Kohler (1960) with 1952 data from forty-eight of 139 ACU-I member union directors found that they spent their time as follows: records and reports (13%), business and financial problems (13%), supervision of personnel (11%), program directing and planning (10%), maintenance problems (8%), student contact (8%), faculty and administration contact (8%), personal supervision of programs (5%), and individual counseling (5%). Kohler also found union directors spent an average of 35 percent (range was from 0 to 80%) of their time on major responsibilities other than direction of the union; Lyons' (1963) figure was 42 percent. Jenkins and McQueen (1973) found that the primary functions of union directors, in order of prevalence, were: student programs and activities, general building services, operation of recreational facilities, and building maintenance.

The educational preparation of union directors and their staff members varies greatly, evidenced by reports of twenty-seven fields of preparation. The two primary areas were student personnel and business with a possible trend towards the former (Jenkins & McQueen, 1973), since a stronger business orientation may not be needed now that many unions are built. Lyons (1963) suggests training should be composed of both areas. While most directors come into the union field with work experience in the field of education, many (41%) have had no previous union experience. Of the other union staff, fifty-two to seventy-seven percent have had no previous union experience, suggesting that they are undertrained, have no underlying union philosophy, and do not know what a union is or what it should be doing (Loomis, 1968a).

Kohler's (1960) directors of unions in 1952 said that the personal qualities they considered important for their job were: liking for people (24%), skill in handling people (22%), sincerity and enthusiasm (15%), good appearance, health, and manners (15%), a pleasing personality (11%), and leadership and organizational ability (9%). They also reported what their most useful experiences or preparations were: business management (46%), individual counseling (45%), student personnel administration (44%), public relations (43%), group work (41%), recreation programming (41%), financial management (40%), recreational administration (37%), accounting (37%), food management (24%), general college administration (24%), and building maintenance (19%).

Among other major union staff are assistant directors, administrative assistants, program directors (Cochran, 1961; Swenson, 1972), food managers, and bookstore managers. Holt (1971) said that generalists are no longer adequate for union needs, and that short-term, issue-oriented staff members need to be brought on the staff, such as part-time lawyers for legal aid, counselors for crisis clinics, and lobbyists for campaigning. In this regard a resource bank has been developed by the professional organization. BACU-I ("President Ronald Barrett," 1973) also recommends the use of outside consultants to lend credibility to staff proposals. Lyons (1963) found that the mean number of total employees (including maintenance, food service, etc.) in a union varied from 33.8 on small campuses (less than 5,000 enrollment) to 294.3 on the largest (more than 10,000). Copeland (1973) recommends one staff member or program advisor for each of three general areas of programming.

D. L. Phillips (1972) found that the average union director is a thirty-seven-year-old man entering his seventh year as director of a facility that is 95,000 square feet and operates an annual budget of $650,000. He is paid over $14,000 and attends about half of the ACU-I conferences. Over half of the directors had previous experience in the union field. Bucci (1970) found the union director to be near the bottom of the student personnel salary scale (see also Lyons, 1963; "Study of the Status of Women in the Union Field," 1974).

FOOD SERVICE

Osterheld (1963) found that sixty-five to seventy-five percent of the union dollar is produced by food operations. In sixteen surveys Butts (1958) found that a place to eat was the number one demand chosen out of a list of some thirty-five needs of unions and that food-related areas accounted for 62 percent of the space in those unions. The food service is the heart of most union programs and has become a specialty within itself — The National Association of College and University Food Services was established in 1960 (see "NACUFS Expands," 1972). Most college student personnel workers do not work in food delivery, but they must be knowledgeable about it in order to work with those who do.

An interesting plan for food services on a small, private campus is described by Hansen (1972). Her food service is handled almost completely by students, primarily by using convenience foods. Since her staff consists of 14 percent of the student body with a payroll of $140,000 and is such a large source of student jobs, the financial aid office cooperates extensively. Student employees who have excelled previously are used by Hansen to train and supervise new students and promotions in pay and responsibility are incorporated to reduce lack of dependability and poor workmanship.

A concern in food services is the serving of alcohol in unions. Most of the reasons for not serving alcohol in the union stem from leftover vestiges of *in loco parentis:* The institution should not sanction alcohol; the opportunity should not be provided for students to go to class inebriated; discipline and damage will increase. However, students now have majority rights, and studies ("Alcohol — To Serve," 1973) have found that few problems result from selling or serving alcoholic beverages nor does the service contribute to discipline problems. These findings collaborate the experiences of those unions which have been selling alcoholic beverages for over forty years — one union was authorized to sell them in 1935. The studies also found that the largest number of unions serving alcohol were public institutions in urban areas with enrollments of under 4,000; less than half of the country's unions sell alcoholic beverages; 41 percent of those who do sell started since 1969; and most unions found an increase in use of union facilities as a result.

CULTURAL AFFAIRS

Cultural affairs is another specialty within the area encompassing union, student activities, and campus auditoria. This specialty has become increasingly important as college campuses have become the major source of support for cultural events and the arts in this country. Cultural affairs has its own professional organization, the Association of College, University and Community Arts Administrators (ACUCAA), which was founded in 1957 as a group of professional presenters of fine arts programming.

ACUCAA (P. O. Box 2137, Madison, Wisconsin, 53701) has monthly publications such as bulletins, supplements, and show reports; provides meetings and workshops; and has published a bibliography on the administration of the arts (Kaderlan, 1970), a profile survey of its membership (Moon, 1971), a monograph on negotiations and contracts for artists and attractions (Taylor, 1972), an analysis of the financial support of professional touring performing arts (Blackburn, 1974), a summary of methods of handling tickets (Phenegar, 1969), a basic handbook (Taylor, 1968). More college student personnel workers should go into this specialty, because in many ways these professionals are responsible for the cultural education of college students (Wockenfuss, 1972), if not of the nation (see also Baumol & Bowen, 1966; Dawson, Haffer, Schneider, Dodge, Beall, & Jones, 1969; "Partnership for the Arts," 1971; J. W. Phillips, 1970; Rockefeller Panel, 1965; Schmidt, Owens, & Tiffin, 1971).

RELATIONSHIP TO OTHER SERVICES

The relationship between student activities and union programming is very unclear (Tinney, 1955), causing problems of overlap and competition. Most (80%) unions of all sizes in Jenkins and McQueen's (1973) study reported that the headquarters for student activities (non-union campus activities) was in the union and that the union director doubled as head of student activities in 65 percent of the unions. As the institution gets larger, the practice of separate union and student activities directors seems to increase, as does the independence of student activities programs from union programs, though 61 percent of Jenkins and McQueen's institutions reported correlation between the two. It is possible that the union program can serve as part of a broader student activities program, particularly since union directors frequently report to the dean of students. On the other hand, Handy (1961) suggests the union should coordinate all campus activities because it knows the students and campus, it has trained staff, the administration wants the buildings used, it can explain the role of the union, scheduling coordination prevents competition and allows little duplication, program standards can be maintained, and it could cut expenses caused by maintaining two program staffs.

Unions on some campuses have found it disastrous to have to compete with other buildings such as snack bars and recreational facilities in the dorms, separate conference and student activities buildings, dining halls, church centers, co-recreational gyms, branch unions in housing centers, and alumni houses ("An Editorial," 1958; Pride, 1959). While Erdahl (1955) suggests that the union should have all food, recreation, theater, and ballroom functions on a campus, he believes that what is primarily needed is a plan for the campus and clear-cut lines between functions. Factors to be considered in deciding which functions belong in the union and which should be housed elsewhere are geographic distances on campus, revenue incomes desired, and dining employee wages. To duplicate services, staff, and facilities weakens the union as well as the institution, reinforces division in the campus community, and can rip the heart out of the union (Lichtenfelt, 1955).

Another area of overlap is with campus religious centers, for which Thomas (1953) suggests the best is much like that of a union. Thomas recommends a combination center that combines the best features and advantages of the home, clubhouse, and chapel. Despite the duplication of union services, he feels that religious centers housed in the unions would cause overburdening administrative responsibilities as well as conflict over space. Koch (1960) in a study of twenty-four religious foundations confirms Thomas' view. Koch says religious centers are "junior unions" with substantial duplication in facilities (lounges, small meeting rooms), in programs (discussion groups, study groups or lectures, outings, retreats, parties), and in staff and student committee personnel. They were not necessarily competitive, however, in that they allowed their small discussion rooms to be used for some union programs and the union allowed the centers to use its large rooms.

Jenkins and McQueen (1973) found that 65 percent of the unions in their study are the headquarters for the campus adult-education programs, sometimes called conferences and institutes. Seventy-nine percent of these programs had non-union personnel in charge of the organization and administration, while the union offered the physical facilities and general services.

In spite of the possible drawbacks, some campuses have built branch or satellite unions. Ditton (1966) found several reasons for branch unions: inconvenience of the main union particularly at night, services were needed in remote areas and were not being provided by off-campus commercial establishments, and lack of land for the main union to expand. While these unions may be physically separate, Tregen (1967) reflects the general view that administration and programs of the two should be combined. However, Haenle (1969) states that the role of the college union is not applicable to decentralized union facilities and they are inconsistent with the living-learning concept.

REFERENCES

ACU-I: Priorities for effectiveness. *Final Report of the Self-Study Commission of the Association of College Unions-International,* February, 1975.

Alcohol — to serve or not to serve? *Bulletin of the Association of College Unions-International,* 1973, *41*(3), 1; 13-15.

Alexander, R. Proper program? Cal Med asks its students. *Bulletin of the Association of College Unions-International,* 1958, *26*(2), 4.

Andrews, M. H. College union programming. *NASPA Journal,* 1969, 7, 12-16.

AuBuchon, J. A. Kansas State College students want "big name" entertainment. *Bulletin of the Association of College Unions-International,* 1972, *40*(4), 8.

Barth, E. L. Comparing union objectives, operational methods, and programs to those of community centers with a view toward sharing reciprocal learnings. *Proceedings of the 38th Annual Conference of the Association of College Unions-International,* 1961, pp. 175-180.

Baumol, W. J. and Bowen, W. G. *Performing arts — the economic dilemma.* New York: Twentieth Century Fund, 1966.

Beaty, R. C. The relationship between a union and the office of the dean of men. *Proceedings of the 20th Annual Conference of the Association of College Unions-International,* 1940, pp. 1-8.

Bell, B. C. Trends in college union operation. *Proceedings of the 40th Annual Conference of the Association of College Unions-International,* 1963, pp. 122-126.

Bell, B. C. Operation and administration of college unions. *Proceedings of the 41st Annual Conference of the Association of College Unions-International,* 1964, p. 218.

Berry, C. A. *Three kinds of unions ... which is yours?* Ithaca, N. Y.: Association of College Unions-International, 1962.

Berry, C. A. The next fifty years of college unions. *Proceedings of the 41st Annual Conference of the Association of College Unions-Intionational,* 1964, pp. 48-57.

Berry, C. A. A model union program — 1965 style. *Proceedings of the 42nd Annual Conference of the Association of College Unions-International,* 1965, pp. 87-105.

Berry, C. A. Open doors — both ways. *Bulletin of the Association of College Unions-International,* 1969, *37*(1), 8-10.

Berry, C. A. No retreat. *Bulletin of the Association of College Unions-International,* 1973, *41*(2), 10-11.

Blackburn, R. *College and university support of the professional touring performing arts.* Madison, Wis.: Association of College, University and Community Arts Administrators, 1974.

Block programming proves successful. *Bulletin of the Association of College Unions-International,* 1972, *40*(4), 13.

Blumberg, M. NSA Congress looks at the union. *Bulletin of the Association of College Unions-International,* 1955, *23*(1), 4-5.

Brewer, F. I. A study of differing perceptions of the functions of college union governing boards. Reported by H. A. Goltz, *Bulletin of the Association of College Unions-International,* Supplement 4, October, 1963, p. 2.

Brugger, A. T. One man's brief against the college union. *Journal of Higher Education,* 1965, *36,* 214.

Bucci, F. A. Union director near bottom of student personnel team. *Bulletin of the Association of College Unions-International,* 1970, *38*(1), 8.

Butts, P. Why student leadership of the union? *Bulletin of the Association of College Unions-International,* 1949, *17*(3), 12.

Butts, P. The case for the continued federal financing of college union buildings. *Bulletin of the Association of College Unions-International,* 1958, *26*(4), 4-6.

Butts, P. State of the union, 1961. *Proceedings of the 38th Annual Conference of the Association of College Unions-International,* 1961, pp. 43-58.

Butts, P. *Planning and operating college union buildings* (Rev. ed.). Ithaca, N. Y.: Association of College Unions-International, 1965.

Butts, P. *State of the college union around the world.* Ithaca, N. Y.: Association of College Unions-International, 1967.

Butts, P. *The college union idea.* Stanford, Calif.: Association of College Unions-International, 1971.

Cameron, A. Is student personnel work obsolete? *Bulletin of the Association of College Unions-International,* 1968, *36*(4), 8-9.

Carlson, J. M. Programming involves risk. *Bulletin of the Association of College Unions-International,* 1973, *41*(2), 6.

Carlson, J. M., Davis, W. J., & Wedell, W. Campus disorder: Dilemma for the union staff. *Bulletin of the Association of College Unions-International,* 1969, *37*(4), 27.

Casse, R., & Burke, J. M. Experimental role of a college union. *Bulletin of the Association of College Unions-International,* 1971, *39*(4), 7-8.

Christensen, E. M. Factors in choosing the union site. *Bulletin of the Association of College Unions-International,* 1970, *38*(2), 12-13.

Cobb, F. M. The "student" union: Myth or reality? *Proceedings of the 44th Annual Conference of the Association of College Unions-*

International, 1967, pp. 87-88.

Cochran, B. J. Analysis of the function of a program director in a college union. Reported by B. Hunt, *Bulletin of the Association of College Unions-International.* Supplement 3, June, 1961, p. 2.

Copeland, A. W. Programming: An ACU-I dilemma. *Bulletin of the Association of College Unions-International,* 1973, *41*(1), 7.

Cowley, W. H. We guarantee satisfaction. *Proceedings of the 14th Annual Conference of the Association of College Unions-International,* 1933, pp. 16-31.

Crabb, G. W., & Handy, R. The food service director and the college union director as a team. *Proceedings of the 49th Annual Conference of the Association of College Unions-International,* 1972, pp. 3: 29-32.

Dawson, W. M., Haffer, D. P., Schneider, R. L., Dodge, P. G., Beall, H. S., & Jones, H. V. Concerts on campus: Should students be involved? *Music Educator's Journal,* 1969, *56*(1), 35-42.

Dees, G. T. Now — programming "in depth." *Bulletin of the Association of College Unions-International,* 1969, *37*(4), 22-23.

Ditton, R. B. The multiversity — will it demand a new kind of union? *Proceedings of the 43rd Annual Conference of the Association of College Unions-International,* 1966, pp. 128-133.

Duncan, D. H. More signs of college activity carry-over. *Bulletin of the Association of College Unions-International,* 1962, *30*(4), 10-11.

An editorial. *Bulletin of the Association of College Unions-International,* 1958, *26*(3), 3.

Erdahl, G. O. T. Dorm — union guide posts. *Bulletin of the Association of College Unions-International,* 1955, *23*(2), 4-5.

Erdahl, G. O. T. The student poll as a tool in programming. *Bulletin of the Association of College Unions-International,* 1959, *27*(2), 6.

Fritz, G. E. Effective utilization of space in the Michigan State University union building. Reported by I. Nanovsky, *Bulletin of the Association of College Unions-International,* Supplement 2, October 1960, p. 2.

Haenle, T. F. The effect of decentralization by residential college on the role of the college union at selected collegiate universities (Doctoral dissertation, State University of New York at Buffalo, 1969). *Dissertation Abstracts International,* 1970, *30,* 3232A. (University Microfilms No. 70-1762)

Handy, B. Should the union coordinate all campus activities? *Proceedings of the 38th Annual Conference of the Association of College Unions-International,* 1961, pp. 164-170.

Hansen, A. Student participation in food service planning. *Proceedings of the 49th Annual Conference of the Association of College Unions-International,* 1972, pp. 3: 35-40.

Harper, E. E. A union credo, based on seven enduring values. *Bulletin of the Association of College Unions-International,* 1960, *28*(2), 8-9.

Hesser, A. L. How do unions operate? *Proceedings of the 35th Annual*

Conference of the Association of College Unions-International, 1958, pp. 83-95.

Hesser, A. L. A study of the operations of college unions. Reported by B. C. Bell, *Bulletin of the Association of College Unions-International,* Supplement 1, February, 1960, p. 1.

Hesser, A. L. Are we taking advantage of our opportunities? *Proceedings of the 40th Annual Conference of the Association of College Unions-International,* 1963, pp. 9-15.

Hinde, D. T. Latest techniques in security and housekeeping. *Proceedings of the 49th Annual Conference of the Association of College Unions-International,* 1972, pp. 2: 58-64.

Holt, C. The new era — staff specialists. *Bulletin of the Association of College Unions-International,* 1971, *39*(4), 9.

Humphreys, E. O. *College unions — a handbook on campus community centers.* Ithaca, N. Y.: Association of College Unions, 1946.

Jenkins, J., & McQueen, S. *Administration and operation of the college union.* Stanford, Calif.: Association of College Unions-International, 1973.

Jones, N. B., Jr. The importance of the college union in campus life. *Bulletin of the Association of College Unions-International,* 1935, *3*(3), 6-7.

Jones, N. B. Faculty-member, guest, or outsider in the college union. *Proceedings of the 42nd Annual Conference of the Association of College Unions-International,* 1965, pp. 155-158.

Kaderlan, N. *Bibliography on the administration of the arts: 1958-1970.* Madison: University of Wisconsin Arts Council, 1970.

Ketter, J. Program study evaluates use of money and time. *Bulletin of the Association of College Unions-International,* 1972, *40*(5), 6.

Koch, H. R., Sr. Union-religious foundation liaison. Reported by F. I. Brewer, *Bulletin of the Association of College Unions-International,* Supplement 2, October, 1960, p. 1.

Kohler, T. M. The college union director and his preparation. Reported by F. I. Brewer, *Bulletin of the Association of College Unions-International,* Supplement 1, February, 1960, p. 5.

Lake, D. E. Operation cross-purposes. *Proceedings of the 38th Annual Conference of the Association of College Unions-International,* 1961, pp. 157-164.

Lancaster, D. D. The union in the personnel program. *Bulletin of the Association of College Unions-International,* 1950, *18*(3), 10; 12.

Lichtenfelt, R. J. Residence halls vs. college unions. *Bulletin of the Association of College Unions-International,* 1955, *23*(1), 9.

Loomis, R. M. The union "feel" at the grass roots. *Bulletin of the Association of College Unions-International,* 1968, *36*(3), 16-17. (a)

Loomis, R. The voluntary fee chaos in New York. *Bulletin of the Association of College Unions-International,* 1968, *36*(3), 19. (b)

Lyons, J. W. The union director and his job. *Proceedings of the 40th Annual*

Conference of the Association of College Unions-International, 1963, pp. 108-116.

Lyons, J. W. A study of the administrative responsibilities, work environment experience, and recommended curricular preparation of the college union director. Reported by E. O. Siggelkow, *Bulletin of the Association of College Unions-International*, Supplement 5, June 1964, p. 2. (a)

Lyons, J. W. The professional nature of the union job. *Proceedings of the 41st Annual Conference of the Association of College Unions-International*, 1964, pp. 151-155. (b)

Maneks, M. Employers rate activity leadership high. *Bulletin of the Association of College Unions-International*, 1963, *31*(3), 6-7.

Martin, T. O. An analysis of the duties and problems of small college union directors with implications for professional preparation (Doctoral dissertation, Indiana University, 1972). *Dissertation Abstracts International*, 1973, *33*, 3417A-3418A. (University Microfilms No. 72-33,276)

McKoane, M. E. A college union as perceived by students and staff: A plan for improving that union. Reported by J. W. Lyons, *Bulletin of the Association of College Unions-International*, Supplement 2, October 1960, p. 3.

McWhorter, R. F. A study of the cooperative relationships of college unions with academic departments. Reported by L. Kottner, *Bulletin of the Association of College Unions-International*, Supplement 1, February 1960, p. 5.

Minahan, A. *The college union and preparation for citizenship.* Ithaca, N. Y.: Association of College Unions-International, 1957.

Moon, R. *Profile survey IV*. Madison, Wis.: Association of College and University Concert Managers, 1971.

Mullins, E. The employers' view of activities. *Bulletin of the Association of College Unions-International*, Supplement 1, February, 1960, p. 8.

NACUFS expands. *Bulletin of the Association of College Unions-International*, 1972, *40*(1), 11.

Noffke, F. Telling the faculty the union story. *Bulletin of the Association of College Unions-International*, 1963, *31*(1), 4-5.

Osterheld, D. C. The organization and administration of college union food service. *Proceedings of the 40th Annual Conference of the Association of College Unions-International*, 1963, pp. 134-144.

Pacific, midwest unions optimistic about future. *Bulletin of the Association of College Unions-International*, 1973, *41*(1), 9-11.

Partnership for the arts. *Music Educator's Journal*, 1971, *57*(9), 51.

Phenegar, J. C. *Tickets and ticket handling procedures* (Rev. ed.). Madison, Wis.: Association of College and University Concert Managers, 1969.

Phillips, D. L. The director in today's college union. *Bulletin of the Association of College Unions-International*, 1972, *40*(4), 1; 14.

Phillips, J. W. Students run a concert series. *Music Journal,* 1970, *28* (December), 38.

President Ronald Barrett discusses plans. *Bulletin of the Association of College Unions-International,* 1973, *41*(3), 2; 4.

Pride, H. The future of the college union. *Bulletin of the Association of College Unions-International,* 1959, *27*(3), 6-7.

Pride, H. E. The future of the college union. *Proceedings of the 37th Annual Conference of the Association of College Unions-International,* 1960, pp. 48-53.

Reynolds, R. C. Labor relations, labor unions, and student labor unions. *Proceedings of the 49th Annual Conference of the Association of College Unions-International,* 1972, pp. 2: 38-39.

Rockefeller panel report on the future of theatre, dance, music in America. *The performing arts: Problems and prospects.* New York: McGraw-Hill, 1965.

Schmidt, F. J., Owens, W. A., & Tiffin, J. Correlates of students attendance at cultural events. *Journal of College Student Personnel,* 1971, *12,* 41-43.

Schoenfeld, C. A. The union — its meaning, its requirements. *Bulletin of the Association of College Unions-International,* 1955, *23*(2), 7.

Siggelkow, E. O. The college union: A model for student power. *NASPA Journal,* 1969, *7,* 7-12.

Spelman, W. H., III. Professionalism and the activities fee. *Bulletin of the Association of College Unions-International,* 1972, *40*(1), 5; 12.

Stevens, G. The college union — past, present and future. *NASPA Journal,* 1969, *7,* 16-21.

Student disruptions of unions more serious than ever. *Bulletin of the Association of College Unions-International,* 1969, *37*(3), 16-17.

Student-faculty "study commission on university governance" at the University of California, Berkeley. *Bulletin of the Association of College Unions-International,* 1968, *36*(3), 12-13. (Summary)

A study of the status of women in the union field and their attitudes. *Proceedings of the 54th Annual Conference of the Association of College Unions-International,* 1974, pp. 172-260.

Sturgell, J. S. Uncommon guide to college union programming. *Bulletin of the Association of College Unions-International,* 1973, *41*(2), 14.

Swenson, M. O. A study of critical roles of full time program advisors employed by college unions in the United States. *Bulletin of the Association of College Unions-International,* 1972, *40*(5), 13.

Swenson, M. O. The director of the small college union: His duties, his problems. *Bulletin of the Association of College Unions-International,* 1973, *41*(4), 5-7.

Taylor, F. *ACUCM workbook: A guide to presenting the performing arts on college and university campuses.* Madison, Wis.: Association of College and University Concert Managers, 1968 (Reissued 1971).

Taylor, F. *Negotiating and contracting for artists and attractions at educational and nonprofit institutions.* Madison, Wis.: Association of College and University Concert Managers, 1972.

Thomas, J. P. Campus religious centers and the union. *Bulletin of the Association of College Unions-International,* 1953, *21*(3), 4.

Tinney, H. The union as an aid to student growth. *Bulletin of the Association of College Unions-International,* 1953, *21*(3), 8.

Tinney, H. The educational role of the union. *Bulletin of the Association of College Unions-International,* 1955, *22*(4), 9-12.

Tregen, F. E. The satellite union. *Proceedings of the 44th Annual Conference of the Association of College Unions-International,* 1967, pp. 62-64.

Union activities part of whole educational development of an individual. *Bulletin of the Association of College Unions-International,* 1940, *8*(2), 7.

Union use policy a major dilemma. *Bulletin of the Association of College Unions-International,* 1970, *38*(1), 1; 6.

Vote approaching on "goals" statement. *Bulletin of the Association of College Unions-International,* 1971, *39*(3), 10.

Wockenfuss, J. Personal communication, 1972.

Wolf, A. G. Basic designs for union activity programs. *Bulletin of the Association of College Unions-International,* 1958, *26*(2), 6.

CHAPTER 7

RELIGION

WILLIAM T. PACKWOOD

HISTORY

UNIVERSITIES emerged in the Middle Ages as an extension of the medieval church school. Of the four faculties within the university, theology was considered queen of the sciences, followed by law, medicine, and the arts (Earnshaw, 1964b). In this country Harvard University was founded to provide an educated ministry for the colonies (Cuninggim, 1947). Of the 182 permanent colleges in the United States before the Civil War, 175 were under religious control (Underwood, 1969).

Religious training and liberal education were intermixed in these early colleges though never to the student's satisfaction. In order to explore religious questions in more depth than the regular curriculum allowed, religious societies were established by students, one as early as 1690 at Harvard and over ninety between 1810 and 1850 (Brubacher & Rudy, 1968). The rebellion from 1830 to 1869 against faculty and clerics was not unlike the tone of the student left protests at Berkeley in the 1960's (Underwood, 1969). From these voluntary student groups grew the Young Men's and Young Women's Christian Associations which were the most influential form of campus ministry from the Civil War to World War I (Underwood, 1969). Also from these groups came the first foreign missionary agency (Eads, 1964), a kind of religious Peace Corps.

Following the Morrill Act of 1862, denominational churches had to come to terms with mushrooming enrollments at the newly formed private colleges because their numbers were outstripping the resources of the "Y's" (Shedd, 1938). What followed was intense denominational competitiveness to protect

206

and save students at the "heathen" universities. Ministers were needed for such a task, so by 1913 the first campus ministry was established at the University of Illinois (Underwood, 1969). This was also about the time that secularization of higher education reached its peak (Cuninggim, 1947). The presence of campus ministers marked a radical shift from the lay, volunteer, student approach of the Y's.

The campus ministry movement caught on and by 1930 and 1934 Miami University and the University of Michigan respectively had full-time religious directors on their university staffs (Olds, 1958). The 1950's and early 1960's were periods of tremendous expansion for the campus ministries and all forms of American church life (Underwood, 1969). Since then there has been more than a decade of decline in the resources and influence of campus ministries as well as increased secularization of American society (Palmer, 1969).

DEFINITION

Campus ministry is the term used throughout this chapter to refer to all religions evidenced on campus. The selection of this name, while inadequate, is the one that has traditionally been used. Although most of the literature concerning religion on campus has been about Protestant Christian Ministries with some concerning Roman Catholic, when used generically, the term denotes campus rabbi, priest, or minister.

Role

The role of the campus minister is fraught with ambiguity and has continually changed since the 1900's when ministers were assigned to campuses. At first they thought they were to perform just like the parish ministers, and they relied heavily for their role definition on the four historic modes of the ministry: priestly or providing church services, pastoral or providing counseling to the church members, prophetic or providing statements regarding how things should or will be, and governance or providing organizational leadership for the church.

Though still prevalent, the old notion of the campus minister being a reflection of the parish minister has been found inappropriate, which prompted Underwood (1969) to redefine the traditional modes. He suggests that the priestly mode might become more a matter of finding new ways to proclaim the faith as well as exploring the human experiences that produced the rituals and language of the traditional services. The pastoral mode might move into research on religious commitments and delineation of the values implicit in professional practices, academic disciplines, and ways of learning. The prophetic mode might move beyond rhetoric into institutes, reordering of priorities, and programs on a national level to help responsibly shape society to better meet the needs of the people. Governance might involve having the highly developed skills as a minister to bring technical fact and moral concern together.

Various other views of the campus minister's role have been suggested. Some say the minister should be a model for students (Biggs, 1968; Evans, 1973; Jospe, 1972; Nouwen, 1969); others, that ministers should be critics, perceiving patterns and places of educational neglect (Lynn, 1969). Asbury (1970) suggests that the campus minister can be conceived as being a procursor or one who seeks new ways to revitalize the church. The precursor role, also called the bellweather, experimental, safety valve, and leavening role of the church (Hammond, 1969), is substantially different from the radical role which seeks to destroy the church. The precursor role is based on the assumption that the campus minister is confronted by problems that the parish minister will face in the following decade after the students get older and start attending parish churches (Underwood, 1969). This view may be ameliorated, however, if the trend in higher education toward commuterism continues and the parish churches become the major service for students and faculty (Earnshaw, 1964a).

Need

Chamberlin (1963) found in a study of five representative

campuses that the Christian church and the modern college have little need for one another. He considers this a sad denouement to twelve centuries of intimate and fruitful relationships between two historic institutions. Their mutual neglect is particularly disturbing considering:

> perhaps the greatest danger in any system of higher education: that a nation's understanding of the universe may become separated from her grasp of the values that make that universe meaningful (John F. Kennedy in Butler, 1963, p. 6).

The tragedy is compounded if Underwood (1969) is correct that "the university is becoming the institution around which the cultural life of modern society is being organized" (p. 49, see Cultural Affairs section). Lynn (1969) agrees that the campus ministers' and rabbis' efforts are increasingly marginal in American education while the centrality of the university grows. Evans (1972a, b) states that orthodoxy is declining and may die out by 2010, though he also suggests an increase in natural religion.

That spirituality has always been an important value or aspect of life and religion a part of the whole life of the student (Milliken, 1964) was recognized in the 1937 Student Personnel Point of View which, in listing twenty-three services that should be provided to students, included attention to the religious aspect of student life in two of the services (Jones, 1967). Additional recognition of religion as part of a student's life is evident on campuses. Ninety percent of the nation's publicly supported, four-year-or-more colleges offer some kind of studies in religion as part of their established curriculums and one fourth of the public universities have special departments of religion (Underwood, 1969).

Students are interested in objective approaches to religion as indicated by their involvement in comparative courses, eastern religions, transcendental meditation, and the Jesus Movement. The university can not pretend to operate in a value vacuum, for in ignoring values it teaches an approach to them. Because the university may be the major institution for the formulation of belief and commitment among key leadership in our society, it has a responsibility to consider the morality of knowledge: to teach the use of "intellectual resources to perceive the truth about the world and one's relation to it and the moral courage to act on such knowledge" (Underwood, 1969, p. 69). Harrod (1960) found that most of the institutions he surveyed saw religious training as an integral part of a student's education.

Legal Basis

The First Amendment to the Constitution requires the separation of church and state by prohibiting Congress from making any law which establishes a particular religion or which prohibits the free exercise of religion. How this and related state laws are interpreted and practiced on campuses is really a matter of individual institutional policy. Most policy statements by colleges regarding religious practice are unwritten with the assumption that they are just understood (Jones, 1973), or the only policy is to have no policy (Rossman, 1960). Nevertheless, it seems clear that at the college level, institutions cannot support or give sanction to any kind of religious orthodoxy, but they can be friendly and encouraging to religion of all kinds. This makes higher education distinctly different from elementary and secondary schools, primarily because of the age difference of the students and the voluntary nature of higher education. Religion courses can be taught at state universities, religious coordinators may be appointed, and religious activities encouraged, as long as no religious group is discriminated against and there is no overt proselytizing (Allen, 1950; Cuninggim, 1947; Earnshaw, 1964b).

ADMINISTRATION

There are three primary approaches to providing for the religious life of a campus. The oldest form, though not the most prevalent, is the college chaplain (Jones, 1973, estimates there are about 600 in the nation). The chaplain is employed by the college itself, is director of the college chapel, has an office in a college building, and has responsibility for the entire college community (see also Smith, 1954). The college chaplain is found most often in the private or church-related colleges (Hammond, 1966) and frequently teaches in addition to performing pastoral duties (Carey, 1962). The second form, the campus minister, is a Twentieth Century phenomenon, is especially predominant in larger public institutions, and is a denominational position with the minister supported by and responsible to a particular church. Campus ministers also have more contact with students from their own denomination than college chaplins do (Hammond, 1966), but the minister is more tenuously connected to the campus, perhaps even peripheral in terms of location, responsibility, and recognition (Chamberlin, 1963).

The religious coordinator, or third form, is hired by and responsible to the institution, usually is not ordained, and is not responsible for a chapel. Again most frequently found in large public institutions (Jones, 1973), the religious coordinator provides a mechanism for the campus ministers connected to the institution to work together. Religious coordinators accept (at approximately 15% of public colleges) a large measure of responsibility for direct sponsorship of various religious functions, or may limit (at approximately 50%) their responsibility to maintaining lines of communication with student religious organizations and sometimes with campus ministers.

Student religious organizations are, however, the most universal expression of religious practice on American campuses (Jones, 1973). It is through recognition of these student organizations that public colleges most frequently approach relating religious practice to the life of the campus. Most colleges in Jones' (1973) survey had from five to nine student religious organizations on campus (50% had 1 to 10 and 28% had 10 to 20) with the usual privileges of using college space and publicity. Recognition granted campus ministers by the college is much less clear. Jones (1973) found that one third of the state colleges grant no recognition to ministers, and those that do usually do so because the ministers are sponsors of student religious organizations or are members of a campus ministerial association.

That nearly all state colleges and universities accept some responsibility for religious affairs functions is attested to by several studies (Balcer, Harris, & Holmgren, 1959; Crouch, 1962; Peterson, 1965). Additionally "nearly two-thirds of America's public colleges designate a staff person as primary liaison with the religious forces serving their campuses" (Jones, 1973, p. 14). In 1968 this religious coordinator was primarily working with student organizations, but by 1972 his or her chief contact was with the campus minister through the campus minister's council. The religious coordinator provides liaison with student religious organizations and campus religious leaders, distributes religious preference information, counsels students regarding religious matters, plans cocurricular programming (lectures, seminars, service-projects), and advises an interfaith council. In 80 percent (Jones, 1973) of the colleges studied, the religious coordinator was the chief student personnel officer. Regional differences in position were evident: In the West the religious coordinator was an assistant dean; in the north central and middle states, a student activities director; and in the north central and southern regions, a director of religious activities. There was a decline from 1968 to 1972 (84% to 55%) in the number of institutions assigning a college staff person to the religious liaison function.

Officially sponsored coordinating councils for religious affairs have also been declining (from 33% in 1968 to 18% in 1972). Of the councils still existing there appears to be no single pattern of organization (Stroup, 1963). However, 43 percent of the institutions surveyed had a council in which student religious organizations plan campus-wide religious programming; only 29 percent had a college officer assigned to the council. Because the director of religious affairs, chaplain, or campus minister helped with program advising and financing for these councils, the councils appear to be more an expression of the religious agencies rather than of the college cocurriculum.

Building

Each of the three forms for providing for the religious life on campus is tied to a unique physical structure as well as a unique program. The chaplain's focal point is the chapel. For a long time, attendance at chapel and worship services was expected. As attendance began to wane, chapel was made compulsory. Then it became one option in a lecture series and finally was dropped (Underwood, 1969). The tax-supported military service academies are the only colleges where chapel is still required (Earnshaw, 1964b).

Ministers operate out of their denominational student centers. Olds (1958) identifies seven kinds of centers ranging from adjacent and isolated to integral and central. The centers may provide a place of worship, a home-away-from-home (Lynn, 1969; Nouwen, 1969), a clubhouse, a mini-union (see Union chapter), or a "small place" on campus (Biggs, 1968). Devor (1969) says the student centers are duplicative because the college has built better unions, student centers, fraternities, and sororities; has better programs for belonging; and has *ad hoc* gatherings for special tasks. He feels it would be better for the building not to be an end in itself and instead use temporary structures for such programs as action groups, tutoring the disadvantaged, study retreats, library work, and meaningful daily worship. The campus ministry then approaches Loats' (1964) definition of working within college structures, unrelated to building or group. Moulds (1969) says that there are only two things the campus ministry can do that the college cannot do: provide a religiously oriented home that is lived in and open and provide a place for worship.

The religious coordinator seems to be without a home, since college owned buildings for religious purposes are the exception (16%). When such religious buildings do exist, they tend to be at the older and larger colleges and have more historical or symbolic than functional significance (Jones, 1973).

Support

Chamberlin (1963) found that the college community for the most part considers religion to be extracurricular. The churches and the colleges by mutual agreement have relegated the campus ministries to peripheral status and there are other forces working against the campus ministry becoming a vital force on campus. As suggested by Hammond (1966), the more acknowledgement given a campus minister by an institution, the more given by the supporting denominational church. This occurs when the campus tends to be local rather than cosmopolitan in orientation and when the role assumed by the minister is more like that of the parish minister, which the denomination understands and supports. At more cosmopolitan campuses the campus ministry frequently receives institutional indifference. These campus ministers tend to have more specialized training, have a better differentiated role conception, and produce more innovations, perhaps as a result of pressure on such campuses to do so. Unfortunately the very campus ministers who lack institutional support also do not receive denominational support.

These problems are indicative of the conflicts present between the campus ministry and the parish ministry and denomination. Hammond (1969) found the campus ministers to be more liberal, more critical of their denomination, more favorable toward ecumenical affairs, better educated, and to have wider interests than their parish counterparts. Bury (1969) describes a pastoral gap existing between what is expected on the parochial level (old formalities) and what takes place on the campus (new principles).

The campus ministers further face differences with their students. Demerath and Lutterman (1967) found that students in fifteen religious groups, including the most liberal Protestant group, were more conservative on all issues surveyed than student samples representing the student body in general and an explicitly nonreligious group. The campus ministers were quite radical at this same campus which created a gap between them and those students who were active in their programs. Hammond (1969) found that 86 percent of the campus ministers he studied met weekly with other campus ministers on their campus for mutual reinforcement — apparently one of the few places they can obtain it.

PROGRAMS

For the most part, public colleges do not assume direct responsibility for the religious programming on campus (Jones, 1973). One-fourth act in an advising role, with one-eighth providing lectures, seminars, and discussion groups on religious topics, concerts of a religious nature, and counseling regarding religious matters. The percent providing religious programming was greater at southern and older institutions. The size of the institution had no relationship to programming, except for Religious Emphasis Week, a shot-in-the-arm approach which is dying out and which was most prevalent at medium-sized (1,000 to 10,000) institutions. (See Overholt, 1970.)

PERSONNEL

In 1968 Jones (1973) calculated that 418 public institutions were served by 5,000 ministers, about half of which were assigned at least two thirds of their time to a ministry on the college campus, the major other responsibility being a town congregation (see also Eddy, 1969).

Full-time religious coordinators (Jones, 1973), or those that devote 50 percent or more of their time to the job, tend to be concentrated in larger (over 10,000) and some smaller (under 5,000) institutions which were publicly supported before 1900. These fifty to sixty people are primarily in the middle, southern, and north central regions; are more likely to teach; and most are clergymen from the major Protestant denominations, graduates from church-related or private colleges with their highest degree being a theological one. Most of these coordinators (86%) have received specialized training for their position and (66%) have expressed a desire for further training.

The part-time religious coordinators devote 10 percent or less of their time to the job and are usually the chief student personnel officer or someone who reports to him or her. They are found at Pacific and new institutions. They are older, hold faculty rank, receive higher salaries, and have experienced longer tenure in their positions. This group also includes more women, more with doctorates in education, psychology, or a related field, and more who attended a public college. Nearly three fourths have no special training for religious affairs and only one fourth desire additional training.

Both groups in Jones' (1973) study expressed preference for the counseling role in their jobs and see themselves as educators rather than clergymen, responders rather than initiators, and facilitators rather than authority figures. Most of the full-time coordinators are members of the Association for the Coordination of University Religious Affairs (ACURA), whereas the part-time coordinators are members of NASPA, ACPA, and NAWDAC.

REFERENCES

Allen, H. E. (Ed.). *Religion and the state university.* Minneapolis: Burgess Press, 1950.

Asbury, B. A. The role of campus ministers in protest and dissent. *Liberal Education,* 1970, *56,* 317-327.

Balcer, C., Harris, J., & Holmgren, M. Religious activities in public colleges. *St. Cloud State College Bulletin,* 1959, *14*(May).

Biggs, D. A. Is the campus ministry dead? *National Catholic Guidance Conference Journal,* 1968, *12,* 273-276.

Brubacher, J. S., & Rudy, W. *Higher education in transition* (Rev. ed.). New York: Harper & Row, 1968.

Bury, H. Newman in campus life: Leading the way or going astray? *Counseling and Values,* 1969, *14,* 54-56.

Butler, R. *God on the secular campus.* Garden City, N.Y.: Doubleday, 1963.

Carey, J. J. Jerusalem and Athens: The religious worker on the college campus. *Personnel and Guidance Journal,* 1962, *40,* 426-431.

Chamberlin, G. *Churches and the campus.* Philadelphia: Westminster Press, 1963.

Crouch, C. *Religious activities in the tax-supported colleges and universities.* Unpublished doctoral dissertation, Arizona State University, 1962.

Cuninggim, M. *The college seeks religion.* New Haven: Yale University Press, 1947.

Demerath, N. J., III, & Lutterman, K. J. The student parishioner: Radical rhetoric and traditional reality. *Abstracts of Proceedings of the American Sociological Association,* 1967, p. 88. *(College Student*

Personnel Abstracts, 1968, *3*(2), 185.)

Devor, R. C. Training for the campus ministry: Another view. *Pastoral Counseling,* 1969, *20*(199), 23-32.

Eads, R. H. A brief history of student christian movements. In G. L. Earnshaw, *The campus ministry.* Valley Forge, Penn.: Judson Press, 1964.

Earnshaw, G. L. *The campus ministry.* Valley Forge, Penn.: Judson Press, 1964. (a)

Earnshaw, G. L. The implications of church and state in public higher education. In G. L. Earnshaw, *The campus ministry.* Valley Forge, Penn.: Judson Press, 1964. (b)

Eddy, J. P. *Comparison of the characteristics and activities of religious personnel employed in selected four-year state colleges and universities in the United States.* New York: Associated Education Services Corporation, 1969.

Evans, J. W. Campus ministry today: Some projections. *Counseling and Values,* 1972, *16*, 81-91. (a)

Evans, J. W. (Ed.). Introduction. *Counseling and Values,* 1972, *16*, 80. (b)

Evans, J. W. Exemplary presence as campus ministry. *Counseling and Values,* 1973, *17*, 195-199.

Hammond, P. E. *The campus clergyman.* New York: Basic Books, 1966.

Hammond, P. E. The radical ministry. In K. W. Underwood, *The church, the university, and social policy.* Middletown, Conn.: Wesleyan University Press, 1969.

Harrod, G. W. Religious activities on campuses of colleges and universities. *Personnel and Guidance Journal,* 1960, *38*, 555-557.

Jones, G. W. A rationale for religious programming in state universities. *Journal of College Student Personnel,* 1967, *8*, 385-389.

Jones, G. W. *The public university and religious practice: An inquiry into university provision for campus religious life.* Muncie, Ind.: Ball State University, 1973.

Jospe, A. Religion in the university — a terminal case? *Religious Education,* 1972, *67*, 123-130.

Loats, L. S. The church alive in the university. In G. L. Earnshaw, *The campus ministry.* Valley Forge, Penn.: Judson Press, 1964.

Lynn, R. W. A ministry on the margin. In K. W. Underwood, *The church, the university, and social policy.* Middletown, Conn.: Wesleyan University Press, 1969.

Milliken, R. L. Religious activities — a forgotten personnel service. *Journal of College Student Personnel,* 1964, *5*, 161-162; 167.

Moulds, G. H. What should be the role of the campus minister on college campuses today? Not to duplicate services. *College and University Journal,* 1969, *8*, 47-48.

Nouwen, H. J. M. Training for the campus ministry. *Pastoral Psychology,* 1969, *20*(192), 27-38.

Olds, G. A. Religious centers. In E. A. Walter (Ed.), *Religion and the state university*. Ann Arbor: University of Michigan Press, 1958.

Overholt, W. A. *Religion in American colleges and universities*. Washington, D. C.: American College Personnel Association 1970. (Student Personnel Monograph Series, No. 14)

Palmer, P. J. A typology of world views. In K. W. Underwood, *The church, the university, and social policy*. Middletown, Conn.: Wesleyan University Press, 1969.

Peterson, H. D. *The role of religion at selected state colleges and universities in the United States*. Unpublished doctoral dissertation, Washington State University, 1965.

Rossman, P. The denominational chaplain in the state university. *Religious Education*, 1960, *55*, 174-181.

Shedd, C. P. *The church follows its students*. London: Oxford University Press, 1938.

Smith, S. A. *The American college chaplaincy*. New York: Association Press, 1954.

Stroup, H. Coordinating councils of religious organizations in public colleges and universities. *Religious Education*, 1963, *58*, 362-365.

Underwood, K. W. *The church, the university, and social policy: The Danforth study of campus ministries*. Middletown, Conn.: Wesleyan University Press, 1969.

CHAPTER 8

OMBUDSMAN

William T. Packwood

HISTORY

THE idea of a civil ombudsman to control bureaucracy for citizens began in Sweden with the appointment of one by Charles XII in 1713 (Stamatakos & Isachsen, 1970) and the election of one in 1809 (Rowland, 1969). However, it is the later developed Danish ombudsman that has served as a model for many governments (Anderson, 1968, 1969; Rowat, 1968). Civil ombudsmen are prevalent in the Scandinavian countries and have been established in other countries such as Canada, states such as Hawaii, counties, municipalities, and other bureaucratic entities.

In the latter 1960's some colleges in the United States adopted the ombudsman idea in an attempt to deal with student dissent (Eddy, 1968). The ombudsman could be added to the administration with little expense and without altering existing structures (Rowland, 1969). East Montana College in Billings in 1966 was apparently the first American higher education institution to use a campus ombudsman (Drew, 1973; Rowland, 1969). Others followed at the State University of New York, Michigan State University, and San Jose State (Buccieri, 1968b). By 1968, Eddy (1970) reported that fourteen nonstudent ombudsmen and four student ombudsmen were appointed at seventeen or more colleges (see also Bloland & Nowak, 1968). California became a national leader with seventeen ombudsmen in its state educational system (Eddy & Klepper, 1972), perhaps because the Berkeley Study Commission on University Governance (California University, 1968) recommended it.

Questions were always raised about the effectiveness of the ombudsman concept, even though Kluge and Smith (1968) found the concept to be the only significant change in the disciplinary structure of American higher education institutions in the 1960's. Evidently the questions were answered in the negative, because by 1973 the topic of ombudsman had disappeared from the literature, though there were 200 in such a position (Drew, 1973).

It is possible that there is no clearer example in the college student personnel literature of the growth and death of an idea. Since the position has been retained n many Scandinavian governments, the significant differences between the college and civil ombudsman probably indicate the seeds of failure for the position on campuses. Stamatakos and Isachsen (1970, see also Isachsen & Stamatakos, 1970) identified several of these differences: The civil ombudsman deals with the law of the land whereas the campus ombudsman deals with vague college administrative policies, rules, and practices; the civil ombudsman is responsible to the people of the state through its legislature rather than to the president of a college; the civil ombudsman's removal is inconceivable whereas the campus ombudsman can usually be removed by presidential action at any time; the civil ombudsman reports to the parliament rather than the college president and uses the public press to publicize the office's findings, which is usually not an option on the campus; the civil ombudsman takes the position at the peak of a distinguished career rather than an intervening short-term activity in a teaching career. All of these adaptations of the civil concept limit the power and effectiveness of the campus ombudsman.

DEFINITION

Various conceptualizations of the ombudsman position on a college campus have been formulated. The psychological value in all of them is that the individual student knows that he or she is not helpless before a large and impersonal bureaucracy (Rowland, 1969), thus humanism is given the edge over bureaucracy (Schlossberg, 1970). Ombudsman literally means one who represents someone (Schlossberg, 1967) and there seem to be two primary ways of representing others: responding and initiating.

Role

The responder role definition assumes that the campus needs an outlet for grievances and someone to help students through the bureaucracy (Barzun, 1968). This kind of ombudsman provides a means to listen to students (Eddy, 1970; London, 1970) and hopefully will sooth tempers and settle grievances more expeditiously (Lehrer, 1969). By giving a hearing to those on campus who feel discriminated against and unfairly treated, an alternative is provided to more violent confrontations (Mundinger, 1967; White, 1969).

In this role the ombudsman also functions as a nonjudgemental pilot guiding each student's efforts through the most effective channels (Gorovitz, 1967). The ombudsman becomes an information source (California University, 1968), a referral agent (London, 1970), and possibly a mediator between the administration with its rules and regulations (Eddy, 1968). However, the ombudsman does not act as a buffer nor liaison between students and administration (Gorovitz, 1967) and does not try to restructure or replace the system (Rowland, 1969). At its best, this role becomes educational in that the ombudsman can teach by example why a large institution has to act as it does as well as how to get from an institution what one is entitled to (Barzun, 1968).

At its worst this role makes the ombudsman a campus protector (Mundinger, 1967) whose first responsibility is to work within the existing system (Eddy, 1970), possibly only aiding in the retention of the status quo and serving as a palliative for dramatic reform (London, 1970). An ombudsman is not needed as a substitute information service (California University, 1968), a buckpasser (London, 1970), a traffic cop, just another stop, nor a gimmick (Clifford, 1970). The ombudsman cannot stop militant radicals (Schlossberg, 1970), but might prevent the liberals from joining them by reducing student alienation, thus becoming an administrative ploy to reduce proliferating headaches (London, 1970).

However, in the process of fulfilling this role, the ombudsman gathers information which can be used to change the role, to serve as a spokesman for inequity or maladministration, to identify wrongdoing by administrative functionaries, to assist the president and board in supervising the administration (Mundinger, 1967), and to discover those practices or policies likely to produce legitimate complaints (White, 1969). These are the first steps to the initiator role definition.

In the initiator role definition the ombudsman does not wait for complaints to come to him or her, but may seek out deficiences in the bureaucracy and try to change them. The ombudsman then becomes an attempt to bureaucratize innovation (Schlossberg, 1970), based on the assumption that the mere operation of large bureaucracies is detrimental to the individual (Schlossberg, 1967). Thus the ombudsman becomes more like the civil ombudsman, defining the role as a change agent within the institution (Stamatakos & Isachsen, 1970). The problem becomes what kind of changes are appropriate. Norman (1970) suggests that the ombudsman must reflect the consensus of the various campus groups regarding proper changes. Few institutions, however, are willing to give the ombudsman such power, and if the position does have such power, it comes close to becoming a second administration (Barzun, 1968).

Need

The rationale behind the ombudsman concept is the college's recognition that the student is subjected to increasing bureaucracy and that the formal structure of the college organization is in reality designed for administrative matters and only secondarily for personal concerns (Stamatakos & Isachsen, 1970). Some say that the ombudsman concept is an admission that the college has failed to meet its responsibilities for equity and communication in the academic community and that there is little likelihood of those charged with such responsibilities to change or regularly evaluate their efforts (Clifford, 1970).

Schlossberg (1970) suggests that such is the case: That in American higher education the current problem is to protect the rights and personality of each person in a power system which is asymmetrical and to modify the system so that it is more symmetrical.

Sandler, Kirk, and Hallberg (1968) suggest that stifling bureaucracy does exist as students must go through four or five persons before finding sufficient authority for a decision. They also suggest that the lateral bureaucracy is a problem perpetuated by specialization with none of the groups (professors, counselors, doctors) having a systematic way to communicate with each other. This view is shared by Rowland (1969) who believes that the diffusion of administrative responsibility required in a quasi-bureaucratic system leads to segmented student services. The problem is further compounded by student lack of access to faculty and administration, student ignorance about procedures, and an inherent elusiveness in the procedures themselves (Rowland, 1969). Consequently, the student, as well as others, feels neglected, abused, and manipulated; these feelings produce anxiety and frustration which can lead to withdrawal or protest. Such a situation requires extraordinary powers in one ombudsman, leading some to call him "ombatman" or suggest that the person needs a halo and wings (London, 1970).

Clifford (1970) believes that rather than an ombudsman, what is needed is rejection of organizational patterns of business and government that produce extensive bureaucracy in colleges. He would prefer a different model of organization with a dean of students who had the conviction, courage, and commitment to be the ombudsman *and more* for students. With such a dean and annual reviews, perhaps the colleges could develop a model for government and business to emulate.

A different concern, though related, is that the ombudsman role is duplicative of functions already performed by others on the campus. Many faculty and staff have always functioned in an ombudsman fashion (Norman, 1970) and many deans of students or vice-presidents for student affairs see the position as a threat or encroachment on their duties (Eddy, 1970). In fact, however, deans have extensive responsibilities and the physical and political realities of their office preclude them from having time as well as the appropriate position to be an advocate for students (Drew, 1973). Rowland (1969) suggests other differences between the ombudsman and the dean of students. The ombudsman frequently has little or no staff, handles academic as well as nonacademic or cocurricular problems, has no discipline or conduct responsibilities, and has more inquiry authority, for example to investigate the dean of students office.

ADMINISTRATION

Unlike many college student personnel services, each decision made about the ombudsman office can increase or decrease its effectiveness.

Selection

The selection of an ombudsman should be made by those to whom the ombudsman is accountable. Ombudsmen appointed by presidents seem to have little likelihood of success, because they appear so closely aligned to the establishment (Johnson, 1972). Ombudsmen should not be selected or elected by the bureaucracy (Schlossberg, 1970) for the same reason. Becoming an arm of the administration results in loss of credibility which undoes any power that may come from a presidential appointment (Sandler et al., 1968).

Students obviously have a stake in the selection of the ombudsman and usually want direct participation in the process (Buccieri, 1968a). However, the ombudsman cannot be representative of, nor attached too closely or exclusively to, any student group (Norman, 1970) or again credibility is lost. Similarly, being hired by a committee of the faculty senate (Gorovitz, 1967) or being considered a one-person senate committee (California University, 1968) also makes the ombudsman appear responsible to one faction.

Rowland (1969) suggests that the way the ombudsman is selected parallels the power emphasis of the college. Broad community support seems crucial (Stamatakos & Isachsen, 1970), whether it is obtained through an election by a faculty-student senate (Drew, 1973) or a procedure such as being nominated by students, cleared by faculty, recommended by the president, and appointed by the college's governing board (Mundinger, 1967; Rowland, 1969).

Powers

The major power of the ombudsman is the use of reasoned persuasion (Rowland, 1969), though hopefully the ombudsman is not limited only to the power of appealing to authority (Stamatakos & Isachsen, 1970). Stamatakos and Isachsen (1970) recommend that the ombudsman have power to initiate investigations without first having to receive a complaint. However, Rowland (1969) says that the ombudsman should only investigate in response to student complaints. Rowland further recommends that where a pattern of grievances exists, the ombudsman should work for change in the regulations, procedures, or personnel to prevent recurrence; supplement but not supersede other means of redress for student grievances; and when rebuffed, have authority to appeal to the chief administrative officers for intervention. There seems to be unanimous agreement that the ombudsman should have access to all campus offices and files, except medical, psychological, and classified documents, but the ombudsman should not have authority to take disciplinary action, reverse decisions, or circumvent regulations (Rowland, 1969). There is no known case where an ombudsman has reversed an academic or administrative action (Eddy, 1970).

Reporting

Closely related to the method of selection and power of the ombudsman is the type and method of reporting on the work done and action attempted or taken. An annual report to those who selected him or her and to those whom the ombudsman is accountable is considered minimal. Reporting is important because a major source of power for the ombudsman is the degree of publicity the reports receive. It should be expected that the public media will be used (Stamatakos & Isachsen, 1970) despite the threatening element of this kind of exposure. At the least, widely publicized, periodic, general reports to all members of the institution (Rowland, 1969) should be made.

Problems Dealt With

If the ombudsman represents all constituencies on campus, then he or she should deal with the concerns of all groups: students, faculty, administration, and staff (Mundinger, 1967). Most problems with faculty such as assignments, class rules, and grades involve the academic freedom of the faculty (London, 1970) and this should be expected and defined. The scope of problems for students includes academic: registration and admission requirements, quality of instruction, advisement, tuition, fees, and grades; and nonacademic: traffic regulations, financial need, housing, use of facilities and services, health care, and employment (Rowland, 1969). Some say the ombudsman should not deal with political concerns nor quell mass student rebellions (California University, 1968; Rowland, 1969), while others see that to be the major area of input (Lehrer, 1969; White, 1969). Rowland (1969) suggests that the ombudsman decide himself or herself about his or her jurisdiction and competence on complaints.

Personal Requirements

Above all, the ombudsman should be someone that students, faculty, administration, and staff can talk to with confidence (Drew, 1973). Some say the ombudsman should have known academic ability and integrity, be a full or tenured professor and have half-time teaching responsibility (Mundinger, 1967). Others feel that this would limit the ombudsman's time too much (Rowland, 1969) and recommend a minimum of committee assignments (Eddy & Klepper, 1972). Faculty who become ombudsmen may find themselves outside of the mainstream of their academic department and college, simply because they are not doing the same things as their colleagues. Candidates that have not been faculty are acceptable as long as they have a thorough knowledge of the campus environment and structure, wisdom and integrity, counseling skills, communication skills, and a basic knowledge of the law (Stamatakos & Isachsen, 1970).

Rowland (1969) surveyed student perceptions of the ombudsman at Michigan State University and found that the following traits were considered important in descending order: knowledge of campus operations and regulations, understanding, effectiveness, authority, and accessibility. A non-teaching faculty member (administrator) was first choice for the position by the students, less than one-fifth favored a professional student personnel worker, and none wanted a student. Rowland found that the typical ombudsman may be identified with any academic department, was not a professional student personnel worker, had spent considerable time teaching, genuinely liked students, and was respected by colleagues. The thread running through all discussion of appropriate candidates is that the ombudsman must have considerable personal prestige, integrity, and persuasive ability (California University, 1968; Eddy, 1970).

Budget and Staff

Staff for the ombudsmen should include an ample supply of secretaries to transact business (Eddy & Klepper, 1972) and legal counsel (Poblana, 1971). Mundinger (1967) recommends an eleven-month appointment with a secretary and an office away from the administration. Norman (1970) suggests a budget which includes travel and luncheon expenses for the public relations necessary for the job. Regarding the salary question and in order for the ombudsman to not seem indebted to any one group, Johnson (1972) recommends that the salary come in fourths from student affairs, faculty, board of trustees, and administration budgets. Rowland (1969) says that while the salary from an outside source may make the ombudsman appear more independent, it will not erase the implications inherent in his or her selection and accountability. Rowland further recommends that the salary and prestige be equivalent to high level academic or administrative positions.

Term of Office

Mundinger (1967) recommends a five-year term of office. Rowland's (1969) suvery found that a term of office longer than two years was highly favored by the students. Rowland himself recommends a two-year term renewable by the ombudsman and the selection committees, and that the decision about continuing be based on a systematic sampling of students who have consulted the ombudsman.

Student Evaluation

Rowland's (1969) survey of students who went to the ombudsman found that they represented the entire range of the student body, although upperclassmen, male students, and married students consulted the ombudsman more proportionally. Half of the 218 students surveyed took their problem to two or more people in authority before consulting the ombudsman. Two thirds said the ombudsman helped in relieving frustration, half said the ombudsman completely or partially solved their problems, half said their problems were not solved, none wanted to see the position abolished, and nearly all reported they would return to the office for help as well as recommend it to others.

Student and Other Ombudsmen

Rothman and Keenan (1970) seem to reflect the prevalent view when they suggest that it would be a naive oversimplification to expect the ombudsman to resolve more than a minimum of difficulties. Clifford (1970) shares this view but suggests three situations where the ombudsman concept might be appropriate: for a new college to help students through unestablished procedures, for an institution in crisis, and as an evaluation of an institution carried out by a college student personnel worker on sabbatical from another institution (see also Mundinger, 1969). He also feels that student government could benefit from an ombudsman since, as Deegan (1972) reports from a survey of ninety-two public junior colleges in California, many student government associations are unrepresentative and ineffective. Some institutions use minority law students as student ombudsmen to cut red tape for minority students and others suggest ombudsmen could be used by the dean of students to obtain student input into plans (Eddy, 1970). Eddy also feels that for the dean to delegate authority to such specialists is good administrative practice. Some student ombudsmen have evidently worked well (Buccieri, 1968a), though others have been accessible but powerless (Sandler et al., 1968). One student ombudsman recommended that the position be filled by a new student each year to capitalize on the unexpected and the advantage of cooperation given a person during the first year in a job. Others do not recommend having one-year terms nor using seniors, because they just learn the job and earn respect when their term is over or they graduate.

REFERENCES

Anderson, S. V. (Ed.), The American Assembly. *Ombudsmen for American Government*. Englewood Cliffs, N. J.: Prentice-Hall, 1968.

Anderson, S. V. *Ombudsman papers: American experience and proposals*. Berkeley: University of California, Institute of Governmental Studies, 1969.

Barzun, J. *The American university*. New York: Harper and Row, 1968.

Bloland, P. A., & Nowak, D. B. The ombudsman: An informal survey of the implementation of the ombudsman concept. (Student Personnel Report No. 4, Office of the Dean of Students, University of Southern California, October 1968.) *College Student Personnel Abstracts*, 1969, *4*(3), 313.

Buccieri, C. H. Campus troubleshooter resetting his sights. *College and University Business*, 1968, *45*(6), 51-53. (a)

Buccieri, C. H. Ombudsman: New troubleshooter on campus. *College and University Business*, 1968, *44*(3), 52-55. (b)

California University Study Commission on University Governance. *The culture of the university: Governance and education*. San Francisco:

Jossey-Bass, 1968.

Clifford, E. W. Second thoughts on the ombudsman in higher education. *NASPA Journal*, 1970, 7, 202-207.

Deegan, W. L. Student and governance: Where are we? Where are we going? *Junior College Journal*, 1972, 42(5), 38.

Drew, J. W. The ombudsman: An unnecessary extra to the dean of students? *NASPA Journal*, 1973, 10, 279-282.

Eddy, J. P. Campus ombudsman in American higher education. *Kappa Delta Pi Record*, 1968, 5, 33-35.

Eddy, J. P. Campus ombudsmen and the dean of students. *NASPA Journal*, 1970, 7, 208-212.

Eddy, J. P., & Klepper, W. M., II. A new model for the chief student personnel worker in higher education. *NASPA Journal*, 1972, 10, 30-32.

Gorovitz, S. (Ed.). *Freedom and order in the university*. Cleveland: Press of Western Reserve University, 1967.

Isachsen, O., & Stamatakos, L. C. Case study: Anatomy of the lingering scholarship. *NASPA Journal*, 1970, 7, 196-201.

Johnson, R. Credibility and the university ombudsman. *Journal of the National Association of Women Deans and Counselors*, 1972, 35, 186-189.

Kluge, D. A., & Smith, J. Recent statements of principles, rights, and procedures in student behavior. *Journal of the National Association of Women Deans and Counselors*, 1968, 31, 64-68.

Lehrer, S. Higher education and the disenchanted students. *School and Society*, 1969, 97, 427-431.

London, H. Underground notes from a campus ombudsman. *Journal of Higher Education*, 1970, 41, 350-364.

Mundinger, D. C. The university ombudsman. *Journal of Higher Education*, 1967, 38, 493-499.

Mundinger, D. C. A brief for a university ombudsman. *Liberal Education*, 1969, 55, 373-380.

Norman, N. F. Ombudsmen: Their job and functions. *NASPA Journal*, 1970, 7, 213-214.

Poblana, R. An ombudsman assesses 3 years of ombudsmanship. *College Management*, 1971, 6(July), 19+.

Rothman, L. K., & Keenan, C. B. Machines, people and ideas: In quest of clarification of the role of the professional student personnel worker. *NASPA Journal*, 1970, 7, 143-150.

Rowat, D. C. The spread of the ombudsman idea. In S. Anderson (Ed.), The American Assembly, *Ombudsman for American government*. Englewood Cliffs, N. J.: Prentice-Hall, 1968.

Rowland, H. R. The campus ombudsman: An emerging role. *Educational Record*, 1969, 50, 443-448.

Sandler, A., Kirk, H. P., & Hallberg, E. C. An ombudsman for the university. *Journal of College Student Personnel,* 1968, *9,* 112-115.

Schlossberg, N. K. An ombudsman for students. *NASPA Journal,* 1967, *5,* 31-33.

Schlossberg, N. K. The ombudsman in current status and theory. *NASPA Journal,* 1970, *7,* 215-219.

Stamatakos, L. C., & Isachsen, O. Towards making the university ombudsman a more effective force in higher education: A comparative study. *NASPA Journal,* 1970, *7,* 190-195.

White, J. B. The ombudsman in practice. *College Student Personnel Abstracts,* 1969, *5,* 47.

CHAPTER 9

DISCIPLINE

MICHAEL DANNELLst380
HISTORY

First Two Hundred Years

DURING the Colonial period in American higher education (1630-1780), discipline was considered a part of the moral and ethical training of students and was used for total behavior control (Leonard, 1956; Schetlin, 1967). Because of the dominance of strict religion (Smith & Kirk, 1971b) and the young age of students (Harvard students were between fifteen and seventeen years, with some as young as eleven, Leonard, 1956), the early colleges had "a veritable straightjacket of regulations governing academic, social and moral conduct" (Smith & Kirk, 1971b, p. 276). Violations of these regulations were met with a wide range of penalties including public confessions and ridicule, fines, corporal punishment, and explusion (Leonard, 1956). Everyone employed by the institution was expected to report violations to the president, who was charged with the major responsibility for discipline and who shared decision making in serious cases with the trustees and in minor ones with the faculty (Leonard, 1956).

The Federal period (1780-1812) was characterized by extreme student misconduct, revolts, and riots (Durst, 1968), and by the establishment of numerous, detailed, and extensive rules and moral codes (Leonard, 1956; Schetlin, 1967). Punishments during this period became somewhat milder, and there was some emergence of persuasion and counseling of student offenders (Leonard, 1956; Schetlin, 1967).

In the years of expansion (1812-1862) the paternalistic and behavior control approach to discipline changed somewhat because of the separation of church and state, broadening aims and objectives of colleges, and increasing enrollments (Leonard, 1956). Trustee participation in disciplinary matters declined, and at some colleges the over-burdened president appointed a faculty member to serve as a disciplinary specialist (Leonard, 1956; Schetlin, 1967). These specialists were apparently the first persons who seriously employed counseling as a way to deal with troublesome students. Previously, the faculty had been harassed by rebellious students to the point of fearing for their personal safety; but during this period, student-faculty relations improved and corporal punishment almost disappeared (Leonard, 1956; Schetlin, 1967).

Civil War to World War II

The mid-1800's to about 1900 saw a major shift away from rigid behavior control to greater emphasis on student self-discipline and self-governance, a result of the introduction of the German university model into American higher education (Brubacher & Rudy, 1968; Durst, 1968; Schetlin, 1967). More humanitarian methods of enforcement and punishment were used, more concern for the individual student was shown, and disciplinary systems were administered more democratically (Schetlin, 1967). As student governments and honors systems developed (Brubacher & Rudy, 1968; Durst, 1968) and student input into the disciplinary process increased, faculty played an increasingly less active role. In addition, the Industrial Revolution dictated that the faculty develop their academic disciplines, which left little time for monitoring student behavior. Consequently, discipline was left more and more to the president, who increasingly delegated it (Smith & Kirk, 1971b).

Between the turn of the century and World War II, the president and faculty on most campuses were relieved of their disciplinary duties by deans of men and deans of women. These specialists, chosen for their rapport with students (Smith & Kirk, 1971b), expanded both the philosophy and programs of discipline in higher education. Most of these pioneer college student personnel workers were idealistic and optimistic about the kind of students they could develop (Fley, 1964). Programs took on the ultimate goals of self-control and self-discipline, methods became more individualized, personalized, and preventative, and the trend toward a more humanistic philosophy with educational and rehabilitative purposes continued (Fley, 1964). The concept of "the student as a whole" began to develop (Durst, 1968) and counseling as a form of corrective action became popular (Fley, 1964).

Through the 1920's most student behavior problems were concerned with either violated institutional rules, such as drinking, gambling, hazing, violations of hours, cheating, or illegal activities, such as graft, forgery, and theft. During the 1930's a new problem, political activism, arose. This problem dissipated with the start of the war (Fley, 1964) and is of interest because of its parallels thirty years later.

The Present

Returning veterans flocked to college when World War II was over, and they found that they "could not digest the traditional palliatives served up by the dean to justify student conduct regulation and discipline" (Smith & Kirk, 1971b, p. 277). A crisis was avoided, however, because the veterans' overriding vocational orientation kept them so busy academically that they had no time to revolt.

During the 1950's, with the increasing emphasis on rehabilitation, professionally trained counselors were delegated more disciplinary responsibility and disciplinary hearing boards composed of both staff and students were established (Sims, 1971).

Movement toward less behavior control and more student input into the disciplinary process has continued to the present. Since the early 1960's the legal and educational conceptions of student rights and responsibilities have broadened considerably and due process safeguards have been introduced.

These more recent developments may be attributed to a variety of factors: older students, the reduced age of legal majority, a general shift in societal attitudes and mores away from the puritanical ethic toward more permissiveness, an increased awareness of student power which arose from the student activism of the 1960's and early 1970's, and court intervention into the disciplinary process.

DEFINITION

Within the context of higher education there are two definitions of discipline (Seward, 1961; Wrenn, 1949). One refers to the external control of behavior and connotes punishment and the placement of restrictions or obligations on violators of laws and mores. The other refers to the internal control of behavior, or self-discipline, and involves a personal sense of responsibility and orderliness.

The evolution of the concept of discipline in American higher education has been from external to internal (Wrenn, 1949). In 1930 it was suggested that "the only real kind of discipline is self-discipline" (Hawkes, p. 253), and that definition is the only one higher education currently recognizes (Mueller, 1961). Of course, theory does not necessarily equal practice, and to many, discipline still connotes forced imposition of external controls.

Philosophy

Discipline, defined as self-discipline, has an educational purpose, a philosophy which has received strong support (Brady, 1965; Clark, Hagie, & Landrus, 1952; DeSena, 1963; Durst, 1968; Gometz & Parker, 1968; Hawkes, 1930; Kroeker & Carver, 1968; Lloyd, 1945; National Education Association, 1971; Rush, 1945; Seward, 1961; Van Houten, 1964; Williamson, 1956, 1961, 1963; Williamson & Foley, 1949). This philosophy holds that college students should be self-disciplining and if they are not, they "should be aided in becoming ... acceptable member[s] of the college community rather than being excluded from it" (Durst, 1968, p. 10).

Suggested components of the educational philosophy are that the individual's welfare is paramount (Brady, 1965;

DeSena, 1963); that sound educational principles (Van Houten, 1964) should be employed to humanistically and rationally teach (Seward, 1961) acceptable behavior (Williamson & Foley, 1949), mastery of developmental tasks (Clark et al., 1952; Kroeker & Carver, 1968), and the development of internal controls (Williamson, 1963); and that the student should be rehabilitated or reeducated (Brady, 1965; Williamson & Foley, 1949). Problems that arise from the philosophy are how to teach without being authoritarian (Rush, 1945) and how to define acceptable behavior.

Two other philosophies affect the actual practice of discipline (DeSena, 1963). One philosophy called pure intellectualism states that the college's duty is to train only the intellect and that it has no responsibility for moral, social, and ethical training. The other philosophy called legalistic or strict constructionist (Williamson, 1961) views discipline as legislative and punitive; broken rules are met with penalties as future deterrents and the institution's needs are of primary importance.

Sources of Student Misconduct

Student misconduct may stem from sources which are largely within the individual, called intrapersonal, and those which have their origins in the institution, called institutional. Intrapersonal sources of misconduct include those which involve actual pathology in the individual, such as neurosis or psychosis (Foley, 1947), and those which are nonpathological (Williamson, 1956).

Nonpathological sources include inadequate development or a gap in learning how to behave properly; lack of information or understanding, as not knowing a given behavior is proscribed (Foley, 1947); and adolescent mischievousness and excess energy (Williamson, 1956).

Institutional origins of student misbehavior include quite an array of campus environmental conditions, but particularly the number and nature of the rules and regulations designed to control student behavior (Foley, 1947; Seward, 1961; Williamson, 1956, 1961; Williamson & Foley, 1949; Wrenn, 1949).

> There is a direct relationship between regulations on the campus and the number of cases called disciplinary cases. This is a function not of the students or their conduct as much as it is of the social structure in which they live and of the regulations provided by the college (Wrenn, 1949, p. 603).

Other institutional factors of student misconduct include the general morale of the institution; the "long tradition of guerrilla warfare between students and administration" (Williamson, 1956, p. 77); the new found freedom a freshman finds on campus; the availability of extracurricular activities, especially athletics, on campus; the difficulty and scope of the curriculum; the degree of vocational seriousness of the students; the amount of student input into the disciplinary process; and the degree of development of the student personnel program (Williamson, 1956, 1961; Williamson & Foley, 1949).

Forms of Corrective Action

Corrective actions taken by the institution in response to violations of rules include punishment or punitive sanctions, rehabilitative activity beyond punishment, and actions aimed at remedying external sources of misconduct.

Punitive Sanctions

Punitive sanctions may be corporal and psychological punishments or deprivation of privileges, liberty, possessions, or student status (Mueller, 1961; Williamson & Foley, 1949). Corporal punishment, though once used liberally, is now considered of little or no value in terms of educational purpose.

Psychological punishment is not usually recognized. Yet the following categories of disciplinary communications, typically considered informative, contain an element of psychological punishment: admonitions, or oral statements of a rule violation; warnings, or oral or written statements of a rule violation accompanied by a reference to more severe sanctions should the prohibited behavior persist or reoccur; and censures, or formal written statements of a rule violation often temporarily placed on the student's disciplinary record or sent to the student's parents.

There is a broad array of sanctions involving punishment through deprivation of privileges, liberty, or possessions. Disciplinary probation is probably the most frequently used sanction for relatively minor or first offenses. It may involve restrictions on social hours or the use of facilities, or be a condition whereby, should another rule violation occur, a more severe sanction will be imposed. At some colleges probation may be conditional on the completion of a forced service task, such as personally repairing what was damaged.

Other deprivations involving loss of possessions which deprive the student of money are: (a) Restitution or monetary compensation paid to the injured party for the damage incurred. Carrington (1971) considers this the least restrictive and most humane of the sanctions, since it allows the student to choose what to do without, as a consequence of misconduct. (b) A fine without an element of compensation. This sanction has been strongly criticized as not being rehabilitative (Williamson & Foley, 1949). (c) The denial of financial assistance. The obvious problem with terminating a student's financial aid is that it may amount to discriminatory expulsion of poorer students (Farer, 1969).

Sanctions which affect the student's status are suspension and expulsion. Suspension is the temporary dismissal of the student, usually reserved for those not considered ready to benefit from the educational offerings of the institution or those considered detrimental to the educational efforts of other students. It has received recent attention as a way to avoid the "creeping legalism" involved in expulsion (Stein, 1974).

Expulsion is frequently considered the capital punishment of student discipline, for it is the permanent dismissal of the offending student. It is applied in only the most serious cases and frequently means that the individual's chances for admission to another college are slim.

Apart from disciplinary probation, suspension and expulsion are probably the most frequently used sanctions on college campuses. However, they are often ineffective because depriving serious campus disrupters of formal status does not necessarily get them away from the college and may, in fact, give them more time to disrupt (Carrington, 1971; Farer, 1969). Further, it is simply not feasible for campus officials to limit ingress and egress of nonstudents on campus, as was learned during the riots of the 1960's and early 1970's.

Suspension and especially expulsion may also be too harsh in many instances (Carrington, 1971). Both not only sever the individual from the useful activity of school, but they may also have long-range, unforeseen consequences, such as the impairment of future earning power because of the lack of a college degree.

Rehabilitative Actions

Corrective actions involving some form of rehabilitative activity beyond punishment include counseling and referral for medical or psychiatric care. Counseling may involve a professionally trained disciplinary counselor, other professionals (an administrator, faculty member, residence hall advisor), or aid from outside sources (parents, friends, religious organizations).

Actions Aimed at External Sources

When the student's living arrangement, financial situation, or the like contribute to misbehavior, it may be more appropriate to address the student's environmental situation than to punish or counsel the student. Courses of action such as changing housing, assisting in job placement, arranging tutorial services, or even changing institutional rules or policies are available when such conditions are present.

Selecting the Appropriate Corrective Action

The action chosen in a disciplinary situation is affected by (Seward, 1961) one's philosophical belief about the nature of man; one's belief about learning and teaching methods; the

nature and amount of external standards used in defining un-
desirable behavior; and the divergence between the standards
used and those of the students.

Other recommendations on selecting and applying corrective
action include: (a) The punishment or treatment should fit the
individual and the particular circumstances and should *not* be
designed to fit the crime (Foley, 1947; Mueller, 1961; Signori,
1966; Whitaker, 1961; Williamson & Foley, 1949); (b) The sanction should be presented as a natural consequence of the
offender's act and not in a retributive manner (Peiffer &
Walker, 1957); and (c) Where a severe sanction such as suspension or expulsion is imposed, it should be the only viable
alternative available (Foley, 1947).

AUTHORITY TO DISCIPLINE

The Theories

There are essentially seven theories regarding an institution's
authority to discipline its students: Statutory, *in loco parentis*,
contract, educational purpose, constitutional, fiduciary or trust,
and status or custom.

Statutory

This theory holds that the institution's power to discipline
arises out of specific statutory grants or laws from the state
legislature to the governing board of higher education in the
state through its charter (Snoxell, 1965), or directly to the institution (Ratliff, 1972). The major types of such legislation are
(Bakken, 1968): (a) a direct grant of disciplinary authority to
the faculty, (b) a direct grant of authority to the board with
authorization to delegate it to faculty or students, (c) a grant of
power to the board without mention of authority to delegate it,
but delegation is implicit, and (d) a general grant of power to
the board without mention of authority to discipline. In reality,
there are many different variations of these types of legislation
and it is not known which is the most prevalent. (For specific

examples of each see Bakken, 1968, who also gives examples of the uncommon practice of specific disciplinary legislation.) Although Bakken (1968) and Snoxell (1965) imply that statutory theory is the practical basis for disciplinary power, others (Ratliff, 1972) claim that it has won only limited support in the courts.

In loco parentis

This doctrine, defined as "in the place of a parent; instead of a parent" (Black, 1968, p. 896) is the oldest rationale for disciplining students and views the college as standing in the place of the parent with respect to all student conduct. It is essentially a court-created fiction which authorizes the college to govern student conduct even when the conduct being regulated has no relation to the college in any practical sense (Yegge, 1968).

For most of the history of American higher education, *in loco parentis* was used as the justification for paternalistic, informal disciplinary procedures which constituted "an open door to arbitrary conduct by those vested with power [to discipline]" (Ratliff, 1972, p. 47). Thus it was a rationale for disciplining students without a hearing or other forms of due process (Gordon, 1971). Despite such abuses of power, the court traditionally deferred to college authorities in the area of discipline because (Van Alstyne, 1966) college administrators were assumed to know best the needs of the student and the college (see *Gott v. Berea College,* 1913); loss of education was not greatly important since education itself was considered a luxury, and the conventional wisdom of the time was that students were immature and should not be allowed to act on their own preferences.

Many current authorities in both law and education consider the *in loco parentis* view of the student-institutional relationship wrought with problems. One criticism is that it is impractical because (Penney, 1967) it is a legal, not an operational concept, which has been extended by popular misconception; it applies the erroneous criterion of legal authority instead of educational effectiveness to the evaluation of the college's actions (see also Ratliff, 1972); and it implies that the institution can do anything that it can legally get away with. The doctrine is also considered detrimental because it detracts from the main purpose of the institution, which is education (Strickland, 1965).

A third criticism is that it is no longer tenable because (Van Alstyne, 1968a) students are older; large, impersonal institutions cannot realistically assume the intimate place of the parent; and parents cannot expel a child from the home. Closely aligned to this is the view that the parent's powers and interests are not the same as those of the college (Van Alstyne, 1966; *Hegel v. Langson*, 1971). But perhaps the single most popular argument against *in loco parentis* is the current feeling of most students and educators that "the personal life of the student is of no concern to the institution as long as his [her] behavior does not interfere with the rights of others" (NEA, 1971, pp. 29-30).

As late as 1967 Bakken stated that the paternalistic approach to discipline is so accepted that it has become common law in the profession and that the courts will not overrule it, and in 1970 Cazier stated that paternalism is inevitable. However, it is clear that if *in loco parentis* does stand, it has severe limitations (Ratliff, 1972). Others have concluded that it is untenable, intolerable, or simply dead because it has been jettisoned by the courts (Beaney, 1968, 1969; Callis, 1967, 1969; Carnegie Commission, 1971; McCay, 1969, 1970; NYU School of Law, 1968; Ratliff, 1972; Sims, 1971; Strickland, 1965; Van Alstyne, 1966, 1968a, 1968b). But just what legal doctrine has taken its place is not clear (Beaney, 1969). Nonetheless, the phasing-out of *in loco parentis* has resulted in less restrictive control over students, which may, in turn, result in more concern with changing the educational environment rather than with remediation and punishment (Carlson & Hubbell, 1971).

Contract

This theory defines the relationship between the student and the institution as a contractual one. The contract is the statement of conditions in the college's catalogue and other publications which the student agrees to by signing the registration card. The student accepts the rules in order to obtain the education and the degree offered by the institution. Should the student violate the rules, the institution can then apply those measures which are enumerated as sanctions in the contract. According to Fisher (1970), this theory is the basis for most of the student-institutional relationship (see also McCay, 1970).

Like *in loco parentis,* the contract theory has been used throughout much of American higher education's history as a justification for oppressive rules and unfair procedures in disciplinary matters (Gordon, 1971; Ratliff, 1972). With respect to discipline in public institutions, it has for the most part been discarded by the courts, but it has been maintained with respect to private colleges (McCay, 1969, 1970).

The contract theory is criticized because, like the doctrine of *in loco parentis,* it is a legal fiction which does not recognize the reality or educational nature of the student-institutional relationship (see Callis, 1967, 1969). Also such a contract is a contract of adhesion (NYU School of Law, 1968; Van Alstyne, 1966) or one that is neither a product of equal bargaining between two parties nor voluntarily entered into. Students really have no choice in the matter because they have no power position from which to disagree with the institution. Because the courts are increasingly likely to regard such contracts as ones of adhesion (NYU School of Law, 1968), colleges will probably continue to move away from this theory of control over students (Beaney, 1968).

Educational Purpose

This theory defines the student-institutional relationship as an educational one, and it thereby limits the institution's disciplinary control to student behavior that adversely affects its educational mission (Callis, 1967; NYU School of Law, 1968; Van Alstyne, 1966). It is founded on the belief that "whatever operational procedures and regulations that a college wishes to

adopt that can be justified as aiding and abetting the education
of students must be considered as proper" (Callis, 1967, p. 232).
Considered the only realistic theory, given the purpose of the
institution and the true nature of its relationship to students
(Callis, 1967, 1969; Carnegie Commission, 1971; NEA, 1971;
NYU School of Law, 1968; Penney, 1967; Van Alstyne, 1966),
the theory allows discipline (Callis, 1969) for maintenance of
order and to prevent conduct unbecoming a student. The obvious difficulties with this view are determining what education is, what behavior is in keeping with the educational
mission, and who decides. This latter difficulty, perhaps more
than any other, is the reason for the theory's relatively uncertain status in the courts.

Constitutional

This theory is actually no more than a legal limitation on
the institution's power to discipline. It

> tells very little about the student-institutional relationship
> *per se*, except that a public institution is prohibited from
> unreasonably proscribing, or requiring the forfeit of, consti-
> tutionally protected rights, as a condition of admission to, or
> continuation at, the academy (Fisher, 1970, pp. 5-6).

The theory's legal limitation was established in *Dixon v. Alabama State Board of Higher Education* (1961, see Due Process
section).

Fiduciary

The fiduciary or trust theory originally proposed by Seavey
(1957, see also Goldman, 1966) considers the institution in the
capacity of a fiduciary to its students.

> A fiduciary is one whose function it is to act for the benefit of
> another as to matters relevant to the relation between them
> .... One of the duties of the fiduciary is to make full disclo-
> sure of all relevant facts in any transaction between them
> (Seavey, 1957, p. 1407, n. 3).

The advantages of this theory are that it prevents the student from having to prove his or her innocence in disciplinary hearings; it prevents the school from hiding its sources of information; and it "demands that [the institution] afford the student every means of rehabilitation" (Seavey, 1957, p. 1410). Despite these advantages, the fiduciary theory has been criticized. First, if extended beyond disciplinary matters, it would become unworkable (Fisher, 1970). Second, although an advancement over *in loco parentis* and contract theory, it is founded on semantics and, therefore, is artificial (NYU School of Law, 1968). Lastly, it has been twice rejected by the courts (Ratliff, 1972).

Status

The status or custom theory will only be defined here, for it has seldom been relied on by the courts. It holds that "the rights and duties of students and colleges are inherent in the status of the parties ... [as] they have developed through custom, tradition, and usage" (Ratliff, 1972, p. 48).

Extent of Jurisdiction and Authority

The major issue with respect to the institution's jurisdiction over its students in disciplinary matters is: Should the institution apply internal sanctions, seek external sanctions, or both in a disciplinary case where internal rules and criminal law both apply (Stein, 1972)? The trend of thought in recent years, especially among students, is that violations of the law both on and off-campus which do not damage the college's pursuit of its educational objectives should be left entirely to the civil authorities ("New Suggestions," 1968; Paulsen, 1968; Van Alstyne, 1968b).

Sims (1971) has argued strongly against civil authority as the sole authority. In his view, the campus is unique and specialized in purpose and nature from the surrounding community and, therefore, has difficult problems which dictate that it should maintain its own regulations and enforcement. He recommends that geography should provide the boundaries for jurisdiction. Then, with the exception of felonies, on-campus violations of campus rules and criminal law (misdemeanors) should be handled on campus. This approach fits quite well with the attitude of most civil authorities, since they generally allow the institution to handle its own, except in cases of extreme behavior or lack of effort to stop criminal violations (Stein, 1972).

Violations of law on campus raise several questions (McKay, 1968): Should the institution try to uncover such violations to aid the civil authorities? If so, to what extent? Under what circumstances should officials of the institution report such violations to the civil authorities? When should the institution leave such matters solely to the civil authorities?

For deciding the last of these jurisdictional questions Stein's (1972) model provides several factors to consider: (a) Does the act interfere with the educational mission of the college? If not, then it is generally best to leave it to the civil authorities. (b) How serious is the act? Here college officials can either use their discretion at the time or employ an artificial guideline, such as felony versus misdemeanor. (c) Does the institution have the resources and the expertise to handle the particular case? If not, then it should probably stay out of it. (d) Is there a need for a unique sanction or will it merely duplicate those of outside agencies?

Double Jeopardy

Occasionally students who have been tried in criminal court and disciplined by their college for the same act have argued that it constitutes double jeopardy, in that they have been tried twice for the same offense (see Amendment V to the Constitution). However, the concept of double jeopardy does not apply to college disciplinary action (Fisher, 1970; A. W. Johnson, 1966; St. Antoine, 1971; Young, 1970a), because double jeopardy is a common law and constitutional prohibition which applies only to criminal proceedings (Fisher, 1970; Young 1970a). For example, if a student steals a book from a store the college could have a hearing and determine penalties and the courts could hold a trial and sentence the student. Such independent, concurrent decisions on the same act are "separate approaches to separate problems which happen to have common elements" (A. W. Johnson, 1966, p. 23).

Even though double jeopardy does not apply, it is recommended that institutions not duplicate punishments imposed by civil authorities (Fisher, 1970), and that institutions either keep an offense within their own systems or turn it over to the appropriate outside agency, but not both (St. Antoine, 1971).

Dutton, Smith, and Zarle (1969) surveyed all NASPA member institutions on their approaches to the adjudication of disciplinary cases. Of the 558 respondents they found: (a) Two thirds did not act on violations of criminal law unless the college was involved; (b) Two thirds delayed disciplinary action until cases were resolved in court; (c) Nearly three fourths kept on-campus violations and misdemeanors within the institution; (d) Only 12 percent left all violations of the law to the civil authorities.

Constitutional Guarantees

Another jurisdictional question is the extent to which an institution can proscribe the conduct of its students. One area of student behavior in which it generally cannot meddle is that of students' constitutional rights. Four principles are fairly well established regarding the extent of the institution's authority in regard to the students' constitutional guarantees. (a) The college cannot put a blanket restraint on students' rights to freedom of assembly and expression (Young, 1970a). But since that right is not absolute, the institution can restrain assembly and expression where it will interfere with its educational and administrative responsibilities (Sherry, 1966; Young, 1970a). (b) The college cannot restrict, prohibit, or censor the content of speech except for extraordinarily impelling reasons, for example, someone's safety (Sherry, 1966). (c) The institution cannot apply its regulations in a discriminatory manner (Sherry, 1966). (d) As citizens, students are protected from unreasonable searches and seizures by Amendment IV to the Constitution. However, the courts will allow the institution to search and seize where it is necessary to foster its educational aims and objectives (Fisher, 1970; Young, 1970a).

DUE PROCESS

Due process may be defined as "an *appropriate protection* of the rights of an individual while determining his [her] liability for wrongdoing and the applicability of punishment" (Fisher, 1970, p. 1). It is a right accorded all citizens with respect to action of the federal government by Amendment V to the Constitution and with respect to action of a state by Amendment XIV.

Procedural due process refers to an individual's rights with respect to the procedures used in adjudicating an offense. While there is no final and absolute definition of just what procedures must be followed in all cases (Young, 1972) and while it varies with the seriousness of the offense and the possible penalty (Fisher, 1970), the standard typically used by the courts is one of fairness or fair play (Bakken, 1968; Callis, 1969; Fisher, 1970; Gordon, 1971; Jacobson, 1963). Substantive due process refers to the nature, purpose, and application of a law, rule, or regulation. Once again, the standard usually used by the courts is fairness. Generally, the law or rule must not be so vague or overly broad as to be unclear; its purpose must be fair, reasonable, and just; and it must be applied in fairness and good faith (Young, 1972).

Procedural Due Process

Prior to 1960 the courts generally held that in dismissal hearings students had a right to present their view, only some evidence needed to be presented, students could be dismissed for the best interests of the college, students had a right to hear the charges, students had no right to counsel, and colleges had to make some effort to investigate a case (Bakken, 1968). Because the student-institutional relationship was viewed as contractual with overtones of *in loco parentis* and because college officials were assumed to be operating fairly and doing their best as educators, their decisions were left untampered with and their methods unquestioned by the courts (Bakken, 1968).

Beginning around 1960 the courts began to take another stance on the matter:

> With the advent of the civil rights movement changes occurred. Students were dismissed from college because they participated in civil rights activities which federal courts decided were legitimate constitutional activities. To support this right of the federal courts to intervene, the analogy of education as property was established. This brought dismissal from college under the due process clause and the Fourteenth Amendment to the U. S. Constitution (Bakken, 1968, p. 42).

This analogy of education as property was based on the recognition that education had become increasingly important to the socioeconomic future of students. Deprivation of education or dismissal from college was thereby viewed as the loss of a property right. This concept does not apply to private colleges nor is it universally accepted by the courts (see *Goldberg v. The Regents of the University of California,* 1967).

The landmark case in this area is *Dixon v. Alabama State Board of Education* (1961). *Dixon* established that in dismissal proceedings from a public college or university, a student has almost a constitutional right to notice and a hearing. The court also suggested the following procedural safeguards: (a) The student should be given notice of the specific charges. (b) A hearing should be held to present both sides of the case. (c) If cross-examination is not allowed, the names of those who testified against the accused and a record of their testimony should be given to the student. (d) The student should have an opportunity to present his or her defense, including evidence and witnesses. (e) The findings and results of the hearing should be reported to the student. (f) The requirements of due process are met in dismissal hearings where the rudiments of fair play are followed.

Many cases following *Dixon* established it as precedent and further specified the procedural due process requirements of dismissal proceedings in public institutions (*Knight v. State Board of Education,* 1963; *Due v. Florida A & M University,* 1963; *Esteban v. Central Missouri State College,* 1969). Subsequent cases also established that the gravity of the offense and of the sanction determines the degree of formality necessary in the hearing (Van Alstyne, 1970).

All of the procedural due process safeguards required in criminal proceedings are not required in student disciplinary hearings, because the hearings are considered civil in nature (*Barker v. Hardway*, 1968). The following rights have *not* been accorded students in disciplinary hearing by the courts (Young, 1970a, 1970b, 1971a, 1971b, 1972): the right to counsel, the right to confront and cross-examine witnesses, the right against self-incrimination, the right to a public hearing, the right to a jury trial, and the right to appeal (Fisher, 1970). However, recommendations have been made for more extensive procedural safeguards, such as the student should have the opportunity to appeal (ACLU, 1970; Beaney, 1969; Byse, 1962; Callis, 1969; Fisher, 1970; Hagie, 1966; Joint Statement, 1968; NYU School of Law, 1968); the student should be allowed to confront and cross-examine opposing witnesses (ACLU, 1970; Byse, 1962, 1963, 1966; Hagie, 1966; M. T. Johnson, 1964; Witmer, 1969); the student should be allowed a representative of the student's choice; and a record of the proceedings should be kept (ACLU, 1970; Byse, 1962, 1963, 1966; Hagie, 1966; M. T. Johnson, 1964; Joint Statement, 1968). Some believe that the representative should not be a member of the bar (Bakken, 1965; Fisher, 1970), and that the hearing should be public if the student requests (Witmer, 1969).

Substantive Due Process

Several principles regarding the nature and purpose of college rules of student conduct are fairly well established. First, the institution has the authority to make necessary and appropriate regulations to maintain order and discipline on campus (Arndt, 1971). Second, the standards of behavior must be in accord with its lawful purpose and function (Callis, 1969; Hanson, 1971; Young, 1970a), including rules regarding off-campus behavior (Arndt, 1971; Callis, 1969). Third, rules and regulations must be constitutionally fair and reasonable and not be capricious or arbitrary (Arndt, 1971; Callis, 1969; Hanson, 1971, Yegge, 1971).

However, the institution can limit constitutionally guaranteed rights of students to enable the institution to carry out its lawful purpose and function. For example, a college cannot ban peaceful demonstrations which are protected by the First Amendment, but it can require a permit and limit such demonstrations as to time and place, require safety and sanitary regulations, and ban those demonstrations that disrupt its specified normal operations (Arndt, 1971; Young, 1970a). Likewise, it cannot arbitrarily ban guest speakers (Arndt, 1971), but it can prevent a person from speaking who intended to incite a riot. Lastly, the institution should publish its rules and regulations for all to see (Arndt, 1971; Young, 1970b).

One aspect of substantive due process which is unresolved in the courts (Arndt, 1971) is the necessary degree of specificity of rules and regulations. Rules may not be vague or overly broad, but whether the standard used on criminal statutes is applicable or not is unclear (Brubacher, 1973; Mash, 1971; "Vagueness in College Rules," 1970; Young, 1972). At this time, the accepted standard is that a rule or regulation must be specific enough to give adequate notice of expected behavior and to allow the student to prepare a defense against a charge under it (Callis, 1969; Hanson, 1971; Young, 1970a, 1971a, 1972). For example, a rule forbidding misconduct, which used to be a common practice, did not give adequate notice of expected behavior to students.

The following are some of the more recent important court cases on substantive due process in higher education: *Soglin v. Kauffman* (1968); *Esteban v. Central Missouri State College* (1969); *Scott v. Alabama State Board of Education* (1969).

Criticisms of the Due Process Model

Numerous arguments have been made against the legalistic or due process model and the type of disciplinary system which it produces. Many people believe it undermines the informal, paternalistic, and friendly relationship between the institution and the student (Wright, 1969, and see Ratterman & Yanitelli, 1963) and that it may destroy many of the relaxed, informal, and unique features of campus life (Carnegie Commission, 1971).

Another criticism of the due process model is that it detracts from the educational function (Snoxell, 1965). According to Brady (1965), legalistic procedures confuse the issue of whose education the student's behavior is hampering. This view is apparently founded on the notion that due process safeguards are unnecessary since disciplinary sanctions are rehabilitative and not punitive (Ratliff, 1972). Not far removed from this approach is the traditional view that colleges should be immune from political and judicial pressures (Ratliff, 1972).

There are other, more practical arguments against the legal model of due process in discipline. One is that it is unduly costly for institutions (Ratliff, 1972; Robert, Brown, & Clemens, 1972; Van Alstyne, 1963) as well as students if they feel a lawyer is required (Robert et al., 1972). Another is that colleges lack several of the elements which are necessary for adversary-type hearings, such as organizational machinery for investigations (Heyman, 1966); legal authority such as, the power to subpoena and compel testimony (Van Alstyne, 1963); and judicial expertise (Robert et al., 1972). Third, such a quasi-legal system may make the students feel as though they are placed in double jeopardy (Robert et al., 1972), the legal reality notwithstanding. Fourth, the public may be angered at the amount of time and money spent on hearings involving demonstrators (Ratliff, 1972). Fifth, some college administrators have felt a decrease in the autonomy they feel they need to function effectively (Stein, 1974). Finally, the fundamental argument against the legal model is that college is a privilege and not a right, and does not need due process protections.

Due Process and Private Institutions

Presently private colleges do not have to meet the due process requirements in student dismissal proceedings, because the courts have held they are not engaged in state action and, therefore, do not fall under the due process clause of the Fourteenth Amendment (see *Greene v. Howard University*, 1967; *Grossner v. Columbia University*, 1968). Thus, attendance at a private college is considered a privilege, to which the *Dixon* analogy of education as a property right does not apply, and the student-institutional relationship is viewed as contractual (see *Anthony v. Syracuse University*, 1928). Many authorities anticipate that private institutions will soon be forced by the courts to meet the due process requirements ("An Overview," 1970; Fisher, 1971; Hanson, 1971; M. T. Johnson, 1964; McCay, 1970; Smith & Kirk, 1971b; Yegge, 1968), and several state that this is the only sensible course the courts can follow ("An Overview," 1970; Jacobson, 1963; M. T. Johnson, 1964).

The courts are expected to abolish the public-private distinction for the purpose of disciplinary due process for a variety of reasons. Federal and state support to private institutions is increasing ("An Overview," 1970; Fisher, 1971; Hanson, 1971; Mash, 1971; McCay, 1970). Private colleges fall under state regulations and charters and perform a public function — education ("An Overview," 1970; Fisher, 1971; Mash, 1971). Private colleges are often vested with quasi-public or quasi-governmental powers ("An Overview," 1970). Even private institutions should not be allowed to take away the constitutional rights of students (Mash, 1971; see *Carr v. St. John's University*, 1962); and dismissal from a private college is no different from dismissal from a public one in terms of the consequences for the individual student.

Even if the courts do not do away with the public-private distinction, the rights of private college students in disciplinary matters may be protected since procedural reforms tend to become normative in higher education irrespective of public-private labels (Hanson, 1971), and the progressive role of higher education in our society would seem to dictate that students be afforded the best possible due process regardless of the court decisions (Fisher, 1971; Jacobson, 1963).

Due Process Research

A survey of seventy-two state institutions revealed that many institutions did not follow adequate due process procedures (Van Alstyne, 1963): (a) 43 percent of the colleges did not provide students with a list of proscribed behavior, (b) 57 percent gave no notice of the specific charges, (c) 16 percent held no hearings, (d) 47 percent allowed administrators who made the charges in disciplinary cases to sit in judgment, (e) 36 percent did not permit the student to have counsel or an advisor, (f) 26 percent did not allow the accused to face opposing witnesses, (g) 85 percent permitted consideration of witness testimony that was not available for cross-examination, and (h) 47 percent permitted consideration of improperly acquired evidence.

In attempting to assess the impact of *Dixon* and *Knight* on disciplinary procedures in 361 institutions, Durst (1968) found the following changes to have occurred from the academic years 1960-61 to 1967-68: (a) More specific information was being provided to students on disciplinary programs, (b) more people were involved in hearing serious cases, (c) the handling of serious cases became more formalized, more trial-like, and (d) student disciplinary records had become more confidential. However, Durst concluded that these changes had resulted from "changing social and philosophical orientations ... rather than the impact of Dixon and Knight cases" (p. 127).

The 1967 NASPA study (Dutton, Smith, & Zarle, 1969) indicated that most of the 558 member institutions informed students of the charges, their rights, and existing procedures; issued a written notice of the charges; allowed counsel; allowed the student to call witnesses and ask questions of them and the judicial body; gave the student written notice of the decision; and provided the names of opposing witnesses. Few institutions considered evidence not presented at the hearing; had case investigators sitting in judgement; did not publish their conduct standards, hearing procedures, nor the student's rights; and did not maintain an official hearing record. Approximately half of the institutions permitted legal counsel, had no policy statement on access to conduct records, and revealed conduct records to government agencies such as the FBI and the military. The authors concluded that large, public universities showed the most concern for procedures to insure fairness and that, although too few colleges really explore the purposes and procedures for their disciplinary process, they generally followed accepted fundamental due process as reflected in the "Joint Statement of Rights and Freedoms of Students" (1968) and the recent court decisions.

The most recent survey of disciplinary procedures supports Van Alstyne's (1963) and the NASPA study's results and indicates little has changed in the area in the past few years. Leslie and Satryb's (1974) findings based on returns from sixty-three public and thirty-five private four-year institutions were: (a) 86 percent of public and 80 percent of private colleges issue written charges; (b) 89/83 percent conduct formal hearings; (c) 86/77 percent receive and present evidence; (d) 25/14 percent do not allow *ex parte* communications; (e) 35/17 percent permit attorney representation; (f) 67/60 percent permit advisor representation; (g) 43/37 percent recognize the accused's right not to testify; (h) 73/60 percent make a transcript of the hearings; (i) 84/57 percent issue a copy of the findings; (j) 84/71 percent recognize the student's right of appeal; (k) 70/54 percent use appeal boards to review; (l) 81/77 percent allow the accused to present and question witnesses; (m) 30/31 percent hold prehearing investigations; (n) 8/9 percent have "informal hearings"; (o) 24/11 percent require a plea; (p) 90/37 percent review by an appeal officer.

Unfortunately, there is apparently nothing to refute the conclusion reached in the *Duke Law Journal* ("Procedural Due Process," 1970) that "many existing procedures fail to satisfy even the minimal current requirements of due process" (p. 793).

Organization Statements

Recommendations concerning conduct regulations, disciplinary procedures, and student rights which go beyond even the most pioneering court decisions have been made by the American Civil Liberties Union (1970), National Education Association (1971), New York University School of Law (1968), and the endorsers of the "Joint Statement on Rights and Freedoms of Students" (1968) which includes a number of professional organizations in addition to the American Association of University Professors, Unites States National Student Association, Association of American Colleges, National Association of Student Personnel Administrators, and the National Association of Women Deans, Administrators, and Counselors.

ADMINISTRATION

For many decades on most campuses the dean served as investigator, prosecutor, judge, jury, counselor, and probation officer for all disciplinary cases. In recent years many different kinds of campus judiciaries have developed. Most are derived from four basic models: the ombudsman, the campus hearing officer, the campus attorney, and the tribunal.

Models

The ombudsman (see Ombudsman chapter) informally handles minor complaints from students or any other member of the campus community, and works independently, without formal connection to other disciplinary bodies. The advantage of this model is that it keeps minor complaints out of campus courts and saves administrators' time (Carnegie Commission, 1971).

The campus hearing officer is a specialized administrator charged with the responsibility of the total disciplinary function. The officer may keep all disciplinary records, organize disciplinary committees and supervise their operation, serve as liaison to the university lawyer in serious matters, investigate the facts in cases, and make provisional decisions on cases subject to review (Carlson & Hubbell, 1971; Carnegie Commission, 1971). This position removes discipline from the dean's office and injects expertise into the disciplinary process through the special training of the officer (Bakken, 1968). The Carnegie Commission has also suggested the position of campus attorney, whose duty it is to prosecute in disciplinary cases, much as the district attorney does in criminal matters. The campus attorney model has essentially the same advantages as does that of the campus hearing officer: specialization and expertise.

Probably every college has some form of disciplinary tribunal which considers evidence, hears arguments, and renders decisions. There are several alternative compositions of such tribunals: faculty/staff only, students only, mixed student-faculty/staff, and persons external to the college community. A tribunal composed entirely of faculty and/or staff members avoids the problem of student turnover, but it has the distinct disadvantage of probably being unacceptable to students.

A tribunal composed solely of students avoids the unacceptability problem; has students "take direct responsibility for group morality and for the constructive education of the individual through the sentences" (Yost, 1945, p. 11); has peers judging peers (Yost, 1945); and has members who are knowledgeable in the ways of the campus life and understand student mores (St. Antoine, 1971). However, such tribunals may also have a student bias against unpopular rules, may be unacceptable to nonstudents (St. Antoine, 1971), and may suffer from turnover and training problems as well as overwork (Yost, 1945). Perhaps the jurisdiction of this type of tribunal should be confined to problems between students and their organizations (St. Antoine, 1971).

Mixed student-faculty/staff tribunals, because they avoid many of the difficulties of the two previous types, may be the most prevalent. In fact, of 558 NASPA institutions, 71 percent had administrators, 78 percent had students, and 85 percent had faculty on their judicial bodies (Dutton, Smith, & Zarle, 1969). Such tribunals provide decisions more acceptable to the community as a whole (Farer, 1969) and represent a variety of viewpoints (St. Antoine, 1971). Of course, the turnover and training problems are not completely avoided, but they are mitigated by the continuing presence of the faculty/staff members. The major disadvantage here is the possibility of factionalism along political lines, students versus nonstudents (St. Antoine, 1971).

The use of tribunals composed entirely of persons who are not members of the campus community has been recommended by the Carnegie Commission (1971) for serious cases involving rights and external legal violations, such as protest cases. Such tribunals have the advantage of impartiality and objectivity since they are not subject to campus pressures. But they may not understand the peculiar mores of the campus or fully appreciate the impact of the sanctions. Also, they may not be acceptable to either side of the dispute because they are not members of the campus community and have no right to sit in judgment (St. Antoine, 1971).

Establishing a Disciplinary System

To establish a judicial tribunal, decisions have to be made concerning the method of member selection, of which there are several alternatives: unilateral appointment, joint student-faculty selection, and random selection; the tribunal's scope of jurisdiction; and the availability of appeal and to whom appeals might be made from the tribunal's decisions (St. Antoine, 1971). Procedures and rules of conduct require consideration of the unique character of the institution and the degree to which the institution is going to insert itself into the lives of its students (Fisher, 1970).

One principle underlies all campus judicial systems. It is the importance of heavy student participation in all phases of the disciplinary process (ACLU, 1970; Beaney, 1969; Clark et al., 1952; Collins, 1967; DeSena, 1963; Farer, 1969; Holmes & Delabarre, 1963; Joint Statement, 1968; Kroeker & Carver, 1968; Prusok, 1961; Rivet, 1967; Smith & Kirk, 1971a; Whitaker, 1961; Williamson, 1956, 1961). For example, one survey of 558 colleges found that 80 percent had student participation in the formulation of conduct standards (Dutton, Smith, & Zarle, 1969).

A completely student-run judicial system allows responsibility for self-direction and recognition of special student problems. The students should have input in deciding the court's purpose, function, and powers, all of which must be clearly delimited and reflective of student values. A training program for court members is necessary and the court's effectiveness should be continuously evaluated (DeSena, 1963).

Difficulties in Discipline

In recent years the college disciplinary function has become increasingly difficult to carry out and to justify to members of the campus community and to the public. For one thing, there is less consensus on standards of conduct in our society than in earlier times (Carnegie Commission, 1971). Also, students' moral values have changed rapidly in the last decade or so (Mash, 1971); they are more conscious of their rights (Caldwell, 1970; Karlesky & Stephenson, 1971); they are more sophisticated and, therefore, they question college policy and tradition more closely (Smith & Kirk, 1971a); they are more mobile, which places off-campus behavior out of the institution's reach (Smith & Kirk, 1971a); and as enrollments decrease, they will gain more consumer powers which may lead to even more "due processitis" (Smith & Kirk, 1971a).

Other difficulties derive from political protest (Carnegie Commission, 1971). Protest cases politicize the procedure (Hanson, 1971); they involve more outsiders; and the proscribed behavior at issue is often in challenge to the authority which governs and structures the institution (Carnegie Commission, 1971). Further, activists often challenge the morality of the rule, and the hearing then becomes a public forum on the institution's morality or values (Carlson & Hubbell, 1971).

Added turmoil comes from the increased interest the courts have taken in the discipline process. Perkins (1967) attributes this to: (a) More public support leads to more public scrutiny, (b) the increasing importance of education has shifted attention from the college's to the student's rights, (c) egalitarianism in higher education or the increased importance of equality of treatment, (d) "the expansion of civil rights protection by public authority" (p. 5), and (e) "the erosion of disciplinary supervision of the young by the family, school, and college" (p. 6). For whatever reason, the courts have taken away the power of administrative fiat (Carlson & Hubbell, 1971), and the constitutional model of the student-institutional relationship has led to greater student freedom which, in turn, has led to more criticism from students (Smith & Kirk, 1971a; Van Alstyne, 1969).

As the sizes of campuses increased in the 1950's and 1960's, not only was there a greater variety of disciplinary cases (Karlesky & Stephenson, 1971; Mueller, 1961) but also, the number of different campus disciplinary committees increased; resulting in confusion over accountability (Carlson & Hubbell, 1971). Finally, discipline is unpopular. And because of its unpopularity, faculty have become more reluctant to serve in a judicial capacity (Carnegie Commission, 1971), and it has not attracted the best efforts of the college student personnel profession (Mueller, 1961).

Administrator Roles

Dutton, Smith, and Zarle (1969) have identified various levels of involvement for those who are responsible for campus discipline: (a) noninvolvement, which frees the college student personnel worker to concentrate on student problems and their education; (b) involvement limited to case investigation and preparation with no adjudicatory decision making, which allows all cases to be referred to the proper judicial body; (c) involvement limited to case investigation, preparation, and decision making in minor cases that are subject to review, which lends itself to quick disposal of less serious offenses; (d) full involvement, with action on all minor cases, referral of major ones to the judicial body on which the administrator sits as chairperson, and final authority.

In choosing a level of involvement, Dutton et al. suggest that several factors be considered: What are the dean's most essential functions? What is the purpose of disciplining and which disciplinary approach is the most desirable? What role should students and faculty play? Should discipline be more of an administrative or a community concern? What procedures best protect the student and the institution?

The Profession and Discipline

The disciplinary function has meant many things to the college student personnel profession over the years. In a way, it is synonymous with the origin of the profession. It has also been the source of more dissension, complaint, distrust, and fear in the profession than probably any other problem (Fley, 1964). It was the cause for considerable embarassment in the 1960's when the courts found it necessary to impose due process safeguards to stop abuses of discretion on the part of some administrators. And it has been a tightrope between community expectations and student demands for independence (Van Alstyne, 1966). But perhaps more importantly, it has been a mirror into which the profession can look, and ask of itself: "Do the methods we use in discipline reflect the training and knowledge we profess?" (Seward, 1961, p. 196, italics omitted).

DISCIPLINARY COUNSELING

Disciplinary counseling is a form of corrective action that is "sympathetic but firm counseling to aid the individual to gain insight and be willing to accept restrictions on his [her] individual autonomy and behavior" (Williamson, 1963, p. 13). While most proponents of disciplinary counseling advocate a directive approach, as does Williamson, some (Rush, 1945) have promoted a Rogerian, or nondirective, approach. The theoretical underpinnings of disciplinary counseling are that disciplinary problems are problems of adjustment (Foley, 1947) and that "within its inherent dimensions, disciplinary counseling is rehabilitation" (Williamson & Foley, 1949, p. 206, italics omitted).

The most commonly stated objective of disciplinary counseling is to help the individual gain insight into the sources and the consequences of his or her misbehavior (Gometz & Parker, 1968; Mueller, 1961; Peiffer & Walker, 1957; Williamson, 1963; Williamson & Foley, 1949). Another objective is to help the individual change to more acceptable behavior

(Gometz & Parker, 1968; Williamson, 1955, 1963) through teaching emotional stability, moral judgment, self-reliance, and self-control (Mueller, 1961) and through teaching that group membership requires certain restrictions on personal freedom and autonomy (Williamson, 1963).

Advantages

The therapeutic advantages of disciplinary counseling over the traditional, sanction-oriented approach to discipline are that reeducation can begin immediately; the student's defenses can be dealt with early so that there is nothing to hide; continuing the educational process with one person lends itself to a relaxed, cooperative relationship; "punishment prior to insight is like the cart before the horse" (Foley, 1947, p. 579); and punishment can never be personalized as can counseling.

Others believe that the advantages of disciplinary counseling derive from the college student personnel point of view in that the student is viewed and treated as a whole and is helped to improve in self-actualization, maturity, social and self-responsibility, social stability, and personal effectiveness (Gometz & Parker, 1968). Likewise, the disciplinary counselor explores all aspects of the student's life adjustment and may thereby deal with deep-seated sources of misbehavior which might never be recognized without the use of counseling (Williamson & Foley, 1949).

The advantages of disciplinary counseling over the punitive approach to discipline are that it avoids the contest between the individual and the institution that frequently follows from the punitive approach (Snoxell, 1960). Also, it avoids the biggest weaknesses in most disciplinary programs (Williamson, 1955): lack of privacy; lack of confidentiality (see Nugent & Pareis in Other Issues section); the use of punishment which is ineffective, repressive, and growth arresting; and the inhuman, impersonal manner of handling and processing the offender. An additional advantage is that screening disciplinary cases through the counseling process prior to administrative or committee action aids in handling minor problems without formality (Wrenn, 1949).

Counseling and Discipline Antithetical?

Many counselors and student personnel administrators believe that counseling and discipline are antithetical, based on several assumptions, all of which have been challenged by Gometz and Parker (1968) and Snoxell (1960).

Disciplinarians are "bad guys" and counselors are "good guys." Gometz and Parker respond that the disciplinary counselor need not be repressive, retributive, harsh, strict, or punitive.

Involuntary counseling is ineffective. Snoxell replies that, in view of its widespread use and the absence of empirical study in support of it, such a conclusion is not warranted. Gometz and Parker also disagree with this assumption because all counseling is, in a sense, forced; in disciplinary counseling the force is just a different kind from a different source, the institution.

The client should be able to terminate the counseling relationship at will. Snoxell ignores the ethical issue and responds that, even though the client may want to terminate the relationship, as long as he or she is kept in counseling, there is a greater likelihood of rehabilitative progress.

Counselors never set limits and must remain nonjudgmental. Gometz and Parker reply that, even if an external authority such as the institution were to impose unwanted limits, the disciplinary counselor could easily circumvent them in the counseling process. Snoxell refutes the judgmental issue by saying that there is adequate empirical evidence to support the idea that a counselor can be both judgmental and effective.

Counselors only care about their clients and not about the institution, and so they do not have the requisite institutional concerns to properly counsel in a disciplinary situation. This just is not true, say Gometz and Parker, if everyone lives up to the college student personnel point of view.

The primary question in regard to discipline and counseling is raised by Gometz and Parker: "Is more to be gained for the discipline function by the semantic alliance with counseling than will be lost to the counseling function" (p. 442)?

Prerequisites for Effectiveness

For disciplinary counseling to be effective, the counselor must be keenly aware of current student and societal attitudes and the differences between them; the client's degree of adherence to both student and societal hierarchies of values; the student's ability to change, which is dependent on the student's personal code of behavior, the student's practice of that code, and the student's level of intelligence; and the effect the case will have on the general campus morale (Mueller, 1958, 1961). Also the good disciplinary counselor must be highly trained in psychotherapy as well as in counseling psychology, must have enough time to devote to a large number of interviews, must exhibit sympathetic and empathic understanding in the interviews, and be able to teach insightful acceptance of accountability of personal behavior to the client (Williamson, 1963).

On the other hand, counselors may lose rapport and consequently, effectiveness, if they have the authority to discipline (Wrenn, 1949). That counselors should not actually select and administer sanctions or punishments to the client-offender, is a view held by 90 percent of 461 counseling service directors and a practice at 84 percent of their services (Nugent & Pareis, 1968).

Other Issues

One issue, confidentiality of information, seems relatively clear in the professional code of ethics (American Personnel and Guidance Association, 1971). However, when counselors are dealing with disciplinary cases, confidentiality may be fraught with problems.

Nugent and Pareis (1968) found that in only 59 percent of 461 counseling services were the files completely confidential. In fact, 10 percent of the services routinely made the discipline files available to the dean of students and 21 percent gave information to administrators for use in disciplinary cases. These data appear to refute Williamson's (1955) claim that disciplinary counseling provides greater confidentiality than traditional disciplinary programs, as well as indicate practices which probably violate the professional code of ethics and in some states may be illegal.

Another issue arises from the involuntary nature of the counseling relationship. How does it fit with the counselor's personal and professional ethics? What is likely to be the student's perception of the counselor in the initial stages of counseling (Snoxell, 1960)? What effect will hostility on the part of the involuntary client have on the desired outcome of counseling (Snoxell, 1960)? Is contrition a valid indication of reformation (Williamson, 1963)? How does a counselor explain and interpret institutionally imposed limits on behavior in the face of widely divergent opinions about the extent of the institution's legitimate interest in student behavior (Snoxell, 1960)?

Another concern is the matter of expense to the institution in relation to the return. Disciplinary counseling is very costly for the estimated 2 percent of the student body directly served (Mueller, 1961; Williamson & Foley, 1949). Without reference to actual cost figures, substantially more than 2 percent of the budget of a counseling service which provides disciplinary counseling goes toward disciplinary cases. Of course, it may still be cheaper for the college than dismissing the student and foregoing the tuition.

Another important issue in disciplinary counseling is where it should be practiced. Does it belong in the counseling service, an administrative office, or the special discipline office on campus? From 20 percent to 40 percent of counseling services surveyed (Anderson, 1970; Oetting, Ivey, & Weigel, 1970) provided disciplinary counseling. The counseling expertise is readily available in the counseling service, but handling discipline cases may have an effect on the reputation of the counseling service and the credibility of the counselor.

Research

The small amount of research on discipline (Bailey, 1941, 1950; LeMay, 1968) is attributed to the fact that the concept or definition of discipline and, therefore, the criteria for judging an individual as a disciplinary case keep changing and to the fact that "the concept involves several variables which cannot be adequately managed for research purposes, granting that they can even be identified" (Woodruff, 1960, p. 381).

Description of Offenders

Disciplinary difficulties are more likely to involve younger students on campus and disproportionately likely to be men (Bazik & Meyering, 1965; Tisdale & Brown, 1965; Williamson, Jorve, & Lagerstedt-Knudson, 1952). Disciplined students have been found to have the same scholastic ability as the rest of the student body (Bazik & Meyering, Williamson et al.) and to have less (Tisdale & Brown); to have lower grade point averages (Bazik & Meyering, Tisdale & Brown) and similar grade point averages (Williamson et al.). Other studies suggest that the fathers of offenders do not have particular occupational backgrounds (Bazik & Meyering); offenders are more likely to get into disciplinary difficulties again (Tisdale & Brown); and offenders are more likely to involve fraternity and sorority members (Lenning, 1970; Tisdale & Brown).

Personality Characteristics of Offenders

Using the California Personality Inventory, differences were found between sixty-six matched pairs of disciplined men and undergraduate residence hall counselors (Work, 1969). The disciplinary cases had spontaneous, expressive, ebullient natures; marked deficiencies in socialization, maturity, responsibility; and difficulty in interpersonal relations. They were aggressive, assertive, and impulsive; had little concern for the wants and needs of others; were easily disorganized under stress or pressure; were pessimistic about their occupational futures; and lacked insight and self-understanding. Their behavior was undercontrolled and their greatest concern was for personal pleasure and diversion.

Using the Minnesota Multiphasic Personality Inventory

(MMPI) to compare seventy undergraduate male offenders to a control group, more father conflict, aggressive or belligerent behavior, and rationalization were found for those involved in alcohol and disorderly misconduct, but no differences were found between those involved in theft, burglary, and other misconduct (LeMay & Murphy, 1967).

Comparing the MMPI scores of forty twice-disciplined first-year female students and controls indicated that neuroticism was not a characteristic of these women but that they had a distorted outlook on life; they reacted to everyday problems in an unusually animated way which might lead to antisocial or irrational manic behavior; and they had a tendency to be sensitive and feel unduly controlled, limited, and mistreated by others. They also had significantly less masculine scores than the nonoffenders (Osborne, Sanders, & Young, 1956). Female offenders have also been found to be more flexible and less dogmatic (Cummins, 1966; Cummins & Lindblade, 1967).

Elton and Rose (1966) concluded from a study of 135 freshmen with varying degrees of disciplinary difficulties that "it is the conforming student who adapts best to our large, impersonal, educational institutions" (p. 434).

Attitudes

The attitudes of students, parents, faculty, and staff toward disciplinary situations, regulations, and processes were surveyed extensively during the 1960's.

SPECIFIC OFFENSES. Studies of attitudes toward specific disciplinary offenses suggest that people are most concerned with behavior that directly affects them. With respect to theft, students (men more than women and older more than younger students) severely condemn such acts for material value (Hodinko, 1964) and do so more than faculty, staff, residence hall counselors, and tribunal members (Murphy & Hanna, 1964). But when the theft was for novelty value, tribunal members and hall counselors were most punitive; and when it was for convenience, faculty and staff were most severe (Murphy & Hanna).

Faculty were more censorious of academic dishonesty, such

as cheating and plagiarism, than were students (Jenison, 1972) and students were more lenient than other groups (Murphy & Hanna). But students condemned cheating involving collusion (Hodinko). Faculty and staff were more severe than students where destruction of property was concerned (Murphy & Hanna), and male and older students were more severe than female and younger students (Hodinko). Female and younger students more than male and older students (Hodinko) and staff members were more severe than other groups in situations involving sexual promiscuity (Murphy & Hanna).

Concerning misuse of alcohol, the ranking of groups from most to least punitive in one study (Prusok, 1961) was parents, students, and student personnel workers, but in another (Murphy & Hanna) faculty and staff were found to be much more severe than other groups. With respect to mass demonstration, student tribunal members most strongly condemned the organizers of them, while participants were most severely viewed by staff members and residence hall counselors (Murphy & Hanna). Situations involving disorderly conduct, violations of probation, and those with civil implications were viewed more severely by parents than by students and personnel workers, while those involving gambling and violations of rules concerning automobiles were seen as more serious by personnel workers than by students and parents (Prusok).

JURISDICTION. Over the entire range of disciplinary situations Prusok (1961, 1963) determined that students, and then parents, most often felt that the institution should have no jurisdiction, while student personnel workers wanted the broadest jurisdiction for the institution. Recently it was found that both students and faculty (student personnel workers were not compared) consistently believed that off-campus behavior was none of the colleges' business (Jenison, 1972).

SERIOUSNESS OF OFFENSES. In surveying thirty-five administrators from nine public institutions in six midwestern and Rocky Mountain states, Sillers and Feder (1964) concluded: (a) There is no relationship between the attitudes toward the seriousness of an offense and the administrator's role, training, age, or experience; (b) Information and knowledge concerning the offender's background had little bearing on the administrator's perceptions of the seriousness of the offense, suggesting that penalties are built-in and that background data collection is merely a ritual; (c) The approaches of the general and student personnel administrators toward the offenses were very similar. As explanation for this last finding, Sillers and Feder suggest that either there is no college student personnel point of view in operation or that general administrators have been won over to the college student personnel point of view.

PURPOSE OF DISCIPLINE. Dutton, Appleton, and Birch (1970) queried 458 chief student personnel administrators, 430 faculty members, 414 presidents, 394 student body presidents, and 347 student newspaper editors in a national survey of all NASPA member institutions in 1966 to determine their opinions as to the purpose of discipline in higher education. They found that more than three fourths of all the groups, including the deans, believed that the main purpose of conduct regulations was "simply to maintain reasonable control and order in the academic community" (p. 10).

REGULATIONS. At the University of Wisconsin during the 1963-64 academic year, Hubbell (1967) found that, of the 590 students sampled, 64 percent were satisfied with the scope of the University's regulations, 23 percent thought the regulations were too strict, and 8 percent felt they were too lenient. In contrast, only 35 percent of the 221 student personnel workers surveyed were satisfied with the regulations, 21 percent thought they were too strict, while 33 percent considered them too lenient. In addition, 58 percent of the student personnel workers felt the University had the prerogative to proscribe out-of-class behavior, while 29 percent felt otherwise. An earlier report (Hubbell, 1966), which included parents and faculty, determined that, with regard to ten misconduct cases, university action was poorly anticipated by all of these sample groups and that there was a great disparity in groups' judgments.

DUE PROCESS. Attitudes of academic community members toward disciplinary processes which meet substantive and procedural due process requirements have been assessed. At a large southwestern state college, Dollar (1969) surveyed 217 disciplined students and found that the majority felt the process was sound, fair, and the hearings courteous. One fourth of them reported that they had not established rapport with the disciplinary coordinator. Dollar concluded that as the severity of the penalty increased, rapport decreased. He also found that one fourth questioned the quality of the hearings and slightly less than that proportion felt the disciplinary measures to which they were subject were harsh, arbitrary, and unjust. But Williams and Rhodes (1969) concluded that the 368 disciplined males at Pennsylvania State University held more favorable attitudes toward the disciplinary process than nondisciplined males and their involvement with the process had no effect on their satisfaction with their collegiate environment.

The attitudes of student personnel workers toward the legal model of due process in the disciplinary process was assessed by Phelps (1968) when he surveyed 518 NASPA delegates in 1967 and 1968. He concluded that student personnel workers were not against the legal model in the disciplinary process, especially when it is applied to a formal hearing, and that favorability toward it has a positive relationship to the size of their institution, to public institutions, and to younger ages of the student personnel workers. He also found, however, that they tend *not* to favor those procedures which cut into their authority or which complicate informal procedures.

REFERENCES

American Civil Liberties Union (ACLU). *Academic freedom and civil liberties of students in colleges and universities.* New York: Author, 1970.

American Personnel and Guidance Association. Ethical Standards. *Personnel and Guidance Journal,* 1971, *50,* 327-330.

Anderson, W. Services offered by college counseling centers. *Journal of Counseling Psychology,* 1970, *17,* 380-382.

Anthony v. Syracuse University, 244 App. Div. 487 (1928).

Arndt, J. R. Substantive due process in public higher education: 1959-1969. *Journal of College Student Personnel,* 1971, *12,* 83-94.

Bailey, H. W. Disciplinary procedures. In M. S. Monroe (Ed.), *Encyclopedia of educational research.* New York: Macmillan, 1941.

Bailey, H. W. Disciplinary procedures. In M. S. Monroe (Ed.), *Encyclopedia of educational research.* New York: Macmillan, 1950.

Bakken, C. J. Student rights as seen by a lawyer-educator. *Journal of College Student Personnel,* 1965, *6,* 136-144.

Bakken, C. J. The legal aspects of *in loco parentis. Journal of College Student Personnel,* 1967, *8,* 234-236.

Bakken, C. J. *The legal basis of college student personnel work.* Washington, D. C.: American Personnel and Guidance Association, 1968. (Student Personnel Monograph Series, No. 2)

Barker v. Hardway, 283 F. Supp. 288 (1968).

Bazik, A., & Meyering, R. A. Characteristics of college students involved in disciplinary problems. *Journal of the National Association for Women Deans, Administrators, and Counselors,* 1965, *28,* 173-176.

Beaney, W. M. Students, higher education, and the law. *Denver Law Journal,* 1968, *45,* 511-524.

Beaney, W. M. Some legal problems of higher education. *Journal of the National Association for Women Deans, Administrators, and Counselors,* 1969, *32,* 162-169.

Black, H. C. *Black's law dictionary.* St. Paul, Minn.: West Publishing, 1968.

Brady, T. A. A university and student discipline. In T. A. Brady & L. F. Snoxell, *Student discipline in higher education.* Washington, D. C.: American Personnel and Guidance Association, 1965. (Student Personnel Monograph Series, No. 5)

Brubacher, J. S. The impact of the courts on higher education. *Journal of Law and Education,* 1973, *2,* 267-282.

Brubacher, J. S., & Rudy, W. *Higher education in transition.* New York: Harper & Row, 1968.

Byse, C. *Procedure in student dismissal proceedings: Law and policy.* Paper presented at the 34th Annual Conference of the National Association of Student Personnel Administrators, Philadelphia, April 1962.

Byse, C. Procedure in student dismissal proceedings: Law and policy. *Journal of College Student Personnel,* 1963, *4,* 130-143.

Byse, C. Procedural due process and the college student: Law and policy. In L. E. Dennis & J. F. Kauffman (Eds.), *The college and the student.* Washington, D. C.: American Council on Education, 1966.

Caldwell, W. F. The changing legal relationship between students and universities. *College and University,* 1970, *45,* 245-265.

Callis, R. Educational aspects of *in loco parentis. Journal of College Student Personnel,* 1967, *8,* 231-233.

Callis, R. The courts and the colleges: 1968. *Journal of College Student Personnel,* 1969, *10,* 75-86.

Carlson, J. M., & Hubbell, R. N. One more time: The future of college student discipline. *NASPA Journal,* 1971, *9,* 127-133.

Carnegie Commission on Higher Education. *Dissent and disruption.* New York: McGraw-Hill, 1971.

Carr v. St. John's University, 231 NYS 2d 410 (1962).

Carrington, P. D. On civilizing university discipline. In G. W. Holmes (Ed.), *Law and discipline on campus*. Ann Arbor, Mich.: Institute of Continuing Legal Education, 1971.

Cazier, S. Student power and *in loco parentis*. In J. Foster & D. Long (Eds.), *Protest! Student activism in America*. New York: William Morrow, 1970.

Clark, S. G., Hagie, D. G., & Landrus, W. M. Discipline in college residence halls. *Personnel and Guidance Journal*, 1952, *31*, 189-193.

Collins, C. C. Student rights and due process. *Community and Junior College Bulletin*, 1967, *37*(7), 34; 36.

Cummins, E. J. Are disciplinary students different? *Personnel and Guidance Journal*, 1966, *44*, 624-627.

Cummins, E. J., & Lindblade, Z. G. Sex-based differences among student disciplinary offenders. *Journal of Counseling Psychology*, 1967, *14*, 81-85.

DeSena, P. A. Constructive discipline through student courts. *Journal of College Student Personnel*, 1963, *6*, 175-179.

Dixon v. Alabama State Board of Education, 294 F. 2d 150 (1961).

Dollar, R. J. Disciplined college students' opinions of the disciplinary process. *Journal of College Student Personnel*, 1969, *10*, 219-222.

Due v. Florida A & M University, 233 F. Supp. 396 (1963).

Durst, R. H. The impact of court decisions rendered in the Dixon and Knight cases on student disciplinary procedures in public institutions of higher education in the United States (Doctoral dissertation, Purdue University, 1968). *Dissertation Abstracts*, 1969, *29*, 2473A-2474A. (University Microfilms No. 69-2910)

Dutton, T. B., Appleton, J. R., & Birch, E. E. *Assumptions and beliefs of selected members of the academic community: A special report of the NASPA Division of Research and Program Development*. Buffalo: National Association of Student Personnel Administrators, 1970.

Dutton, T. B., Smith F. W., & Zarle, T. *Institutional approaches to the adjudication of student misconduct*. Buffalo: National Association of Student Personnel Administrators, 1969.

Elton, C. F., & Rose, H. A. Personality characteristics: Their relevance in disciplinary cases. *Journal of Counseling Psychology*, 1966, *13*, 431-435.

Esteban v. Central Missouri State College, 290 F. Supp. 622 (1969).

Farer, T. J. The array of sanctions. In G. W. Holmes (Ed.), *Student protest and the law*. Ann Arbor, Mich.: Institute of Continuing Legal Education, 1969.

Fisher, T. C. *Due process in the student-institutional relationship*. Washington, D. C.: American Association of State Colleges and Universities, 1970.

Fisher, T. C. The rights and responsibilities of students in private institutions: The decline and fall of an artificial distinction. In D. P.

Young (Ed.), *Higher education: The law and individual rights and responsibilities.* Athens: University of Georgia, Institute of Higher Education, 1971.

Fley, J. Changing approaches to discipline in student personnel work. *Journal of the National Association for Women Deans, Administrators, and Counselors,* 1964, *27,* 105-113.

Foley, J. D. Discipline: A student counseling approach. *Educational and Psychological Measurement,* 1947, *7,* 569-582.

Goldberg v. The Regents of the University of California, 248 Cal. App. 867 (1967).

Goldman, A. L. The university and the liberty of its students — a fiduciary theory. *Kentucky Law Journal,* 1966, *54,* 643-682.

Gometz, L., & Parker, C] A. Disciplinary counseling: A contradiction? *Personnel and Guidance Journal,* 1968, *46,* 437-443.

Gordon, K. W. Due process: A swing toward student rights. *Journal of College Student Personnel,* 1971, *12,* 95-101.

Gott v. Berea College, 156 Ky 376 (1913).

Greene v. Howard University, 271 F. Supp. 609 (1967).

Grossner v. Columbia University, 287 F. Supp. 535 (1968).

Hagie, D. G. The law and student dismissal procedures. *Educational Record,* 1966, *47,* 518-524.

Hanson, D. J. Student rights and the institutional response. *Journal of the National Association for Women Deans, Administrators, and Counselors,* 1971, *35,* 40-48.

Hawkes, H. E. College administration. *Journal of Higher Education,* 1930, *1,* 245-253.

Hegel v. Langson, 273 N. E. 2d 351 (1971).

Heyman, I. M. Some thoughts on university disciplinary proceedings. *California Law Review,* 1966, *54,* 73-87.

Hodinko, B. A. A study of student opinion regarding collegiate discipline situations. *Journal of College Student Personnel,* 1964, *5,* 217-219; 225.

Holmes, J. E., & Delabarre, P. M. Discipline in residence halls. *Journal of College Student Personnel,* 1963, *4,* 188-189.

Hubbell, R. N. Varying perceptions of alleged misbehavior and resultant disciplinary action. *Journal of College Student Personnel,* 1966, *7,* 260-265.

Hubbell, R. N. Sociological and attitudinal factors relating to perception of college student misconduct. *Journal of College Student Personnel,* 1967, *8,* 318-321.

Jacobson, S. The expulsion of students and due process of law. *Journal of Higher Education,* 1963, *34,* 250-255.

Jenison, L. M. Attitudes of students and faculty toward selected disciplinary situations. *NASPA Journal,* 1972, *9,* 291-294.

Johnson, A. W. Double jeopardy — a misnomer: The relation of the student to the college and the courts. *Journal of Higher Education,* 1966, *37,*

274   *College Student Personnel Services*

16-23.

Johnson, M. T. The constitutional rights of college students. *Texas Law Review*, 1964, *42*, 344-363.

Joint statement on rights and freedoms of students. *AAUP Bulletin*, 1968, *54*, 258-261.

Karlesky, J. J., & Stephenson, D. G. Student disciplinary proceedings: Some preliminary questions. *Journal of Higher Education*, 1971, *42*, 648-656.

Knight v. State Board of Education, 200 F. Supp. 174 (1963).

Kroeker, L. L., & Carver, G. H. A developmental paradigm for discipline. *Journal of the National Association for Women Deans, Administrators, and Counselors*, 1968, *31*, 111-115.

LeMay, M. College disciplinary problems: A review. *Journal of College Student Personnel*, 1968, *9*, 180-189.

LeMay, M., & Murphy, T. A. MMPI patterns of college disciplinary referrals. *Journal of College Student Personnel*, 1967, *8*, 85-89.

Lenning, O. T. Understanding the student lawbreaker. *Journal of College Student Personnel*, 1970, *11*, 62-68.

Leonard, E. A. *Origins of personnel services in American higher education.* Minneapolis: University of Minnesota Press, 1956.

Leslie, D. W., & Satryb, R. P. Due process on due process? Some observations. *Journal of College Student Personnel*, 1974, *15*, 340-345.

Lloyd, A. The dean and discipline. *Journal of the National Association for Women Deans, Administrators, and Counselors*, 1945, *9*, 3-5.

Mash, D. J. Student discipline in higher education: A collision course with the courts? *NASPA Journal*, 1971, *8*, 148-155.

McCay, W. T. Legal pot pourri. Paper presented at the 21st Institute of Higher Education. Nashville, June 1969. *College Student Personnel Abstracts*, 1970, *5*, 380-381.

McCay, W. T. Student protest and discipline in private institutions. In D. P. Young (Ed.), *The law and student protest.* Athens: University of Georgia, Institute of Higher Education, 1970.

McKay, R. B. The student as private citizen. *Denver Law Journal*, 1968, *45*, 558-570.

Mueller, K. H. Theory for campus discipline. *Personnel and Guidance Journal*, 1958, *36*, 302-309.

Mueller, K. H. *Student personnel work in higher education.* Boston: Houghton Mifflin, 1961.

Murphy, R. O., & Hanna, N. Campus views of male student conduct. *Journal of College Student Personnel*, 1964, *6*, 74-78.

National Education Association Task Force on Student Involvement. *Code of student rights and responsibilities.* Washington, D. C.: National Education Association Publications, 1971.

New suggestions on disciplinary authority, *Intellect*, 1968, *96*, 62-64.

New York University School of Law. *Student conduct and disciplinary proceedings in a university setting.* New York: New York University

Press, 1968.

Nugent, F. A., & Pareis, E. N. Survey of present policies and practices in college counseling centers in the United States of America. *Journal of Counseling Psychology*, 1968, *15*, 94-97.

Oetting, E. R., Ivey, A. E., & Weigel, R. G. *The college and university counseling center.* Washington, D. C.: American College Personnel Association, 1970. (Student Personnel Monograph Series, No. 11)

Osborne, R. T., Sanders, W. B., & Young, F. M. MMPI patterns of college disciplinary cases. *Journal of Counseling Psychology*, 1956, *3*, 52-56.

An overview: The private university and due process. *Duke Law Journal*, 1970, pp. 795-807.

Paulsen, M. G. *Implications of recent court decisions involving rights and responsibilities on campus.* Paper presented at the 8th Annual Meeting of the American Association of State Colleges and Universities, Washington, D. C.: November, 1968. (ERIC Document Reproduction Service No. ED 029 603)

Peiffer, H. C., & Walker, D. E. The disciplinary interview. *Personnel and Guidance Journal*, 1957, *35*, 347-350.

Penney, J. F. Variations on a theme: *In loco parentis. Journal of College Student Personnel*, 1967, *8*, 22-25.

Perkins, J. A. *The university and due process.* Paper presented at the 82nd Annual Meeting of the New England Association of Colleges and Secondary Schools, Boston, 1967. (ERIC Document Reproduction Service No. ED 030 379)

Phelps, F. D. Personnel workers' attitudes toward the legal model of due process in campus discipline cases (Doctoral dissertation, Northwestern University, 1968). *Dissertation Abstracts*, 1969, *29*, 3839A-3840A. (University Microfilms No. 69-6976)

Procedural due process and campus disorder: A comparison of law and practice. *Duke Law Journal*, 1970, pp. 763-794.

Prusok, R. E. Students, student personnel worker, and parent attitudes toward student discipline. *Personnel and Guidance Journal*, 1961, *40*, 247-253.

Prusok, R. E. An investigation of attitudes toward student discipline. *Journal of College Student Personnel*, 1963, *5*, 12-19.

Ratliff, R. C. *Constitutional rights of college students: A study in case law.* Metuchen, N. J.: Scarecrow Press, 1972.

Ratterman, P. H., & Yanitelli, V. R. A dialogue on discipline. *NASPA Journal*, 1963, *1*, 7-10.

Rivet, H. L. Student discipline. *NASPA Journal*, 1967, *5*, 215-216.

Robert, O. D., Brown, C. W., & Clemens, B. T. Procedural due process: One institution's plan and how it is working. *NASPA Journal*, 1972, *9*, 207-214.

Rush, H. P. The dean and discipline. *Journal of the National Association for Women Deans, Administrators, and Counselors*, 1945, *9*, 6-9.

Schetlin, E. M. Disorders, deans, and discipline: A record of change. *Journal* of the National Association for Women Deans, Administrators, and Counselors, 1967, *30*, 169-173.

Scott v. Alabama State Board of Education, 300 F. Supp. 163 (1969).

Seavey, W. A. Dismissal of students: "Due process." *Harvard Law Review*, 1957, *70*, 1406-1410.

Seward, D. M. Educational discipline. *Journal of the National Association for Women Deans, Administrators, and Counselors*, 1961, *24*, 192-197.

Sherry, A. H. Governance of the university: Rules, rights, and responsibilities. *California Law Review*, 1966, *54*, 23-39.

Signori, E. I. Some social psychological aspects of discipline. (Proceedings of the Canadian Association of University Student Personnel Services, Vancouver, December, 1965, pp. 36-37) *College Student Personnel Abstracts*, 1966, *1*, 196.

Sillers, D. J., & Feder, D. D. Attitudes of general and student personnel administrators toward student disciplinary problems. *Journal of College Student Personnel*, 1964, *5*, 130-140; 145.

Sims, O. S. Student conduct and campus law enforcement: A proposal. In O. S. Sims (Ed.), *New directions in campus law enforcement*. Athens: University of Georgia, Center for Continuing education, 1971.

Smith, G. P., & Kirk, H. P. Student discipline for tomorrow. *NASPA Journal*, 1971, *9*, 28-31. (a)

Smith, G. P., & Kirk, H. P. Student discipline in transition. *NASPA Journal*, 1971, *8*, 276-282. (b)

Snoxell, L. F. Counseling reluctant and recalcitrant students. *Journal of College Student Personnel*, 1960, *2*, 16-20.

Snoxell, L. F. Due process and discipline. In T. A. Brady & L. F. Snoxell, *Student discipline in higher education*. Washington, D. C.: American Personnel and Guidance Association, 1965. (Student Personnel Monograph Series, No. 5)

Soglin v. Kauffman, 295 F. Supp. 978 (1968).

St. Antoine, T. J. The administrative tribunal. In G. W. Holmes (Ed.), *Law and discipline on campus*. Ann Arbor, Mich.: Institute of Continuing Legal Education, 1971.

Stein, R. H. Discipline: On campus, downtown, or both, a need for a standard. *NASPA Journal*, 1972, *10*, 41-47.

Stein, R. H. The nature of temporary suspension. *NASPA Journal*, 1974, *11*(3), 16-23.

Strickland, D. A. *In loco parentis* — legal mots and student morals. *Journal of College Student Personnel*, 1965, *6*, 335-340.

Tisdale, J. R., & Brown, F. G. Characteristics of college misconduct cases. *Journal of College Student Personnel*, 1965, *6*, 359-366.

Vagueness in college rules. *College Law Bulletin*, 1970, *2*, 59-62.

Van Alstyne, W. W. Procedural due process and state university students. *UCLA Law Review*, 1963, *10*, 368-389.

Van Alstyne, W. W. The prerogatives of students, the powers of universities and the due process of law. *Journal of the National Association for Women Deans, Administrators, and Counselors,* 1966, *30,* 11-16.

Van Alstyne, W. W. The judicial trend toward student academic freedom. *University of Florida Law Review,* 1968, *20,* 290-305. (a)

Van Alstyne, W. W. The student as university resident. *Denver Law Review,* 1968, *45,* 582-613. (b)

Van Alstyne, W. W. The tentative emergence of student power in the United States. *American Journal of Comparative Law,* 1969, *17,* 403-414.

Van Alstyne, W. W. Student activism, the law, and the courts. In J. Foster and D. Long (Eds.), *Protest! Student activism in America.* New York: William Morrow, 1970.

Van Houten, P. S. A positive approach to better student conduct. *Journal of the National Association for Women Deans, Administrators, and Counselors,* 1964, *28,* 88-91.

Whitaker, B. E. Helping students achieve high moral values by combining discipline and guidance. *Community and Junior College Journal,* 1961, *32,* 35-36.

Williams, G. D., & Rhodes, J. A. Satisfaction with the environment and attitudes toward the disciplinary process. *Journal of College Student Personnel,* 1969, *10,* 391-396.

Williamson, E. G. The fusion of discipline and counseling in the educative process. *Personnel and Guidance Journal,* 1955, *34,* 74-79.

Williamson, E. G. Preventative aspects of disciplinary counseling. *Educational and Psychological Measurement,* 1956, *16,* 68-81.

Williamson, E. G. *Student personnel services in college and universities.* New York: McGraw-Hill, 1961.

Williamson, E. G. A new look at discipline. *Journal of Secondary Education,* 1963, *38,* 10-14.

Williamson, E. G., & Foley, J. D. *Counseling and discipline.* New York: McGraw-Hill, 1949.

Williamson, E. G., Jorve, W., & Lagerstedt-Knudson, B. What kinds of college students become disciplinary cases? *Educational and Psychological Measurement,* 1952, *12,* 608-619.

Witmer, D. R. *Right of notice and hearing, "due process," and related constitutional rights of students.* Madison: Wisconsin Board of Regents of State Universities, 1969. (ERIC Document Reproduction Service No. ED 027 005)

Woodruff, A. D. Discipline. In C. W. Harris (Ed.), *Encyclopedia of educational research.* New York: Macmillan, 1960.

Work, G. G. CPI patterns of college male disciplinary cases and a comparison group. *Journal of College Student Personnel,* 1969, *10,* 223-226.

Wrenn, C. G. Student discipline in college. *Educational and Psychological Measurement,* 1949, *9,* 625-633.

Wright, C. A. The constitution on the campus. *Vanderbilt Law Review,* 1969, *22,* 1027-1088.

Yegge, R. B. Emerging legal rights for students. In G. K. Smith (Ed.), *Stress and campus response*. San Francisco: Jossey-Bass, 1968.

Yegge, R. B. Constitutional dimensions of student protest. In D. P. Young (Ed.), *Higher education: The law and individual rights and responsibilities*. Athens: University of Georgia, Institute of Higher Education, 1971.

Yost, M. Discipline at Stanford University. *Journal of the National Association for Women Deans, Administrators, and Counselors*, 1945, *9*, 10-11.

Young, D. P. *The legal aspects of student dissent and discipline in higher education*. Athens: University of Georgia, Institute of Higher Education, 1970. (a)

Young, D. P. Student discipline and due process. In D. P. Young (Ed.), *The law and student protest*. Athens: University of Georgia, Institute of Higher Education, 1970. (b)

Young, D. P. Due process standards and guidelines for student discipline in higher education. *Journal of College Student Personnel*, 1971, *12*, 101-106. (a)

Young, D. P. *Student rights and responsibilities*. Paper presented at the Conference on the Law and Higher Education: Where the Action Is! Tuscaloosa, Alabama, March 1971. (b)

Young, D. P. The colleges and the courts. In L. J. Peterson & L. O. Garber (Eds.), *The yearbook of school law 1972*. Topeka, Kan.: National Organization on Legal Problems of Education, 1972.

CHAPTER 10

SECURITY

William T. Packwood

HISTORY

Colleges have always had to maintain order and protect life and property. In the medieval university, murder, rape, robbery, and bloody riots were common, daily occurrences (Patrick & Perricone, 1974). "Bedels," servants of the chancellor and proctors in Fifteenth Century Oxford, served writs, exacted fines, and escorted students to prison (Gelber, 1972). A Massachusetts Act in 1656 empowered the president and faculty of Harvard to punish all student misdemeanors. Nevertheless, Harvard often found it necessary to request the governor or the sheriff of Middlesex for aid and the Cambridge justices of the peace to provide a constable and additional men to prevent disorder around the college hall (Gelber, 1972).

In early American colleges, faculty, if not the president, were required to live in and patrol dormitories, forcing entrance into student rooms which were not opened after knocking (Leonard, 1956). Even into the Twentieth Century, the president and faculty had maintenance functions such as repairing broken locks, replacing light bulbs, and recovering lost mattresses (Gelber, 1972). Watchmen were also hired at times to reduce the threat of fires, night prowlers, and wandering cattle, and to prevent wood-burning stoves from going out. Janitors served similar functions on some campuses with duties ranging from sweeping floors and carrying water to serving as the unofficial campus advisor. Sometimes private detectives were hired, as the Wisconsin Board of Regents did in 1880, to search out student ringleaders who were opposed to military drill on campus (Gelber, 1972). The first campus security officer was hired in 1894 when Yale University borrowed two New Haven Police

Department officers, called Campus Cops, to patrol the grounds and work directly with students (Gelber, 1972; Holloman, 1972).

During the 1920's the stereotype of the friendly, old retired watchman who looked the other way was prevalent. Student proctors were usually more feared as they enforced rules and regulations of student conduct (Holloman, 1972). The advent of the automobile and its resulting parking problems began to change the security requirements of the campus. After World War II, the need for campus security increased in direct proportion to the increase in motor traffic (Holloman, 1972), and consequently, retired police officers were frequently employed. Gelber (1972) found that the increased number of buildings was also related to the change from the watchman-guard function to traffic and crime control. Most of the functions of these various positions were natural responses to the need for order that occurs whenever groups of people gather together, but they also found support in the principle of *in loco parentis* (see Discipline chapter).

In the 1960's the campus protest demonstrations, disruptive student activities, violence, and increase in campus crime (a spillover from the general society itself) made the need for professional campus police departments and the inadequacies of the previous approaches vividly clear.

DEFINITION

Roles

There are a variety of roles for campus security officers. While these roles appear to fall on a continuum from watchman to professional policeman, usually a security service borrows something from each of the roles with one role predominating. The particular selection of roles is related to size and type of campus and the philosophy and financial backing of the administration. Thus, no one role or model is appropriate for all campuses.

Watchman

The first role is almost stereotypic. It is based on the philosophy that the campus is basically a safe place and needs minimal security. Watchmen are low-paid, frequently retired from another job such as city police, and have little or no training for the job. The watchman's main duties consist of controlling access and parking, locking doors, protecting transfer of monies, detecting fires, vandalism, and other maintenance problems, and escorting a variety of university employees during the night hours (Kakalik & Wildhorn, 1971). This model is frequently found at small colleges and colleges that have ready access to municipal police forces.

Old Educative

The old educative model frequently includes the functions of the watchman model, but adds some repressive capabilities as well as efforts to identify law breakers. It derives from an ivory-tower conception of the institution: Students should have an opportunity to try out different behaviors, to learn from mistakes, and to be protected from the consequences of unlawful behavior unlike their nonstudent counterparts. In this model deans of students act *in loco parentis,* have working relationships with local police forces, and may even provide bail for students. The campus security service in this model does much of the leg work and has close working relationships with the student affairs service and individualizes its action by trying to provide guidance and treatment for offenders (Gelber, 1972; see Disciplinary Counseling).

Police

Based on the assumption of equality before the law, the third model views students as having full responsibility for any unlawful act performed, like all citizens. It further assumes that there are no differences between the campus community and the community surrounding it. Thus, the campus security officer is a full-bodied representative of law enforcement (Gelber, 1972) and functions in the college community similar to the municipal police officer. This model is most prevalent on large, urban campuses where distinctions between the campus and city are blurred. Powell ("Ten Important Questions," 1969) believes that public universities lean too much toward real police operations, but agrees with others (Iannarelli, 1968; Nielsen, 1971; Powell, 1972) that full police powers for campus security officers are an absolute must.

Professional

This model assumes that the college community differs in important respects from the community surrounding it, that the college community's primary purpose is educative, and that the campus security service should provide the very best model of law enforcement available (Kassinger, 1974). The emphasis is on prevention of unlawful behavior which requires highly paid and trained officers who may give lectures on campus, teach courses like self-defense, and be highly involved in an academic police science training program.

Public Safety

The public safety model is based on the concept of eliminating campus environmental hazards (Kassinger, 1971) by combining the police, safety, and fire-fighting functions (Michigan State University Department of Public Safety, 1974). It may derive from the Occupational Safety and Health Act (OSHA) which places on the institution the responsibility for safety of its employees (see Gorda, 1973). The safety division organizes safety campaigns and educational programs for the faculty and staff and provides mobilized first aid centers ("Georgia's Security Staff," 1970). This type of program is usually found at institutions with large police, fire, and safety staffs and requires the capability of organizational coordination. Because of the importance of safety, such a model should not simply be added to a police unit, as safety might become secondary for those trained and interested primarily in another function (Nielsen, 1971).

Public safety programs include fire safety control, accident prevention control, laboratory safety control, radiation safety control, sanitation safety control, food handling inspection, sanitation and safety inspections, lighting surveys, pest and rodent control, civil defense and disaster programs, campus pollution study, campus first aid, narcotics and drug control (apart from law enforcement), driving inspection, and safety training classes. In other words, public safety programs are concerned with all environmental conditions that may negatively affect the purposes of the community (Kassinger, 1971).

Need

The over-all need for campus security forces has been recognized by colleges. Particular needs were clearly drawn in the 1960's, such as in the 1968-69 academic year when 6 percent of the nation's colleges experienced violent protests and 16 percent experienced nonviolent but disruptive protests. While at most times on most campuses disruption was absent, the majority of American colleges experienced at least one incident of protest, peaceful or otherwise (Linowitz, 1970). The following year, the FBI determined that the damages directly attributed to demonstration and unrest on campus exceeded $1.5 million. They also found that one in three private colleges and one in eight public colleges experienced violent protests, that 78 percent of the private colleges and 43 percent of the public colleges experienced peaceful protests, and that few colleges with under 1,000 students had any protests (Kassinger, 1971).

Aside from protests, major problems on campuses are thefts in dormitories, thefts of bicycles, thefts of autos, and vandalism ("Campus Police Offer," 1971; Patrick & Perricone, 1974). Dukiet (1973) estimated that larceny accounted for 60 percent of the criminal incidents on campuses. Patrick and Perricone (1974) found in their survey of deans and security officers that the incidence of crime was lower for college students than for the total U. S. population and considerably lower for persons eighteen to twenty-two years old, though the three violent crimes, murder, rape, robbery, as well as assault (all types), burglary, theft, and auto theft did occur at the 164 institutions reporting. They also found that many of these crimes were committed off campus, that approximately a third of the campus crimes were committed by outsiders, and that a significant number of colleges had professional thieves operating on their campuses. Anderson (1971) found that only 10 percent of 400 apprehensions on his campus were of campus members.

While campuses are not crime laden, all the crimes that occur in the rest of society occur on college campuses. Colleges are communities (Bernitt, 1971) with urban-like characteristics and problems requiring urban-like responses (Kassinger, 1971). The president of the college is actually a mayor of a city (Powell, 1972). Providing for security on a campus requires that the rights and responsibilities of both students and institution be determined (Grossman & MacGregor, 1973). In fact, institutions can be held responsible for the quality of security they provide (see Feld, 1971). Several liability suits have been brought against institutions; in one case a watchman talked to a rapist and locked the door after him to allow the rapist privacy.

Although the need for protection in the campus community is clear, it is not the primary function of campus security. In fact, 70 percent of deans and security officers in Patrick and Perricone's (1974) study said that crime was not a serious problem on their campuses.

It has been suggested that 80 to 90 percent (Daniels, 1974; Kassinger, 1971) of campus security officers' responsibilities are devoted to service and that 75 percent of their time is involved with traffic control (Patrick & Perricone, 1974). Service may include such things as dealing with dead batteries, flat tires, locked cars, transportation to health services, stuck elevators, blocked cars, and kittens in trees ("Campus Police Offer," 1971).

ADMINISTRATION

Where campus security fits into the institutional administrative structure depends primarily upon the function it serves. If the operation primarily involves watchmen providing security for buildings, then it may belong in the physical plant. Those forces having substantial responsibilities in student discipline should report to the dean of students; whereas those with broad community police powers should report to the vice-president or president. Whitehead and Van Meter (1969) in their survey of 184 public and private colleges found that 6 percent of campus security directors reported to the president, 29 percent to the vice-president, 10 percent to personnel deans, 27 percent to the physical plant, 14 percent to the business manager, and 14 percent to other administrators. Nielsen (1971) found at 120 institutions that 41 percent reported to the physical plant, 18 percent to the dean of students, and 24 percent to a vice-president.

Nielsen (1971) also found that 60 percent of the campus security directors reporting to the physical plant director suggested a change to reporting to the vice-president. The only advantage mentioned for remaining in the physical plant was that the budget for that department was large enough to allow greater flexibility. The disadvantages stated were that the physical plant director is not familiar with police matters and the status is considered low.

Campus security directors who report to the dean of students were mostly found in the smaller colleges in Nielsen's (1971) study. Chandler and Shainline (1969) give a privacy rationale for this administrative structure: Since the dean of students is charged with student conduct, the campus police must operate within the philosophy established by the dean and consequently can best handle most infractions of the law by referral to the dean's office. If this structure is utilized, both the dean of students and campus security officer need to establish territories and completely separate operational functions (Nielson, 1974). Nielsen (1971) found that 50 percent of the campus security officers reporting to the dean of students advocate change. As deans continue to disappear and discipline is handled by more legally trained personnel, this structure will probably decrease in frequency.

If campus security has responsibility for a broad spectrum of the campus community, then reporting to the vice-president seems the most appropriate administrative structure, especially because policy decisions can be obtained quickly and the security chief can remain relatively free from campus political pressures (Nielsen, 1971). The major disadvantage is the unavailability of the vice-president.

Psychological Aspects

Daniels (1974) compares the work of the policeman to that of the doctor. Both provide emergency, preventive, counseling, and referral services. Both draw on experts and specialists, work long hours, sacrifice normal family life, and are resource persons for the community. They have to deal in an intimate way with people with wisdom and tact. Kirkham (1974), a professor who became a policeman, found that the public demanded that he be an authority, giving guidance, control, and direction. Powell ("Ten Important Questions," 1969) agrees that the campus security officer must present a competent image. The policeman (and the doctor) deals frequently with people who are upset and requires someone who can take charge and inspire confidence. Consequently, the policeman constantly deals with tension and anxiety as well as abuse, an aspect that is perhaps different from the doctor, particularly if the abuse is physical. As a policeman, Kirkham found that he had to make spot decisions with no time to consider and that because there was always the possibility of harm, he was constantly living with fear.

Hamann (1969) believes that police on campus are limited by administrator and student lack of confidence in them. As a result, recognition for prevention of crime is hard to obtain (Gunson, 1974). With these attitudinal battles to fight, the campus policeman must earn trust, respect, and public support in a job that also requires it (Nielson, 1974). Increasing professionalization is probably a reflection of the campus security officers' need for recognition in the academic community (Kassinger, 1974) and need for a sense of belonging, which Gunson

(1974) suggests is a state of mind fostered through training and guidance.

Holloman (1972) says that campus policemen must be perfectionists in that they have no second chances in their decisions and their mistakes are magnified. They can reduce crime but have no control over its causes, because they take over after society has failed. Their job is people, but those they would die for would destroy them. They must also enforce all laws equally or become a dictator or a god.

Police Aspects

As campus security moves away from a watchman operation toward a professional police operation, a variety of decisions must be made, most of which depend upon the philosophy of the institution about its security force and the functions it is to perform.

Title

During stages of transition even simple things such as what to call the security force chief become complex. Whitehead and Van Meter (1969) found that fifty-six titles were used in 184 institutions, the most prevalent being Chief Security Officer (18%), Director of Security (15%), Chief of Police (11%), and Director of Safety and Security (8%).

Police Authority

If campus security officers are to be full-fledged police with power to make arrests, their authority must be legalized. Until recently, most campus security officers were deputized by the local sheriff or municipal police. Gelber (1972) found that for public institutions twenty-seven of the fifty states permit the state governing body for higher education to appoint campus police officers with power to arrest. The remaining twenty-three states permit deputization through one of the following: the governor, the court, a law enforcement agency, or a city government. Private institutions receive little statutory consideration, with only seven states providing direct authority. Nielsen (1971) strongly recommends obtaining state legislation for campus police authority. Being deputized by the municipal police chief is not the answer because the campus officer is never really independent, in effect has two superiors, and can be controlled by the municipal chief's threat to revoke the commissions.

Training

Standards pertaining to campus security administration and personnel have been developed by the International Association of College and University Security Directors (Professional Standards Committee, 1974). In practice, the training required of campus security officers is not consistent. Abramson (1973) found in a survey of campus police training practices at 286 institutions that 52 percent required formal training, 83 percent required in-service training, 48 percent had a part- or full-time training officer, and 28 percent required continued education. Only two states, New York and Texas, require or provide special training for campus security on a regular basis (Gelber, 1972). However, if campus security officers will be operating with police powers, they must attend and complete police academy training.

There has been an increasing requirement for campus officers to have a college degree (A.A., B.A., M.A.) or to be working towards one. The requirement of a college education is designed to make the officers better understand the needs of students, having been one themselves, and also help them to obtain more respect. Nielsen (1971) questions a college education requirement because he doubts that many college graduates will be satisfied with the drudgery of patrol work with the number of years presently required before promotion.

Uniforms

The image conveyed by dress has been a concern of campus

security officers. The prevalent view seems to be that they wear modified police uniforms, a requirement in some states in order for their arrests to be legal. The idea is that the police uniform provides a presence and clear identification, though some have found this image too militaristic and softened it by using blazers with an appropriate emblem. Dumas (1970) considers the blazers and other modifications of the police uniform as phoney — either you are a policeman or you are not. He does not feel that dress is as important as the quality of service provided. Patrick and Perricone (1974) found that 90 percent of the forces they surveyed did wear uniforms. Gelber (1972) found only 20 to 30 percent support among campus security officers, administrators, students, and faculty for replacement of the standard police uniforms with civilian-like attire. Powell ("Ten Important Questions," 1969) says that the director should never wear a uniform.

Guns

The view that campus police should not be armed probably prevails on campus today. Those who hold this view believe that guns are not appropriate to the educational atmosphere, they invite retaliation, escalate criminal armament, and encourage violent crime. From the professional viewpoint, however, campus police should be armed, especially if they have police powers, they are adequately trained, and the policy is clear that the gun is used only to protect human life. In addition, guns are needed, as society is presently structured, because it is naive to assume that armed criminals who go on college campuses see them as separate environments (Iannarelli, 1968; Nielsen, 1971; "Should Campus Security," 1969).

Nielsen (1971) quotes a study by Marchant which found that at 140 institutions, 75 percent of the urban and 67 percent of suburban campus police carried sidearms at all times. One campus' student-faculty committee determined that arms would not be carried on foot patrol or during demonstrations but could be at other times and particularly at night (Kennedy, 1972). Alternatives to carrying sidearms are for the gun to remain in the patrol car or for the policeman to carry batons (Koga & Nelson, 1968). The use of a gun from a professional point of view has limits. For example, if a campus policeman was beaten and shot when trying to prevent an armed robbery in a college building, he would not use his gun to prevent the robbers' escape since it would not be a case of protecting life at that point ("Part II: Security," 1971; "Should Campus Security," 1969).

Intelligence

In order for police to function effectively they must have reliable information. Gelber (1972) found that 55 percent of the private colleges and 76 percent of the public colleges use undercover agents. The most frequent sources for undercover agents were outside police (45%), regular staff (25%), and the student body (20%). The most frequent sources of intelligence were outside police (84%), informants (67%), and personnel from other colleges (54%). Undercover agents who pose as students are irritants on some campuses and create a climate of fear which destroys academic and political freedoms and the trust necessary in a community whose primary function is inquiry (Kakalik & Wildhorn, 1971). Nielson (1974) considers the use of undercover agents to be hypocritical, but Brest (1971) considers some intelligence gathering functions as natural and necessary. Regardless of the view taken, the policy should be clearly defined and limitations identified.

Relationship to Municipal Police

Defining the relationship between the campus and municipal police forces is necessary since tensions and rivalries frequently occur. Limiting the campus police to a certain campus geographical area or a certain clientele seems unrealistic (Nielsen, 1971) though it has worked at one institution in the heart of an urban area (McDaniel, 1971). The suggestion that the city and college use the same police force (Hamann, 1969;

O'Neil, Morris, & Mack, 1972) seems to have grown more out of need for the coordination necessary to handle campus disturbances than any assessment of the particular needs of the college.

Planning

While Switzer (1967) suggests that the degree of preparedness seems to bear little relation to the likelihood of trouble on a campus, there seems to be almost unanimous agreement on the necessity of planning ahead (Hamann, 1969; Stevens, 1971) to effectively deal with campus problems. During the sixties many colleges developed elaborate and extensive plans for dealing with disturbances. Most campuses also have detailed and effective plans for traffic control. Well-thought-out policies and detailed plans seem to be the foundation of a secure campus and a professional campus police force.

PROGRAMS

Although students probably arrive at college with negative attitudes toward police, if they leave with them, campus security has failed (Nielson, 1973) according to the professional view of police work. To shoulder such a responsibility requires the assumption of an educator role with campus security being a vital part of the educational team (Anderson, 1971). Nielson (1973) says that campus security must teach responsibility and integrity so that each individual citizen feels responsible for developing a personal security system for body and possessions (Michigan State University Department of Public Safety, 1974) and there must be equal application of the laws if true education is to occur (Kassinger, 1974).

The educational role can have many forms. Powell ("Ten Important Questions," 1969) suggests campus security officers take part in orientation of students and use the campus newspaper to inform students of campus security work. Gross (1974) suggests working with campus publications to produce posters, brochures, and stickers to help the campus become security conscious. Gunson (1974) suggests having a policeman of the week in the newspaper as recognition for prevention of crime. Other suggestions have included help for protecting possessions, such as providing electric pens for making identifying marks and brochures on the rights and duties of members of the community (Stuart, 1974).

Other ways in which campus security officers are educators are by example (Nielson, 1974), maintaining a good departmental library, teaching in classrooms, and participating in orientation (McDaniel, 1971).

PERSONNEL

Most campus security forces are composed of full-time males (Gelber, 1972). With the budget squeezes on colleges, students have been added to the force and with affirmative action programs, women have also been recruited.

Students

Powell (1972) reports a trend in campus security to include students as the eyes and ears of the campus. Students over twenty-one (Freeman, 1970) and those in criminal justice academic programs are preferred candidates. Most security forces report successful use of students (Nielsen, 1974; "Stop! In the Name," 1969) primarily because they are young, are available for night patrols, can move fast, and have an immediate rapport with fellow students. However, Littrell (1969) stopped using students on his campus security force because he felt it was unfair to place student against student in investigative matters. He also found scheduling problems because classes prevent shift rotation and examination periods create time pressures, plus students are not available during summer months. In addition, some stealing and selling of exams occurred because students had keys to sensitive areas. Using students on campus security forces successfully probably hinges on their selection and training as well as the degree of campus support for such a program.

Women

Women on campus security forces are performing the same job as men, probably because most of a police officer's time is concerned with public relations (Hocutt, 1974). Stuart (1973) reports that 15 percent of all police-citizen encounters in the nation involved physical strength, while the other 85 percent involved a more sophisticated interpersonal type of skill. While possible lack of muscle may be considered a disadvantage for women, Hocutt reports no difference in the number of persons resisting arrest by female or male officers. However, women did not make as many arrests as men. Hocutt found other differences between men and women officers: Fewer women were accused of being discourteous, using abusive language, obstructing civil rights, or using too much force.

RELATIONSHIPS

To the Community

A perennial problem for colleges is the development of good town-gown relations. While the city and the college may of necessity depend upon and need one another, inevitably, negative feelings between the two exist because of their differing purposes. This tension is most visible in the campus security sphere of responsibilities (Nielsen, 1971) because the community believes, rightly or wrongly, that it has greater expectations for order and lawfulness than the college, or at least the students who go there. On the other hand the college feels that the community is not tolerant enough or at least that its members cannot understand the unique problems of the campus (Anderson, 1971).

Several factors hamper good town-gown relationships in the campus security area (Bernitt, 1971). The first is the double standard of justice for college members, a carry-over from the old *in loco parentis* view, which allowed both experimentation and protection. An example of this philosophy is the dean of students putting up bail for those university members, primarily students, who are arrested (Anderson, 1971). Municipalities often feel they do not have such a luxury and resent paying taxes which can be used as bail money for those who break the laws of the community and state.

A second deterrent to good town-gown relations is the tax exempt status of colleges coupled with their demand for services. Many colleges rely on the community for fire protection, road maintenance, garbage collection, and, in some cases, police protection. The community resents paying for those services while the college does not see itself able to spend the funds nor desire to duplicate such services. Lastly, unlike cities in which the police chief is responsible to the mayor, campus security is often buried in the adminstrative structure and is therefore less visible and effective and is unable to respond quickly and appropriately. One area where campus security effectiveness is recognized is in the control of traffic, both on a routine basis and at major athletic or cultural events.

Town-gown tensions can be dealt with through public relations work such as speakers' programs (Nielsen, 1971). Grossman and MacGregor (1973) recommend that the public relations director of the university participate in planning and organizing of campus security arrangements. This recommendation is a recognition that the concerns of the municipality, as well as those of the campus, must be responded to.

To the University

Kassinger (1974) among others believes that campus security should have no part in enforcement of student conduct regulations. Sims (1971) suggests changing from a student-ward to a student-citizen concept which would allow the campus to become more legally a community which regulated in exemplary fashion its unlawful behavior. Under this concept the state legislature would codify ordinances for its student citizens. The campus could then provide a model of enforcement and could handle infractions with its own judiciary. Although this is an appealing concept for teaching students about law enforcement, most colleges would probably not view such a legal approach as appropriate for an institution dedicated to inquiry.

REFERENCES

Abramson, S. A. Campus police: A survey of training practices. *Campus Law Enforcement Journal,* 1973, *3*(4), 13-17.

Anderson, B. R. Patrol's job: Keeping the campus cool. *College Management,* 1971, *6*(5), 15-17.

Bernitt, R. O. Campus law enforcement: Town-gown relations. In O. S. Sims, Jr. (Ed.), *New directions in campus law enforcement: A handbook for administrators.* Athens: University of Georgia, Center for Continuing Education, 1971.

Brest, P. A. Intelligence gathering on the campus. In G. W. Holmes (Ed.), *Law and discipline on campus.* Ann Arbor, Mich.: Institute of Continuing Legal Education, 1971.

Campus police offer wide variety of services help. *College Management,* 1971, *6*(4), 42.

Chandler, C. L., & Shainline, J. W. Campus police emphasis is shifting from security to enforcement, from parking problems to problem people. *College and University Business,* 1969, *46*(3), 90-92.

Daniels, C. B. The policeman's image. *Campus Law Enforcement Journal,* 1974, *4*(2), 3-5.

Dukiet, K. H. Awareness is key to prevention of campus crime. *College Management,* 1973, *8*(9), 16-17.

Dumas, P. J., Jr. Police relationships with the campus community. In *Campus unrest: Dialogue or destruction.* Washington, D. C.: International Association of Chiefs of Police, 1970.

Feld, L. G. How much liability does a college have in student injury? *College Management,* 1971, *6*(9), 34.

Freeman, G. W. Student security. *College Management,* 1970, *5*(8), 26-27.

Gelber, S. *The role of campus security in the college setting.* Washington, D. C.: United States Department of Justice, National Institute of Law Enforcement and Criminal Justice, 1972.

Georgia's security staff stresses service. *American School and University,* 1970, *42*(11), 28-29.

Gorda, B. L. Georgetown University has model safety program for low budget institutions. *Campus Law Enforcement Journal,* 1973, *3*(4), 26-56.

Gross, P. J. Community awareness continued. *Campus Law Enforcement Journal,* 1974, *4*(2), 13.

Grossman, R. J., & MacGregor, A. Public relations in campus security. *College and University Journal,* 1973, *12*(2), 25-27.

Gunson, H. P. The need to be recognized. *Campus Law Enforcement Journal*, 1974, *4*(3), 27-28.

Hamann, A. D. A plan for more effective police control of campus disturbances. *NASPA Journal*, 1969, *6*, 205-207.

Hocutt, D. Police acknowledge women's capabilities as officers. *Campus Law Enforcement Journal*, 1974, *4*(3), 32-33.

Holloman, F. C. The new breed: College and university police. *Campus Law Enforcement Journal*, 1972, *2*(2), 10-13.

Iannarelli, A. V. *The campus police.* Union City, Calif.: Precision Photo-Form, 1968.

Kakalik, J. S., & Wildhorn, S. *Special-purpose public police* (Vol. 5:R-873/DOJ). Santa Monica, Calif.: Rand Corporation, 1971.

Kassinger, E. T. Alternative to chaos: The need for professionalization of campus law enforcement. In O. S. Sims, Jr. (Ed.), *New directions in campus law enforcement: A handbook for administrators.* Athens: University of Georgia, Center for Continuing Education, 1971.

Kassinger, E. T. New directions in campus law enforcement. *Campus Law Enforcement Journal*, 1974, *4*(2), 30-34.

Kennedy, V. C. Setting up a strong university security department. *American School and University*, 1972, *44*(6), 30.

Kirkham, G. L. What a professor learned when he became a "cop." *Campus Law Enforcement Journal*, 1974, *4*(3), 22-23.

Koga, R. K., & Nelson, J. G. *The Koga method: Police baton technique.* Beverly Hills, Calif.: Glencoe Press, 1968.

Leonard, E. A. *Origin of personnel services in American education.* Minneapolis: University of Minnesota Press, 1956.

Linowitz, S. M. (Chm.). *Campus tensions: Analysis and recommendations.* Washington, D. C.: American Council on Education, 1970.

Littrell, W. O. Denver nixes students. *College Management*, 1969, *4*(9), 55.

McDaniel, W. E. Law enforcement: The officer as educator. In O. S. Sims, Jr. (Ed.), *New directions in campus law enforcement: A handbook for administrators.* Athens: University of Georgia, Center for Continuing Education, 1971.

Michigan State University Department of Public Safety. Protective services objectives defined at Michigan State University. *Campus Law Enforcement Journal*, 1974, *4*(3), 14-15.

Nielsen, S. W. *General organizational and administrative concepts for university police.* Springfield, Ill.: Charles C Thomas, 1971.

Nielson, R. C. Student and teacher: The dual role of the campus police officer. *Campus Law Enforcement Journal*, 1973, *3*(4), 57-58.

Nielson, R. C. My first year in campus law enforcement. *Campus Law Enforcement Journal*, 1974, *3*(4), 3-4.

O'Neil, R. M., Morris, J. P., & Mack, R. *No heros, no villains: New perspectives on Kent State and Jackson State.* San Francisco: Jossey-Bass, 1972.

Part II: Security tries for a low profile at Penn. *College Management,* 1971, *6*(9), 32-33.

Patrick, C. H., & Perricone, P. J. Crime and the changing role of the campus policeman. *Campus Law Enforcement Journal,* 1974, *4*(1), 43-48.

Powell, J. W. Campus security today: Progressive but sensitive. *American School and University,* 1972, *45*(2), 17-20.

Professional Standards Committee. Standards pertaining to administration and personnel. *Campus Law Enforcement Journal,* 1974, *4*(3), 8-10.

Should campus security police be armed? *College Management,* 1969, *4*(10), 44-50.

Sims, O. S., Jr. Student conduct and campus law enforcement: A proposal. In O. S. Sims, Jr. (Ed.), *New directions in campus law enforcement: A handbook for administrators.* Athens: University of Georgia, Center for Continuing Education, 1971.

Stevens, W. W. The police. In G. W. Holmes (Ed.), *Law and discipline on campus.* Ann Arbor, Mich.: Institute of Continuing Legal Education, 1971.

Stop! In the name of the students. *College Management,* 1969, *4*(9), 51-55.

Stuart, C. G. Women in campus law enforcement: An analysis of a survey investigation. *Campus Law Enforcement Journal,* 1973, *3*(2), 38-39.

Stuart, C. G. Crime prevention campaign at Tufts in full swing. *Campus Law Enforcement Journal,* 1974, *4*(1), 20-31.

Switzer, L. Battle plans for urban colleges threatened by civil upheaval. *College and University Business,* 1967, *43*(3), 63-65.

Ten important questions colleges are asking about security today. *College Management,* 1969, *4*(10), 35-38.

Whitehead, A. T., & Van Meter, C. *Security services analysis, 1968-1969.* Knoxville, Tenn.: International Association of College and University Security Directors, 1969. (Available through Whitehead, University of Tennessee)

CHAPTER 11

HEALTH

WILLIAM T. PACKWOOD

HISTORY

THE educational institutions "of the early seventeenth century were notorious for their unhygienic conditions" (American Medical Association, 1936, p. 3). There was very little concern for the body, devastating epidemics occurred, and rooms were dark, gloomy, and smelly (Williams, 1896). With advances in medicine came improvements, but none were substantial until the latter part of the Nineteenth Century.

The early developments of health work among college students can be divided into three periods (American Medical Association, 1936). The first, the gymnastic period, began in 1825 when German and Scandinavian methods of physical exercises, which were practiced *en masse* and by command, were introduced into the United States. It was not until 1861, however, that the first well-organized, comprehensive department of hygiene and physical education was established at Amherst College by Dr. Edward Hitchcock (Boynton, 1971; Bruyn, 1969). This program provided for annual medical examinations of each student, instruction in hygiene, regular prescribed physical exercise throughout the four years, treatment of the sick, and an annual report on the number and kind of illnesses.

The second period was characterized by faculty committees on sanitation which inspected student boarding houses, sought to control communicable diseases, and supervised the hygiene of the college community. The third period began in the 1890's when "team doctors," physicians hired to supervise the medical treatment needed by athletic teams, found themselves caring for other students as well. This led to medical services for ambulatory patients, then to infirmaries (the first was established at

Princeton in 1893), and finally to courses in hygiene.

In 1901 the University of California opened a health service after a study indicated that student absence from class was primarily due to illness and not to idleness or lack of interest (Boynton, 1962). Other influences which assisted the college health movement included epidemics or deaths on campus; the finding that of the first 2.5 million draftees in World War I, 29 percent were rejected on physical grounds; the appointment of Dr. Thomas A. Storey as the first Executive Secretary of the Interdepartmental Social Hygiene Board to deal with venereal diseases after World War I; appropriations to college health programs for army units stationed on campuses; and the establishment of the American Student Health Association in 1920 (Boynton, 1962, 1971). Additional impetus for the development of the college health movement came from increased interest in prevention and public health in education, the development of medical schools, the principle of *in loco parentis*, the fact that many colleges were built away from communities which could provide health care, and the notion that college work endangers health with its accompanying stereotype of the college student being an anemic, frail, bespectacled anthropoid (American Medical Association, 1936).

DEFINITION

The World Health Organization (1947, p. 3) defines health "as a state of complete physical, mental, and social well-being, not merely the absence of disease or infirmity." Wiechmann (1970) believes that health and fitness approach self-actualization since health behavior speaks to the total needs of man as a growing, striving, developing, integrating organism. Each individual owes it to his or her self and to society to keep the self and energy at a peak. These laudable definitions or goals have not been achieved by any society, much less a college or a college health service. Yet human health is a foremost ingredient in learning (Wiechmann, 1970).

Colleges vary enormously in the degree of health care they provide. Moore and Summerskill (1954), in one of the best designed research studies conducted in the college student personnel field, found that 17 percent of the colleges in the United States claimed no responsibility for student health. Farnsworth (1965) said that there were probably no major changes since that time. Nichols (1973) found that 59 percent of 482 public community colleges had no health service on their campuses. Moore and Summerskill's (1954) major conclusion was that there is no uniform or standard health program for college students. This conclusion is supported by Cooke, Hekhuis, Huntington, and Knisely's (1969) finding that of the eighteen Michigan campuses they visited, there were eighteen different health care approaches. They suggested five factors which were primary influences on a college's health service: number of students, extent of on-campus housing, locale of surrounding community, availability of nearby health facilities and community-university relationships, and presence and relationship of a medical school. Colleges that do assume responsibility for health care provide programs that range from first aid and physical exams to complete medical care (American Medical Association, 1936).

Diehl and Shepard (1939) found that the more complete health service programs include: health examinations of entering students, periodic health examinations of other students, health inspections of participants in physical activities, follow-up care of physical defects leading to remedy or amelioration, medical care of minor illness and injury (dispensary), bed care for the acutely ill (infirmary), medical advice on health problems not associated directly with illness or injury (mental, sexual, marital, and vocational hygiene), medical and nursing care in rooming houses and dorms, public health protection against cases and carriers of epidemic diseases, and sanitary inspection of campus environment.

The American College Health Association (1969) has recommended standards for college health programs and for college health officials' ethical and professional relationships.

Need

College students are generally considered one of the healthiest subgroups in society. Farnsworth (1964) reports that college health services are quantitatively concerned with relatively few illnesses: respiratory infections and other infections such as mononucleosis, skin disorders, injuries, and psychological conflicts. There are few degenerative or chronic diseases and few psychoses. Also, there is an unrivaled opportunity for immunization, evidenced by the fact that one third of all the visits to the health service at Harvard were for immunizations or desensitization shots.

However, Diehl and Shepard (1939) found in the reports of thirty-five colleges with 4,800 students that 30 percent of the students were underweight, 5 percent were overweight, 11 percent had defective vision, 70 percent had dental pathology, 35 percent had nasal obstructions, 19 percent had posture defects, 19 percent had flat feet, less than 2 percent had heart diseases, and 7 percent had high blood pressure primarily due to excitement or fatigue of exam periods with 3 percent persisting.

Comstock and Slome (1973) tabulated the prevalence of health service problems in one year at their college. They found that 74 percent had colds, sore throats, and headaches; 39 percent had upset stomach, diarrhea, or vomiting; 23 percent had dental needs; 23 percent had menstrual problems; 19 percent (28% for females and 8% for males) had contraceptive needs; 17 percent had other injuries; 11 percent had bone injuries; 16 percent had skin problems; 10 percent had visual problems; and all the others were less than 10 percent each.

On the other hand, at a Florida college where inflated figures may have been produced because of the attractiveness of the climate, Egolf (1969) found the following number of cases of permanent illnesses and disabilities among 10,000 students: 99 had asthma; 19, other congenital defects; 15, diabetes mellitus; 12, rheumatic heart disease; 10, fracture or dislocation of the spine with paralytic effects; and all others, less than 10. Nichols (1973) received reports from 482 public community colleges that in the past five years, 69 percent of them had epileptic seizures occur on their campuses, 50 percent had laboratory accidents, 36 percent had cases of drug overdose, 25 percent had heart attacks, and there had been a total of 27 incidences of suicide.

At a college which gave medical examinations to all faculty, Tupper (1962) found that 75 percent had a health defect of which they were not previously aware. Sickle-cell (Yeager, Johnson & Gynn, 1973) and tuberculosis screening programs for all college members have been recommended (Durfee, 1972; Farnsworth, 1964). The occurrence of emotional disturbances is discussed in the section on Mental Health, but the range appears to be between 6 and 16 percent with an average of 12 percent (Farnsworth, 1957; Reifler, 1971).

Farnsworth (1964) found that a third of the student body at Harvard visited the health service each year and that the average number of visits was three per student per year. But Osborne (1970) suggests a health service, which limits itself to caring for the overt illnesses and injuries that may arise and may present themselves for care, will fail to meet, let alone recognize, from 40 to 50 percent of both the real and felt community health needs. He feels (1973) that this kind of laissez-faire approach to college health care does not take into account the college community's ignorance, youth, or lack of money, as well as the fact that disorganized and expensive services can act to reduce effective service to the college population.

Since the very beginning of college health care, health services and health instruction have been inadequate (Meylan, 1908; Storey, 1927). The American Medical Association (1936) was struck by the superficiality of medical care provided on campuses and concluded that it was largely the result of low finances. Farnsworth (1964) suggests that the problems are larger than lack of finances and include such things as apathy or inertia and opposition. Opposition comes from those who believe that when the illness is serious, students will go to a private physician or away from the campus. According to this point of view, colleges, and particularly the medium-sized colleges, may be wasting money on health services ("Colleges May Be," 1972) and might do better to utilize community resources.

ADMINISTRATION

Farnsworth (1964, 1965) recommends that the health service director report directly to the president and that the office be parallel in structure to the dean of students' office, so as to protect physicians from administrative decisions. A better organization would be to have the health service director report to the chief student personnel officer, in order for coordination with the rest of the campus' college student personnel program. Of course, the administrative structure must reflect the purpose and breadth of the health service on each campus.

Moore and Summerskill (1954) found that 42 percent of the health services had a committee or board on student health whose primary concerns were (94%) operating policy and (54%) overall supervision of the health service (see also Bobilya & Yarver, 1974). Other recommended committees are executive or staff committees, pharmacy committees, as well as professional practices committees, which can scrutinize any health service function (Farnsworth, 1964). The major thrust in any committee structure is to have a coordinated campus health program, rather than the usual lack of unification of those who attend to health on a campus (Diehl & Shepard, 1939).

Moore and Summerskill (1954) found that the directors of health services came from the fields of medicine (42%), nursing (23%), and education and physical education (25%). Only 39 percent of the directors were full-time and only 21 percent of the health services had full-time physicians, of which 54 percent had only one physician.

Fees

Most college health services are supported primarily by student fees. Thirty percent of the colleges had a special health fee and 50 percent had a tuition fee or used general college funds. The average amount of the fee or amount allotted from general funds per student was $7.25, though the range was from zero to twenty dollars or more (Moore & Summerskill, 1954).

A more recent figure at colleges with comprehensive health services is $50 to $100 (Farnsworth, 1965).

While originally most health services were probably provided free, as costs increased, fees were imposed. Fees which are prepayments are preferred by many because they place the emphasis on prevention and treatment rather than illness and finances (Edison, 1970; Farnsworth, 1964). An objection to fees came in the 1960's when many students demanded voluntary or at least separate health fees. Like other adults not in college, they wanted to know exactly what they were paying their money for and to plan for their own health care or health insurance. One college that went to a voluntary health fee found that 70 percent of the student body participated at $7 a semester (Cox, 1974).

Most colleges also charge additional fees for services other than routine, such as laboratory work and prescriptions. Edison (1970) found that 45 percent of 111 colleges charged fees for some services. Frequently there is also a separate student hospitalization insurance plan available, sometimes arranged by student governments with private insurance companies.

Health Maintenance Organizations

A Health Maintenance Organization (HMO) is defined as "an organization which operates or manages a health service delivery system designed to provide comprehensive health care economically and effectively on a prepaid capitation basis for an enrolled population group" (Louden, 1973, p. 210). The primary emphases are on prevention of disease and economy. Since they are prepayment plans, they have in some way been present on campuses for half a century (Hair, 1972).

Perhaps the best known college HMO is the Yale Health Plan which is open to all students, faculty, staff, and dependents at $9.36 per month per individual and $22.00 per month per family (Davie, Goldberg, & Rowe, 1974). Offered as one answer to the medical care crisis in the country and on college campuses, the plan appears to have been quite successful. Faculty participated more than staff and joined because of the comprehensiveness of the plan, the cost, and the convenience. The primary reason for not joining was the necessity of relinquishing one's choice of physician.

The benefits of an HMO are that cost can be predicted for the duration of the contract, the possibility of medical audits and quality control are increased, accountability and responsiveness to the consumer and community are increased, and paramedical personnel can be included. In addition, there is ease and availability of consultation and coverage for weekends and holidays, there is more continuity of care, and hospital days can be reduced by 20 to 25 percent (Rosenberg, 1972). However, there appears to be no assurance that the quality of care is better, more available, or less expensive, nor that the disadvantages of one of the oldest HMO's, Kaiser Permanente, such as long waits, getting sufficient staff, physician motivation, and impersonality, can be eliminated (Hair, 1972).

To have a campus HMO requires a change in attitude about the way health care is provided on campuses. The emphasis must shift to prevention; the notion of the student as a minor must be rejected; and all elements of the college community must be included (Forbes, 1972). A. Bloom (1972) identifies four elements which must be present and active: an organized health care delivery system, an enrolled population, a financial plan, and a managing organization. Further, at least 10,000 people are needed in the first three years for the rural college HMO to survive and 25,800 to 30,000 subscribers are needed for a profit (Hair, 1972). Alternatives suggested for the urban college are to have an HMO like Yale, be a satellite of a parent HMO, contract for services through medical foundations or organizations, or set up a county network system (Forbes, 1972).

Information Processing

The computer is finding its place in the college health service primarily because of the indispensability of medical records (Farnsworth, 1964). It is possible to put the student's registration and entire health service file on computer for ease of obtaining the information as well as storage (Matte, 1970).

Confidentiality of the records must be maintained, however, (Farnsworth, 1965) allowing no release of information without the student's permission.

Computer based scheduling systems have been developed (Averill, Rising, McBride, Gage, & Piedmont, 1972). Combined with nurses handling half of the walk-ins, such a system has allowed for varying of appointments according to walk-in loads, a 15 percent increase in patient utilization, a 13 percent increase in physician contact, and a 40 percent increase in physician appointments. Such systems can also yield weekly diagnostic and utilization reports which can be used to plan and develop better administrative practices (Averill, 1970).

Legal Aspects

The legal aspects of health services, which are becoming more complex with expansion of medical facilities, include employer responsibility, liability, malpractice, consent, records, privileged communications, negligence, workmen's compensation, involuntary confinement, civil liberties, constitutional rights, and others (Farnsworth, 1964).

Involvement of Students

In order to meet rising costs with decreasing budgets and to provide more health care services, some college health services have employed students. These students, called health aides, are trained in a one to two credit academic course and paid twenty dollars a month as members of the health service staff. They may organize health education programs in the student living units (Helm, Knipmeyer, & Martin, 1972) or care for minor aches and pains. They are provided with first aid kits and carefully selected over-the-counter medications.

One college which implemented such a program (Martin & Newman, 1973) found that the majority of complaints (54%) of those who saw the health aides were for upper respiratory problems followed by injuries. The health aides had a median of five visits per week, utilized drugs in 62 percent of the visits, and made referrals to the health service in 7 percent of the cases. Sixty-eight percent of those referred to the health services went and 7 percent of those who were not referred also went. The $10,800 cost of the program which had 135 aides produced an average direct cost of $1.12 per visit and was substantially lower than the $25,855 cost that would have resulted if all the visits had been made to the health service.

At a junior college, students led or established a health advisory board, student advice center, child care center, crash pad, and other drug programs (Leavitt, 1973). At another college students developed a peer sex education program after receiving a three credit course (Baldwin & Wilson, 1974; Zapka, 1972).

Utilization

The more students are aware of the various programs offered by the health service, the more they may utilize them (see also Franklin & McLemore, 1970; Weiner, 1974). Sidhu and Klotz (1971) found that student awareness was low. The majority were not aware of the programs offered, the hours available, nor the details of the programs. Of the twenty-eight programs, nonawareness percentages went from 7 percent for emergency care and first aid to 78 percent for minor surgery with an average of 43 percent.

Assuming that awareness leads to utilization, some public relations efforts have been suggested. McKay (1972) suggests using videotape or closed circuit advertisements on television before classes, radio announcements, and personal contacts.

Evaluation

The most frequently reported method of evaluating a college health service is questionnaires sent to students asking about their attitudes toward the service. Scales or questionnaires have been published for this purpose (Franklin & McLemore, 1967; Lopater & Hursh, 1972).

The range of satisfaction among students varies from study to study, but usually half or more consider the health service adequate, good, or excellent. There are negative attitudes, of course, but a frequent interpretation is that they are more the result of hearsay than personal experience (Bobilya, 1974; Franklin & McLemore, 1968; Lopater & Hursh, 1972). Women have been reported to use the service more frequently than men (Burke, 1974), to use private care more frequently (Lopater & Hursh, 1972), and to be more dissatisfied with the health service (Franklin & McLemore, 1968; King, 1973). Sometimes no differences in attitudes across class, sex, and race are found (Comstock & Slome, 1973); sometimes older students are more pleased (Bobilya, 1974) and sometimes less pleased (Storrs, 1972). Frequently a need for more information on the part of the students is indicated (Bobilya, 1974; King, 1973; Storrs, 1972).

Other evaluative methods have been suggested: a health service self-evaluation guide which rates principles and practices (Kilander & Brown, 1964); a problem-oriented approach for medical records to facilitate audits (Scott, 1974); procedures for determining unit cost or Relative Value Units which allows comparison of the costs of college health services with those offered off-campus by private physicians (Gray, Snively, Healy, & McNece, 1967); many possibilities utilizing a computerized health service (Hall, 1970); and a yearly visit by a committee outside the college to inspect the health service and make recommendations (Farnsworth, 1964).

Perhaps the most sophisticated evaluative approach has been suggested by Dubois (1970, 1973). He suggests that the health service's control of future illness or health impairment must be evaluated by how much a particular health problem is reduced or prevented. To make these determinations, the population at risk and the expected amount of the health problem in the population must be estimated. A disease prevented is a Chargeable Health Impairment Unit (CHIMPU) and the difference between expected and observed CHIMPU's is the Attributable Effect Unit (AEU). The more AEU's the better. For example, if a health service expected 40 percent of the student body and 30 percent of the faculty to get the flu, gave flu shots, and obtained lower percentages, then its expected CHIMPU's would be higher than its obtained CHIMPU's and it would accumulate lots of good AEU's.

DuBois' preventive approach assumes that the goal is no illness on campus and that anything a health service does to reduce illness it should get credit for and be evaluated by. In the flu example above, the number of days of student classroom time and faculty time could be computed. The cost of the health service's administration of the flu shots and publicity could be compared to the cost of the loss of say 5,000 student classroom days. Decisions could be made on the basis of the savings involved and the effectiveness of the action taken by the health service.

Such an approach also indicates areas deserving increased attention by following four steps: (a) Estimate the quantity of health impairment among the population at risk which has not been controlled as well as it should have been; (b) classify each incident of attributable health impairment in terms of what went wrong; (c) derive from the data an appraisal of the program's effectiveness; and (d) conduct an analysis by the class of the problem to determine where the problems are in the system.

PROGRAMS

Medical Exams

One of the earliest health care functions of colleges was the medical exam. It was required for admission, sometimes was repeated annually, and in some cases used to reject students. Rationales for requiring medical exams were that they provided needed care for the students, insured that the student was able to benefit from the education received, protected the community from communicable diseases, provided needed information when the student got sick later, and satisfied any legal need that might arise concerning pre-existing conditions. Providing an exam is also an excellent preventive measure, a foundation upon which to build health education, and a demonstration of concern (Bruyn, 1969). Moore and Summerskill (1954) found that 90 percent of colleges with health services required physical exams for entering students and half requested them for enrolled students. Lohr (1973) found that 70 percent of public community colleges required an exam of all the full-time students.

Required physical exams by the health service have decreased not only because of increasing expense, but also because few students had positive findings, the process became crowded and impersonal, and the demands on time and staff became too great. An alternative of having off-campus physicians conduct the exams was always questionable regarding completeness and validity (Farnsworth, 1964) because of the lack of standardization, the physician's view of the exam as relatively unimportant, and the physician not wanting to jeopardize the student's chance for admission (R. M. Schwartz, 1973b). Another alternative of having nurses conduct the exam creates a question regarding validity. (See also Duncan, 1971.)

With the possibility of automated or computerized entrance record systems (R. M. Schwartz, 1973b), an interview could replace the physical exam (Bergy, 1969; Hathaway, Milone, & White, 1961) which would give information that would allow for a more thorough, personal exam to be done only when needed. Although health should not be a basis for rejecting a student's admission, some mechanisms are needed to plan adequately for the problems encountered primarily for those severely handicapped or terminally ill and their roommates (Egolf, 1969; McMurrer & Clark, 1973).

Women

Increasing concern about the health care of women has raised questions about the adequacy of the college health service. From a survey of the directors of college health services at the 107 medical schools in the United States which grant medical degrees, it was concluded that there were not enough women doctors for female patient visits and that the pelvic exam was considered beyond routine for many of the services (Howell & Hiatt, 1975). One suggestion has been to make the gynecological examination a positive educational experience (G. D.

Miller, 1974).

Injuries and Athletes

For people between the ages of one and thirty-five, the leading cause of death in the United States is accidents. One quarter of all college students or one million are injured each year (Burg & Douglass, 1970). While the college environment is similar to the home environment in number of accidents (Scheffler, 1967), according to available data, intramural sports account for the largest single group of on-campus injuries, with touch football being the major contributor (Kraus & Colberg, 1971). Another estimate is that half of the accidents for college students occur in sports and recreation, while only 10 percent are academically related (Scheffler, 1967). Despite the prevalence of accidental injuries related to sports, Thomasson (1973) found that in fifty-one major colleges, less than one quarter had courses on the medical aspects of sports. Some responses to this lack of attention to athletic injuries have been the identification of the legal responsibilities of team physicians (Feurig, 1962) and a Bill of Rights for the College Athlete (Farnsworth, 1964, 1965).

Drugs

The problem of cigarette smoking has been attacked on most college campuses. Smoking has been outlawed inside health services and has been reduced in classrooms by college policies. Smoking, however, has been on the increase. Dunn (1973a, b, c) found that more students were smoking in 1969 than in 1964 and that they were smoking more. Fifty-eight percent of the seniors smoked a pack or more a day compared to only 28 percent earlier.

The most abused drug of all is alcohol (Johnson, 1974; Sanford & Singer, 1968). Milman and Su (1973) found at ten undergraduate campuses of a large mid-Atlantic university that 91 percent of the students used alcohol and that 21 percent were heavy users. Penn (1974) also found a very high frequency of alcohol use and that it increased with class standing and was higher in social fraternity and off-campus situations.

Marijuana is the second highest drug used with a 23 percent use rate and a 4 percent heavy use rate. The rate of marijuana use has increased since 1970 and has not been accompanied by a reduction of alcohol (Milman & Anker, 1971; Rouse & Ewing, 1974). Innumerable other drugs are used on a college campus (Farnsworth, 1966b) as in the rest of society and expertise and programs for all of them are needed.

Sex

There are a variety of sources which support the need for sex education programs on campuses. One of these sources concerns the degree of sexual activity of college students, otherwise called the sexual revolution (Davis, 1971). At a southern college Vincent and Stelling (1973) found among unmarrieds 66 percent of the men and 49 percent of the women were not virgins and 30 percent had intercourse once a week or more. Oswalt (1974) found that 65 percent of college females were not virgins and only 40 percent were protected by contraceptives all the time. Guttmacher and Vadies (1972) found a 70 percent premarital sex rate for males and females. Vincent and Stelling (1973) also found that the pill was the most popular method of birth control, followed by condoms for the seldom active; approximately two thirds of both sexes received information about contraceptives by reading on their own; of those very sexually active, 82 percent of the females and 62 percent of the males seriously discussed and planned contraceptive procedures with their partners; and the less sexually active the less reliable the method used.

Another source of data comes from the fact that venereal disease is reaching epidemic proportions (Garner, Gerald, & Turner, 1974; Turner & Garner, 1974; Yarber, 1974), with gonorrhea exceeding all other forms of VD combined, and that adults between the ages of twenty to twenty-four account for most of the infectious syphilis cases. An entirely student-run program for screening was developed (Garner et al., 1974), but no cases of VD were found probably because such information would have to be reported by state law. Hood (1973) found a low incidence (.5) of unsuspected gonorrhea at Stanford and concluded that whole scale screening was not warranted.

·Data from pregnancy counseling services provide additional support for sex education programs (Amdur & Oreschnick, 1972; Siddall & Cann, 1973). Services at two colleges found that there was a great deal of misinformation, lack of knowledge, relying on chance, and, perhaps the main problem, denial. There was also a lack of utilization of effective contraception, with rhythm and withdrawal being the main methods used. Most women had a long, continuing relationship with one male, with frequent and regular sex, were reluctant to or did not tell their parents, and chose to have abortions for which the males were supportive and helped pay.

The profession has been slow to respond to such needs, evidenced by the first article in the *Journal of the American College Health Association* dealing primarily with family planning or its contraceptive aspects occurring in 1967 (Klein, see also Farnsworth, 1966b). This was at a time when 24 percent of the total American college population was married. Despite the Birth Control Movement (Donald & Kinch, 1974), a survey of ACHA members found that 55 percent did not prescribe oral contraceptives and 76 percent would not prescribe the pill for any purpose for unmarrieds (Committee on Ethical and Professional Relationships, 1968). A later study including non-ACHA members found that only 30 percent of the institutions had pharmacies and half of these were at institutions of less than 5,000 and that there was a change in unmarrieds getting contraceptive prescriptions to 40 percent for majority age and 35 percent for nonmajority (Barbato, 1971). In another survey, 90 percent of the parents said information should be dispensed and 66 percent said contraceptives should not be available at health services. However, 80 percent of the students in the same study said contraceptives should be available (Dutton, 1971).

There have been a variety of contraceptive and sex education programs (Baldwin & Wilson, 1974; Guttmacher & Vadies,

1972; Packard, 1974; Taylor & Fox, 1974) including a Peer Sex Education Program where students were given a three credit course and then carried out education programs in the dorms (Zapka, 1972). Perhaps the best known program is the sex counseling service established at Yale and the accompanying sex education course (Sarrell & Sarrell, 1971).

Gendel (1974) says that an optimal sex program on campus would be a comprehensive and broad-based or multisponsored program which provided information, counseling, services, and education to students and faculty. There are, however, coordination, staffing, and content problems in developing a multidisciplinary sex-education program (Amdur, Nichols, Boroto, & Shay, 1974; see also Rapp, 1974). Regarding another possible problem, Rees and Zimmerman (1974) found that sexual promiscuity did not increase as a result of sex education, but that attitudes did change toward more tolerance, more responsibilities were identified, and females changed their attitudes more than males. In 1974 (Sheppard), 88 percent of 213 colleges had some type of formal or informal provision for students to learn something about human sexuality, with the larger the college the greater the chance.

Dental Care

Almost 100 percent of the college population in the United States is known to have experienced tooth decay. There is a documented peak need of four fillings per person in the fifteen to twenty-four age group, but only one in ten colleges have dental clinics (Dunning, 1968). Since the need for dental care is clear, the major issue is how much of the dental needs of the college community the institution is willing to meet (Dunning, 1968; Farnsworth, 1964). In Finland 45 percent of the total expenses of the Student Health Foundation go to dentistry (Gaverick, Bonghi, Phipps, & Bissell, 1973).

Thirteen college dental programs in the United States have been described by Pelton (1971). The major services recommended for college dental care are case finding, emergency care, and preventive and educative measures (Dunning, 1968; Farnsworth, 1964, 1965). Of the latter, one of the most frequent services is mouth-guard programs for body-contact sports (Dunning, Giddon, & Greene, 1963).

Medical Excuses, Pharmacies, and Nurses

The practice of requiring medical excuses for absence from class has been recommended for abolishment (Farnsworth, 1964), primarily because it wastes valuable health service time and builds hypochondriacs and antagonistic attitudes towards the service. One college (McCoy in Farnsworth, 1965) reduced its health service visits by 25 percent by dropping the medical excuse system.

The best method for the health service pharmacy to provide drugs to the students has had considerable discussion (Farnsworth, 1964) primarily in regard to preventing long waits and making the process personal. The efficiency problem has prompted prepackaging and conveyor belt approaches, which some reject (Parker, 1974). Some health services at colleges in urban areas have stopped dispensing drugs because of the large number of thefts of controlled substances.

The role of nurses in a college health service has received considerable attention (Campo, 1974; Dutton, 1970; Farnsworth, 1964) both in regard to the peculiarity of the college setting, which at a junior college may mean the nurse is the entire health service, and in regard to the changing views and demands upon the nurse in the society at large.

Safety

The American College Health Association has developed minimum standards for student housing ("Student Housing Standards," 1962). These standards were developed in coordination with the Campus Safety Association and the Association of College and University Housing Officers. There has also been discussion regarding fire safety design in high-rise campus buildings (Maatman, 1972), though the primary responsibility for determining adequacy of exits, alarms, and ventilation would lie with the housing authorities or buildings and grounds. Frequently, however, there is cooperation with the health service or department in implementing the federal Occupational Safety and Health Act (Kilpatrick, 1974; Loofbourow, Holdstock, & Cooper, 1973; Wyatt, 1972; see Campus Security). Particularly important is the OSHA requirement for adequate medical facilities for employees and record-keeping (Satterfield, 1972).

Purdue seems to have anticipated the problem by establishing in 1958 an Environmental Health and Sanitation Officer, as a member of the student health staff (Jones, 1974), an administrative organization also recommended by Farnsworth (1964). A survey of twenty-three schools found that only six had formalized environmental health codes and eight had health and safety codes. Purdue's officer deals with air, noise, and water pollution control; building and grounds sanitation; review of construction plans for new and existing facilities; food and housing sanitation; animal and pest control; occupational health; control of communicable diseases; swimming facilities; solid wastes; water supplies; and general health hazards. Whether such broad responsibilities should be administratively located in student health is questionable. J. M. Miller (1972), however, suggests that an environmental health and safety program is intimately interwoven into the fabric of a good college health program. He says the college ought to be a model, teaching environmental control by example.

The disposal of wastes on college campuses is a particular problem since they come from such a variety of sources: residence halls, hospital, radioactive substances, experimental animals, power plant and industrial discharges, pesticides, and others (Fish, 1972). Regarding radioactive wastes, one university found that radioisotopes were used by 225 approved users in 325 labs in the university system throughout the state (Wollan, Boge, & Staiger, 1969). Protective use and disposal procedures had to be developed in each case. Michigan State University says it established the first waste control authority on any college campus (Rosenhaft & Shafer, 1975). The authority dealt with solid chemical waste disposal and antipollution procedures, environmental protection, recycling, and safety.

Many campuses have civil defense disaster plans and some have riot control plans, but few apparently have epidemic disaster plans. Bruyn (1967) reports that the University of California at Berkeley went through three epidemics in one year and recommends developing plans which emphasize a sensor system for anticipating epidemics, definition of executive action, and simplified hospital procedures.

Health Education and Prevention

Health education courses had their beginning in ancient Greece, but it was 1818 in this country before Harvard required a hygiene course (Richardson, 1974). In the middle part of the Twentieth Century, public health courses were required at many colleges. In recent times the courses have fallen into disrepute and have been dropped for a variety of reasons some of which are irrelevant content, unclear conceptualization, close relationship to physical education, and low status (Carlyon, 1974). Farnsworth (1964), however, considers health education and health service to be equally necessary and important (see also Heyns, 1974). Health education can occur anywhere from the doctor's office to the dorm program to a health course. He also says that health service staff should consider themselves educators. Moore and Summerskill (1954) found that courses in health education were offered at 80 percent of the colleges with a student health service and were required of all students at over 50 percent of those colleges.

There are differing views regarding the purposes of a college health course: to help students stay well in college, learn how to cope, learn how to get help when needed; to serve as a preparation course for the health-related professions; and to help fulfill the overall objectives of the institution which include knowledge and understanding to help students achieve and maintain a range of functioning throughout life that is loosely referred to as being healthy (Carlyon, 1974). Haro (1972) sees the purposes differently: to inform the students about the health service and how to avail themselves of its programs; provide information which builds trust and confidence; make health education an ongoing element of the health service; and provide programs which aid students in making decisions. The purpose of such programs are varied and there are innumerable departments within the college that can have input or responsibility for such a course.

There are other problematic areas of health education. The information is not seen as immediately needed and so relevance for the future must be clearly identified. The concepts within the content are diffuse, with cause and effect not readily apparent. There is also lack of interest in American society as a whole in general health (Haro, 1972). That these problems can be overcome is indicated by an evaluation of one course where students taking the course applied health concepts better, had more positive attitudes toward health, and more positively practiced the concepts (Sorochan, Ulrich, & Coleman, 1971).

Wirag (1973) has rank ordered fifty-seven health education responsibilities. He also found that of 285 directors of college health services which had ACHA membership, only thirty-seven employed a full- or part-time health educator (18 were nurses or physicians and 19 were professional health educators). Whether the college had a professional health educator or not was related to the size of the college and the budget. Health services offered almost as many lectures on health as colleges, but not as many courses. In twenty-nine California community colleges there were 138 health education instructors. Only 19 percent had degrees in health education and 35 percent had degrees in physical education (Eiseman & Marshall, 1972).

It has been suggested that Peace Corps training has some implications for college health education. The Peace Corps approach is preventive in that it tells what to expect, suggests how to handle problems, and provides some trial experiences (Leviton, 1967). The Peace Corps example has primarily to do with mental health but the approach is sound for other health areas as well.

There are a variety of reasons for preventive approaches to health. One is that colleges have a responsibility to teach students to take care of themselves and establish habits to remain healthy (Rose, 1973). An example of this view is in regard to heart attacks, which have risen by 14 percent since 1950 for men between the ages of twenty-five and forty-four (Russek, 1973). Predisposing characteristics of males to heart disease have been identified (Paffenbarger, 1967). Through education those males with the characteristics can be taught better dietary habits, ideal weights, the need for exercise, the need to not smoke, ways to avoid stress, and ways to control blood pressure (Wolf, 1973). Hopefully these changes in habits will lower the incidence or at least delay the onset of symptoms (Dawber, 1973), even though the problem is more complex than this suggests.

MENTAL HEALTH

As early as 1910 Stewart Paton at Princeton was inviting students to conferences about their personal problems (Farnsworth, 1957). But the first full-time psychiatrist appointed to a college staff was H. M. Kerns at the United States Military Academy at West Point in 1920 (Reifler, Liptzin, & Fox, 1967).

By 1932 only twenty-one colleges furnished mental health facilities (Thompson, 1971) and by 1947, while about 550 psychiatrists did occasional consulting in colleges, only about twenty-five were engaged in college psychiatry on a full-time basis (Farnsworth, 1957). Nine years later, in 1956, Gundle and Kraft conducted the last complete survey of mental health programs (Thompson, 1971).

Amada (1975) found that 62 percent of California junior colleges did not offer mental health or counseling services. B. L. Bloom (1970a) found that in the four-year colleges and universities in the western states, the mental health services had doubled since 1953, but more than 60 percent of them had no full-time staff. Seven modalistic or outstanding college mental health programs have been described in detail (Glasscote & Associates, 1973).

College psychiatry or mental health can be conceived as the prototype for community psychiatry (Farnsworth, 1966b; Larson, Barger, & Cahoon, 1969), for many of the psychological concerns of students are simply developmental (Reifler, 1967). Some consider the self-expressed inadequacies as a student to be indistinguishable from the self-expressed inadequacies as a person (Crabbe & Scott, 1972). Even regression in the face of change (or demands of college) is considered a necessary step in maturation (Berns, 1966).

There are, however, special environmental conditions imposed by colleges that augment student problems (Farnsworth, 1957) and various college environments have different impacts (Chickering, 1974). Broadly conceived student tensions in college are produced by dilemmas of choice, increase in the accumulation of knowledge, feelings of anonymity or helplessness, perception of college as a means of social and economic advancement, and crises in meaning and purpose of life (Farnsworth, 1966a). Conceptualized differently, the developmental tasks required of college students include: independence, authority, ambiguity, sexuality, adequacy, standards, and value systems (Farnsworth, 1966b).

Need

The percentage of the college population which needs psychiatric services is difficult to determine, but the accepted estimate appears to be about 12 percent, with a range from 6 to 16 percent (Pearlman, 1966; Reifler, 1971; Reifler & Liptzin, 1969b; Segal, 1966; Thompson, Bentz, & Liptzin, 1973). Schuckit, Halikas, Schuckit, McClure, & Rimmer (1973) found a 20 percent prevalence rate of emotional disturbance among freshman at a midwest university. Another college population was found to have 58 percent well, 30 percent subclinical, 12 percent clinically disturbed and none severely disturbed, as determined by the College Health survey (Smith, Hansell, & English, 1963). Using the Health Opinion Survey, only 5 percent of the undergraduates at another institution scored in the psychiatrically disordered range (Thompson, Bentz, & Liptzin, 1973).

Deutsch and Ellenberg (1973) take issue with the notion that the typical student visiting the college mental health clinic is well and undergoing only transient situational or developmental problems. They found that 60 percent of the freshmen students they saw had psychological problems in high school. Most of the remaining 40 percent were seen again later in their cóllege career and had some psychological difficulties.

The usage rate of mental health services has been found to vary from fifteen to ninety-nine per 1000 with a median of 63/1000 (Reifler, Liptzin, & Fox, 1967). In another study a 48/1000 usage rate was found for smaller schools and a 33/1000 rate for larger schools (Reifler & Banning, 1973; see also Ellis, 1968; Rust & Davie, 1961; Snyder & Kahne, 1969). Pearlman (1966) also suggests that the more organized the mental health services are, the fewer percentage of students seen. It has been estimated by Farnsworth (1966b) that 2/1000 college students will become psychotic each year. He (Farnsworth, 1965) also found one to three suicides per year at Harvard, with five to eight attempts for every one completed (see Sims & Ball, 1973).

Most of the problems presented at college mental health services are depressions and anxieties (Ellis, 1968; Farnsworth, 1957; Schuckit et al., 1973). Although there is difficulty in classifying problems, the primary presenting complaints (more than one could be given) at the University of Chicago were 64 percent affective (equally divided between depression and anxiety), 59 percent interpersonal (more in regard to the opposite sex than to family), 46 percent academic (including some sleep disturbance), 34 percent self-inadequacy, 24 percent somatic, and 13 percent alienation (Winer & Dorus, 1972). The University of Illinois found that their two primary classifications were personality disorders 36 percent and psychoneurosis 29 percent (Walters, 1970). At the University of Michigan it was 35 percent psychoneurotic, 25 percent personality disorder, and 22 percent schizophrenia (Selzer, 1960).

The number of visits to a mental health clinic ranged from 2.8 to 8.2 per year (Reifler et al., 1973) with an average of five (Farnsworth, 1966b). The average yearly cost was $3.27 per student with a range of $2.09 to $4.60 (Farnsworth, 1966b). Most of the students were self-referred (40% to 43%), followed by physician referral (20% to 27%), faculty referral (9%), and deans, dorm staff, and academic counselors referral (22%), (Ellis, 1968;

322   *College Student Personnel Services*

Selzer, 1960; Walters, 1970).

Mental health services are used more by women, younger, foreign, first-year graduate students, and Jewish students (Braaten & Darling, 1961; Reifler, 1971; Walters, 1970; Wogan & Amdur, 1974); sometimes more by older students and married couples (Wogan & Amdur, 1974). At times a strong similarity of problem areas independent of class and sex is reported (Kramer & Berger, 1974). Usually fewer athletes and social organization members seek services (Reifler, 1971; Wogan & Amdur, 1974).

Some suggest that commuter students have greater pathology than residential students in that they are postponing developmental tasks of leaving home (Kysar, 1964), but this hypothesis was found to be true only for females, if at all, at one college (Bown & Richek, 1968). Another college found that commuters used the campus counseling and psychiatric services less (Reinhold, 1973), which may have been because they utilized off-campus services. Believing that junior college students sounded a lot like Kysar's description of the pathology of commuter students, Bown and Richek (1966) found some statistically significant differences between junior and four-year college students.

Mental Health Education

Farnsworth (1966a) says that good mental health is promoted by good education with an involved faculty which teaches by example. He further believes that the psychiatrist should be a teacher whose duty it is to aid in the emotional aspects of maturity (1966b) with every contact an opportunity for learning and teaching (1964). The emphasis on prevention and development rather than therapy and remediation has returned (Falk, 1971; McCarthy, 1970). In a survey of thirteen western states' mental health services, 92 percent said preventive services were at least as important if not more important than client clinical services (B. L. Bloom, 1970b). Research to identify the stress producing areas in the campus community (Falk, 1971), efforts to improve the learning community (Yamamoto, 1970), and teaching mental health as part of a basic health course (Fusco, 1974; see also Leviton, 1971) have been called for. Recognition of changes in student mood during the academic year (Nelson, 1971) and identification of characteristics of the mentally healthy (Grinker, Grinker, & Timberlake, 1962) have been dealt with.

Perhaps the most well-developed approach to the prevention of mental illness in a college population is one outlined by Whittington (1963). He has identified methods (such as referrals and workshops) for agents (such as faculty and student leaders) to use for target groups or problems (such as the peer-group misfits and the married undergraduate) to achieve certain aims or objectives. He provides a conceptual model from which a campus can build its own preventive mental health program.

Screening

Some colleges used to screen entering students regarding their psychological well-being. A Personal Rating Scale was developed as a quick screening device (Wright, 1967). The rationale for early information was to help the student achieve academically and to prevent larger problems (Whittington, 1963). Some evidence exists that students who had psychotherapy during adolescence are subject to increased risk of academic failure, with the highest risk existing for those who inform the college of their history before being admitted (Averbach, 1973).

Psychological screening of college applicants appears to be recommended now only if prior psychiatric illness interrupted the student's education or if the student was hospitalized (Reifler & Liptzin, 1969a). The legal implications of such screening need to be very carefully explored before a college initiates such a program. Further, Farnsworth (1964) believes that no questions regarding present or previous mental illness should be included on applications sent to administrative offices. Rather, information about all health problems should be sent to the health service director.

Other Programs

One way to expand mental health staff is to hire students who have natural expertise in the area. Such students are called indigenous subprofessionals and have been used as resident advisors to lead groups (Davis, 1974; Wolff, 1969), in rehabilitation living units as an alternative to hospitalization for disturbed students (Sinnett & Niedenthal, 1968), and as crisis health aides to answer a crisis help telephone (Grant, Hubble, & Helm, 1973). Other staff expansion methods include using the dean of students and student activities personnel to provide information and serve as a referral system (Craig, 1974) and training faculty in mental health practices (Farnsworth, 1966b; Kuehn, 1974). Each of these programs place the mental health staff in the role of consultants.

Small colleges have developed programs to meet their specialized needs. At one college the student health service and the counseling service shared a psychiatrist and developed programs together (Cary & Papalia, 1974). Fifty small colleges with over 100,000 students and faculty in one geographic locale pooled their resources to form a multiple college mental health center (Soloman, Patch, Sturrock, & Wexler, 1967), which provided anonymity for those seeking help as well as a unique opportunity for research.

Consultant

The role of the mental health consultant has been a topic of considerable discussion, primarily because such a role involves divided loyalties, confusing role definition, and difficult ethical decisions. The consultant has a responsibility to help the student but also to help the administration of the college protect the institution and other students (Blaine, 1964; Blaine & Miller, 1969; Caplan, 1963; Farnsworth, 1957, 1964, 1965, 1966b). Obtaining students' written permission for use of information about themselves and having a policy statement have been suggested as aids in the dilemma (Blaine & Miller, 1969;

Farnsworth, 1965), though most services have not developed any printed set of policies (Curran, 1969).

The moral and political implications of the college psychiatrist's role need to be explored (Halleck, 1967; Szasz, 1967; see Disciplinary Counseling section). Students can see the psychiatrist as a double agent who is willing to breach their confidences whenever the psychiatrist personally considers it in the best interests of either the student or college. Curran (1969) found that most of the services (at a time when most college students were not of majority age) notified parents of hospitalization, serious illness, or suicide attempts; only 25 percent kept separate mental health records with most making notations in the central file; and often gave information to the central administration — all possibly unethical practices.

Evaluation

Little evaluative research is reported in the literature (see Brigante, 1969; Farnsworth, 1966b). An Index of Emotional Stress (Estes, 1973) and a Twelve-Problems Scale (Rust, 1960) were developed for descriptive purposes. One clinic described itself by tabulating the characteristics of the average patient: where the patients came from, why they came, their diagnosis, their treatment, how they spent their time, and how they were terminated (Friedman & Coons, 1969). An extensive procedure for systematic recording of relevant clinical data has also been reported (Whittington, 1963). The caseload reporting method for evaluation has been considered unsatisfactory (Friedman & Reifler, 1974), because the staff engage in many activities other than direct patient care, the proportion of time spent in indirect service is greater than in direct service, and the impact of indirect service on the total patient count is impressively greater. It has been suggested that a better approach is to account for hours, rather than patients. One follow-up study to determine therapy effectiveness was unclear in its conclusions (Brush & Nelson, 1968) and the other was generally positive (Whittington, 1963).

Relationship with Counseling Service

Frequently there is little contact between the college mental health service and the college counseling service. Each views the other with suspicion and distrust and questions the level of competency. B. L. Bloom (1970b) found that most mental health units in the western states felt that relationships with other agencies were poor. The lack of relationship may result from lack of personal contact, campus geographical distance, and fear of duplication or loss of territory. Regrettably few campuses have good, working, mutually agreed on, and well-documented relationships. Where mergers do occur, they are frequently the result of financial necessity rather than of planned policy. Sometimes mutual referrals do occur and a psychiatrist comes a few hours a week as consultant to the counseling service. Telephone crisis lines and provision of regular in-office service after hours (Mason & Curtis, 1973) are two other areas in which cooperation has occurred.

A study (Reinhold, 1973; see also Whittington, 1963) of users and nonusers of college counseling and psychiatric services found that 19 percent of the students who graduated with continuing registrations used one or both of the services. The counseling service was used by 13 percent and the student health service psychiatric clinic was used by 9 percent. The users visited the medical service significantly more than the nonusers, but there was no user syndrome. The users of the counseling service had more difficulty with studying, concentrating, and career planning (and appeared more conservative, like the nonusers) and the psychiatric service users had more feelings of depression and anxiety, thoughts of suicide, and fears of a nervous breakdown. The users of both services were similar regarding concerns about interpersonal relationships, sexual behavior, trouble with sleep, lack of confidence, loneliness, and apathy. Also the counseling service users acknowledged fewer sources of help than the psychiatric service users. The data from the Reinhold study suggest that a close working relationship between the two services could be very beneficial to the student.

RELATIONSHIPS TO OTHER SERVICES

The American College Health Association has been aware for a long time of the relationships that can and probably should exist between a college health service and at least fifteen other college student personnel services. These other services (and indications of the primary aspects of the relationship) are:

Registrars and academic deans (admissions, enrollment, contacts);

Deans or vice-presidents of students (consultation, contacts, rooming house supervision, facilities for disabled, discipline);

Board in control of athletics (physical education cooperative service, care of athletes);

Student operated organizations (cooperative projects such as lectures);

Counseling service (consultations, referrals, programs);

University business office (all financial dealings, fees);

University high school (examinations, inspection service);

Building and grounds department (sanitation, safety, inspections, disposals);

R.O.T.C. commandant (examinations of approval, excuses, investigations);

Director of university hospital (certain bed care, consultations);

Superintendents of other hospitals (occasional bed care, consultations);

Administration of the medical school (pathology, other less regular services);

City health officer (sanitary inspections, quarantines);

Dormitories (care of student illness through resident part-time nurses, food handler examinations);

Members of county medical societies (may use any health service facilities for care of their student patients, see also Alexander, 1972); and

Campus security (escort, safety);

(American Medical Association, 1936).

ACHA suggested that representatives from these areas form

an Advisory Health Council for the college health program. Relationships with other college student personnel services can be formal or informal depending upon the expertise of the staff. R. M. Schwartz (1973a) suggests that usually there are none at all. He also suggests that the health service should at least be involved in the college's orientation and participate in the regular speaker's bureau.

The primary relationships probably exist between the health service's mental health unit and the counseling service and residence halls (Davis, 1974). Many cooperative programs can be developed between mental health and counseling services (though seldom are), particularly in regard to training and providing consultative services. R. K. Schwartz (1973) describes the total integration of the health and counsewing services into a resource center.

REFERENCES

Alexander, S. B. The responsibility of the campus to the community. *Journal of the American College Health Association,* 1972, *20,* 171-175.

Amada, G. The paucity of mental health services and programs in community colleges: Implications of a survey. *Journal of the American College Health Association,* 1975, *23,* 345-349.

Amdur, M. J., Nichols, M., Boroto, D. R., & Shay, B. L. Issues in developing a multidisciplinary sex education program in a public university. *Journal of the American Health Association,* 1974, *22,* 364-369.

Amdur, S. B., & Oreschnick, R. W. A descriptive study of a pregnancy counseling service in a university health service. *Journal of the American College Health Association,* 1972, *21,* 149-151.

American College Health Association. Recommended standards and practices for a college health program. *Journal of the American College Health Association,* 1969, *18,* 41-106.

American Medical Association. *University and college student health services.* Chicago: Author, 1936.

Averbach, I. J. History of psychiatric disorder and risk of academic failure in freshman. *Journal of the American College Health Association,* 1973, *21,* 252-256.

Averill, B. W. Use of automated information systems in the management and evaluation of college health programs. *Journal of the American College Health Association,* 1970, *19,* 67-74.

Averill, B. W., Rising, E. J., McBride, T. C., Gage, R. W., & Piedmont, E.

B. The outpatient care delivery system — a new approach. 1. Developing a new system. *Journal of the American College Health Association,* 1972, *20,* 334-339.

Baldwin, B. A., & Wilson, R. R. A campus peer counseling program in human sexuality. *Journal of the American College Health Association,* 1974, *22,* 399-404.

Barbato, L. Study of the prescription and dispensing of contraceptive medications at institutions of higher education. *Journal of the American College Health Association,* 1971, *19,* 303-306.

Bergy, G. G. Is medical examination of the "well" person effective and valuable? *Journal of the American College Health Association,* 1969, *17,* 194-197.

Berns, R. S. Regressive emotional behavior in college students. *American Journal of Psychiatry,* 1966, *122,* 1378-1384.

Blaine, G. B., Jr. Divided loyalties: The college therapist's responsibility to the student, the university and the parents. *American Journal of Orthopsychiatry,* 1964, *34,* 481-485.

Blaine, G. B., Jr., & Miller, J. M. College health psychiatry — a resource for administrators: A panel discussion. *Journal of the American College Health Association,* 1969, *18,* 152-155.

Bloom, A. The HMO and college health services. *Journal of the American College Health Association,* 1972, *21,* 115-116.

Bloom, B. L. Characteristics of campus community mental health programs in Western United States — 1969. *Journal of the American College Health Association,* 1970, *18,* 196-200. (a)

Bloom, B. L. Current issues in the provision of campus community mental health services. *Journal of the American College Health Association,* 1970, *18,* 257-264. (b)

Bobilya, L. J. Students' views of the Indiana University student health service. *Journal of the American College Health Association,* 1974, *23,* 19-21.

Bobilya, L. J., & Yarber, W. L. Reflections on the role of the advisors to the health service. *Journal of the American College Health Association,* 1974, *22,* 177-181.

Bown, O. H., & Richek, H. G. Mental health of junior college students. *Junior College Journal,* 1966, *37*(4), 18-21.

Bown, O. H., & Richek, H. G. The mental health of commuter college students. *Mental Hygiene,* 1968, *52,* 354-359.

Boynton, R. E. Historical development of college health services. *Student Medicine,* 1962, *10,* 294-305.

Boynton, R. E. The first fifty years: A history of the American College Health Association. *Journal of the American College Health Association,* 1971, *19,* 269-285.

Braaten, L. J., & Darling, C. D. Mental health services in college: Some statistical analyses. *Student Medicine,* 1961, *10,* 235-253.

330 *College Student Personnel Services*

Brigante, T. R. The assessment process in campus community mental health programs. *Community Mental Health Journal*, 1969, *5*, 140-148.

Brush, A. L., & Nelson, M. J. A followup study of students seen for psychiatric counseling: Ten or more years later. *Journal of the American College Health Association*, 1968, *16*, 270-280.

Bruyn, H. B. Practical disaster planning: The impact of acute epidemics on a health service and the community. *Journal of the American College Health Association*, 1967, *16*, 109-115.

Bruyn, H. B. Medical and health evaluation upon enrollment in college: A foundation for the ideal program in student health. *Journal of the American College Health Association*, 1969, *17*, 198-206.

Burg, F. D., & Douglass, J. The role of college health in injury control. *Journal of the American College Health Association*, 1970, *18*, 278-281.

Burke, W. M. Attitudes and the utilization of health services. *Journal of the American College Health Association*, 1974, *22*, 320-324.

Campo, I. T. Role expectations of a community college nurse. *Journal of the American College Health Association*, 1974, *22*, 192-193.

Caplan, G. Types of mental health consultants. *American Journal of Orthopsychiatry*, 1963, *33*, 470-481.

Carlyon, W. H. The health education course. *Journal of the American College Health Association*, 1974, *22*, 259-260.

Cary, G., & Papalia, A. S. A college mental health program that works. *Journal of the American College Health Association*, 1974, *22*, 288-294.

Chickering, A. W. The impact of various college environments on personality development. *Journal of the American College Health Association*, 1974, *23*, 82-93.

Colleges may be wasting money on health services survey shows. *College and University Business*, 1972, *53*(2), 48.

Committee on Ethical and Professional Relationships. Dispensing of birth control information, devices and medications in college health services: A panel discussion. *Journal of the American College Health Association*, 1968, *16*, 233-245.

Comstock, L. K., & Slome, C. A health survey of students. *Journal of the American College Health Association*, 1973, *22*, 150-159.

Cooke, J., Hekhuis, L., Huntington, C., & Knisely, W. Profile of eighteen university health services. *Journal of the American College Health Association*, 1969, *17*, 257-260.

Cox, J. The University of Kentucky's experience with a voluntary health fee. *Journal of the American College Health Association*, 1974, *22*, 311-314.

Crabbe, J. L., & Scott, W. A. Academic and personal adjustment. *Journal of Counseling Psychology*, 1972, *19*, 58-64.

Craig, T. J. Evaluating utilization and outcome in a small college mental health service: Implications for future planning. *Journal of the American College Health Association*, 1974, *22*, 295-301.

Curran, W. J. Policies and practices concerning confidentiality in college mental health services in the United States and Canada. *American Journal of Psychiatry,* 1969, *125,* 1520-1530.

Davie, J. S., Goldberg, B., & Rowe, D. S. Consumer acceptance of Yale Health Plan. *Journal of the American College Health Association,* 1974, *22,* 325-331.

Davis, K. Sex on campus: Is there a revolution? *Medical Aspects of Human Sexuality,* 1971, *5*(1), 128.

Davis, K. L. Mental health consultative services in residence halls. *Journal of the American College Health Association,* 1974, *23,* 98-101.

Dawber, T. R. Risk factors in young adults. *Journal of the American College Health Association,* 1973, *22,* 84-95.

Deutsch, A., & Ellenberg, J. Transience vs. continuance of disturbances in college freshmen. *Archives of General Psychiatry,* 1973, *28,* 412-417.

Diehl, H. S., & Shepard, C. E. *The health of college students: A report to the American Youth Commission.* Washington, D. C.: American Council on Education, 1939.

Donald, I. R., & Kinch, R. A. H. The birth control movement and oral contraceptives in the college population. *Journal of the American College Health Association,* 1974, *22,* 375-383.

Dubois, D. M. Evaluation of health service systems with special emphasis on college health services. *Journal of the American College Health Association,* 1970, *18,* 182-191.

DuBois, D. M. Measuring the effects and qualities of college health programs. *Journal of the American College Health Association,* 1973, *21,* 282-286.

Duncan, W. R. Medical examination — complete? *Journal of the American College Health Association,* 1971, *19,* 239-240.

Dunn, D. F. Cigarette smoking: Health knowledge and practices. *Journal of the American College Health Association,* 1973, *22,* 124-125. (a)

Dunn, D. F. Cigarettes and the college senior. *Journal of the American College Health Association,* 1973, *21,* 224-226. (b)

Dunn, D. F. Cigarettes: College freshmen in 1964 and 1969. *Journal of the American College Health Association,* 1973, *22,* 126-127. (c)

Dunning, J. M. Dental care for the student: How far shall we go? *Journal of the American College Health Association,* 1968, *17,* 97-99.

Dunning, J. M., Giddon, D. B., & Greene, F. B. Prevalence and characteristics of college dental health services. *Journal of the American College Health Association,* 1963, *11,* 189-196.

Durfee, M. Proposed guidelines for tuberculosis control in colleges. *Journal of the American College Health Association,* 1972, *20,* 233-236.

Dutton, R. C. The legal aspects of college health nursing. *Journal of the American College Health Association,* 1970, *18,* 218-221.

Dutton, R. C. Sex and the college health nurse. *Journal of the American College Health Association,* 1971, *19,* 313-314.

Edison, G. R. Prepayment versus fee for service. *Journal of the American College Health Association,* 1970, *18,* 325-329.

Eiseman, S., & Marshall, L. The status of professional preparation of health educators in selected California community colleges, 1970-1971. *Journal of the American College Health Association,* 1972, *20,* 280-282.

Egolf, R. L. Admissions screening and the health evaluation report. *Journal of the American College Health Association,* 1969, *18,* 138-140.

Ellis, V. Students who seek psychiatric help. In J. Katz (Ed.), *No time for youth: Growth and constraint in college students.* San Francisco: Jossey-Bass, 1968.

Estes, R. Determinants of differential stress levels among university students. *Journal of the American College Health Association,* 1973, *21,* 470-476.

Falk, R. B. Innovations in college mental health. *Mental Hygiene,* 1971, *55,* 451-455.

Farnsworth, D. L. *Mental health in college and university.* Cambridge: Harvard University Press, 1957.

Farnsworth, D. L. (Ed.). *College health administration.* New York: Appleton-Century-Crofts, 1964.

Farnsworth, D. L. *College health services in the United States.* Washington, D. C.: American College Personnel Association, 1965. (Student Personnel Monograph Series, No. 4)

Farnsworth, D. L. The liberal arts college's responsibility for the emotional stability of students. In E. J. McGrath (Ed.), *The liberal arts college's responsibility for the individual student.* New York: Teachers College Press, 1966. (a)

Farnsworth, D. L. *Psychiatry, education, and the young adult.* Springfield, Ill., Charles C Thomas, 1966. (b)

Feurig, J. S. Legal liabilities of team physicians. *Student Medicine,* 1962, *10,* 479-483.

Fish, J. O. Campus wastes — a community problem. *Journal of the American College Health Association,* 1972, *20,* 186-189.

Forbes, O. Z. In the urban setting. *Journal of the American College Health Association,* 1972, *21,* 108-109.

Franklin, B. J., & McLemore, S. D. A scale for measuring attitudes toward student health services. *Journal of Psychology,* 1967, *66,* 143-147.

Franklin, B. J., & McLemore, S. D. Attitudes toward and reported utilization of a student health center. *Journal of the American College Health Association,* 1968, *17,* 54-59.

Franklin, B. J., & McLemore, S. D. Factors affecting the choice of medical care among university students. *Journal of Health and Social Behavior,* 1970, *11,* 311-319.

Friedman, W. H., & Coons, F. W. The mental health unit of a student health service: A study of a clinic. *Journal of the American College Health Association,* 1969, *17,* 270-283.

Friedman, W. H., & Reifler, C. B. How come you guys in mental health don't see more patients? *Journal of the American College Health Association,* 1974, *22,* 274-278.

Fusco, R. A. Developing a course in mental health. *Journal of the American College Health Association*, 1974, *23*, 106-108.

Garner, W. R., Gerald, M. C., & Turner, H. S. A student conducted VD education and syphilis screening program. *Journal of the American College Health Association*, 1974, *22*, 409-411.

Garverick, C. M., Bonghi, J. J., Phipps, G. T., & Bissell, G. D. Consumer evaluation of a university dental health program for students. *Journal of the American College Health Association*, 1973, *22*, 146-148.

Gendel, E. S. Introductory statement: Perspectives on human sexuality. *Journal of the American College Health Association*, 1974, *22*, 356-360.

Glasscote, R. M., & Associates *Mental health on the campus: A field study.* Washington, D. C.: Joint Information Service, American Psychiatric Association and the National Association for Mental Health, 1973.

Grant, C. H., Hubble, K. O., & Helm, C. J. The utilization of peers in a college crisis intervention program. *Journal of the American College Health Association*, 1973, *21*, 327-332.

Gray, T. J., Snively, S. A., Healy, C. F., & McNece, E. R. Comparative cost accounting for college health services. *Journal of the American College Health Association*, 1967, *16*, 125-130.

Grinker, R. R., Sr., Grinker, R. R., Jr., & Timberlake, J. "Mentally healthy" young males (homoclites). *Archives of General Psychiatry*, 1962, *6*, 451.

Gundle, S., & Kraft, A. Mental health programs in American colleges and universities. *Bulletin of the Menninger Clinic*, 1956, *20*, 63.

Guttmacher, A. F., & Vadies, E. E. Sex on the campus and the college health service. *Journal of the American College Health Association*, 1972, *21*, 145-148.

Hair, J. E. The relationship of the HMO to the college and university health service in the rural setting. *Journal of the American College Health Association*, 1972, *21*, 105-107.

Hall, W. A. The role of electronic data processing in the evaluation of college health programs. *Journal of the American College Health Association*, 1970, *19*, 125-130.

Halleck, S. L. Psychiatric management of dangerous behavior on a university campus. *American Journal of Psychiatry*, 1967, *124*, 303-310.

Haro, M. S. The health educator and the campus health service. *Journal of the American College Health Association*, 1972, *20*, 293-298.

Hathaway, J. S., Milone, H. S., & White, C. Health problems and health surveys of college students. *Student Medicine*, 1961, *9*, 211-217.

Helm, C. J., Knipmeyer, C., & Martin, M. R. Health aides: Student involvement in a university health center program. *Journal of the American College Health Association*, 1972, *20*, 248-251.

Heyns, R. W. The changing climate of higher education. *Journal of the American College Health Association*, 1974, *23*, 3-6.

Hood, A. F. Prevalence of unsuspected gonorrhea in female students. *Journal of the American College Health Association*, 1973, *21*, 370-372.

Howell, M. C., & Hiatt, D. Do student health services discriminate against women: A survey of services in the United States medical schools. *Journal of the American College Health Association*, 1975, *23*, 359-363.

Johnson, R. D. Alcohol and the college campus. *Journal of the American College Health Association*, 1974, *22*, 216-219.

Jones, K. K. Status and use of codes and regulations on campus. *Journal of the American College Health Association*, 1974, *22*, 302-307.

Kilander, H. F., & Brown, W. C. A college health services self-evaluation guide. *Journal of the American College Health Association*, 1964, *13*, 218-226.

Kilpatrick, F. J. Establishing priorities for scheduled elimination of environmental hazards. *Journal of the American College Health Association*, 1974, *23*, 7-13.

King, S. H. How students view the health services. *Journal of the American College Health Association*, 1973, *21*, 351-352.

Klein, E. The need for family planning as a student health service. *Journal of the American College Health Association*, 1967, *16*, 95-98.

Kramer, H. C., & Berger, F. Utilization of assessment data for program planning. *Journal of the American College Health Association*, 1974, *23*, 138-142.

Kraus, J. F., & Colberg, G. Some epidemiologic factors associated with intramural football injuries on a rural college campus. *Journal of the American College Health Association*, 1971, *20*, 106-114.

Kuehn, J. L. A pilot program of mental health education for faculty. *Journal of the American College Health Association*, 1974, *23*, 109-112.

Kysar, J. E. Mental health in an urban commuter university. *Archives of General Psychiatry*, 1964, *11*, 472-483.

Larson, E. A., Barger, B., & Cahoon, S. N. College mental health programs: A paradigm for comprehensive community mental health centers. *Community Mental Health Journal*, 1969, *5*, 461-467.

Leavitt, A. Student-organized health programs at City College of San Francisco. *Journal of the American College Health Association*, 1973, *21*, 296-305.

Leviton, D. What the Peace Corps has to suggest about college mental health services. *Journal of the American College Health Association*, 1967, *16*, 74-79.

Leviton, D. A course on death education and suicide prevention: Implications for health education. *Journal of the American College Health Association*, 1971, *19*, 217-220.

Lohr, J. G. Community college health services. *Journal of the American College Health Association*, 1973, *21*, 407-411.

Loofbourow, J. C., Holdstock, R. S., & Cooper, T. Y. Occupational health; organization and function. *Journal of the American College Health Association*, 1973, *21*, 317-320.

Lopater, D., & Hursh, L. M. Report on student views of the Illinois health service. *Journal of the American College Health Association*, 1972, *20*,

299-301.

Louden, T. L. The role of college health in planning for health maintenance organizations. *Journal of the American College Health Association,* 1973, *21,* 209-212.

Maatman, G. L. Fire safety design in high-rise campus buildings. *Journal of the American College Health Association,* 1972, *20,* 193-196.

Martin, G. L., & Newman, I. M. The costs and effects of a student health-aide program. *Journal of the American College Health Association,* 1973, *21,* 237-240.

Mason, R. L., Jr., & Curtis, J. R. A night mental health clinic. *Journal of the American College Health Association,* 1973, *21,* 358-360.

Matte, P. J. Implementation of a data processing system. *Journal of the American College Health Association,* 1970, *19,* 55-66.

McCarthy, B. W. New approaches to mental health services in colleges and universities. *Psychological Reports,* 1970, *27,* 420-422.

McKay, E. R. Health services — consumer awareness leads to utilization. *Journal of the American College Health Association,* 1972, *21,* 140-141.

McMurrer, J., & Clark, F., Jr. Psychiatric intervention in the case of a terminally ill college student. *Journal of the American College Health Association,* 1973, *22,* 134-137.

Meylan, G. L. Status of hygiene in American colleges. *Journal of the Proceedings of the Second Annual Congress, American School Hygiene Association,* 1908, *1,* 77-79.

Miller, G. D. The gynecological examination as a learning experience. *Journal of the American College Health Association,* 1974, *23,* 162-164.

Miller, J. M. The development of an environmental health and safety program in a comprehensive health program for the campus community. *Journal of the American College Health Association,* 1972, *20,* 183-185.

Milman, D. H., & Anker, J. L. Patterns of drug usage among university students: IV. Use of marihuana, amphetamines, opium, and LSD by undergraduates. *Journal of the American College Health Association,* 1971, *20,* 96-105.

Milman, D. H., & Su, W. Patterns of drug usage among university students: V. Heavy use of marihuana and alcohol by undergraduates. *Journal of the American College Health Association,* 1973, *21,* 181-187.

Moore, N. S., & Summerskill, J. *Health services in American colleges and universities, 1953.* Ithaca, N. Y.: Cornell University Press, 1954.

Nelson, T. M. Student mood during a full academic year. *Journal of Psychosomatic Research,* 1971, *15,* 113-122.

Nichols, D. D. Some recent data on community college health service programs. *Journal of the American College Health Association,* 1973, *22,* 61-64.

Osborne, M. M. Discussion. *Journal of the American College Health Association,* 1970, *18,* 194-195.

Osborne, M. M., Jr. That's not where the problem is, but that's where it hurts. *Journal of the American College Health Association*, 1973, *21*, 287-295.

Oswalt, R. M. Sexual and contraceptive behavior of college females. *Journal of the American College Health Association*, 1974, *22*, 392-393.

Packard, R. A. The evolution of a contraceptive program. *Journal of the American College Health Association*, 1974, *22*, 389-391.

Paffenbarger, R. S., Jr. Chronic disease in former college students: VI. Implications for college health programs. *Journal of the American College Health Association*, 1967, *16*, 51-55.

Parker, H. E. The pharmacy in a university atmosphere. *Journal of the American College Health Association*, 1974, *23*, 181-183.

Pearlman, S. Mental health in higher education. In L. E. Abt & B. F. Riess (Eds.), *Progress in clinical psychology.* (Vol. VII). New York: Grune & Stratton, 1966.

Pelton, W. J. Concept to action: Student dental health programs. *Journal of the American College Health Association*, 1971, *20*, 77-93.

Penn, J. R. College student life-style and frequency of alcohol usage. *Journal of the American College Health Association*, 1974, *22*, 220-222.

Rapp, C. E. An example of a presentation to a university administration recommending gynecological and contraceptive services. *Journal of the American College Health Association*, 1974, *22*, 361-363.

Rees, B., & Zimmerman, S. The effects of formal sex education on the sexual behaviors and attitudes of college students. *Journal of the American College Health Association*, 1974, *22*, 370-371.

Reifler, C. B. Some psychiatric considerations in the case of college students. *Southern Medical Journal*, 1967, *60*, 171-176.

Reifler, C. B. Epidemiologic aspects of college mental health. *Journal of the American College Health Association*, 1971, *19*, 159-163.

Reifler, C. B., & Banning, J., et al. A student mental health data bank: Report of a pilot project. *Journal of the American College Health Association*, 1973, *21*, 405-406.

Reifler, C. B., & Liptzin, M. B. Entering college with a psychiatric history. *The American Journal of Psychiatry*, 1969, *125*, 1625-1632. (a)

Reifler, C. B., & Liptzin, M. B. Epidemiological studies of college mental health. *Archives of General Psychiatry*, 1969, *20*, 528-540. (b)

Reifler, C. B., Liptzin, M. B., & Fox, J. T. College psychiatry as public health psychiatry. *American Journal of Psychiatry*, 1967, *124*, 662-671.

Reinhold, J. E. Users and nonusers of college counseling and psychiatric services. *Journal of the American College Health Association*, 1973, *21*, 201-208.

Richardson, C. E. The college health education course: Its status and future. *Journal of the American College Health Association*, 1974, *22*, 262-264.

Rose, K. To keep the people in health. *Journal of the American College Health Association*, 1973, *22*, 80-83.

Rosenberg, C. A functioning HMO. *Journal of the American College Health Association,* 1972, *21,* 103-104.

Rosenhaft, M. E., & Shafer, C. A. A comprehensive overview of university waste control. *Journal of the American College Health Association,* 1975, *23,* 333-339.

Rouse, B. A., & Ewing, J. A. Student drug use, risk-taking, and alienation. *Journal of the American College Health Association,* 1974, *22,* 226-229.

Russek, H. I. Emotional stress as a cause of coronary heart disease. *Journal of the American College Health Association,* 1973, *22,* 120-123.

Rust, R. M. Epidemiology of mental health in college. *Journal of Psychology,* 1960, *49,* 235-248.

Rust, R. M., & Davie, J. S. The personal problems of college students. *Mental Hygiene,* 1961, *45,* 247-257.

Sanford, N., & Singer, S. Drinking and personality. In J. Katz & Associates, *No time for youth.* San Francisco: Jossey-Bass, 1968.

Sarrell, P. M., & Sarrell, L. J. A sex counseling service for college students. *American Journal of Public Health,* 1971, *61,* 1341-1347.

Satterfield, R. W. The responsibilities of institutions of higher education under the Occupational Safety and Health Act of 1970. *Journal of the American College Health Association,* 1972, *21,* 121-122.

Scheffler, G. Student accidental injury experience. *Journal of the American College Health Association,* 1967, *16,* 85-90.

Schuckit, M. A., Halikas, J. A., Schuckit, J. J., McClure, J., & Rimmer, J. Four year prospective study on the college campus: II. Personal and familial psychiatric problems. *Diseases of the Nervous System,* 1973, *34,* 320-324.

Schwartz, R. K. Integration of medical and counseling services. *Personnel and Guidance Journal,* 1973, *51,* 347-349.

Schwartz, R. M. The college health service and the college health course. *Journal of the American College Health Association,* 1973, *22,* 143-145. (a)

Schwartz, R. M. A new system for entrance health evaluations. *Journal of the American College Health Association,* 1973, *21,* 213-220. (b)

Scott, S. R. The use of problem oriented medical records in college health services. *Journal of the American College Health Association,* 1974, *22,* 332-334.

Segal, B. E. Epidemiology of emotional disturbance among college undergraduates: A review and analysis. *Journal of Nervous Mental Diseases,* 1966, *143,* 348-362.

Selzer, M. L. The happy college student myth. *Archives of General Psychiatry,* 1960, *2,* 131-136.

Sheppard, S. A survey of college-based courses in human sexuality. *Journal of the American College Health Association,* 1974, *23,* 14-18.

Siddall, L. B., & Cann, M. A. Pregnancy on a university campus. *Journal of the American College Health Association,* 1973, *21,* 247-251.

Sidhu, S., & Klotz, A. L. Student awareness and utilization of a college student health service. *Journal of the American College Health Association,* 1971, *19,* 298-302.

Sims, L., & Ball, M. J. Suicide among university students. *Journal of the American College Health Association,* 1973, *21,* 336-338.

Sinnett, E. R., & Niedenthal, L. K. The use of indigenous volunteers in a rehabilitation living unit for disturbed college students. *Community Mental Health Journal,* 1968, *4,* 232-243.

Smith, W. G., Hansell, N., & English, J. T. Psychiatric disorder in a college population. *Archives of General Psychiatry,* 1963, *9,* 351-361.

Snyder, B. R., & Kahne, M. J. Stress in higher education and student use of university psychiatry. *American Journal of Orthopsychiatry,* 1969, *39,* 23-35.

Soloman, P., Patch, V. D., Sturrock, J. B., & Wexler, D. A new approach to student mental health in small colleges: A multiple-college mental health center. *American Journal of Psychiatry,* 1967, *124,* 658-661.

Sorochan, W. D., Ulrich, C., & Coleman, G. Assessment of a basic required health education course. *Journal of the American College Health Association,* 1971, *19,* 315-318.

Storey, T. A. *The status of hygiene programs in institutions of higher education in the United States.* Stanford, Calif.: Stanford University Press, 1927.

Storrs, R. T. A survey of attitudes of students toward utilization of the university health center. *Journal of the American College Health Association,* 1972, *20,* 204-206.

Student housing standards. *Student Medicine,* 1962, *10,* 363-393.

Szasz, T. S. The psychiatrist as double agent. *Trans-action,* 1967, *4*(10), 16-24.

Taylor, K. R., & Fox, S. C. Cooperation in the area of birth control. *Journal of the American College Health Association,* 1974, *22,* 372-374.

Thomasson, G. O. Educational programs in sports medicine. *Journal of the American College Health Association,* 1973, *21,* 325-326.

Thompson, J. R. Psychological services at a small liberal arts college. *Journal of the American College Health Association,* 1971, *20,* 141-147.

Thompson, J. R., Bentz, W. K., & Liptzin, M. B. The prevalence of psychiatric disorder in an undergraduate population. *Journal of the American College Health Association,* 1973, *21,* 415-422.

Tupper, C. J. The college professor — his health and health care habits. *Student Medicine,* 1962, *10,* 414-421.

Turner, H. S., & Garner, W. R. Gonorrhea: A review of the problem at a large state university. *Journal of the American College Health Association,* 1974, *22,* 419-424.

Vincent, M. L., & Stelling, F. H. A survey of contraceptive practices and attitudes of unwed college students. *Journal of the American College Health Association,* 1973, *21,* 257-263.

Walters, O. S. Prevalence of diagnosed emotional disorders in university students. *Journal of the American College Health Association*, 1970, *18*,204-209.

Weiner, H. A comparison of frequent and non-frequent health service users. *Journal of the American College Health Association*, 1974, *22*, 315-319.

Whittington, H. G. *Psychiatry on the college campuses*. New York: International Universities Press, 1963.

Wiechmann, G. H. Education for health behavior: A philosophical model. *Journal of the American College Health Association*, 1970, *19*, 89-100.

Williams, S. *History of modern education*. Syracuse, N. Y.: S. Bardeen, 1896.

Winer, J. A., & Dorus, L. W. Complaints patients bring to a student mental health clinic. *Journal of the American College Health Association*, 1972, *21*, 134-139.

Wirag, J. R. The role of the health educator in health service centers of selected colleges and universities. *Journal of the American College Health Association*, 1973, *21*, 393-398.

Wogan, M., & Amdur, M. J. Changing patterns of student mental health, 1964 to 1972. *Journal of the American College Health Association*, 1974, *22*, 202-208.

Wolf, G. L. Adolescent hypertension and cardiovascular disease prevention. *Journal of the American College Association*, 1973, *22*, 113-119.

Wolff, T. Undergraduates as campus mental health workers. *Personnel and Guidance Journal*, 1969, *48*, 294-304.

Wollan, R. O., Boge, R. J., & Staiger, J. W. Radioactive waste disposal at a large university. *Journal of the American College Health Association*, 1969, *17*, 315-324.

World Health Organization. *Constitution of the World Health Organization*. Geneva: Author, 1947.

Wright, J. J. Reported personal stress sources and adjustment of entering freshmen. *Journal of Counseling Psychology*, 1967, *14*, 371-373.

Wyatt, G. L. The Williams-Steiger Occupational Safety and Health Act of 1970. *Journal of the American College Health Association*, 1972, *21*, 117-120.

Yamamoto, K. Healthy students in the college environment. *Personnel and Guidance Journal*, 1970, *48*, 809-816.

Yarber, W. L. College women and the prevention of venereal disease. *Journal of the American College Health Association*, 1974, *22*, 412-418.

Yeager, L. B., Johnson, E., & Gynn, T. Feasibility of sickle-cell screening and research in a private university community. *Journal of the American College Health Association*, 1973, *21*, 278-281.

Zapka, J. M. Student involvement in university health programs. *Journal of the American College Health Association*, 1972, *20*, 252-256.

CHAPTER 12

COUNSELING

Lynette Daniels Schneider

HISTORY

THE origins of the modern counseling service are somewhat obscure. The earliest form of counseling in American institutions of higher education was the private discussion of student and faculty advisor. It was not until after World War I, when diagnosis and testing techniques and other psychological advancements had been widely developed and implemented, that a trend toward supplementing and replacing faculty advisors with professionally trained counselors could be identified on college campuses.

Counseling as an organized service in the public school system can be traced to the work of Frank Parsons in the Boston YMCA after World War I (Williamson, 1961), but information is scarce regarding the history of organized counseling services on the college campus. It is likely that the concept emerged from the same source as the guidance program in the public school system. The model Frank Parsons proposed centered on vocational counseling and incorporated diagnosis and testing techniques. Since then, counseling on the college campus has broadened to include what is categorized as personal counseling. This growth parallels the general development of counseling psychology as a specialty (Thrush, 1957).

Today, counseling services are available at approximately two thirds (Oetting, Ivey, & Weigel, 1970) to three fourths (Oetting, 1970) of four-year institutions of higher education in the United States.

DEFINITION

Purpose

According to Mueller (1961) the goals of a college counseling service are the composite expression of the staff's interests and training and the preferences of the college's administrative personnel combined with traditions which have given foremost advantage to certain personalities and departments.

Wrenn (1951) says that the primary purpose of the counseling service is to serve as a campus-wide agency for students and as a resource agency for faculty who seek aid in dealing with their students. Taking a broader view, Danskin (1969) suggests that the counseling service should help focus attention on the educational process, both in the classroom and through other instructional resources, and its effect on the students. A counseling service organized for this purpose would demand a greater time commitment on the counselor's part to conduct research and develop programs and less time to deal directly with students.

Others suggest that the college counseling service should be concerned mainly with the adjustment of students to the campus and academic environment. Mueller (1961) proposes that the college counseling service should function as the conscience of student welfare on campus, providing a service to anyone in need of any kind of help and insuring the availability of adequate preventive and developmental programs. In its "Guidelines for University and College Counseling Services," 1970, The University and College Counseling Center Directors Task Force stated that the counseling services staff should be involved in the planning and implementation of the academic and administrative aspects of student life (Kirk, Free, Johnson, Michel, Redfield, Roston, & Warman, 1971). The major responsibility of a counseling service is to be aware of the shifting needs of its college population, especially of students, faculty, graduate training students, and staff. The overall objective is to help students receive the maximum benefits from their academic environment (Kirk et al., 1971).

In general, the effect of these definitions of purpose is to insure that the student can adjust well to and receive the maximum benefits from an accepted institution of our society. But Adams (1973) raises the question as to whether the counselor as an individual committed to safeguarding the welfare of his or her clients should facilitate a student's adjustment to a system which is competitive, profiteering, and highly individualistic.

Models

Several organizational and administrative models can be found among college counseling services, but the range of possible models (Oetting et al., 1970) is broader than that represented by current counseling services.

Vocational Guidance

The oldest counseling service model is the vocational guidance or counseling model in which the counseling service is concerned primarily with vocational choice, testing, and information giving. A full-time psychometrist is usually available. Counseling services which adhere to this model usually do not view therapy as their proper function. Services with this orientation may also be involved with freshman orientation and testing, remedial reading, and study skills programs (Oetting et al., 1970).

Psychotherapy

Unlike the vocational counseling model, a counseling service with a psychotherapy orientation will place little emphasis on vocational guidance, testing, and information giving. The primary concern is with a student's emotional problems and concerns. Counseling service staff more likely would be composed of clinical psychologists than would be the staff of a vocational counseling service (Calgary University, 1968; Oetting et al., 1970).

Personnel Services or Student Affairs

Counseling services designed after this model are more often found among smaller colleges. Financial and personnel limitations create the necessity for pooling several student personnel services under one organization. Counselors are assigned duties in several student personnel areas as housing, financial aid, and foreign student advising. The staff is more likely to have earned degrees in education rather than psychology or counseling psychology. Junior colleges, especially the smaller ones, more frequently employ the personnel services model (Calgary University, 1968; Oetting et al., 1970).

Training

A college counseling service may be an administrative part of an academic department, usually psychology or education. Under the training model the primary function of the counseling service is to provide experience for the department's graduate students under departmental faculty supervision. Such services are usually found at large institutions with graduate programs (Calgary University, 1968; Oetting et al., 1970).

Research

Oetting et al. (1970) report that an operational research model cannot presently be found on college campuses. But Danskin (1965, 1969) and others have proposed the need for a counseling service designed after this model. Its primary concern would be research and not direct service to students. Danskin (1969) suggests that the counselor's objective should be to guide faculty towards the means and resources for focusing upon the human concerns of their students. This objective can best be implemented if counselors are educational personnel researchers who assess educational effects on students; educational communications specialists who make information available to students, faculty, and administration; and student development specialists who create developmental programs.

Teaching

Paar (1962) argues for the necessity of reestablishing the faculty-student relationship. The director and an assistant would be the only personnel necessary to carry out the functions of counseling, testing, research, and teaching in a counseling service of this type. Teaching is the most crucial function aimed at the services' primary public, the faculty. The overall purpose is to train faculty members to become sufficiently proficient as counselors themselves.

Academic Affairs

The academic affairs model is rarely found in four-year colleges and universities, but does occur in junior colleges, although it is not the predominant mode of counseling service among junior colleges either. In this model the counseling service resembles a division of the college. Although counselors do not function as teaching faculty members, they are identified with other academic functions as registration, program planning, and academic advising. The counseling service is oriented more toward vocational concerns than therapy (Oetting et al., 1970).

Religious Counseling

The religious counseling model is also rare among four-year colleges. As a separate model, not included within the functions of a broader counseling service model, religious counseling may only be identified in smaller church colleges. The primary concern of this type of service is with the religious concerns and questions of the students (Calgary University, 1968).

Student Development Center

A more recent trend has been the establishment of a Human Growth and Development Center (Guinan & Foulds, 1969) or a Student Development Center (Morrill, Ivey, & Oetting, 1968).

Morrill et al. (1968) stress that this is a model for mental health intervention. The primary goal is to facilitate human growth and development. Counselors' efforts are aimed at expanding human awareness and experience and maximizing human potentials for each student within the academic community (Guinan & Foulds, 1969). Staff members have a humanistic orientation (Guinan & Foulds, 1969) and may have had interdisciplinary preparation and training (Nygreen, 1962).

According to Guinan and Foulds (1969) the functions of a Student Development Center are service to the academic community, education through involvement in counselor education programs, and research and evaluation. Implementation of the goals and functions can be accomplished through several means that distinguish the developmental model from those previously mentioned. First, emphasis is placed on the expansion of consultative services to the academic community (Guinan & Foulds, 1969). Oetting et al. (1970) even list the counseling service based entirely on the consultation model as a separate design. Secondly, implementation of the student development model is facilitated through expanded graduate training programs, especially at the internship level. Thirdly, emphasis is placed on developmental and educational group experiences through outreach programs (Guinan & Foulds, 1969).

Outreach

The outreach concept of a college counseling service has acquired various definitions and designs, but maintains the central goal of expanding services to a larger population within, and sometimes beyond, the academic community. An outreach program may be established that merely decentralizes the counselors and counseling service facilities. Counselors no longer remain cloistered in cubbyholes in one central location, but locate themselves in areas closest to students as dorms or libraries. This design may not be universally accepted as more desirable by students and faculty. At Wisconsin State University, Hamann (1970) found that students surveyed preferred the established centralized counseling service to an outreach program. Students ranked dorms as the least desirable place to locate counselors and faculty ranked the library and classroom as least desirable.

Physical decentralization also may follow the UCLA design for their Student Counseling Services in which each major program usually provided by a counseling service on a large university campus is located in a separate, but generally centralized, location (Palmer, 1970). It may also take the form of a mobile counseling service in which a van and a group of counselors can go out to local schools, etc. (Dole, 1970).

When designed as a basic model for a counseling service, the outreach concept may take the form of the community mental health model described by Morrill et al. (1968) as a foundation for their conceptualization of a Center for Student Development. Again, the central objective is to move the mental health center directly into the community and to work toward facilitating personal development and mental health prevention rather than treatment. Consultation is emphasized as the primary vehicle for mental health intervention with the entire academic community including students, faculty, administration, and residence hall staff (Oetting et al., 1970).

The relationship between the counseling service and other student services can be more easily facilitated when the counseling service adopts the outreach-consultative role. Russell, Hallberg, & Krofcheck (1970) propose that counseling personnel should establish contacts with various campus subcultures and then aid the university community in interpreting and understanding these groups of students. Other outreach-consultative activities might include student leadership training, in-service training programs for residence hall staff, and helping financial aid officers work with students on problems such as assessment of work load and parents' reactions to student requests for loans. Close cooperation and coordination between the counseling service and the placement service could provide for both early exploration of a student's vocational choice and consideration of the world of work and job or graduate school placement (Russell et al., 1970).

Perhaps the counseling service is most effective in its service to the community when the outreach and centralized service models are combined. Maes (1967) suggests that in the future the counseling service will be a consortium of professionals with a flexible team approach to situational problems, but with permanent centers for specific educational and therapeutic purposes. The stable centralized services would be concerned with testing, training, research, and individual and group counseling, while the flexible operations would involve a team of experts in group processes, discussion groups, etc., who move on request to any area of the campus.

Traditional Counseling Model

The traditional counseling service is the most common model found on campuses today (Albert, 1968; Clark, 1966; Nugent & Pareis, 1968; Oetting et al., 1970). It combines, to varying extents, the vocational guidance and counseling and psychotherapy models as well as various concepts from other models previously defined. Its major functions, vocational, educational and personal counseling, are seen as overlapping and not distinct categories of service. The traditional counseling service operates as a separate campus agency, usually not clearly identified with a particular academic department. Its central purpose is service to students, but the service usually will sponsor internships and practicums for graduate students (Guinan & Foulds, 1969; Oetting et al., 1970).

According to Guinan and Foulds (1969) the traditional services have played reactive, reparative, and adjustive roles. They have been isolated from the mainstream of student growth and development and the overall educational process (Morrill & Oetting, 1970). They have maintained a position of providing services primarily to the troubled student, rather than broadening their scope to a wider student population (Lombardi, 1974). They have provided a narrow range of services to a small percent of the student population and have served as an arm of the administration in performing evaluative services (Guinan & Foulds, 1969). Although the creation of Student Development

Centers is an attempt to avoid these pitfalls, the newer models have yet to supplant the traditional counseling services on college campuses.

ADMINISTRATION

College counseling services are generally administered through a student personnel department or division. Albert (1968) found that 57 percent of 415 colleges said their counseling services were connected in some way with a student personnel division. The counseling service director generally reports to the dean of students who, in turn, reports to a vice-president for administration. Occasionally, especially in the smaller colleges, the director may report directly to the president of the college (Oetting et al., 1970).

Most services have a centralized location, and students, who are usually self-referred, come to the service for one-to-one counseling (Guinan & Foulds, 1969). Most services have established cooperative referral arrangements with other agencies such as student health services. For example, Nugent & Pareis (1968) found that 75 percent of 461 institutions felt that their relationship with their health services was adequate (see Health chapter).

While the traditional model has come under attack in recent years, counseling service directors report that they are satisfied with this organization (Nugent & Pareis, 1968; Oetting et al., 1970). The major problem with the traditional organizational structure is that it isolates the counseling personnel from the academic faculty so much so that counseling becomes an auxiliary service of secondary educational relevance (Oetting et al., 1970).

Variations of this organizational structure can be found. Albert (1968) found that 12 percent of 415 institutions had counseling services as separate independent units and 6 percent were affiliated with departments of psychology. Several were subunits of other departments or services: health and medical departments, 2 percent; larger broad-scale psychological services, 12 percent; and college employment offices, 17 percent.

Kirk et al. (1971) argue in favor of an autonomous arrangement whereby the counseling service director is directly responsible to the president and there are no ties to other services. If counseling services are to function in a special relationship to students, they say, then students must perceive the service as independent of medical, instructional, and disciplinary units.

Decentralization

As the college campus has steadily increased in size and student population, the demand for counseling services has also grown. In order to reach more students and other members of the academic community, some counseling services have decentralized their operations. Decentralized facilities are supported by those students who say that counselors should be available to see students in the students' own environments (Snyder, Hill, & Derksen, 1972). Decentralization can also be implemented through outreach programs designed to reach various student groups, increase the counseling services' relationships with other services (Russell et al., 1970), and work with faculty (Nygreen, 1962).

There are many who still prefer the single unified counseling service. Pustell (1965) argues that there is a need to integrate psychological and vocational services rather than compartmentalize the student among various agencies and locations. Physical decentralization also tends to isolate counseling personnel from one another, thus discouraging consultation and exchange of views.

Counseling service facilities, when centralized, need to be well marked (Oetting et al., 1970) and easily accessible to as many students as possible (Kirk et al., 1971). Oetting et al. (1970) note that a physical proximity with psychology or education departments may work to increase communication and help identify counseling staff as faculty, but at the same time, such identification with these departments may lead students to believe that the service will handle only certain types of problems.

Staffing

The internal organization of counseling services varies greatly in the number of assistants, counselors, and student trainees involved (Oetting et al., 1970). The ratio of counselors to students varies considerably, but on the whole, counselor/student ratios found on college campuses do not approach the ideal. The ideal ratio according to Oetting (1970) is 1:500 to 1:1000. Clark (1966) reported a mean ratio of 1:3000 while Albert (1968) found a median ratio of 1:770. Nugent & Pareis (1968) found that 25 percent of 461 institutions did not have even a 1:2000 ratio. With so few counselors and increasing amounts of time spent per student (the mean number of hours spent with a student in Clark's 1966 study was 3.3 hours), the counselor faces an impossible task. The smaller the college the more likely it is that the counselor/student ratio approaches the ideal (Oetting, 1970).

The most consistent difficulty facing counseling services in institutions of all sizes is lack of personnel (Clark, 1966). Counselors tend to be spending less time seeing individual clients and more time in other counselor-related activities outside the counselor's office. Yet, there is also pressure for counselors to see more individual clients. This situation intensifies the problem of personnel shortages. Services have handled the increasing demand with waiting lists and various in-take counseling procedures (Oetting et al., 1970). The only alternatives are to limit which students can be seen (Albert, 1968) or hire more counselors.

Finances

Most counseling services are college financed (Guinan & Foulds, 1969). Clark (1966, 1970) found that 58 percent of thirty-six services were fully supported through direct appropriations. The mean operating budget for the total service in 1962 to 1963 was $96,555 and the average amount allotted by the institution per student enrolled was $6.49.

Most colleges lack adequate financing to handle institutional growth. Among the thirty-six institutions surveyed by Clark (1966), salaries and financial support were listed as major problems. In an effort to overcome financial restraints, several colleges have turned to charging fees for their services. The idea has not been universally well received and in 1968 only 4 percent of 461 colleges charged for counseling, while 19 percent charged for testing (Nugent & Pareis, 1968). Proponents argue that long-term treatment would occur if fees were charged. Payment might motivate clients to use therapy more effectively (Oetting et al., 1970). Opponents argue that fees are unfair to poor students and inappropriate to the counseling role. Since the service is provided for them, usually through student fees, students should not have to pay for them. More importantly, requiring a fee may discourage those who need help (Oetting et al., 1970).

Clientele

Generally, services offered by a counseling service are available to all students, faculty, and other members of the academic community. Albert (1968) reported that 8 percent of 415 institutions limited the availability of their services to certain groups of students such as noncredit and evening students. But Albert (1968) also found that 178 out of 389 institutions reported that some or all of their facilities were open to nonstudents.

Publicity and Source of Information

The degree of knowledge regarding the counseling service, as well as of any other student service, may depend on how well it has been publicized. Over half of the thirty-six colleges surveyed by Clark (1966) said they advertised in the student newspaper. More formal notice often was given at freshman orientation and listed in the college catalog (Clark, 1966). However, students are more likely to obtain information regarding the counseling service from other people than from printed material (McMillan & Cerra, 1972). At Washington State University, friends were the main source of information and few students heard about the counseling service from faculty, advisors, head residents, or instructors (Minge & Cass, 1966). Virginia Polytechnic Institute established a Student Advisory Panel to its counseling service to help interpret the service and its image to other students (Canon, 1964). Continuous publicity is needed not only to increase student usage, but to reach the one fourth of the population that is new every year (McMillan & Cerra, 1972).

Referrals

Clark (1966) reported that 78 percent of thirty-six colleges said that students were self-referred; 54 percent said their second most frequent source of referrals was peers and friends; 10 percent listed administration and faculty as third; and 95 percent placed last referral by physicians.

Redding (1971) questioned whether counseling services should urge faculty and administration to refer more students. In a comparison of self-referred students with other-referred students, Redding discovered that students in self-referred groups improved their grade point average after counseling more than did students in the other-referred groups. Also, the self-referred students graduated in significantly larger numbers. Redding (1971) concluded that counseling services should develop a better public relations approach to inform both faculty and students and attract more students.

Confidentiality

Perhaps the most serious problem to confront a counseling service is the provision for confidentiality. If confidentiality is not available, students may be reluctant to use the counseling service. Nugent & Pareis (1968) found that among 461 counseling services, only 59 percent had complete confidentiality; 21 percent gave information to administrative heads for use in disciplinary actions and recommendations; 10 percent made information regularly available to deans of students for use at their discretion; 5 percent gave faculty access to information; and 2 percent made information available to prospective employers and other outside agencies. These statistics refer to situations in which information is given without a student's permission and are unethical.

Counselors are committed to professional confidentiality expressed in statements of ethical conduct by the professional organizations such as the American Personnel and Guidance Association (1971) and the American Psychological Association (1953). A separate but related problem is that counselors in most states do not have legal confidentiality and records can be subpoenaed (Bakken, 1970).

Counseling Services at the Small College

Size is directly related to whether the college has a counseling service (Oetting, 1970). Counseling services appear less frequently among smaller colleges because of the greater opportunity for close, personal contact between faculty and students (Goertzen & Strong, 1962). The number of services or activities does not vary with size, but the kind of activity offered will vary with size.

The student personnel model is most commonly found in the small college with most functions handled by one or two staff members (Oetting et al., 1970). Another model may occasionally be observed in colleges in the eastern states. Here, the center is administered within the psychology department, headed by the department chairman, and staffed by psychology department faculty members (Oetting et al., 1970).

In the student personnel model counseling personnel are often given the title "dean," which indicates that counseling personnel also perform administrative functions (Oetting et al., 1970). In addition to administrative duties, counseling staff are often indistinct from the teaching staff as the counselors have strong ties with the academic life on campus, sometimes to the point where in smaller colleges only one-fourth time is spent in counseling. The average level of training for these counselors is the Master's degree (Goertzen & Strong, 1962).

The counseling activity itself is treated broadly, combining it with several other student personnel functions. Intensive therapy is generally not available, but counseling will include curricular guidance, vocational choice, and educational and academic counseling (Goertzen & Strong, 1962).

Some activities are more likely to be found in counseling services at small colleges than in larger ones, such as supervision of residence hall counselors, evaluation of discipline cases, student scholarships and loans, incorporation of the dean of women and men's offices, and probationary counseling (Anderson, 1970). Because these counseling services are less differentiated from other campus services, they tend to be more totally involved in aspects of student behavior other than that seen strictly as counseling (Oetting et al., 1970).

The small college counseling service is beset with problems similar to that of a counseling service at a large college. Both usually suffer from a lack of finances and adequately trained personnel (Goertzen & Strong, 1962). But since the counselor in the small college is also responsible for administrative and teaching duties, limited time and energy are more critical (Oetting et al., 1970). To deal more effectively within these limits set by finances and personnel, Oetting et al. (1970) stress the necessity of establishing clearly defined purposes and goals' consistent with the overall goals of the college. They also suggest that with the limited budget, counselors should devote most of their time to the normal students.

PROGRAMS

In 1970 Anderson found that the number of programs available to students, as indicated by responses from 219 counseling service directors, ranged from three to twenty-nine. Only 10 percent reported more than eighteen different programs.

Counseling

The counseling function may focus on one or more of several

areas. Categorical names are often used to ease communication and occasionally pinpoint differences; but on the whole, the types of counseling defined below are overlapping and difficult to separate for an individual. Clark (1966) found that 50 percent of thirty-six institutions reported that three or more areas of counseling, usually vocational, educational, and personal, were offered. When asked to list their main functions, the colleges indicated some overlap: 71 percent said vocational-educational counseling was their main function; 67 percent indicated educational and occupational information; 60 percent said personal adjustment; and 6 percent indicated psychotherapy. In 1968 Albert found that 71 percent of 415 services offered some combination of vocational, educational, and personal counseling.

Educational counseling usually refers to remedial skills programs, test-taking workshops, and academic advising, although in many institutions, especially the larger ones, academic advising is handled by a separate agency. Vocational or vocational-educational counseling may incorporate activities included in the above category and further refer to developmental counseling involving vocational choice or exploration and discovery of skills and abilities and other similar activities. Personal counseling deals with student's emotional problems. Marital conflicts, drug problems, and human sexuality counseling would fall in this category, as would the emotional aspects and identity concerns in vocational and educational counseling.

Psychotherapy is also offered in many college counseling services and may be included in the personal counseling category, but its definition and the context in which it is used will vary. Albert (1968) found that 3 percent of 415 institutions provided complete medical-psychological treatment as needed; 15 percent offered full-scale psychotherapy; 37 percent dealt with some unconscious material, but limited it to normal personality dynamics; and 45 percent restricted themselves to clearly conscious level problems. Clark (1966) found that distinguishing between counseling and psychotherapy was an issue for 48 percent of the colleges in his survey and that the distinction was most often made on the basis of time involved with the student and the depth of the problems encountered. Albert (1968) also found that when asked which counseling orientation was preferred, 72 percent indicated "eclectic," while the next largest category, "Rogerian," was indicated by only 22 percent.

Other categories of counseling may be found in counseling services in varying proportions. Of 461 colleges 51 percent offered group counseling centered on any of the three major areas of counseling (Nugent & Pareis, 1968). In a 1972 study the majority of 129 responding counseling services provided two to five different types of group experiences (Conyne, Lamb, & Strand, 1975). Oetting et al. (1970) reported that less than 20 percent of 268 institutions had religious counseling and 20 percent had some form of disciplinary counseling (see Disciplinary Counseling section). Finally, many colleges have established an efficient referral system with resources in the larger community to handle situations and problems the college counseling service may not be equipped to handle (Gallagher, 1970).

Other Programs

Counseling services also perform functions not considered as primary areas of counseling, but which are often integrated into counseling programs. Remedial programs usually involve reading and writing skills and perhaps study habits. Oetting et al. (1970) found that 25 percent of the colleges had reading programs; Nugent and Pareis (1968) reported that 67 percent had reading and study habits programs. Consultation to faculty regarding student problems (Gallagher, 1970) was reported to be available in 69 percent of the colleges (Oetting et al., 1970). Oetting et al. (1970) also found that 4 percent of the colleges provided some precollege student contact. Approximately one-third had a summer orientation program. Although testing was listed as a major function by only 14 percent of the institutions (Clark, 1966), its use is still widespread. Albert (1968) reported that 80 percent of the colleges test entering freshmen for academic aptitude; 60 percent test for personality; and 84 percent offer, but do not require, intelligence tests. Some services also provide exit interviews for disqualified, withdrawing, and readmitted students.

Counseling services may also provide academic advisement. Only 14 percent of the institutions (Nugent & Pareis, 1968) furnished this program through the counseling service. Usually it is performed by faculty members of the respective departments. The use of faculty as academic advisors, as opposed to using counselors, has caused some conflict especially in the junior colleges. There are too many academic programs and requirements especially in a large institution for a faculty member to keep up to date, nor does the faculty have the counseling skills and broader knowledge of vocational choice to help the undecided student. Where faculty are employed for this purpose, some services arrange for counselors to consult with faculty for instruction on interview technique and explanations of college-wide procedures and polity (Nugent & Pareis, 1968, see Hardee, 1970).

Graduate student training programs are provided by 33 percent of the colleges (Nugent & Pareis, 1968). Also, many counseling services provide programs for special groups of students as the educationally disadvantaged, women, older students, foreign students, and married students (Dole, 1970). Some services provide an orientation for college seniors. While the placement office handles questions of immediate employment, it does not handle the developmental, life-planning type of inquiries the counseling service handles best (Dole, 1970). Finally, services also have outreach programs, but few have become involved with such programs (Oetting et al., 1970).

Research

Most counseling services are involved to some degree in research. In 1966 Clark reported that 60 percent of the services did research; Nugent & Pareis (1968) found that 54 percent were involved in research. Most research efforts revolve around studies of student characteristics within a particular institution;

fewer efforts are geared toward academic and counseling areas; and 24 percent of the institutions surveyed did provide research consultation to other departments (Oetting et al., 1970).

Research could be conducted over a wide range of activities. Counseling services could be involved in studies on methods, treatments, and effects of counseling. Applied research studies could be conducted for specific programs such as remedial skills or study skills. Institutional research in areas as demographic factors or why students withdraw might also become part of the counseling services' research program. Larger colleges may have a separate office or director for institutional research which provides the data collection function (Gallagher, 1970).

PERSONNEL

Most counseling service directors have a Ph.D. or Ed.D. degree. As college size increases, the likelihood of the director having earned a Ph.D. rather than an Ed.D. is greater, except in those colleges with a heavy teacher-training emphasis. There is also a direct relationship between size of the college and the amount of time a director will spend in administration. Few have full-time counseling duties, nor are the teachers given part-time duties as administrative heads of a counseling service. It has also been noted that directors in institutions of 5,000 to 15,000 students will have the strongest commitment to research (Oetting et al., 1970).

Whereas directors generally have earned the Ph.D., staff may have earned either the M.A. or Ph.D. (Oetting et al., 1970), but it has been suggested that those who emphasize personal counseling should have a Ph.D. (Gallagher, 1970). Albert (1968) found that 18 percent of 415 colleges used graduate student trainees as counselors. Some colleges, like UCLA, are using paraprofessionals to supplement their staff (Palmer, 1970). In studies done in 1970 and 1973 almost all of the 192 responding counseling services directors said that the use of paraprofessionals was acceptable, but only in four areas of student problems: study skills, college adjustment, freshmen orientation, and drug problems (Crane, Anderson, & Kirchner, 1975).

Duties

According to Glazer (1964) most counseling service directors see counseling and teaching as the major counselor roles. In most cases emphasis in counseling is on short-term cases, spanning one to six appointments (Nugent & Pareis, 1968). The majority of services have faculty who engage in teaching. Clark (1966) found 80 percent, Nugent and Pareis (1968) found 65 percent, and Giddan, Price, and Healy (1976) found 75 percent of the colleges had counselors who regularly taught. Gallagher (1970) warns that counseling services should be careful not to become too closely identified with faculty or administration if they seek to achieve their counseling objectives. Finally, counselor duties may also involve some research (Oetting et al., 1970).

Academic Rank

Although Gallagher (1970) opposes identification with faculty, counselors and directors support academic rank for counselors whose training and experience is commensurate with that of other faculty (Glazer, 1964; Kirk et al., 1971). In the Nugent and Pareis study (1968) 77 percent of the institutions said their counselors had academic rank.

There are several arguments in favor of faculty status for counselors. First, it is easier to recruit staff with the appropriate academic training. Second, faculty status should lead to greater counselor participation on faculty university-wide, policy-making committees. Third, faculty status might bring about a wider acceptance of counseling services by faculty and students by giving the appearance of university approval or of having achieved a certain status or recognition. Similarly, it should help to assure faculty cooperation and acceptance of counseling service functions (Oetting et al., 1970).

Granting faculty status to counselors also poses problems. The academic rank granted counselors may limit the benefits counselors are eligible for. Conflicts over salaries and salary increments are likely to occur between service directors and department heads (Nugent & Pareis, 1968). Faculty status may deprive counselors of time needed for counseling in order to pursue research efforts often necessary as requirements for advancement. Also counselor qualifications are not always comparable to the academic qualifications of other faculty, especially for counselors with Master's degrees. Finally, counseling services have traditionally been part of student personnel services and student personnel staff do not frequently hold rank. If counselors are granted academic rank, the question might also be raised as to whether other student personnel workers should be eligible for academic rank (Oetting et al., 1970).

Counselor Salaries

Not surprisingly, larger institutions pay higher salaries. Directors' salaries vary with nine- or twelve-month appointments, academic degree, and institutional size. Those with nine-month appointments tend to identify more with faculty (since faculty are often paid on a nine-month basis) while those with twelve-month appointments will identify more with the role of providing services to students. Oetting et al. (1970) note that nine-month appointments seem to be divided almost equally in number of M.A.'s and Ph.D.'s, while twelve-month appointments are held by twice as many M.A.'s as Ph.D.'s. In addition large institutions will pay higher salaries to Ph.D.'s than smaller colleges, but M.A.'s will get higher salaries in a smaller institution (Oetting et al., 1970).

Professional Association

Most counselors identify themselves with the American Personnel and Guidance Association with the exception of those with the Ph.D. Of the Ph.D. holders, 70 percent identify with the American Psychological Association (Oetting, 1970).

RESEARCH

Perceptions of Functions

In 1957 Thrush reported that the University Counseling Center at Ohio State University had experienced a change of emphasis in their agency point of view within the past five years. From an emphasis on vocational counseling, the center moved toward counseling for personal adjustment. Thrush postulated that the staff found clinical problems more interesting and therapy more prestigious than vocational counseling. He also suggested that this trend paralleled the mushrooming growth of counseling psychology.

In 1961 Warman reported the results of a national study of counseling services selected from the 1958 to 1960 issue of the *Directory of Vocational Counseling Services*. His sample was selected by geographic distance, size, and type of financial support. Among the twenty-one counseling services responding, counselors viewed Vocational Choice as a more appropriate function than College Routine and Adjustment to Self and Others. Counseling trainees, on the other hand, saw adjustment problems as more appropriate. The Vocational Choice function was considered appropriate regardless of the size of the institution but counseling services that did not train students saw Vocational Choice as more appropriate than did services that were involved in training programs. Counselors at smaller colleges saw Adjustment problems as more appropriate than did counselors at larger colleges.

At Wisconsin State University responses were solicited from faculty and students, rather than counselors (Hamann, 1970). Although both groups felt that all three traditional programs were the most important functions, students ranked low in importance the personal growth and development functions.

At the University of Wyoming, Wilcove and Sharp (1971) sampled students, parents, student personnel workers, faculty, and counselors. Counselors saw Adjustment problems as most important followed by Vocational Choice and College Routine while students' priorities were just the reverse: College

Routine, Vocational Choice, and then Adjustment. But students who had used the services of counselors saw Adjustment problems as more appropriate than those who did not.

While it is difficult to generalize from single institution studies and studies with small sample size, the change over ten years in counselor responses seen in these studies is similar to the change Thrush (1957) found at Ohio State University in 1957. This suggests a growing trend among counselors to prefer adjustment problems. Further study is required to determine what changes in goals, training programs, student services, publicizing of services, or personnel may be implied by this change.

Student Knowledge of the Counseling Service

Knowledge and perception of counseling service functions are crucial to its use (Frankel & Perlman, 1969). While the majority of students in several studies were aware of their college's counseling service, considerable proportions of each student body were unaware of its existence or poorly informed about its programs. At the University of Utah, one fourth of the students were unaware of the counseling service (Rickabaugh & Heaps, 1970). At a large midwest state university, 25 percent or more were unfamiliar with the service and those who knew of its existence were poorly informed about its programs (McMillan & Cerra, 1972). Only 14 percent had not heard of the counseling service at Washington State University, but considerably fewer had correct specific information about it (Minge & Cass, 1966).

Rickabaugh and Heaps (1970) found that a greater proportion of students living off-campus were aware of the service than students living in on-campus dorms, but Minge and Cass (1966) found the reverse situation to be true. Rickabaugh and Heaps (1970) also found that more men had been to their counseling service than women, yet Minge and Cass (1966) reported that men were less aware than women of their college's counseling service. They also reported that the most informed groups with regard to the counseling service were females, unmarried students, sorority and dormitory residents, and juniors and seniors.

Frankel and Perlman (1969) found that knowledge of counseling service functions is not dependent on experience or contact with the service. Perhaps with short contact, students receive a narrow view of service functions and the memory is short-lived. Most perceptions of services are derived from hearsay rather than experience. Salisbury (1972) found that even the title of the counseling service will affect students' perceptions of its functions. He argued that the term "Counseling Center" as opposed to "Guidance Center" or "Psychological Services Center" should be employed if a service wishes to be perceived as offering a breadth of programs. In the mid-1970's "Counseling Service" is the preferred title.

Several colleges have conducted studies to determine the perceptions students have of their particular counseling service functions, as opposed to the functions they feel the services should have. At the University of Utah students mainly perceived their counseling service as a place to discuss problems of Vocational Choice and College Routine. Only one eighth of the students surveyed thought Adjustment problems were commonly discussed. Class in college was related to differential perceptions. Utah freshmen were more concerned with College Routine questions, while older students put greater stress on problems of career choice. Also, students who had heard of the counseling service felt that Vocational Choice was most frequently discussed, while those who were unfamiliar with the service felt that College Routine concerns were most frequently discussed. Students who had actually been to the counseling service felt that Adjustment problems were less frequently discussed than those who had never been (Rickabaugh & Heaps, 1970).

In a study of counseling service functions in an urban commuter university complex, Frankel and Perlman (1969) found that students saw individual counseling as dealing with personal problems and correctly perceived that the freshmen guidance program dealt with vocational and academic discussions. At Washington State University students also correctly perceived that the major type of problem handled at the counseling service was personal counseling (Minge & Cass, 1966).

Here again it is difficult to generalize, but within a college there probably are varying perceptions of service functions among different groups and some colleges have projected more successfully an image that agrees with their functions than have others.

Student Usage

The mean number of students seen per year at the larger colleges is approximately 1,800 or 12 percent of the student body (Clark, 1966). The proportion of the student body seen in the counseling service is inversely related to the size of the institution (Oetting et al., 1970). It might appear that a service that serves only 12 percent of the student body is either woefully inefficient or unnecessary and, hence, wasteful when the limited monies available for student services could be rerouted to other services which handle large numbers of students.

Why do so few students use the counseling service? Rust and Davie (1961) suggested that students may feel their problems are not appropriate or important enough to seek a counselor's help. Fear that conversations or test scores may not be kept confidential might also deter students. Form (1953) thought that some students might have negative attitudes toward a counseling service. Studies have shown that students will usually approach their friends first for help with all kinds of problems, rather than go to a counselor (Rust & Davie, 1961; Snyder, Hill, & Derksen, 1972). But perhaps the main reason, as indicated above, is a simple lack of knowledge either of its existence or its functions.

Therefore, a counseling service that perceives that too few students avail themselves of its services has several avenues open to it, most of which revolve around better publication and communication of its existence and programs. Another alternative is to assume that if the proportion of students seen is all that can be handled with present facilities to ensure quality programs, then the service is doing an effective job in providing a necessary service. The question is one of quality v. quantity and whether there is a need to justify a service that reaches few students, but does provide essential programs to those it can serve.

REFERENCES

Adams, H. J. The progressive heritage of guidance: A view from the left. *Personnel and Guidance Journal,* 1973, *51,* 531-539.

Albert, G. A survey of college counseling facilities. *Personnel and Guidance Journal,* 1968, *46,* 540-543.

American Personnel and Guidance Association. Ethical standards. *Personnel and Guidance Journal,* 1971, *50,* 327-330.

American Psychological Association. *Ethical standards of psychologists.* Washington, D. C.: Author, 1953.

Anderson, W. Services offered by college counseling centers. *Journal of Counseling Psychology,* 1970, *17,* 380-382.

Bakken, C. J. Counseling services and related operations from a legal viewpoint. In P. J. Gallagher & G. D. Demos (Eds.), *The counseling center in higher education.* Springfield, Ill.: Charles C Thomas, 1970.

Calgary University. *Models of counseling centers.* Alberta, Canada: Calgary University, 1968. (ERIC Document Reproduction Service No. ED 027 555)

Canon, H. J. Student counsel for a counseling center. *Journal of College Student Personnel,* 1964, *5,* 251-252.

Clark, D. D. Characteristics of counseling centers in large universities. *Personnel and Guidance Journal,* 1966, *44,* 817-823.

Clark, D. D. Current emphasis and characteristics of counseling centers in universities of over 10,000 enrollment. In P. J. Gallagher & G. D. Demos (Eds.), *The counseling center in higher education.* Springfield, Ill.: Charles C Thomas, 1970.

Conyne, R. K., Lamb, D. H., & Strand, K. H. Group experiences in counseling centers: A national survey. *Journal of College Student Personnel,* 1975, *16,* 196-200.

Crane, J., Anderson, W., & Kirchner, K. Counseling center directors' attitudes toward paraprofessionals. *Journal of College Student Personnel,* 1975, *16,* 119-122.

Danskin, D. G. My focus for a university counseling center. *Journal of College Student Personnel,* 1965, *6,* 263-267.

Danskin, D. G. *The university and a fully functioning counseling center.* Las Vegas, Nev.: Annual Convention of the American Personnel and Guidance Association, March 30 to April 2, 1969. (ERIC Document Reproduction Service No. ED 030 905)

Dole, M. B. Special programs offered by university and college counseling centers in the United States. In P. J. Gallagher & G. D. Demos (Eds.), *The counseling center in higher education.* Springfield, Ill.: Charles C Thomas, 1970.

Form, A. L. Measurement of students' attitudes toward counseling services. *Personnel and Guidance Journal,* 1953, *32,* 84-87.

Frankel, P. M., & Perlman, S. M. Student perceptions of student counseling service function. *Journal of College Student Personnel,* 1969, *10,* 232-235.

Gallagher, P. J. Major responsibilities of the counseling center and core duties of counselors. In P. J. Gallagher & G. D. Demos (Eds.), *The counseling center in higher education.* Springfield, Ill.: Charles C Thomas, 1970.

Giddan, N. S., Price, M. K., & Healy, J. M. The status and future of joint appointments in counseling centers. *Journal of College Student Personnel,* 1976, *17,* 2-6.

Glazer, S. H. College and university counseling centers: Pragmatic questions of mutual concern. *Journal of College Student Personnel,* 1964, *5,* 168-169.

Goertzen, S. M., & Strong, D. J. Counseling practices in the small colleges and universities of the Pacific Northwest: A 12 year follow-up study. *Personnel and Guidance Journal,* 1962, *41,* 254-259.

Guinan, J. F., & Foulds, M. L. The counseling service as a growth center. *Personnel and Guidance Journal,* 1969, *48,* 111-118.

Hamann, J. B. Desired counseling center functions as perceived by faculty and students. *Final Report* (Cord Project). Stevens Point: Wisconsin State University, Consortium of Research Development, February, 1970, (ERIC Document Reproduction Service No. ED 053 429).

Hardee, M. D. *Faculty advising in colleges and universities.* Washington, D. C.: American Personnel and Guidance Association, 1967. (Student Personnel Monograph Series, No. 9)

Kirk, B. A., Free, J. E., Johnson, A. P., Michel, J., Redfield, J. E., Roston, R. A., & Warman, R. Guidelines for university and college counseling services. *American Psychologist,* 1971, *26,* 585-589.

Lombardi, J. S. The college counseling center and preventive mental health activities. *Journal of College Student Personnel,* 1974, *15,* 435-438.

Maes, J. L. *The cloudy crystal ball: A projection of the nature of the university counseling center in the year 2000.* 1967 (ERIC Document Reproduction Service No. ED 044 716)

McMillan, M. R., & Cerra, P. Student knowledge about a college counseling center. *NASPA Journal,* 1972, *10,* 138-141.

Minge, M. R., & Cass, W. A. Student perceptions of a university counseling center. *Journal of College Student Personnel,* 1966, *7,* 141-144.

Morrill, W. H., Ivey, A. E., & Oetting, E. R. The college counseling center: A center for student development. In J. C. Heston & W. B. Frick (Eds.), *Counseling for the liberal arts campus.* Yellow Springs, Ohio: Antioch Press, 1968.

Morrill, W. H., & Oetting, E. R. Outreach programs in college counseling.

Journal of College Student Personnel, 1970, *11,* 50-53.

Mueller, K. H. *Student personnel work in higher education.* Boston: Houghton Mifflin, 1.61.

Nugent, F. A., & Pareis, E. N. Survey of present policies, and practices in college counseling centers in the United States. *Journal of Counseling Psychology,* 1968, *15,* 94-97.

Nygreen, G. T. The college counseling center of the future. *Journal of College Student Personnel,* 1962, *4,* 32-34.

Oetting, E. R. Problems and issues in the administration of college and university counseling services. *Final Report.* Fort Collins, Colorado State University, 1970. (ERIC Document Reproduction Service No. ED 010 553)

Oetting, E. R., Ivey, A. E., & Weigel, R. G. *The college and university counseling center.* Washington, D. C.: American College Personnel Association, 1970. (Student Personnel Monograph Series, No. 11)

Paar, H. J. The counseling center: Its psychology, personnel, publics, and promise. *Journal of College Student Personnel,* 1962, *3,* 185-187.

Palmer, D. A university counseling center. In P. J. Gallagher & G. D. Demos (Eds.), *The counseling center in higher education.* Springfield, Ill.: Charles C Thomas, 1970.

Pustell, T. E. A unified college counseling center. *Journal of College Student Personnel,* 1965, *6,* 171-174.

Redding, R. Self-referred students and other-referred students using college counseling services. *Journal of Counseling Psychology,* 1971, *18,* 22-25.

Rickabaugh, K., & Heaps, R. A. Student awareness of the University of Utah counseling center. *Research Report* (No. 25). Salt Lake City: Utah University, 1970. (ERIC Document Reproduction Service No. ED 046 016)

Russell, N. M., Hallberg, E. C., & Krofcheck, J. L. Relationships with student services. In P. J. Gallagher & G. D. Demos (Eds.), *The counseling center in higher education.* Springfield, Ill.: Charles C Thomas, 1970.

Rust, R. M., & Davie, J. S. The personal problems of college students. *Mental Hygiene,* 1961, *45,* 247-257.

Salisbury, H. Counseling center name and type of problem referred. *Journal of Counseling Psychology,* 1972, *19,* 351-352.

Snyder, J. F., Hill, C. E., & Derksen, T. P. Why some students do not use university counseling facilities. *Journal of Counseling Psychology,* 1972, *19,* 263-268.

Thrush, R. S. An agency in transition: The case study of a counseling center. *Journal of Counseling Psychology,* 1957, *4,* 183-189.

Warman, R. E. The counseling role of college and university counseling centers. *Journal of Counseling Psychology,* 1961, *8,* 231-237.

Wilcove, G., & Sharp, H. Differential perceptions of a college counseling center. *Journal of Counseling Psychology,* 1971, *18,* 60-63.

Williamson, E. G. *Student personnel services in colleges and universities.* New York: McGraw-Hill, 1961.

Wrenn, C. G. *Student personnel work in college.* New York: Ronald Press, 1951.

CHAPTER 13

PLACEMENT

BETTY BLASKA AND MARLIN R. SCHMIDT

HISTORY

FROM their inception American colleges have assumed a vocational advising function. Their geographic isolation and the religious nature of their administration fostered a fatherly sort of advice service. The university president acted as chief personnel officer, placement director, and religious and moral leader.

Vocational advice was not systematic and elaborate as student bodies were small and curriculum programs limited. The fact that students and faculty lived and ate together fostered intimate relations between them and encouraged the continuance of personal and individual counsel regarding vocational planning and placement (Leonard, 1956).

The first model of modern placement activity may have begun in the 1770's with George Washington, who visited colleges to recruit men for the Engineers Corps of the Continental Army, or in the late 1800's with research scientist George Steinmetz, who sought college graduates to work in his labs at General Electric in New York (Lansner, 1967), and with George Westinghouse who recruited college students as employees of Westinghouse Corporation (Boynton, 1949). The earliest established college placement service was the Committee on Appointments at Oxford University in 1899 (Wrenn, 1951) and in the United States the first vocational counselor was Jesse B. Davis of Detroit in 1898 (Stephens, 1970).

In the 1900's, the specialization and departmentalization of the various professions, agriculture, business, technical, and industrial training, pinpointed "the need for extensive educational and vocational guidance both before and after matriculation in the colleges" (Leonard, 1956, p. 78). Frank Parsons (1909), a Boston educator and social worker, was the driving force behind the vocational guidance movement and outlined the first theory of vocational choice. Academic and vocational counseling, once the domain of faculty and general administration, began to require new personnel specifically trained.

> The complexity of the occupational world, the rapidly changing needs of commerce and industry, and the recent advances in psychological measurement were factors about which most faculty counselors were uninformed. This state of affairs pointed unequivocally to the need for a professionally trained university officer who could give adequate occupational and educational advice (Williamson & Sarbin, 1940, p. 18).

In 1913 a body of vocational specialists founded the National Vocational Guidance Association. Six years later at Yale University the first placement service opened (Teal & Herrick, 1962). The years 1924 to 1926 saw the beginnings of the first regional placement association, the Eastern College Personnel Officers; seven others were to follow (Stephens, 1970).

In the 1930's the economic depression showed that the college degree did not guarantee employment. More and more college graduates were desperately in need of placement assistance and realized at graduation the need for better vocational planning earlier (Teal & Herrick, 1962).

After World War II, the demands for employees by business, industry, and government and the great numbers of veterans made job counseling, training, and placement a tremendous task (Teal & Herrick, 1962). The federal government assumed responsibility in this area, as indicated in 1943 by the founding of the Veteran's Administration and the funding of the Vocational Rehabilitation and Educational Counseling Program. In 1944 the VA contracted with 429 colleges to establish counseling services. The first *Occupational Outlook Handbook* was published in 1945 as a VA manual with cooperation from the Vocational Rehabilitation and Educational service and the Bureau of Labor Statistics (Brayfield, 1961).

The veterans administration counseling services consisted

primarily of educational monitoring and job placement. Procedures were routine and standards of counseling minimal (Warnath, 1971). Nevertheless, most of the services were continued and expanded by the colleges after the VA contract was terminated. Dreese (1949) considers the VA program as having advanced vocational guidance in higher education by more than fifteen years of normal development.

The period of greatest growth occurred after 1946; and as a result, by 1950 the majority of colleges had some form of placement service (Wrenn, 1951). New technologies created new occupations, and increased demands for consumer goods caused business and industry to have greater needs for employees. While fifty businesses were recruiting on colleges at the turn of the century and 600 were involved at the end of World War II (Lansner, 1967), by 1960, over 2,000 business and government organizations were involved in nationwide recruiting, with many more times that number recruiting locally and regionally (see Dempsey, 1970; Hackamack & Iannone, 1969; McEneaney, 1973).

During this time coordination of placement associations seemed desirable and the College Placement Council (CPC) was created in 1957. The CPC has served as a clearinghouse for placement publications and a stimulus for communications and research; has originated GRAD, a computer based referral program; and has published a number of materials relevant to placement and recruiting, such as *A Manual for Campus Recruiting, The Directory of College Placement Offices, Organizing Workshops, The Fundamentals of College Placement* (Teal & Herrick, 1962), and *Career Counseling and Placement in Higher Education* (Stephens, 1970). Its ongoing publications are the professional journals, *Journal of College Placement,* the *Placement Perspective,* a report of council meetings and current issues, and the *College Placement Annual,* a directory of major employers of college graduates which assists students in their job search.

The College Placement Services, Inc. (CPS) is a relatively recent development. Started in 1965, it acts as an advisory body to initiate and expand placement services at black colleges. The CPS has given suggestions and guidelines to black college placement services, has supported a fellowship program to train guidance workers at black colleges, and has developed a career-guidance film depicting job concerns of black students.

During the late 1960's with affluence, the leisure climate, and student activism, an antibusiness attitude emerged on college campuses (Dempsey, 1970). Because they felt business was "where the action isn't" and they sought to avoid the draft (Blue, 1968), many college graduates went to graduate school rather than interview for jobs. Campus recruiting was not the single most important method of obtaining new employees in the 1960's as it had been in the 1950's. The 1970's have seen a reversal of this situation. Employers interview something like 20 applicants for each opening (McEneaney, 1973). With inflation, austerity programs, and reduced hiring, the student more than the recruiter must be competitive. Placement services have responded by increasing their efforts to assist students to find jobs and to make vocational plans earlier in their college career.

DEFINITION

Parsons viewed placement activities as a three-pronged approach to vocational guidance: self-understanding or man-analysis, job-analysis or knowledge of the work world, and the merger of the two (McDaniel, Lallas, Saum, & Gilmore, 1959). One or the other has at times been preeminent, but it is the integration of the two, the understanding of the self in relation to the work world, that is the essence of career planning and placement.

Specifically, Parsons stated that the task of the Vocational Bureau (as it was called then) is to "aid young people in choosing an occupation, preparing themselves for it, and building up a career of efficiency and success" (Brewer, 1942, p. 61). Increasing attention is being paid to the first of these objectives as placement services move away from the limited role of matching students to jobs. Counseling, guidance, and advising from freshman orientation through graduation and often after are key concerns of the placement service. Placement means counseling students to know themselves, their interests, abilities, values, and needs; guiding them to a determination of their vocational goals and life-long objectives; and advising them of educational and training requirements, job market trends, and employment openings (Stephens, 1970).

According to Wrenn (1951) the placement service relies upon many other student personnel professionals and college faculty. In turn the placement service serves many others — students, employers, college, and community. It brings together students and their interests, abilities, and life styles; professors and their recommendations; employers and their opportunities.

In its broadest sense, placement means learning. Within an institution whose role is to prepare individuals for rewarding lives, vocationally as well as intellectually, placement is an integral part of the student's educational experience.

Philosophy

Placement philosophy has evolved from a post-World War II instrumentalist concern for uses of knowledge and training with a job-matching orientation to a pragmatic recognition of student needs and interests utilizing a trait-and-factor approach. The current humanistic philosophy emphasizes the individual as a person with unique attributes who needs to develop in his entirety as a whole person (Penney, 1972).

Whereas the employer wants qualified employees, it is the student, not the employer, who is the placement officer's first concern. Although society needs intelligent citizens and competent workers, placement's responsibility to students lies in furthering their self-fulfillment and achievement of their highest goals. The placement service's goal must be the implementation of each student's self-concept in a unique and important way. Its attitude is that there is a place for everyone somewhere.

The philosophy of placement as stated by the College Placement Council is that

> the focus of the Career Planning and Placement Services is upon the student not only immediately before and after graduation, but during the earlier undergraduate years in the

quest for self-understanding, appraisal of interest and abilities, and efforts to determine vocational objectives which are most meaningful and satisfying (McEneaney, 1973, p. 56).

This statement reveals the newer view of vocational development as a life-long process of dynamic growth. It could be more accurately labelled "life-development." In an increasingly complex world where job trends and societal needs are in constant flux, students need or will need assistance in making not only the transition from college to job, but from job to college. Greater efforts in the area of continuing education (see Alumni chapter) will be important and students will need help both earlier and later in life than ever before.

Woody (1973) emphasizes the concept of student development in which students are helped to gain self-insight and to acquire problem-solving and decision-making skills in order to learn self-appraisal and self-management. They also need the expert counseling, advice, and reliable occupational information offered by placement professionals. "Placement has to be regarded as a process which puts people in situations for further growth" (Odell, Pritchard, & Sinick, 1974, p. 145). Thus the number of job placements effected becomes less important than the number of students helped to crystallize their career conceptions.

Roles

There was a time when the number of job hunters and employers in the placement service became so heavy that "few placement directors found the time to do little more than direct the traffic" (Stephens, 1970, p. 202). The role of the placement officer involved little more than gathering information, arranging interviews, directing students to job routes, and matching employers with employees. However, few placement officers of today are willing to accept such a limited function (Bishop, 1966).

Indicative of the changing attitude, many placement services are adopting new titles, such as Career Planning and Placement Service and Career Development Service (Bishop, 1966; McEneaney, 1973). These new titles are meant to reflect the increasing concern of placement officers with the function of counseling and life planning. Placement per se is de-emphasized. There is interest in early involvement with students, closer contact with faculty, and the development of credit courses in career planning, cooperative education, and internship programs. Toomes and Frisbey (1972) note that of the three principal placement functions, campus recruiting, career counseling, and dissemination of occupational information, the first has been adequately handled but the latter two functions are in need of development and improvement.

Sovilla (1972) defines the duties of placement counseling in terms of four key tasks in which the placement counselor helps the student: identify and transfer career interests to a plan of action, relate interests and goals to opportunities in the community, relate career plans to overall life goals, and evaluate progress toward career goals throughout academic preparation and active life. Through its counseling programs the placement service aids in the development of career and life goals; through its interviewing and job placement programs the placement counselor helps the student implement those goals. Even after graduation, the student, as an alumnus, is assured assistance in assessment and reassessment of vocational pursuits (see Alumni chapter).

Additional aims are suggested by Sovilla (1972). First, it is a necessity to provide a career resource center consisting of relevant and timely occupational and vocational information to enable the student to understand the career planning process, explore vocational fields, and compare specific opportunities. The second aim is "to bridge the gap between the university faculty, students and employer groups so as to enhance understanding in areas of mutual concern" (Sovilla, 1972, p. 65). Placement serves the faculty by helping them to understand the realities of the work world and thereby facilitate needed changes in academic preparation. Facts about salaries and entry-level positions may be relayed from faculty to students. Likewise, placement interprets the college to industry and business. The curriculum, the student body, and student attitudes are presented to employers in hopes of bridging the gap between the academic and the real world. Third, placement functions "to serve the university, in whatever capacity, as the complete university center for career relations and professional development" (Sovilla, 1972, p. 65). Placement serves primarily its students and alumni, and in so doing, it meets the opportunity for partnership with business and industry, the professions and government.

Fitzgerald (1962) asked a random sample of 150 Michigan State University faculty members their views of placement's role. The rank ordering of those most to least important for higher education were: (a) Data are available to potential employers regarding the student's educational preparations, job and extracurricular experience, and letters of recommendation. (b) Information is communicated to staff and students about the job market, salaries, and placement trends in a wide variety of fields. (c) All student vocational functions are coordinated. (d) Alumni are assisted in further professional programs by acquainting them with opportunities for advancement in their fields. Also, faculty who worked more closely with students as opposed to those who did not indicated greater approval for most functions.

In terms of public accountability placement receives the onus of responsibility for evidence of the performance and success of college graduates. As Robb (1971) points out, a university may have an excellent academic program, but it is an institutional failure if the students get no assistance with career planning.

Versus Public Employment Agencies

In an era of increasingly complex economic and social structures the relationship of the college placement service to the services of public employment agencies becomes important. Which is more efficient? Which best meets the needs of business and industry? Of students? Which is likely to prevail over the coming years?

Sinick (1955) suggests that state employment agencies are more effective because they have greater access to all sources of occupational and economic information; are more economical since they would eliminate a duplication of services; have more time to devote to placement since they do not emphasize the counseling function; and initiate students into an agency with which they will eventually deal and thus wean the student from dependence on the college. On the other hand, the college placement service is closer to the actual needs and interests of its students and is better able to gauge the employment for which the students are prepared, and to suggest additional training if needed.

Also, Sinick (1955) fears that if government assumes the job of placement, it will put short-term manpower needs over the long-term needs of students. Penney (1968) sees this matter as a question of "whether the placement-oriented counselor can be free enough to allow himself [herself] to place primary emphasis on the needs of his [her] client" (p. 290). Through the sharing, interpretation, and intelligent use of informational resources, government employment services and college placement services can work together to facilitate choice-oriented movement into the employment world (Odell, Pritchard, & Sinick, 1974).

Attitudes of recruiters regarding public and college placement services were assessed by Dennis and Gustafson (1973). From seventy-two randomly selected firms in the 1971 College Placement Annual, results indicated that college placement services are the most often chosen and best source of young, educated talent. More graduates were chosen through campus recruiting than all other sources combined. Employers found college-recruited applicants no less qualified and no less expensive than those obtained through employment agencies.

ADMINISTRATION

Some placement directors come under the direction of the dean of students or the particular deans of the various colleges; others report to the vice-president of administration or directly to the college president. More and more placement services are being administered by the office of student services in line with the adoption of the student personnel philosophy.

Placement operations vary according to the kind of student body served. The nature of the operation is different for prospective teachers than it is for future engineers. Operations also differ depending on the kinds of employers utilizing the service, their methods, and the kinds of information desired. If employers wish to interview students, then interview space is crucial; if employers merely wish to obtain personal resumes, then good clerical services are more important. Williamson and Sarbin (1940) concluded that no standard methods exist in placement.

Tasks

The placement service typically includes the following tasks: job solicitation, student applicant recruitment and registration, applicant interviewing and referral, accumulation of records and recommendations, scheduling of student-recruiter interviews, record keeping of applicant referrals and job placements, and reports and studies of working students (Mohs, 1962). Testing, part-time employment, summer employment, educational and alumni activities, and financial aid are programs sometimes offered by placement services, depending on the size and scope of the institution and its student affairs services (McEneaney, 1973).

Thomas (1966) found that eighty-two placement services on campuses having 4,000 students or more ranked these tasks in order of most to least in importance: to assist students in the investigation of career opportunities, to assist in the fulfillment of the purposes of the institution, to maintain liaison between the university and employers of its products, to assist alumni in matters pertaining to employment opportunity, to provide part-time, temporary, and/or summer student placement services, to act in a public relations capacity, and to perform research in areas related to placement activity.

As the link to the world of work, placement services provide valuable data on business and industrial trends. Placement personnel explain occupational information to university departments, deans, faculty, and the counseling service (Teal &

Herrick, 1962; Thomas, 1966). Employer information and alumni feedback aid in curriculum planning and revision as it pinpoints deficiencies and suggests appropriate emphasis in college preparation for work (Simpson & Harwood, 1973). However, in Thomas' (1966) study of eighty-two placement directors' perceptions of their role, he found that placement does not utilize the opportunity for placement staff to participate in faculty committees: "It is not common practice to initiate suggestions on the redirection of academic programs in relation to the demands of the employment market" (p. 90).

Nevertheless, placement staff can facilitate dialogue among faculty members, department heads, and employers through conferences and luncheons (Breslin, 1969; Edwards, 1968; Teal & Herrick, 1962; Wyatt, 1966-67). Also, Edwards (1968) suggests that faculty actually participate in the placement and recruitment processes in order to better advise students, to adjust course content according to the needs of the work world, and to better present practical, applied course material.

A final function of placement professionals is to communicate with business so as to build an attitudinal base of support and understanding for the college and its programs. Thomas (1966) notes that more than 60 percent of the eighty-two placement officers he surveyed foster employer support of university research projects, scholarships, fellowships, and endow-. ments.

Centralization Versus Decentralization

Placement services may be centralized or decentralized and they may be with or without central coordination. Bishop (1966) delineates four main variations: a centralized student personnel service; a coordinated and centralized function distinct from, but related to academic affairs and student personnel service; a decentralized service with several placement offices in each of several main university colleges, with or without central coordination; and one function in an office of many other student services. This last variation is most often found in small institutions. In the centralized office all programs, staff, and records are under one roof, while in a decentralized system, each college maintains its own records and network of employer contacts. Faculty advising and informal placement efforts may remain within individual departments. According to Stephens (1970) and Teal and Herrick (1962), the centralized service is the most common type of operation. The Calvert and Menke (1967) survey showed that only one in eight placement services was decentralized. In some cases placement operations are separated by type of student, such as underclassmen, upperclassmen, graduate, or alumnus rather than separation by college.

Centralization

A variety of authors (Boynton, 1949; Stephens, 1970; Swaim, 1968; Teal & Herrick, 1962; Wrenn, 1951) are in favor of the centralized operation. First, centralization makes for efficiency in the use of office space, facilities, records, and personnel. The ability to handle a greater volume of student needs is thereby an important by-product. Second, the placement service that is centralized is more effective and convenient for students. The pooling of resources and the interdisciplinary approach makes for a more comprehensive service. Third, the services of a centralized office engender equality of opportunities for all students. The decentralized service, on the contrary, makes for gaps where some groups of students do not receive any service. The uncommitted undergraduate or the miscellaneous major, for example, are both assured of counseling at the centralized service (Swaim, 1968). "Evenness of opportunity among the total group of students, and correspondingly, the greatest range of possible applicants for an employer, can be insured only by centralized placement" (Wrenn, 1951, p. 395).

Fourth, centralization suggests that placement is an integral part of the educational process. Students get the message that the university has a determined interest in helping them enter the work world. Finally, the centralized service is a convenient point of referral for all placement and employer information. One employer favoring centralized placement is Boynton (1949) of Standard Oil, who advised employers against recruiting at decentralized services. Too much time and effort as well as expense, he thought, are wasted for the college, the students, and the employer when it is necessary for the recruiter to engage with as many as a half-dozen separate department heads in one school.

Decentralization

Decentralized placement results in each specialty, such as college, department, or curriculum, having its own placement director, facilities, staff, and employer contacts. Decentralization goes back to the time when, for instance, engineering and education were two separate educational institutions and hence had their separate placement services. Today they may be part of the same institution, but in some instances each has retained its own placement service (Stephens, 1970).

Arguments in favor of decentralization are several. First, on large multi-university campuses where geographical access is limited, decentralized services ensure ease of access for students and employers. Second, decentralization is more personal, less mechanical, and more effective in relations with students. Third, contact with faculty and employers is more direct and hence, there is closer communication between representatives of the work world and those in their respective academic field (Swaim, 1968; Teal & Herrick, 1962). Career counseling and educational advising is more meaningful when ties between faculty and placement are strong. Fourth, evaluations of students are more qualitative and hence more valid than in a centralized service. Swaim notes

> not only is [the department head] responsible for [the placement service's] effectiveness, but he [she] has a personal and professional interest in the careers of "his [her] graduates" (p. 126).

And fifth, since more specialized opportunities avail themselves, decentralized services can offer more specialized placement assistance. For instance, it is argued that disciplines as different as education and engineering need to have two different approaches to employment counseling.

Recruiting Procedures

It is the responsibility of the placement staff to foster a wide range of employer relations, paralleling student needs and interests, to attract recruiters to the campus. Usual recruitment procedure is to contact the company well in advance to establish dates of visits to the campus (Lee, 1970; McEneaney, 1973). Depending on size and needs of the student body, visits will be twice a year, in the fall about mid-November and in the spring about mid-February. Dates must be scheduled early enough to attract January and June graduates, but late enought to insure the crystallization of students' career objectives (A. C. Shaw, 1969). The placement service publicizes the company visits, posts requirements, develops an interview schedule, and displays company literature.

Attitudes Regarding Recruiting

Good, Hunt, and Vokac (1974) surveyed employers' attitudes concerning campus recruiting. Questionnaires filled out by 5,934 employer representatives at 113 placement services revealed that the reception and assistance given recruiters was highly rated, while preparation of students prior to interviews was rated poorly. Rated favorably was the adequacy of physical facilities, information on students available to employers, and information about employers available to students.

In another study (Dennis & Gustafson, 1972) 33 percent of 100 employers felt students needed more counseling and greater awareness of the available jobs. A small number (17%) felt interview schedules were not handled well because of an absence of prior prescreening, no restriction on number of interviews per student, and too short a time allotment. Overall the majority had favorable attitudes toward college campuses and placement services as the prime source of talent.

Another study (Jamie, 1957) examined companies that failed to return to particular campuses for recruiting. The reasons given for discontinuance included failure to properly prescreen interviewees in advance; failure of interviewees to have read the company literature before the interview; failure to set interview schedules according to time limits; failure to provide a private space for interviewing; and filling interview schedules with students planning graduate study or students that are "hard-to-place."

Students have also been surveyed. They view with disdain the interviewer who talks too much; they question the validity of interviews as selection devices; and they doubt that they can be thoroughly evaluated in so short a time as that of the interview (Windle, Kay, & Van Mondfrans, 1971). With 152 students in the graduate schools of business at Northwestern and the University of Chicago, Downs (1971) reported these complaints about recruiting: interviewer's deficiency in knowledge of specific jobs and their requirements, lack of time to establish rapport, lack of privacy, and failure of interviewer to listen to the student or an interviewer who argues.

Varney and Galloway (1974) queried 308 placement directors, 184 campus recruiters, and 100 company managers. All three groups thought college recruiting was moderately effective. Placement directors believed the campus interview, cooperative work-study programs, and direct referrals are among the most effective approaches, while recruiters felt casual drop-ins and referrals by letter to be more important. In the future, placement directors believe that federal government intervention will become important, although they do not favor such intervention. Recruiters believe important future programs will be professional specialty days, resumé books, and placement service referrals. There is general agreement upon the expansion of cooperative programs and development of employers' information banks.

Problems

Among the problems Dempsey (1970) outlines include the fact that not all students are using the placement service and that many private employment agencies are doing as good a job as the college placement service. Some employers use the first job as a screening device by hiring more applicants than are needed. Attrition from students' first jobs is then very high and many new employees are disillusioned. Dempsey suggests that the placement staff make special efforts to reach all students and that they undertake follow-up studies on students to see if the job is meeting the expectations outlined by the recruiter. In addition, employers should assess their manpower needs, question whether its entry-level positions actually require a college degree, and allow mobility and job changes.

Staff

Stephens (1970) recommends one professional counselor for every 100 students registered with the service, plus adequate clerical help. Calvert and Menke (1967) suggest one to two professionals and one to two secretaries for each 1,000 students receiving the Bachelor's degree. They report that the average placement service has about 1.4 secretarial and clerical workers per professional. Most services (66%) also use part-time or temporary help.

Budget

There are four main ways in which placement services are budgeted: The budget is predetermined by the dean of students or vice-president; the placement director makes requests for each expenditure; expenses are paid by the alumni association; or the placement service operates on its own annual budget (Baker, 1968). Baker notes that most placement directors favor the fourth type. Teal and Herrick (1962) add that the most stable and acceptable method is to allow the placement service to establish its own annual budget.

Placement budgets range from several thousand dollars at colleges with less than 100 annual graduates to over $100,000 at larger universities. Some colleges charge students a fee for registration. These may range from one dollar to twenty-five and are usually used to cover clerical costs connected with registration (Calvert & Menke, 1967).

Space and Facilities

The location of the placement service should be one of heavy student traffic, such as near the student union, so as to attract students. Easy access to business representatives and recruiters should also be a consideration. If possible, a location near the counseling service and the student services office is desirable in terms of cooperation and coordination of services (Lansner, 1967; Stephens, 1970).

Adequate space is needed for the functions of interviewing, counseling, occupational information, clerical help, storage of files and records, and staff offices. There should be space for reception and waiting areas for students to make appointments, sign up for interviews, and wait to see counselors and recruiters.

The career library demands a lot of space as it houses vocational information, employer information, company brochures, and job listings. T ese materials should be attractively displayed in a variety of ways so as to stimulate interest. Area for browsing and study is required also (Souther, 1969-70).

The offices of placement counselors need to be quiet and private. Proximity to the reception area and career library facilitate movement and afford the counselor and student use of occupational resources. The director's and other administrative offices should be large enough for staff meetings and conferences, but small enough to insure intimacy if also used for counseling (Lansner, 1967).

Testing and interviewing rooms should be near the reception-waiting room also. They need to be sound-proofed and well-lighted. Stephens (1970) voices the concern that this space is used only half the time. Some services share or borrow office space from other offices during their peak recruiting times so as to avoid wasting space. Calvert and Menke (1967) report that 68 percent of 640 placement directors borrow space, up to 2,000 sq. ft., from other administrative offices.

Forms and Records

The placement director should study and review the particular purposes of data collection for use by employers, students, and the services. Usually forms are needed for student registration, letters of recommendations, employer-contact, and intraoffice communication.

Teal and Herrick (1962) note four areas of placement activity where careful records need to be maintained: (a) services to students: the number involved, classification (undergraduate, graduate, alumnus), degree of placement assistance, and number of interviews; (b) services to employers: number recruiting on campus, correspondence, interviews, and field visits; (c) jobs available: number of openings, variety of jobs available, and geographic location; and (d) public relations: reports given, speeches made, conferences attended, and amount of literature distributed.

Keeping careful records of this sort will greatly facilitate the preparation of annual reports or periodic review of the programs undertaken by the placement service. These reports, when compared with similar reports of other placement services, can aid the placement director in examining and improving procedures and activities of the service in terms of effectiveness and efficiency.

A key feature of placement services is the placement file kept for each student registrant. Biographical data, educational and vocational records, personal interviews, letters of recommendation, and correspondence are all maintained in the student's file. Research (Windle, Van Mondfrans, & Kay, 1972) reveals that both employers and placement officers feel biographical data, educational history, and work experience are important parts of the file. Grades are of some importance to employers. The file is usually cross-indexed for vocational fields so that the student can be notified of possible job opportunities or of companies who are coming to campus for interviews. Some of the information in the placement file may overlap with the records of other services, such as admissions, registrar, or counseling. Centralization of records may be desirable but impossible, especially at large universities (Arbuckle, 1953).

It is of some advantage to start the student's file earlier than the senior year (Spolyar, 1972; Wrenn, 1951). For instance, the placement officer might keep the admissions folder and then add to it relevant data throughout the college years until it is finalized the senior year. Submitting recommendations directly after students' performance insures greater accuracy and completeness and encourages more detailed letters. The student evaluation is more thorough when based on three to four years rather than only on the senior year. Starting the file early encourages earlier and better familiarization of the placement service by the student.

Somewhat disconcerting, however, is the finding by Windle, Van Mondfrans, and Kay (1972) that far fewer employers than placement directors believe the student file is important. They conclude that "since the file generally requires considerable time and money to maintain, further study should be made to determine if it should be discontinued or modified" (p. viii).

Advisory Committee

Establishing a student advisory board could be a step toward guaranteeing the fit between student needs and placement services. Additionally, an advisory committee can help formulate policies, report trends in business and industry, investigate new areas in the employment field, assist with follow-up surveys, assess institutional and departmental cooperation, help plan expansion, and establish liaison between placement and various departments (Teal & Herrick, 1962).

Annual Reports

Segal and Klos (1970) analyzed responses from 354 placement directors as to what they include in their annual reports. They found that six main categories of material are covered: placements, starting salaries, recruitment activity, office activity, class profiles, and student's reasons for job choices. Information about placements detail "who took what job" and list students by class, major, and type of placement, such as company, government, and further education. Starting salaries are grouped according to occupation, sex, academic degree, and geographic location. The names and locations of recruiters' organizations and number of positions offered are listed under recruiting activity. Office activities indicates the number of students registered with the service, the number of interviews held, and the number of placements made. Class profiles give a demographic summary of all the classes. The final category delineates students' reasons for their job choice, those qualities of a job for which they sought, and those persons who helped them make their choice and their vocational plans, both long-range and short-term.

Segal and Klos believe that the placement director reveals his or her conception of function in the annual report, and they criticize the typical annual report for omitting items crucial to the placement role, such as the research activities indigenous to placement, the coordination of other university offices with placement, and the details of the counseling and advising aspects. According to Segal and Klos the tone of the report should be evaluative and conclusive; and the perspective should be in terms of long-range goals. Present trends and their implications for the future of the profession need to be analyzed.

Information Processing

The potentials for computerization are many, some of which are: (a) the library system, or storage and retrieval of occupational-educational information; (b) the client data system, or storage and retrieval of student data; (c) the student-employer system, or prescreening of students for interviews; (d) the personal utility system, or aiding students in decision-making processes; and (e) the counseling system, or selective use of simple counseling skills (Loughary, 1970).

An example of the first, the library system, is the Career Information Project (Kroll, 1969). It uses a computer to produce a bibliographic indexing system for classifying and storing materials for occupations. Searles (1971) describes a computerization of occupational materials that allows students to readily find desired materials and receive photo-offset copies of them.

Stephens (1970) gives an example of the second use of the computer. Complete data on registered students is fed into the computer. As job opportunities or recruiting schedules appear, student qualifications are matched and letters of notification sent out to qualifying students. Harmon (1967) has found such a procedure to be better than notices in the student newspaper and announcements in campus and placement bulletin boards. A greater use of company literature and greater volume of interviews resulted from weekly computer-assisted mailings.

With placement's new philosophy emphasizing counseling over matching, staff time is a serious limitation. The computer comes to the rescue as it can more efficiently perform the job-matching process and free staff time for counseling. Essentially, students describe themselves and state their goals and employers describe their organizations and state their opportunities and needs. The computer then performs the analysis and matching (Shingleton, 1970). Grad II, a national computerized matching system, has been considered successful in this venture and favorable responses have been received from both placement directors and employers (Holcomb, 1970).

Auto-instruction is an example of how the computer can be used for personal utility. Systems have been developed to help students explore their values, to facilitate the decision-making process, and to assess students' probability of success in chosen fields (Harris, 1970; Katz, 1969). To those who would object that such methods are mechanized and impersonal, Harris (1970) would reply:

> with good script-writing and adequate interchange between student and computer, computers can add a dimension of student involvement and excitement to self-appraisal, decision-making, vocational exploration, and educational exploration seldom attained in traditional counseling conferences (pp. 163-164).

Harris does not see the computer as a replacement for the counselor and notes that "the computer cannot, and should not in my opinion counsel" (p. 163).

Helm (1967), however, believes computers can simulate the counseling process. Computer techniques can process and analyze verbal data with precision and efficiency. Simulations of various occupations and work environments can aid vocational exploration. Helm's "black box" model of counseling posits that input such as grades, test scores, and interests can be transformed by computer procedures to output in the form of therapeutic statements and suggestions of job search behavior.

Some placement professionals may find these computer applications untenable or radical. Nevertheless, all or some of these practices are likely to be increasingly considered and implemented in the placement service of the future, as technology advances, as placement demands increase, and as emphasis on counseling continues.

Computerization's advantages are that it makes for more efficient and economical recruiting by reducing employer's time spent in prescreening (Hoy, 1971; W. E. Kauffman, 1967; Stephens, 1970). The efficiency of automation also saves counselors' valuable time. Less time needs to be spent on clerical tasks and paper work, so they can provide more services to more students (Harris, 1970; Hoy, 1971; W. E. Kauffman, 1967; Lohnes, 1969; Stephens, 1970). Automation has enhanced the placement service's programs rather than eliminating them as some feared (W. E. Kauffman, 1967).

Legal Aspects

There are several legal sanctions against discrimination in the administration and activities of the placement service. Title VII of the Civil Rights Act of 1964 prohibits discrimination based upon race, color, religion, sex, or national origin. Since it applies to employment agencies, this law concerns the placement service. In addition, the Employment Act of 1967 forbids discrimination relating to persons between the ages of forty and sixty-five. Although most college students presently do not fall between these ages, the return of older persons to college study makes this law applicable to college recruiting procedures.

Several executive orders compel organizations which receive

federal funds, as do most public colleges, to agree by contract not to discriminate on the basis of race, color, religion, sex, age, or national origin. Also Title VI of the Civil Rights Act prohibits denial of benefits on the basis of race, color, or national origin by persons or institutions receiving federal financial aid (Purdy, 1972).

By example, the placement officer would probably be violating the law if he or she engaged in prescreening of company applicants in such a way as to develop notices implying that certain persons are ineligible, to review student records and make selections, or to give a special test to determine who should be interviewed. In terms of pretesting, placement personnel "may not make referrals or appraisals of applicants based on the results of psychological tests or other selection standards not validated in accordance with the [Equal Employment Opportunity] Commission's guidelines" ("Placement and Its Legal Implications," 1974, pp. 43-44).

It is recommended that the placement director review the forms used in order to eliminate the possibility of employers stating religious, sex, or national origin preferences for applicants unless the employer can present evidence that such is a bona fide occupational qualification. And "if the prospective employer furnishes such information, legal counsel should review it because it probably cannot stand up under the [EEOC] commission's opinions, of which placement directors are charged to be knowledgeable" (Purdy, 1972, p. 49).

Title IX of the Education Amendments Act of 1972 applies to colleges receiving financial assistance and prohibits discrimination in educational programs and activities. Specifically covered are "academic research, extracurricular and other offerings, housing, facilities, access to programs and activities, financial aid and employment assistance to students" (U. S. Dept. of HEW, 1974, p. 22228). Section 86.35 of Title IX requires that "assistance in making outside employment available to students, and employment of students by a recipient must be undertaken in a non-discriminatory manner" (p. 22230).

The College Placement Council discusses the legal complications concerning the confidentiality and privacy of student records. It suggests that the placement director review student files in order to remove any potentially damaging statements for which libel might be claimed. Concerning privacy of records, the college as well as the placement service needs to formulate a policy regarding the information contained in student records. According to the Council of Student Personnel Associations in Higher Education

> the policies should ... pay proper respect to the legal principles of privacy and confidentiality; ... reflect a reasonable balance between the obligations to the student for personal growth and welfare and the responsibilities of the institution to society; ... be flexible enough not to hinder the student, the institution, or the community in legitimate pursuits; ... permit individual professional judgments under appropriate circumstances; ... be clear and concise, and be communicated by appropriate means, including official publications, to those to whom it applies; and, ... make provision for maximum security of records from unauthorized accessibility and from loss or damage by fire and other hazards ("Placement and Its Legal Implications," 1974, pp. 45-46).

Specific recommendations are that only those records should be maintained for which there is a demonstrable need, and further, academic, medical, counseling, and disciplinary records are not pertinent to the placement file. Letters of recommendation should be discussed by student and author. Those recommendations submitted as confidential are to remain so unless agreed to in writing by both the writer and the student. Within the institution, staff members with legitimate interest and need might be allowed access to a student's confidential file. The placement director must use discretion and professional judgement in this regard. Formal consent of the student is needed for access by persons or organizations outside the institution.

The Family Educational Rights and Privacy Act of 1974 (the "Buckley Amendment") specifically protects the student's right of privacy regarding college records including the placement file. Students may elect to review letters of recommendation written for them or to waive this right and retain confidentiality of these letters. In some cases placement officers may keep dual student files, one for confidential letters and another for nonconfidential ones. The amendment also details students' right to a hearing where the accuracy of records is in question. Release of information from a students' file requires the student's written consent. It is advised that the placement service keep records of when and to whom records are sent (Herrick, 1975).

Student Activism

The student ferment on campuses in the 1960's and 1970's included dissent and picketing aimed at placement services. Students' activism raised the question of placement's role at academic institutions. A major feeling common among students was that placement existed to serve business, industry, and government rather than serving students. There was a strong feeling that the ethics of business were questionable. Some demanded that big business put money into social services and humanitarian causes. Students saw organizations such as the CIA and Dow Chemical as war-related and hence picketed their recruiters in attempts to prevent them from recruiting students. Correspondingly, they charged the college as being pro-war and thus in violation of academic neutrality (Liebers, 1970; Steele, 1971).

The reactions of placement officers and administrators had been to defend the practice of open forum and to reiterate the rights of students to interview with those recruiters that they wished (W. E. Kauffman, 1969; Morgan, 1969). Morgan has urged colleges to determine the actual extent of their complicity and has recommended putting students on committees of advising and governing.

Those students who decry big business' lack of ethics or who want meaningful work engaged in social change can find assistance at some placement services. For instance, a nonprofit organization in Canyon, California, Vocations for Social Change, counsels youth concerning jobs which work to change institutions from within or work outside the system to create alternative institutions. Examples of careers for social change include free medical clinics, the New York Media Project, Radio Free People in Media, and the Bay Area Radical Teachers Organizing Project in Education ("Careers for Social Change," 1971).

Placement services at Sacramento State College, the University of Washington, and Michigan State University also disseminate information about opportunities for jobs outside the mainstream. The Other Placement Office at Oberlin College and an Alternatives Festival at Columbia offer students alternative job possibilities ("The Vanguard," 1971). These activities foster a new approach to the conception of "job." They allow students to determine the nature of their own job and create their own lifestyle.

Research

To improve its programs and the programs of the university, the placement service may undertake three basic forms of research. These are: follow-up of all students, including those not registered; evaluation of placement techniques, communication channels, and field services; and examination of job market conditions, vocational trends, and employer requirements (Wrenn, 1951). Four methods used are conferences and correspondence with graduates; an active file of students and alumni; placement services to alumni; and visits and correspondence with employers (Hagerty & Brumbaugh, 1951).

Research designed to investigate the role of placement in the student's educational life can be framed in a variety of questions: To what extent does the college recognize its responsibility in placement? To what extent does the college endeavor to secure placements? To what extent does the college actually place its graduates? To what extent are students familiar with the college placement activities? (Berger, 1944). In addition, research on job trends is vital in order to facilitate the vocational advice given students. Counseling, programming, and job placement activities must be continuously evaluated in light of changing conditions and requirements (Thomas, 1966). Statistics gathered and disseminated by local, state, and government sources, such as U. S. Employment Service and the U. S. Department of Labor, provide valuable information pertinent to this need.

Another form of research with feasible application to the placement operations is the investigation of career development and vocational decision making. The placement director can easily sponsor such research and encourage graduate students or professors in other departments to do so (Simpson & Harwood, 1973).

PROGRAMS

Placement personnel assist students with vocational decision-making and related educational-occupational questions. Employer contacts through job listings and interview schedules are offered, as well as information about occupations and employer organizations. In implementing career decisions, students learn to sharpen their interview and job-search skills. In general, students are given encouragement in attaining their individual vocational and employment goals (Teal & Herrick, 1962). Placement personnel attempt to develop on-going relationships with students throughout their college career, offering interest, objective information, personalized individual and group counseling, and placement programs that are educational and resource-building.

Counseling

A major program for students is vocational counseling, defined as:

> a process by which an individual is stimulated to: (1) Evaluate himself [herself] and his [her] opportunities; (2) make a feasible choice in the light of his [her] unique characteristics and opportunities; (3) accept responsiblities for his [her] choice; and (4) initiate a course of action consonant with his [her] choice. (Froehlich, 1961, pp. 370-371).

Vocational counseling is a relatively new adjunct to placement advising, which has dealt primarily with the availability of jobs (Wrenn, 1951).

Stevens' (1966, 1972) conceptualization further specified the placement counseling function. Based on the assumption that vocational development is an expression of self-actualization and the implementation of self-concept, she infers that job-seeking behavior is an indication of placement readiness. Placement readiness (PR) is measured on two continuums, from vague to crystallized goals and from passive and confused behavior to goal-oriented behavior. The implication for placement counselors is that they must differentially counsel students according to their level of placement readiness. For example, the student high in PR will want primarily detailed information about specific jobs, while low PR students will need increased self-awareness, maybe improved self-concept, or even in-depth counseling or referral.

Counseling students for graduate study has increased because more students are seeking advanced degrees, due perhaps to the tight economy and manpower needs (Riegel, 1966), the proliferation of advanced programs, and the availability of fellowship resources (Bishop, 1966). Although faculty assumed the job of advising the student on graduate study in the past, the increased numbers of students have complicated the advisement process.

Counseling college seniors about graduate study is equally as important as counseling high school seniors about college. In fact, a greater proportion of students with a Bachelor's degree are likely to go to graduate school than are high school graduates to go to college: Three fourths of graduating college students continue their education (J. A. Davis, 1964).

> Except for a minority of students who attend graduate school because they do not know what else to do with themselves, graduate and professional study is decidedly a career decision. It is inevitably bound up with vocational counseling and career guidance (J. F. Kauffman, 1964, p. 357).

Interview Training

In special counseling sessions, seminars, workshops, classes,

etc., students practice role-playing with each other, with placement staff, or with real recruiters in simulated interview sessions. Sometimes they use tape recordings or videotapes to
increase effectiveness of feedback. They may listen to tapes or
watch films of real or simulated interview sessions. The main
purposes of these sessions are to help alleviate students' anxiety
about interviewing and to increase their self-confidence. Interview training educates students as to what it is all about, what
goes on in an interview with recruiters. In the practice sessions,
students learn to articulate their vocational goals and to develop good listening skills. Further, this practice stimulates
them to become aware of their competencies and qualities (Gilmore, 1973; Hess, 1971; Raanan & Lynch, 1974; Rossen, Nash,
& Miller, 1971).

Babcock and Yeager (1973) consider interview training a
form of cheating that destroys the individuality of each interview in that all students sound the same. Also it raises employer expectations to the detriment of the student who may
not be as qualified as would appear in the coached interview.
Babcock and Yeager assert that since recruiter interviews have
questionable validity as selection devices, the false facade engendered by interview training further decreases validity. They
see some benefits in interview training but urge a careful analysis of its uses and limitations. However, both Soltys (1971) and
E. A. Shaw (1973) contend that interview practice preserves
student individuality in that it alleviates anxiety and teaches
students to relax and be themselves. Student reactions have
been favorable and interview preparation was found to be informative and helpful in improving skills (Gilmore, 1973;
Hess, 1971; Rossen, Nash, & Miller, 1971).

Academic Vocational Courses

The need for earlier educational and vocational counseling
and more broadly reaching counseling services is an acute one.
Traditional approaches as reading pamphlets and signing up
for interviews are often insufficient (Salinger, 1969). Yet coun-

selors' time is scarce and valuable. Vocational or career development courses reach more students while economizing on time and availability of placement staff.

A survey (Calvert, Carter, & Murphy, 1964) of 1,023 colleges found that 7 percent offered courses in occupational adjustment. They list four types of vocational courses: those centered on personal vocational choice or career planning, those giving an introduction to the world of work, those presenting job search techniques, and those dealing with career adjustment.

A more recent study (Devlin, 1974) found these courses to be increasing: 10 percent of 756 colleges had career development courses and an additional 15 percent had courses in the planning stage. Of the seventy-eight existing courses forty-three were interdisciplinary, fifteen were in teacher education departments, and ten each were in business and psychology. Placement counselors taught forty of the courses, faculty in education taught fourteen, and counseling service counselors taught twelve. The primary role of placement staff in teaching these courses indicates that placement is moving into formal academia. As Powell (1971-1972) sees it, career planning is the "interrelationship between advising, counseling, teaching and placement" (p. 31). When career planning is integrated into the classroom it more clearly becomes an integral part of student life.

Career Counseling Groups

A similar vehicle for furthering career exploration that also maximizes staff time is vocational counseling groups. The specific goal of career discussion groups at the Career Development Center of Rhode Island College was the transmission of occupational information (Haney, 1963). The groups met twice a week and consisted of guest speakers from varied occupations, career counselors, faculty, and students from many majors. Information presented included requirements for various occupational fields, methods of entry, salaries, etc. Aiken and Johnston (1973) sought to facilitate information-seeking behavior or to teach developmental skills that enable clients to independently shape their lives. In two to three group sessions of one and one-half hours each, ninety-four career undecided freshman and sophomore males received positive reinforcement counseling for information-seeking behaviors.

In terms of participants' satisfaction with groups the research is mixed. Sprague and Strong (1970) report overall enjoyment and positive reactions to group counseling. Their study did not, however, compare the group counseling method to individual counseling. Students in Adams' study (1974) were satisfied with the attention given them in both the Career Planning Group and the individual counseling session, with the greatest gains found in the group situations. Although the data did not indicate statistical differences between groups, the students in the group were more positive about college than those individually counseled, were more satisfied with their major, were more certain about completing the program, and were making more appropriate educational and vocational choices.

Banikiotes and McCabe (1972) report more positive reactions to individual counseling sessions than to groups. In the Simpson, Pate, and Burks study (1973) both clients and counselors rated individual counseling more favorably than group. Graff (1971) compared individual and group counseling with self-instruction and found the latter to make students more satisfied with their career decisions. Both self-instruction and group approaches were more effective than individual counseling in terms of transmission of occupational information, teaching how to make educational-vocational decisions, teaching self-appraisal, and setting goals consistent with abilities and interests.

Most studies point to greater effectiveness with the group method as compared to individual counseling. The exception is the study by Simpson, Pate, and Burks (1973) which found no differences between those counseled in groups and those individually helped and found employment interview evaluations remained lower for both groups than for those in the control group. Comparing pre- and post-test results for members of a vocational counseling group, Andersen and Bennie (1971) found occupational aspirations to be higher at the termination of the group. There was also a greater incidence of decisive commitment to occupational choice.

Occupational Information

Disseminating occupational information is another key function of the placement service. In the context of student vocational development more than facts are needed when personal vocational decisions are made, for example, attitudes and values are important affective determinants of vocational choice and satisfaction. For developing individuals, occupational information is most beneficial "if it is acquired in experential as well as didactic modes .... The total experiencing, feeling, and thinking person is the appropriate focus of information reception" (Reardon, 1973, p. 497). Brayfield (1948) notes the readjustive and motivational applications of occupational information as well as its informational role. And Christenson (1948) sees the function of occupational information to be instructional, instrumental, distributional, and therapeutic.

Typical sources of occupational information for the placement library are the Department of Labor, the U. S. Government Printing Office, and the Women's Bureau. The *Occupational Outlook Handbook*, published by the Department of Labor annually, describes the nature of work and employment opportunities in almost all fields. *The Occupational Outlook Quarterly* supplements the *Handbook* with the most recent labor market trends. The Occupational Outlook Report Series publishes single pamphlets in specific careers. The Occupational Outlook Service also publishes materials that relate college major to occupational areas, such as "English and Your Career" (Counselor's Guide to Manpower Information). Printed information from publishers, professions, and business associations and pamphlets from national and state employment firms are two other sources (Bishop, 1966).

Placement professionals can also rely on the College Placement Council's publications with which to build a solid base of knowledge. Other basic reference materials include the *Dic-*

tionary of Occupational Titles, an encyclopedia of job definitions and related information; the *Occupational Thesaurus;* the *Guide to Listings of Manufacturers;* and the *Dunn and Bradstreet Reference Book,* a listing of business organizations (Austin, 1973). Additional references of value to the career resource area include directories of business, department stores, social agencies, university and graduate schools, and telephone directories (Bishop, 1966). Company literature and recruiting materials and actual first-hand visits to companies and agencies are excellent ways of acquiring occupational information essential to the job of career advising.

Faculty members should not be overlooked as a possible source of valuable occupational information. Arbuckle (1953) finds that they are often superior to vocational personnel for their grasp of their own particular field. Professors often have unique individual relationships with employers. Since some students are closer to their professors than to counseling or placement staff, they may turn to them first.

Instructive occupational literature is useless without an effective communication system. Bishop (1966) recommends constant communication with students via the student newspaper, radio, bulletin boards, special flyers, and placement newsletters. Some placement services send out mimeographed pamphlets detailing specific areas to students in certain majors and publish a listing of new occupational resources received. Exposing students to information in their area "helps students to help themselves" (Searles, 1971, p. 59). Other means of communication are panel discussions by representatives in various occupational fields, individual guest speakers, clubs or discussion groups for particular areas, workshops or seminars, occupational courses, and career days or career fairs. Tapes, films, and computerized information have been developed as well (Handville, 1953-1954).

A note of caution has been expressed in the extensive use of written materials. Davison (1968) suggests that written materials should not be considered as a substitute for a close interpersonal relationship between students and counselor. More efficient tools for information dissemination, such as the computer, are seen as freeing counselor time to enable more individual face-to-face relationships so important for goal setting, identity information, and career information.

Testing

Thomas (1966) says that "placement offices rarely provide personality, aptitude, attitude, and/or interest testing" (p. 92). He hypothesizes that such services usually come under the aegis of the counseling service. Placement directors themselves appear to view testing for placement purposes as obsolete and anachronistic. A recent decline in this use of testing is seen, though within business firms, testing for counseling and placement is on the rise (Treible, 1969).

Treible (1969) assessed attitudes toward testing of 125 students placed in a Chase Manhattan Training Program. They criticized testing for the lack of professional administration, lack of relativism of test results, failure to use a control, poor testing conditions, and improper use of test results. Opposition of undergraduate and graduate students toward aptitude, achievement, interest, and personality testing ranged from 40 percent to 75 percent with least opposition to interest tests and most disfavor towards achievement tests. Careful use of tests necessitates proper motivation and attitudes of the student, professional administration of the test, proper testing conditions, and informed and intelligent interpretation of test results (Newsome, Thorne, & Wyld, 1973; Stephens, 1970; Treible, 1969). Some authors suggest that interest tests are effective tools for initiating students into the self-exploration process. They can serve as a stimulus for discussion and involvement with the counselor (Newsome, Thorne, & Wyld, 1973).

Full-Time Recruiting

The placement service offers students the opportunity to meet with representatives of business, industry, and government agencies. In the interview the student learns about the company or agency, its needs and openings, and the recruiter learns of the applicant and possible relationship with the company. The two discuss entry level positions, promotion and advancement, company history, salary and fringe benefits, company's training program, among other things. They explore the student's educational and vocational background, hobbies and leisure pursuits, needs, values, interests, and goals as they relate to the interviewer's company.

The actual interview is a preliminary screening. As well as evaluating the student's suitability for employment, the interviewer wishes to create a favorable impression of the organization to the student and also to placement staff and faculty. If acceptable, the student is then considered by the company management. The student is usually invited to the home office for a day where interviews and possibly testing takes place. If the interview is successful the student is given an offer of employment to accept or reject.

Avenues of employer contact other than the campus interview are being encouraged as well. Placement workshops on the Job Search assist students with resumes, letters of application, etc. Whether in an interview or on a resume, the injunction "Know Thyself" describes the task the students face in analyzing themselves and relating and selling that self to the work world. "Here at last, in confrontation with the recruiter, is the challenge to bring into play all he/she has learned" (Stephens, 1970, p. 177).

Student Work Experiences

Another area servicing both students and employers is the rapidly developing and expanding field of student work experiences. Career-related programs implemented include work-study, cooperative education, job internships, summer employment, part-time employment, voluntary community activities, and independent study projects. These programs afford the students actual on-the-job experiences and can, therefore, acquaint them with potential career opportunities as well as giving employers a source of labor. Students gain insight into their vocational aptitudes and areas of occupational satisfaction, hence facilitating career decision making (Walters, 1969). Better prospects for job placement await these students at graduation (Babbush, 1966). Some of these programs offer academic credit. Some provide financial remuneration thereby assisting the student in financing his or her education. Placement services vary from institution to institution as to responsibility for these programs. Some services share responsibility with other personnel services such as financial aid and counseling, or with academic departments and faculty (see Financial Aid chapter).

Cooperative education alternates semesters of academic study with semesters of job placement. While work-study is primarily a means of financial assistance and is a program usually administered by the financial aid service, cooperative education programs are mainly educational. "Educational institutions and employers engage cooperatively in the education of the student, hence the term 'cooperative education'" (J. R. Davis, 1971, p. 140). Co-op programs are increasingly being developed and implemented. Cross (1973) estimates that over 350 colleges now offer co-op programs, and some 200 more are in the planning stage. That placement plays a large role in their development is inferred from the fact that 80 percent of the colleges with cooperative education cite career development as its most important goal. Additional advantages to the student besides career exploration, financial assistance, and job placement are personal growth, maturation and professionalization, more thorough and deeper understanding of work skills, increased meaning to one's academic pursuits, application of academic learning to an applied situation, gain in knowledge from established professionals, and an attractive option to those who claim the classroom is irrelevant (Borman, 1967-1968; Cross, 1973; J. R. Davis, 1971; Reitman, 1970).

In providing students real-life experiences in the work world and offering them the chance to test out their career interests, placement can "become more fully involved in assisting students to develop a solid foundation from which a career may be launched. The time has never been better for placement to be an *active* partner with students in meeting these needs" (Simpson & Harwood, 1973, p. 229).

Several advantages accrue to the employer as a result of cooperative education and other work experience programs. Since most cooperative program students continue as company employees, cooperative education assists the company in attracting potential employees. Companies may use the program to train or update their own employees and thus save time and money. Also, students often bring new ideas and fresh perspectives to the job. The program supplements a company's staff and aids expansion of the organization, and it gives business and industry a share in the educational process (Addison, 1970; Borman, 1967-68; Cross, 1973; J. R. Davis, 1971).

The college sponsoring cooperative education benefits also. These programs enrich the educational offerings, keep faculty aware of new developments in their fields, better utilize college facilities through year-round operation, increase student enrollments, extend new relations to employers, and enhance college-community relations (Cross, 1973; J. R. Davis, 1971).

Problems dealing with student attitudes and program administration have been cited. Student attitudes include initial skepticism, resistance to maturation, and reservations about missing out on extracurricular college life. In terms of administration, problem areas may be in finding reliable and trained supervisors, surmounting high initial and continuing costs, scheduling the irregular flow of employment, and finding adequate job sites with high educational potential (Borman, 1967-68; J. R. Davis, 1971; Reitman, 1970; Smithers, 1971).

PERSONNEL

Placement officers have not usually come from student personnel programs since the placement service is not often part of their graduate programs (Bishop, 1966). Calvert and Menke (1967) found that almost half of 534 placement directors obtained their position through transfer from some other campus position. They have come out of the academic disciplines, business, industry, government, or personnel work in other settings (Bishop, 1966).

In the Calvert and Menke (1967) study 53 percent had backgrounds in business, 61 percent had experience in college teaching or administration, and 18 percent had worked in some other placement office. In a summary of research bearing on this issue, Windle, Van Mondfrans, and Kay (1972) found that the most frequently given reason for entering placement was "by chance." Of course, "earlier identification and training, perhaps at the undergraduate or graduate student level [is needed before such persons become] accidentally involved" (Windle, Van Mondfrans, & Kay, 1972, p. viii).

Consequently 52 percent of Calvert and Menke's (1967) respondents favored specific professional preparation for prospective placement directors. However, there were some who preferred directors *not* from a unified professional training route. They maintained that a diversity of backgrounds strengthens the field, and others feared rigid stereotyping of placement professionals or questioned the value of professionalization. Those favoring specific training placed experience over degree and recommended training in vocational counseling, tests and measurement, and data processing.

Characteristics

The typical placement director is male, forty-five years old, has a Master's degree, has been on the job less than four years, and has attained faculty rank at a college other than his alma mater (Calvert & Menke, 1967). Though based on older data and a smaller sample, Vokac's (1959) findings were quite similar except his composite typical director is positioned at a centralized placement service that is his alma mater.

Possessing an advanced degree and holding nonplacement duties, such as teaching, are two factors that determine high status for the placement director (Vokac, 1959). Placement directors are likely to be a member of the academic faculty with tenure and other benefits; part of an administrative staff; or a part-time placement officer with other duties, such as teaching, administration, or other student personnel functions (Baker, 1968).

Bucci's evidence (1970-71), however, shows that placement

directors frequently do not have academic rank. They also are not eligible for tenure and do not receive sabbatical leave. Calvert and Menke (1967) report the frequencies of 534 placement directors whose salaries are on a par with other college personnel: department head (75), full professor (97), associate professor (140), assistant professor (104), instructor (50), administrative assistant (40), secretary (11), and other (17). Highest salaries are obtained at state universities with state colleges next highest and private institutions the lowest.

Training

In 1909 Parsons said the placement director should be

> qualified to test the abilities and capabilities of young men [and women], apply good judgement, common sense and scientific method to the various problems a vocation bureau has to deal with, and give appropriate counsel with the insight, sympathy, grasp and suggestiveness the service calls for (Parsons, 1909, p. 94).

Today, training in individual differences and measurement, understanding of the normal personality and of society, vocational psychology, occupational knowledge, and expertise in counseling techniques are all important skills. Simpson and Harwood (1973) add knowledge of higher education, especially of the placement service's own institution and its students. They stress background, experience, and outlook toward life as variables more important than academic degree. Lansner (1967) advocates experience in business so that the director is sensitive to the problems of employers in recruiting and of students in their roles of job aspirants and new employees.

Stevens (1965) laments the absence of a specific graduate level training program in placement counseling, as distinguished from vocational counseling. The latter stresses the process of occupational choice while placement counseling deals with personal mobilization of resources to obtain the job that is one's career choice. She notes very few specialized programs in placement counseling and administration.

Concerning formal training programs in placement, Vokac (1959) surveyed 1,000 placement directors at graduate level institutions who belonged to the Midwest College Placement Association. The top five weaknesses mentioned were: lack of any placement training internships or workshops; lack of specialized academic training in guidance, personnel, and counseling; too narrow a field of specialization; insufficient knowledge of the job market; and lack of depth in informal liberal arts training. These results suggest that placement directors desire the kind of background most writers in the field are advocating: that is, a broadly based knowledge of the individual and of the work world, specialized training in placement counseling and office administration, and actual field work or practicum experience.

Actual qualifications mentioned by Vokac's sample of 440 placement directors and the number of times mentioned were: business or industrial experience (197), academic training in personnel, guidance, and/or psychology (154), teaching experience (88), personal qualifications (65), knowledge of job market opportunities (54), interest in and appreciation of student viewpoint (49), administrative ability (46), a Master's degree (44), placement experience and training (43), and ability to work with people (36). The emphasis is upon business experience, a facility for relating to the work world and its representatives and aspirants. An academic background in the helping fields is seen as important. Teaching experience is weighted somewhat heavily and the ability to work with people is considered essential.

In a later study, Stevens (1965) surveyed the qualifications forty-five placement personnel in the greater New York area would consider in hiring placement staff. In terms of academic degree 75 percent would require an M.A., 41 percent a B.A., and 34 percent the Ph.D. or Ed.D. Fifty percent prefer the degree to be in the field of vocational counseling, 29 percent in college student personnel administration, and 20 percent in business. Ninety-one percent favor college work experience, 77 percent want business experience, and 40 percent would hire industrial personnel. The ideal age range was twenty-five to thirty years (43%) or thirty to thirty-five years (32%) while 27 percent said that it "doesn't matter." The composite ideal placement director would then be a man or woman, about twenty-five to thirty-five years old, who has a Master's degree in counseling with work experience in business and college.

Vokac's (1959) study reveals a greater relative demand for a business experience background than does Stevens', which emphasizes a counseling background. Vokac's (1959) study is six years earlier than Stevens' (1965). This indicates the earlier conceptualization of placement as a business enterprise contrary to the present emphasis on the counseling function. Also there is a greater concern for academic qualifications in the more recent study: 75 percent of Stevens' sample demand a Master's degree while only 10 percent in Vokac's study mention the M.A. as a preferred qualification.

An even more recent study is McLaughlin's (1973). He surveyed 160 college and university placement directors. The most preferred academic background for a placement director was a Master's degree (72%) while 10 percent preferred a Bachelor's and 6 percent a doctoral degree. Sixty-five percent favored a degree in counseling, psychology, or college student personnel administration. This substantiates the observed trend toward counseling-based placement professionals. Further, the desire for a background of work experience in business is decreasing, according to this study. Here only 31 percent preferred a business background compared to larger proportions in both Vokac's and Stevens' investigations.

Tyler's (1961) vision of the body of knowledge needed "encompasses vocational guidance resting on a much broader base of knowledge about individual development in a complex, changing society" (p. 70). This approach would utilize many disciplines in the behavioral sciences, such as psychology, sociology of occupations, testing, economics, labor market analyses, counseling theory, and group dynamics. Knowledge would be drawn from computer science, personnel research, business and management, and placement service operation.

Professional Activities

Calvert and Menke (1967) sent questionnaires to 1,136 placement directors. Of those placement directors in state universities, 89 percent belong to their regional placement association, whereas in small colleges only 50 percent belong to a placement association. The placement director may spend anywhere from ten to 300 hours a year on professional activity. The placement directors wanted the regional associations to work for a positive image of placement, help sell the college administration on the importance of placement, provide in-service training for personnel, stress the need for vocational counseling, and help involve more people in placement programs. They said the College Placement Council might set up a clearinghouse for jobs in the field of placement, help sell the "top brass" on the importance of placement, help keep directors better informed on new trends in placement, further develop GRAD, organize placement associations by size and interest rather than by areas, and develop a means of accreditation of placement services.

Code of Ethics

General ethical guidelines for placement professionals, including recruiters as well as placement directors, are outlined in "Principles and Practices of College Placement and Recruitment," adopted by the College Placement Council and the Chamber of Commerce of the United States. It was updated in 1964, 1968, and 1970 (Stephens, 1970). An excerpt follows:

> It is in the best interest of students, colleges, and employers alike that the consideration of careers and selection of employment opportunities be based on an understanding of all the relevant facts and that these considerations be made in an atmosphere conducive to objective thought.
>
> The recruiting of college students for employment by business, industry, government, and education should be carried out by the employers, candidates, and college authorities to serve best the following objectives:
>
> 1) The open and free selection of an employment opportunity that will provide the candidate with the optimum long-term utilization of his [her] talents, consistent with his [her] personal objectives.
> 2) The promotion of an intelligent and a responsible

choice of a career by the candidate for his [her] own greatest satisfaction and the most fruitful long-range investment of his [her] talents for himself [herself], for his [her] employer, and for society.

3) The development of the placement function as an integral part of the educational system so that it, as well as the total recruiting process, may be oriented toward the establishment of high standards of integrity and conduct among all parties (Stephens, 1970, p. 228).

RELATIONSHIPS WITH OTHER SERVICES

Placement and Counseling

Although the placement service has been distinct from the counseling service on campus for over thirty years, the question arises: Whose function is it to do counseling (H. P. Kirk, 1971)?

In career counseling the placement officer is likely to emphasize occupational and job information while the counseling service contributes information and data about the student. As Merrill (1954) points out, both aspects are needed. Often the realities of the job market are ignored by the counselor, while the placement worker may lack counseling expertise and often gets the students too late — in their senior year. Although this pattern is changing, the placement service has been more of a business office, with the counseling service being more clinically oriented (McLaughlin, 1973).

Hoppock (1963) discusses the need for career counseling to be closely related to the placement function. He notes that the counselor's effectiveness becomes accountable at the time of placement. Similarly, Sinick (1955) speaks of the necessity for placement personnel to do counseling and testing. By so doing "the worker gains a rounded view of the agency's mission, a view which is more likely to include the individual client, his [her] basic needs and capacities, and his [her] long-range goals" (Sinick, 1955, p. 39).

Results from two studies provide perceptions of counseling service directors as to the locus of vocational counseling. Of thirty-six counseling service directors who returned question-naires to Clark (1966), 71 percent indicated that vocational counseling was a primary concern of the counseling service, with educational and occupational information counseling second at 67 percent, and personal counseling third with 60 percent.

In B. A. Kirk's study (1965) respondents were participants at a meeting of counseling services directors representing sixty-seven institutions. Their perceptions of placement service functions in addition to placement were vocational counseling (6%), employment counseling (75%), nothing more or none (14%), or not known (6%). Respondents differentiated vocational counseling from employment counseling and overwhelmingly delegated the latter to placement while retaining vocational counseling as their duty. When asked where employer information was maintained, 88 percent answered the placement service, only 1 percent said the counseling service, 9 percent indicated both services, and 1 percent said neither had employer information. However, to "Where is occupational information maintained?" responses were mixed: 23 percent responded the counseling service, 5 percent the placement service, and a majority, 56 percent, both (5% neither, 11% both and library). According to these studies, counseling service directors see vocational counseling as a primary function of their services, but share with placement services the development and maintenance of occupational information.

Since placement and counseling are both major student personnel services directed toward students' vocational development, it is often felt that they should be coordinated in order to best meet the goals of the individual student. McLaughlin (1973) found that 14 percent of counseling directors have combined placement and counseling facilities on their campuses. Personal problems are most often inseparable from vocational-educational problems. A unified service would make such a distinction obsolete and hence prevent questions of jurisdiction and problems of referral. It might also encourage students to seek help earlier due to the lessened stigma once attached to psychological or counseling assistance. Additionally, more adequate research can be undertaken when a close relationship exists between counseling and placement. And, simply enough, the elimination of wasteful overlap and duplication is an obvious benefit.

Although coordination of the two services is rare and occurs mainly on small campuses, it is logical to expect some kind of working relationship to exist between counseling and placement. B. A. Kirk (1965) asked sixty-seven counseling service directors about the relationship between counseling service and placement service. The responses were "work closely together" — 19 percent, "sometimes communicate regarding a student" — 57 percent, and "rarely have contact" — 75 percent. Communication seems to be mainly a case-by-case approach as seen in the referral process. It was found that 19 percent of the counseling service directors referred students to the placement service "frequently" with 59 percent doing so "occasionally," and 22 percent only "rarely." On the other hand, 30 percent of the placement service directors referred students to the counseling service "frequently" and 56 percent did so "occasionally," with 37 percent making referrals "rarely."

The counseling service may refer students to the placement service who need career exploration or who need more specificity in their career planning. Likewise, the placement officer might refer to the counseling service students who are uncertain of their direction or who do not know "what there is within themselves which needs fulfillment in work" (B. A. Kirk, 1965, p. 290). B. A. Kirk emphasizes that a "cooperative relationship is vital for career placement as an extension of counseling and as a final culmination of the counseling of the student throughout his [her] college career" (p. 291). She notes that a start has been made. Counseling service directors were asked "By what means do you attempt closer working relations with placement?" Sixty-six percent answered "telephone" and 33 percent said "special joint meetings and/or field trips." Thirty-seven percent "interchange reports and information," 19 percent conduct "informal interpersonal communication," and 16 percent report "contact via third party meetings, e.g. general student personnel meetings."

Placement and Other Services

In addition to the counseling service, other student personnel services overlap with placement in their functions. These include: precollege counseling and admissions, orientation, financial aid, part-time employment, student activities, personnel records, and follow-up studies (Johnson, 1949).

Personnel involved with precollege counseling and admissions are in fact dealing with placement objectives since they are making decisions concerning the student's goals for higher education. It is at this point that they are evaluating the student's potential, not only for college work, but for career placement. Wrenn (1951) notes that the admissions officer serves the functions of vocational counseling to the high school students and of public relations with parents, teachers, and community in selling them the benefits of their particular institution. At Oberlin College, for example, admissions merged with placement. Visits to high schools were seen to involve placement as well as admissions functions. The admissions officer engaged in vocational counseling at the high schools as well as thinking about the placement potential in recruiting new freshmen (Wrenn, 1951).

The orientation program for freshman and other new students undoubtedly emphasizes the vocational aspects of the college experience. Usually the program allows the personnel to publicize its services, show students what it has to offer, and discuss with students their long-term college goals. It is logical that there be ties between the placement service and financial aid and part-time employment services because both are concerned with the employability of students. New Mexico State University is an example of one institution where the two functions were joined under one director. Due to heavier responsibilities engendered by the new federal financial aid programs, the two functions were split into separate offices, though close working relations still exist (Sanchez, 1968).

As the social development of students is an important addition to vocational effectiveness, placement has an interest in the office of student activities. Wrenn (1951) suggests that placement counselors recommend to the student activities office, activities and social skills of benefit to student vocational growth. Student personnel records and follow-up studies and evaluation are maintained by the placement services and hence, access to the registrar's office is essential.

The educational advisory office is an important adjunct to the placement service. Both are involved in guiding students throughout their years of college. Regrettably the placement service usually sees students only towards the end of the final year while the advisory office deals with students only on an intermittent basis. Both offices could integrate their services so as to provide more continued and coordinated counseling. Curricular committees are a source of benefit to placement personnel who need to keep informed of educational policy. In exchange, the placement personnel may be of benefit to curricular planning in that they have knowledge of business and industry and governmental needs.

At the University of Florida not only placement and counseling, but also academic advising, residence halls advising, and faculty advising joined to make for better communication and cooperation. The "Career Counseling, Planning and Placement Center," as it was called, became the central agency that directed all student advisory services on campus. It worked with the faculty in developing career models and advised them on educational policy matters. The Center supplied feedback to academicians from its work contacts and implemented work-study programs. The Center established close ties between the educational world and the vocational (Hale, 1973-1974). Such examples show how horizontal coordination of other student services can be accomplished.

REFERENCES

Adams, G. A. "Preventative" career counseling — proving it works. *Journal of College Placement*, 1974, *34*(3), 26-30; 32-33.

Addison, A. Work-study graduate programs in personnel management. *Personnel Journal*, 1970, *49*, 209-212.

Aiken, J., & Johnston, J. A. Promoting career information seeking behaviors in college students. *Journal of Vocational Behavior*, 1973, *3*

(1), 81-87.

Andersen, D. G., & Bennie, A. A. Effects of a group vocational guidance class with community college students. *Vocational Guidance Quarterly,* 1971, *20*(2), 123-128.

Arbuckle, D. S. *Student personnel services in higher education.* New York: McGraw-Hill, 1953.

Austin, S. F. The employment market and you. In P. W. Dunphy (Ed.), *Career development for the college student.* Cranston, R. I.: Carroll Press, 1973.

Babbush, H. E. The work-study program in action. *Journal of College Student Personnel,* 1966, *7,* 271-274.

Babcock, R. J., & Yeager, J. C. Coaching for the job interview: Does it change students into puppets? *Journal of College Placement,* 1973, *33*(3), 61-64.

Baker, R. Placement counseling. In M. Siegel (Ed.), *The counseling of college students: Function, practice and technique.* New York: Free Press, 1968.

Banikiotes, P. G., & McCabe, S. P. Facilitating vocational planning. *Journal of the National Association of Women Deans and Counselors,* 1972, *35,* 133-135.

Berger, M. A yardstick for your placement program. *Occupations,* 1944, *25,* 163-165.

Bishop, J. F. Portents in college placement. In G. J. Klopf (Ed.) *College student personnel work in the years ahead.* Washington, D. C.: American Personnel and Guidance Association, 1966. (Student Personnel Monograph Series, No. 7)

Blue, R. J. New recruitment advertising — image making or breaking. *Journal of College Placement,* 1968, *28*(3), 93-94; 97.

Borman, A. K. Cooperative education moves up to graduate study. *Journal of College Placement,* 1967-1968, *28*(2), 97-99; 102-103.

Boynton, P. W. *Selecting the new employee.* New York: Harper, 1949.

Brayfield, A. H. Putting occupational information across. *Educational and Psychological Measurement,* 1948, *8,* 485-495.

Brayfield, A. H. Vocational counseling today. In M. S. Viteles, A. H. Brayfield, & L. E. Tyler (Eds.), *Vocational counseling: A reappraisal in honor of Donald G. Paterson.* Minneapolis: University of Minnesota Press, 1961.

Breslin, J. A college administration looks at placement. *Journal of College Placement,* 1969, *29*(4), 33-36.

Brewer, J. *History of vocational guidance.* New York: Harper, 1942.

Bucci, F. A. The placement director: Middle man on the totem pole. *Journal of College Placement,* 1970-1971, *31*(2), 73-82.

Calvert, R., Jr., Carter, E. M., & Murphy, I. College courses in occupational adjustment. *Personnel and Guidance Journal,* 1964, *42,* 680-682.

Calvert, R., Jr., & Menke, R. F. Placement, 1967. *Journal of College Placement,* 1967, *27*(4), 29-31; 119-121; 123; 125-126; 129; 131; 135.

Careers for Social Change. *Personnel and Guidance Journal,* 1971, *49,* 740-745.

Christenson, T. E. Functions of occupational information in counseling. *Occupations,* 1948, *28,* 11-14.

Clark, D. D. Characteristics of counseling centers in large universities. *Personnel and Guidance Journal,* 1966, *44,* 817-823.

Cross, K. P. *The integration of learning and earning: Cooperative education and nontraditional study.* Washington, D. C.: American Association for Higher Education, 1973. (ERIC Higher Education Research Report No. 4)

Davis, J. A. *Great aspirations: The graduate school plans of America's college seniors.* (National Opinion Research Center Monographs in Social Research, No. 1). Chicago: Aldine, 1964.

Davis, J. R. Cooperative education: Prospects and pitfalls. *Journal of Higher Education,* 1971, *42,* 139-146.

Davison, A. W., Jr. How to provide occupational information and still be a counselor. In J. C. Heston & W. B. Frick (Eds.), *Counseling for the liberal arts campus: The Albion Symposium.* Yellow Springs, Ohio: Antioch Press, 1968.

Dempsey, F. K., Jr. College recruitment — a reassessment. *Personnel Journal,* 1970, *49,* 746-749.

Dennis, T. L., & Gustafson, D. P. How do employers really rate the placement office? *Journal of College Placement,* 1972, *33*(1), 73-76.

Dennis, T. L., & Gustafson, D. P. College campuses vs. employment agencies as sources of manpower. *Personnel Journal,* 1973, *52,* 720-724.

Devlin, T. C. Career development courses. *Journal of College Placement,* 1974, *34*(4), 62-64; 66; 68.

Downs, C. W. Perceptions of the selection interview. In J. L. Windle, R. S. Kay, & A. P. Van Mondfrans, Project 200: A research review. *Journal of College Placement,* 1971, *31*(4), 95-99.

Dreese, M. Policies and plans of college guidance centers operating under VA contract. *Education Record,* 1949, *30,* 446-457.

Edwards, R. M. Faculty members need placement participation. *Journal of College Placement,* 1968, *28*(4), 46-49.

Fitzgerald, L. E. Faculty perceptions of student personnel functions. *Journal of College Student Personnel,* 1962, *3,* 169-179.

Froehlich, C. P. Paper 45: Counseling, its use and abuse. In G. F. Farwell & H. J. Peters (Eds.), *Guidance readings for counselors.* Chicago: Rand McNally, 1961.

Gilmore, R. G. Video-taping the real interview. *Journal of College Placement,* 1973, *33*(3), 52-56; 58.

Good, W. A., Hunt, D. C., & Vokac, R. B. An "A" for hospitality. *Journal of College Placement,* 1974, *34*(4), 71-74; 76.

Graff, R. W. *A comparison of the effectiveness of three kinds of vocational counseling with a college population.* Paper presented at the American Personnel and Guidance Convention. Washington, D. C., 1971.

Hackamack, L. C., & Iannone, C. R. Selecting, recruiting, retaining today's college graduate. *Personnel Journal,* 1969, *48,* 988-991.

Hagerty, W. J., & Brumbaugh, A. J. *The student in college and university.* (North Central Association of Colleges and Secondary Schools, Publication No. 13). In C. G. Wrenn. *Student personnel work in college.* New York: Ronald Press, 1951.

Hale, L. L. A bold, new blueprint for career planning and placement. *Journal of College Placement,* 1973-1974, *34*(2), 39-40.

Handville, R. Twenty-two ways of disseminating career information. *Vocational Guidance Quarterly,* 1953-1954, *2*(2), 45-48.

Haney, T. At Rhode Island, they track career paths via informal groups. *Journal of College Placement,* 1963, *34*(1), 62-63.

Harmon, N. F. Arkansas uses computer to help curb apathy toward interviews. *Journal of College Placement,* 1967, *27*(3), 57-58.

Harris, J. A. Can computers counsel? *Vocational Guidance Quarterly,* 1970, *18,* 162-164.

Helm, C. Computer simulation techniques for research in guidance problems. *Personnel and Guidance Journal,* 1967, *46,* 47-52.

Herrick, R. F. Presentation by Thomas S. McFee on Family Education Rights and Privacy Act of 1974 at CPC National Meeting. Bethlehem, Pa.: College Placement Council, 1975.

Hess, H. R. Preparing for the effective interview. *Journal of College Placement,* 1971, *32*(1), 49; 50; 52.

Holcomb, J. R. Keysort: Another application in campus data processing. *Journal of College Placement,* 1970, *30*(4), 55-60.

Hoppock, R. *Occupational information.* New York: McGraw-Hill, 1963.

Hoy, W. A. Computerizing the small campus placement function. *Journal of College Placement,* 1971, *31*(3), 67-72.

Jamie, W. *Placement — a model program for corporate recruitment of collegiate personnel.* Reprint of a serialized presentation in the *Journal of College Placement,* 1957.

Johnson, N. A. Integrating placement with the student personnel program. *1948-49 Proceedings of the American College Personnel Association,* Chicago, 1949, pp. 602-613.

Katz, M. R. Can computers make guidance decisions for students? *College Board Review,* 1969, *72,* 13-17.

Kauffman, J. F. Student personnel services: Some questions and recommendations. *Educational Record,* 1964, *45,* 355-365.

Kauffman, W. E. Senior placement — the story of a successful 3-year experiment by a large firm and university. *Journal of College Placement,* 1967, *27*(4), 42-44; 47; 49.

Kauffman, W. E. Special report: College recruitment demonstrations.

Placement Perspective, 1969, *3,* 8 pages.

Kirk, B. A. Relations between counseling and placement. *Journal of College Student Personnel,* 1965, *6,* 289-292.

Kirk, H. P. Bringing counseling and placement together. *Journal of College Placement,* 1971, *31*(4), 44-49.

Kroll, A. M. A computer-generated bibliography of occupational information. *Vocational Guidance Quarterly,* 1969, *18*(1), 3-9.

Lansner, L. A. Evening college placement. In M. L. Farmer (Ed.), *Student personnel services for adults in higher education.* Metuchen, N. J.: Scarecrow Press, 1967.

Lee, S. M. Job selection by college graduates. *Personnel Journal,* 1970, *49,* 392-395.

Leonard, E. A. *Origins of personnel services in American higher education.* Minneapolis: University of Minnesota Press, 1956.

Liebers, D. E. Can placement and recruiting survive? *Journal of College Placement,* 1970, *30*(3), 41-44.

Lohnes, P. R. Learning about opportunities for adult activities and roles at the college level. *Computer-based vocational guidance systems: Summary of papers presented at the fourth symposium for systems under development for vocational guidance.* Washington, D. C.: U. S. Department of Health, Education, and Welfare, Office of Education, 1969.

Loughary, J. W. The computer is on! *Personnel and Guidance Journal,* 1970, *49,* 185-191.

McDaniel, H. B., Lallas, J. E., Saum, J. A., & Gilmore, J. L. (Eds.), *Readings in guidance.* New York: Winston, Holt, 1959.

McEneaney, T. J. On campus recruiting. In P. W. Dunphy (Ed.), *Career development for the college student.* Cranston, R. I.: Carroll Press, 1973.

McLaughlin, W. L. Placement's emerging role. *Journal of College Placement,* 1973, *33*(4), 79-82.

Merrill, R. The interrelations of counseling and placement services. In R. F. Berdie (Ed.), *Counseling and the college program.* Minneapolis: University of Minnesota Press, 1954.

Mohs, M. C. *Service through placement in the junior college.* Washington, D. C.: American Association of Junior Colleges, 1962.

Morgan, W. R. *Faculty mediation of student war protests.* Paper read at American Sociological Association, San Francisco, September 1969.

Newsome, A., Thorne, B. J., & Wyld, K. L. *Student counseling in practice.* London: University of London Press, 1973.

Odell, C. E., Pritchard, D. H., & Sinick, D. Whose job is job placement? *Vocational Guidance Quarterly,* 1974, *23,* 138-145.

Parsons, F. *Choosing a vocation.* Boston: Houghton Mifflin, 1909.

Penney, J. F. Vocational Guidance in Europe and the United States. *Vocational Guidance Quarterly,* 1968, *16,* 287-291.

Penney, J. F. *Perspective and challenge in college personnel work.* Springfield, Ill.: Charles C Thomas, 1972.

Placement and its legal implications. *The secretarial manual for career planning and placement offices.* Bethlehem, Pa.: College Placement Council, 1974.

Powell, C. R. At Indiana University — a 30 year success story for business students. *Journal of College Placement,* 1971-1972, *32*(2), 30-36.

Purdy, C. H. Placement and the law. *Journal of College Placement,* 1972, *33*(1), 43; 46-51.

Raanan, S. J., & Lynch, T. H. Two approaches to job-hunting workshops: "Job Scene" helps students get ready for interviews. *Journal of College Placement,* 1973-1974, *34*(2), 67; 71-72; 74.

Reardon, R. C. The counselor and career information services. *Journal of College Student Personnel,* 1973, *14,* 495-500.

Reitman, A. Students talk about intern experiences. *Journal of College Placement,* 1970, *30*(4), 79-80.

Riegel, P. S. Counseling for graduate study. *Journal of College Student Personnel,* 1966, *7,* 86-90.

Robb, F. The three P's: Preparation, placement and performance. *Journal of College Placement,* 1971, *31*(3), 28-34.

Rossen, J. G., Nash, P. A., & Miller, C. D. Candid camera — video tape's role in interview training. *Journal of College Placement,* 1971, *32*(1), 63-64; 66.

Salinger, M. What are you doing after graduation? I'm not sure. *Journal of College Placement,* 1969, *29*(3), 104-108.

Sanchez, A. A. Why one senior no longer wears two sombreros. *Journal of College Placement,* 1968, *28*(4), 97-98; 100.

Searles, A., Jr. Helping students to help themselves. *Journal of College Placement,* 1971, *32*(1), 59-60; 62.

Segal, S., & Klos, D. The placement annual report. *Journal of College Placement,* 1970, *30*(4), 62-72.

Shaw, A. C. College recruiting: Some basic questions and answers. *Personnel Journal,* 1969, *48*(7), 523-524; 554.

Shaw, E. A. Behavior modification and the interview. *Journal of College Placement,* 1973, *34*(1), 52-57.

Shingleton, J. D. Campuses, computers, careers. *Journal of College Placement,* 1970, *31*(1), 38-49.

Simpson, L. A., & Harwood, R. K. Placement: From employment bureau to career development center. *NASPA Journal,* 1973, *10,* 225-230.

Simpson, L. A][Pate, R. H., Jr., & Burks, H. M., Jr. A new approach — group counseling with trained subprofessionals. *Journal of College Placement,* 1973, *33*(3), 41-43; 45; 47; 50.

Sinick, D. Placement's role in guidance and counseling. *Personnel and Guidance Journal,* 1955, *34,* 36-40.

Smithers, A. Students' experience of thick sandwich courses. *Educational*

Research, 1971, *13*, 171-178.

Soltys, M. P. Video-taped role-playing. *Journal of College Placement*, 1971, *31*(3), 55-58.

Souther, J. The new look at Washington. *Journal of College Placement*, 1969-1970, *30*(2), 33-36.

Sovilla, E. S. A new functional balance for career planning activities in the '70s. *Journal of College Placement*, 1972, *33*(1), 62-66.

Spolyar, L. J. The students flexible "holding file system." *Journal of College Placement*, 1972, *32*(3), 75-76.

Sprague, D. G., & Strong, D. J. Vocational choice and group counseling. *Journal of College Student Personnel*, 1970, *11*, 35-36; 45.

Steele, J. E. Changes and innovative response. *Journal of College Placement*, 1971, *31*(3), 46-52.

Stephens, E. W. *Career counseling and placement in higher education: A student personnel function.* Bethlehem, Pa.: College Placement Council, 1970.

Stevens, N. D. A changing concept of college placement. *Journal of College Student Personnel*, 1965, *6*, 233-235.

Stevens, N. D. Counseling for placement readiness. *Journal of College Student Personnel*, 1966, *7*, 27-32.

Stevens, N. D. The effect of job-seeking behavior on obtaining a job. *Journal of College Placement*, 1972, *32*(4), 46-50.

Swaim, R. Centralization or decentralization: Two approaches to placement receive an up-to-date review. *Journal of College Placement*, 1968, *28*(3), 119-120; 122; 124; 126.

Teal, E. A., & Herrick, R. F. (Eds.), *The fundamentals of college placement.* Bethlehem, Pa.: College Placement Council, 1962.

Thomas, W. G. Placement's role in the university. *Journal of College Placement*, 1966, *26*(4), 87-92.

Toomes, W., & Frisbey, N. Placement: A study in futures. *Journal of College Placement*, 1972, *33*(1), 36-41.

Treible, R. R. On the firing line — psychological testing. *Journal of College Placement*, 1969, *29*(3), 74-80.

Tyler, L. E. The future of vocational guidance. In M. S. Viteles, A. H. Brayfield, & L. E. Tyler (Eds.), *Vocational counseling: A reappraisal in honor of Donald E. Paterson.* Minneapolis: University of Minnesota Press, 1961.

United States Department of Health, Education, and Welfare. Education programs and activities receiving or benefiting from federal financial assistance. *Federal Register*, 1974, *39*(120), 22228-22240.

The vanguard in the field of activism. *Personnel and Guidance Journal*, 1971, *49*, 780.

Varney, G. H., & Galloway, J. L. The changing character of college recruiting. *Journal of College Placement*, 1974, *34*(2), 53-57.

Vokac, R. B. Directors suggest their own qualifications. *Journal of College

Placement, 1959, *19*(3), 71-72; 76.

Walters, R. W. Let's stop manpower waste. *Journal of College Placement,* 1969, *29*(4), 72-73.

Warnath, C. F. *New myths and old realities: College counseling in transition.* San Francisco: Jossey-Bass, 1971.

Williamson, E. G., & Sarbin, T. R. *Student personnel work in the University of Minnesota.* Minneapolis: Burgess, 1940.

Windle, J. L., Kay, R. S., & Van Mondfrans, A. P. Project 200: A research review. *Journal of College Placement,* 1971, *31*(4), 95-99.

Windle, J. L., Van Mondfrans, A. P., & Kay, R. S. *Review of research: Career planning and development, placement and recruitment of college-trained personnel.* Bethlehem, Pa.: College Placement Council, 1972.

Woody, R. H. Self-help experiences. *NASPA Journal,* 1973, *10,* 339-343.

Wrenn, C. G. *Student personnel work in college.* New York: Ronald Press, 1951.

Wyatt, G. M. Employers/Faculty. *Journal of College Placement,* 1966-1967, *27*(2), 69-70; 72; 74; 76; 78.

CHAPTER 14

GRADUATION

WILLIAM T. PACKWOOD

HISTORY

ALL academic degrees in the Western World derive from the conferring of the title, "Master Teachers," by medieval corporations or guilds with tacit or explicit authorization of a pope, emperor, or king (Brubacher & Rudy, 1968). The occasion at which these degrees were awarded and new members were welcomed into the guild was called Ceremonies of Inception (Powicke & Emden, 1936). Processions beginning and ending these ceremonies, like the processions of today, originated with the clerics (Sheard, 1962). Even the traditional black robes date from the earliest days of the oldest universities. For example, a 1321 statute of the University of Coimbra required all "Doctors, Licentiates, and Bachelors" to wear gowns (American Council on Education, 1973). Whether gowns were necessitated by the lack of warmth in unheated medieval buildings or derived from hooded clerical dress seems unclear.

The first American colonial college commencement on record is described in a 1643 English pamphlet. At this commencement Harvard college students attended two solemn "Acts" and the governor, magistrates, ministers, and others came to hear the students' exercises, answers, and disputations (Brubacher & Rudy, 1968). Those who were Master's candidates at Harvard gave oral Latin dissertations.

Commencement was one of the great events of the year in provencial society. Called Public or Exhibition Day, it was an occasion in which every student could display the literary and forensic skills learned through four years of argumentation in the classrooms. These events could run for two days, include activities such as horse races and cock fights, and result in laments about the students drinking too much (Earnest, 1953; Rudolph, 1962).

Changes occurred in the 1850's when literary societies assumed major responsibility for the student exhibitions and controversial speakers became important. Because most of the country was still isolated, a visiting speaker from the state university or seat of government was eagerly anticipated. His speech might last two hours, since the occasion was a significant one, and be discussed and rehashed for months (Turbeville, 1966).

After the Civil War, the Land Grant Act, the beginnings of modern transportation and communication, and the decrease in cultural barriers diminished the need to bring news from the outside. In 1884 students gave addresses on topics such as irrigation and drainage and diseases of ox or horse feet. Eventually, the commencement ritual became an exhibition by professionals, particularly the new academic specialties such as agriculture, designed to underline their newly acquired status within the ancient tradition of learning (Rudolph, 1962).

From the latter part of the Nineteenth Century until 1960, the traditional model of graduation, described below, developed. In the turbulent sixties, graduation services provided settings for protest. Some student dissenters walked out during the main address and wore red antiwar tassels on their mortarboards. They protested policies prevalent in the U. S., particularly those concerning the Vietnam War and civil rights, and wanted a greater student voice in the college. Since that time there has been a steady decline in the importance of graduation ceremonies.

TRADITIONAL MODEL

The traditional model of graduation in our era has included a procession, invocation, commencement address, awarding of earned and honorary degrees, benediction, and recession. The preceeding companion event, Baccalaureate, a sectarian religious program with compulsory attendance, has generally been eliminated, primarily because of its doubtful constitutionality

(Turbeville, 1966). Hanhila (1970) found that only 17 percent of the forty-five junior colleges he surveyed retained Baccalaureate services. Planning for graduation touches many departments of the college: university relations, alumni offices, registrar, buildings and grounds, security, campus ticket office, chaplain's office, office of each dean of a school or faculty, president's staff, etc. (Gunn, 1969).

Graduation is viewed by those involved in a variety of ways. Some students plan for their graduation for years, dream about it, and view it as a symbol of their achievement (Kinnick, 1973). Many parents appreciate the ceremony and its dignity and view it as a capstone of four years of investment and hard work. Others find graduation silly, an occasion with no personal relevance, or find the format antiquated. Hall (1973) found in his survey of 244 public community colleges that students over twenty-one years of age and those in vocational-technical training had the greatest desire to take part in graduation exercises, with racial and ethnic minority students also interested. Those least interested were younger or transfer students.

PROBLEMS

The usual spring graduation has become less important and inconvenient, particularly with students graduating every quarter or at the end of the fall semester. One option is to let students graduate whenever they meet the requirements and return for the full-dress ceremony in the spring. Some institutions prefer to go through the elaborate plans and expense of graduation ceremonies two to five times a year to avoid the problem of finding a facility large enough to accommodate a full year of graduates.

The mechanical details of determining actual graduates has become an unmanageable problem. Time pressures require faculty to report grades early. Such pressures may be resisted or produce errors and result in last minute changes. Students have been cancelled from graduation exercises, even removed from procession lines, resulting in embarassment and dissatisfaction for students and parents. To reduce such problems, some institutions have defined graduation as the university's public convocation to recognize students who are at the time or soon to be granted degrees (Constance, 1965). This permissive approach allows the ceremony to be held even before final exams if desired. This solution, while practical, can further reduce the meaningfulness of the ceremony.

The major difficulty in maintaining graduation is student lack of interest in attending. Hall's (1973) study of junior colleges, which is indicative of other institutions, found a drop in average participation from 90 percent in 1962 to 58 percent in 1972. The initial response to this lack of interest was to require attendance and excuse only by petition. Hanhila (1970) found 64 percent of forty-five junior colleges required attendance of their students and 71 percent required faculty attendance. However, Hall (1973) found only 30 percent of 224 junior colleges required attendance. Regional differences in the attendance requirement were striking: 58 percent in New England, 54 percent in the South, 47 percent in North Central, 10 percent in Northwest, and 2 percent in the West. Apparently with increased number of students graduating, institutions have a large enough gathering without requiring attendance or feel the effort necessary to enforce attendance is not worth it.

One of the most clearly related variables to graduation attendance is size of institution (Hall, 1973). Institutions with fewer than 2,000 students had an 81 percent participation rate, institutions with 2,000 to 3,999 had 64 percent, 4,000 to 6,999 had 62 percent, 7,000 to 9,999 had 42 percent, and those with over 10,000 had 33 percent participate. Apparently the larger the institution, the less commitment and allegiance to it and the less meaningful and relevant is participation in graduation.

CHANGES

Even with the many problems connected with graduation exercises, all reporting institutions in both Hall and Hanhila's studies (the only ones available) acknowledge completion of the associate degree with some kind of planned recognition. The primary change has been to substitute students for outside speakers or to eliminate the speeches altogether. Only 10 percent of Hall's 224 junior colleges had discontinued the graduation ceremony in favor of luncheons, dinners, or teas and eliminated the wearing of regalia. Substitutions for the speech have included slide presentations, playlets by professional actors, modern music presentations, poetry readings, and audiovisual programs about the campus and student activities, particularly those of the graduating class.

Changes in apparel have included the use of paper caps and gowns and the wearing of occupational uniforms by vocational-technical students. Diplomas at some insitutions are mailed later and at some are handed out prior to the processional. One of the most responsive changes, which relates to the institutional-size hypothesis, has been to have graduation in each academic unit on the campus rather than with the student body as a whole. Some institutions have developed student-faculty-administration "Think Tanks" to make each graduation unique from the previous year.

These changes and other like them are in the minority and relatively superficial. Most colleges adhere to the traditional graduation ceremony, though there have been trends towards greater brevity and increased student involvement.

REFERENCES

American Council on Education. *American universities and colleges* (11th ed.). Washington, D. C.: Author, 1973.

Brubacher, J. S., & Rudy, W. *Higher education in transition* (Rev. ed.). New York: Harper & Row, 1968.

Constance, C. L. Commencement exercises for recognition rather than for diplomas. *College and University*, 1965, *40*, 314-318.

Earnest, E. *Academic procession.* New York: Bobbs-Merrill, 1953.

Gunn, M. K. *A guide to academic protocol.* New York: Columbia University Press, 1969.

Hall, L. H. Commencement: Sacred tradition or irrelevant vestige? *Community and Junior College Journal*, 1973, *43*(9), 20-21.

Hanhila, M. O. Graduation week: Selected junior colleges. *Community and Junior College Jounal*, 1970, *40*(6), 88.

Kinnick, B. J. Are commencements obsolete? *Today's Education*, 1973, *62*(5), 42-43.

Powicke, F. M., & Emden, A. B. *The universities of Europe in the middle ages*

(Vol. 3). London, England: Oxford University Press, 1936.

Rudolph, F. *The American college and university.* New York: Random House, 1962.

Sheard, K. *Academic heraldry in America.* Marquette: Northern Michigan College Press, 1962.

Turbeville, G. Is the commencement address an anachronism? *Peabody Journal of Education,* 1966, *44,* 130-131.

CHAPTER 15

ALUMNI

TERRY F. GANSHAW

HISTORY

ALUMNI services have emerged primarily in the Twentieth Century, although informal activities existed previously. The early motivation for alumni work was clearly financial in that established sources of revenue from foundations and family fortunes were seriously depleted and new sources had to be located (Turner, 1947). Colleges turned naturally to those who had attachments to the institutions and involvement in their continuance: the former students.

The first local alumni club was the Cincinnati Club of Marietta College, formed in 1855 (Sailor, 1944). By 1913 interest in alumni work had developed to the extent that the Association of Alumni Secretaries was organized and four years later, the American Association of College News Bureaus was formed to assist its members in publicizing their institutions to the general public. Together, these organizations formed the dual track along which professional alumni work developed for the next half-century.

Increased interest in alumni following World War I resulted in the existence of nearly fifty alumni magazines and ten alumni funds by 1918, with the formation of alumni associations as defined groups beginning three years later at Williams (Sailor, 1944). However, the Yale University Alumni Fund, built upon a long history of publications coupled with the nurturance of sentimental ties with the university, was the precursor of modern alumni fund raising.

The initiation of education programs for alumni was somewhat tardy (Danilov, 1959) with the earliest reported attempt originating at Amherst in 1922. It was a plan developed by

428

Robert A. Woods, then president of the Alumni Council, for alumni reading and study (Shaw, 1929). Prior to that time, education had been considered as ending at graduation. It was not the classroom but the reunion and traditional college friendships from which alumni associations originated.

In 1927 the Association of Alumni Secretaries combined with three other groups, Alumni Magazines Associated, the Association of Alumnae Secretaries, and the Association of Alumni Funds, to form the American Alumni Council or AAC (Finehout, 1966). The merged organization had as its goal "mobilizing behind education the full strength of organized alumni support in all its spiritual, moral and practical manifestations" (p. 9). By 1938 there were 150 alumni magazines and 100 alumni funds, and the number of alumni offices had increased by 40 percent. Six years later, 55 percent of the nearly 300 members of AAC had established alumni funds and 64 percent were publishing some form of alumni magazine (Sailor, 1944).

In 1946 the American Association of College News Bureaus, which had changed its name in 1930 to the American College Publicity Association, became the American College Public Relations Association or ACPRA (Seller, 1964). although ACPRA traditionally served a somewhat broader spectrum of the population than AAC, they followed nearly parallel courses until the post-World War II boom in fund raising and the proliferation of expensive forms of communications media resulted in a merging of their interests (Radock & Rhodes, 1974).

Through the years, institutional and alumni concern with continuing education ebbed and flowed. In the 1950's a revival of interest came about as a result of the appointment of professional directors of alumni affairs on most campuses, increased interest in the alumni on the part of the institutions, and a growing awareness of the need for intellectual stimulation among the alumni (Danilov, 1959). By 1959, of 800 alumni associations surveyed, 54 percent responded and of these, 27 percent had some form of intellectual stimulation included as part of their reunion programs and an additional 35 percent had some plans in that direction (Danilov, 1959).

By the 1960's the AAC represented over 1,500 colleges, uni-

versities, and independent secondary schools ("New Alumni
Council," 1969) and virtually all had funds and magazines. In
addition to regular national and district conferences, the AAC
inaugurated a series of Special Conferences in 1963 to provide
in-depth programming on topics of special interest, such as the
implications of revised tax laws for prospective large donors
(Finehout, 1966).

Illustrative of the magnitude and rapid growth of alumni
support, the AAC survey of capital giving in 1964 to 1965
reported that over 1.7 million alumni gave $284 million to
1,167 colleges and 111 independent secondary schools. This
figure had more than quadrupled since 1954 when alumni
donations totalled $63 million. Annual drives for funds to meet
operating expenses experienced similar, but slightly smaller
growth ("Alumni Gifts For Colleges," 1966).

AAC and ACPRA merged in 1974 with the formation of the
Council for the Advancement and Support of Education
(CASE). The purpose of this union was to "concentrate on our
major goal; improving the professional competence of people
in the fields of college and university publications, information, fund raising and advancement management" (V. L. Carter
quoted in Radock & Rhodes, 1974, p. 19). As AAC and ACPRA
developed, they published a series of technique-oriented journals. The primary publication of AAC was *Alma Mater* and
ACPRA published the *College and University Journal*. During
the merger deliberations the groups jointly published *Technique* for a brief period, after which it became the CASE publication, *Interim*.

DEFINITION

Quoting R. F. Berdie, Dehne (1972) notes that, if the task of
student personnel workers is to "bring into balance the world
of the student, that of the university, and the enveloping 'real'
world that encompasses all, then it stands to reason that student personnel administrators must take alumni into consideration" (p. 250). The alumni are, after all, former students and
one of the friendly links between the present students and the

real world. Although alumni relations may not be included in many lists of student personnel services, there are similarities in function. Practitioners in both areas form an interface between the institution and administration, various external publics, and their own respective reference groups.

Goals

Sailor (1944) characterized alumni work as sales, as indeed it is. The notion of merchandising an institution to its graduates stems from Turner's (1947) concept of the "living endowment." This concept suggests that the institution belongs to the alumni and it is their responsibility to support it. In order to ensure acceptance of the concept, Turner borrowed from Sailor (1944) the notion of "banding the squab" or developing the tendency of future alumni to identify closely with the institution while still in attendance (see also Fluckiger, 1962, 1963). The loyalties thus built are based largely upon emotional and nostalgic grounds.

In spite of the common belief that alumni work is directed at the Old Grad, who as a student survived on football and five-day weekends with little time for academics and, hence, fond memories of campus life, Sailor (1944) stresses the development of pride in the alma mater based upon facts. The goal of the alumni director is to interpret the college to the alumni and the alumni to the college in order to generate goodwill, gifts, prospective students, and protection from adverse legislation and hostile regents.

Alumni may be the best friends a college can have, especially during a period in which higher education and students are under attack from much of the rest of society. However, in general the role of the alumni is perhaps most ambiguous and least understood of any of an institution's many publics. Dehne (1972) observes that there is consensus that alumni represent a critical source of economic power and must be kept happy, but the means suggested differ considerably, from catering to alumni and protecting them from the truth, to giving them a voice in institutional policy formation. Further supporting the importance of favorably disposed alumni, Massey and Fawcett (1969) in a survey of the presidents of institutions of the Southern Association of Colleges and Schools, report that alumni ranked fourth after accrediting agencies, faculty groups, and student groups as a source of influence exerting substantial pressure on the institution.

Major Emphases

Alumni have traditionally been organized according to class units, as this was considered the most logical way of perpetuating and building upon undergraduate social relationships. In addition to class organizations, alumni who live at some distance from the institution are provided a local alumni club. Although such clubs generally attract a very small proportion of the alumni, they possess considerable strength as a source of personal contact for those who are attracted. One advantage of such clubs to the institution is the economy of fund raising efforts among club members, compared to those classmates who are geographically, if not emotionally and developmentally dispersed. However, at least one authority (Sailor, 1944) believes that such organizations are more effectively utilized to motivate alumni to work for the institution than to donate funds.

Even if the necessity for fund raising is ignored, some form of continuing mutually beneficial relationship with the alumni is essential (Rowland, 1974). That this is true is due to the fact that the image of an institution is formed in part by the alumni and how they perform in their occupations, function as community citizens, and whether or not they display continued knowledge and understanding of their alma mater.

Furthermore, J. L. Nelson (1964) points out the potential value of alumni input for improving the effectiveness of educational offerings through programs of continuing institutional self-evaluation and improvement and through formulation of purpose and policy. By following up its alumni, the institution also gains public relations materials and some basis for comparison of itself with other institutions, as well as supportive

material for use during accreditation visits (Weisman, Snadowsky, & Alpert, 1970), even though the success or failure of
its graduates cannot be definitely tied to an institution or department.

In considering the future course of alumni work, Rowland
(1974) raises several issues. Assuming some consensus regarding
institutional objectives, how well does the alumni program
meet them? Is the program sufficiently diversified to meet the
interests of all alumni? How can the program be best organized, governed, and administered? How can it be most efficiently financed? How can the interests and concerns of the
most recent alumni be made compatible with those of ten,
fifteen, and even fifty-year alumni? Has the alumni club out-
lived its usefulness? How should alumni be related to fund
raising, legislative relations, admissions, and similar activities?
Finally, Rowland asks, is the alumni program being evaluated
on a continuing basis by both the alumni and the institution?

ADMINISTRATION

The specific location of the alumni office within the organizational structure varies greatly among institutions. Frequently,
the alumni relations function falls among the responsibilities
of the vice-president for administration or the director of development. At other institutions, it may be included in the responsibilities of the business manager or director of finance, while
at still others, the alumni director is responsible directly to the
president.

Fundamentals for success in alumni relations include "effective organization, complete and automated records, adequate
financing, sufficient and qualified staff, and a broad program
of services and activities" (Rowland, 1974, p. 12). As a basis
from which to build these characteristics, Sailor's (1944) handbook provides detailed guidelines for the organization of the
alumni service and selection of personnel, as well as required
hard and software, and J. L. Nelson (1964) provides recommended procedures to locate alumni through class agents and
personal contacts.

Staff

Many alumni secretaries began their duties on a part-time basis, with additional responsibilities in admissions, athletics, public information, placement, the union, and other administrative capacities (Sailor, 1944). Although such an arrangement may continue to exist at smaller institutions having relatively few alumni, at most colleges the position of alumni director is a full-time job requiring substantial additional staff. As for the nonprofessionals who work for their alma mater, they possess myriad backgrounds, and provide their services as a hobby, for fun, relaxation, and a host of other reasons.

Tasks

Fund raising and student recruitment consume the bulk of the time and effort of most alumni offices (Meyer, 1974). A 1969-1970 survey conducted by ACPRA found that the median alumni office devoted from 20 to 40 percent of its time to fund raising. For private colleges the figures ranged from 30 to 40 percent and for private and public universities it was 20 to 30 percent. Recruiting of students consumed 65 percent of the time available to alumni offices of private universities, 27 percent for private colleges, and 17 percent for state universities. Private college and university alumni offices both devoted an additional 12 percent of their time to alumni placement (Bacon & Pride, 1971, see Placement chapter).

Fund Raising

Although a few institutions have relieved the alumni relations office of the responsibilities for the annual fund drive, with those offices devoting time to advancing the institution and serving the alumni in other ways (Meyer, 1974), nevertheless, fund raising continues to be a primary activity for most alumni offices (Bacon & Pride, 1971).

Sailor (1944) describes the annual alumni fund drive as one which canvasses all alumni, seeking 100 percent contributions, regardless of the amount. The idea behind this approach is that, since the size of the average donation seems to remain relatively constant, the main task is to increase the number of donors.

Of the two major types of charitable funds, the alumni office is usually least concerned with capital gifts, which are intended to defray expenses associated with major capital investments. The second type of alumni fund, geared toward meeting annual operating expenses, is used by those institutions at which prior attendance or graduation does not automatically constitute membership in the alumni association (Sailor, 1944). In funds of this type the donation includes membership in the association, a subscription to the alumni magazine, as well as a gift to the institution.

As institutions have become increasingly dependent upon charitable gifts for operating funds, individual alumni associations, as well as the American Alumni Council, have devoted considerable time and effort to the task of devising better means of obtaining more and larger donations. Means explored have included the advantageous application of the various tax laws, deferred giving programs, bequest programs, pooled income trusts, and charitable remainder trusts (Cassell, 1972; Finehout, 1966).

Information Processing

In 1971 the alumni record storage system at Ohio State University was totally revamped. The new system permits closer contact through more rapid information retrieval and has been credited with an increase in alumni giving from $3.5 million to $10 million during the first year of operation. In this system, information which is used regularly but is subject to frequent and rapid change is stored on discs, and all of the remaining information is microfilmed, a departure from the common practice of storing all information on costly computers. In a comparison of time required to enter vital information on graduates into storage, the Class of 1971 had 39 percent more graduates who were processed in 46 percent less time at an absolute cost reduction of 35 percent compared to the class of 1967 ("Microfilm Keeps Alumni," 1972; Miller, 1972). The benefits of such automation in alumni placement, location of alumni who occupy important positions in government and business, and in stimulating donations are substantial.

Activities of Alumni Associations

To assist in building goodwill, Sailor (1944) recommends the use of broadcast media for addresses, athletic events, and major happenings, as well as films depicting the institution as it really is today, direct mail to contact large numbers of the alumni, and a variety of programs including alumni placement, continuing education, honor awards to deserving alumni, and inclusion of alumni representatives on governing boards. To coordinate dissemination of public statements and to reduce the amount of misinformation, particularly in time of crisis, Dehne (1972) suggests regular, weekly meetings between the dean of students and the alumni director. Also, alumni publications are suggested as an appropriate place to solicit reactions to planned programs, facilities, and changes.

Whereas some alumni associations may engage only in such traditional pursuits as fund raising, continuing education, placement, and special group trips, others involve alumni actively in the administrative and policy-making functions of the university. Some associations which are independent from the institution support a lobbyist at the seat of state government and apportion membership on the alumni council to coincide with state senatorial districts (Meyer, 1974).

It is likely that independence from the institution is essential for those alumni associations of public colleges and universities which are active in politics. In their survey, Bacon and Pride (1971) report that 73 percent of the state universities, 40 percent of private universities, and 24 percent of private colleges reported having legally independent alumni associations. When the question concerned the financial independence of the alumni associations, 20 percent of the state universities, 8 percent of the private colleges, and none of the private universities answered in the affirmative. Regarding whether the alumni association contributed to the operating expenses of the alumni office, 78 percent of the state universities, 10 percent of the private universities, and 14 percent of the private colleges gave affirmative answers.

Alumni groups from different institutions are beginning to unite with each other with increasing frequency. Lang (1972) observed that, "professional alumni workers in ever increasing numbers seem to be recognizing that an organization of individual associations has the potential to advance the cause of higher education far beyond the ability of any single association to do so" (p. 5). Such confederations, which are able to deal more directly and specifically with local problems by focusing their efforts more precisely than is usually possible for larger national groups, have been instrumental in the passage of legislation, as well as in attempts to establish full-time alumni directors at several state universities (Lang, 1972).

Research

In the AAC Fifty Colleges Study (Barcus, 1968) fifty of the most active members of the AAC were selected on the basis of being established, well-known institutions which were thought to be above average in the quality of their professional approach to alumni administration. The study found that alumni programs at private institutions tended to stress continuing education, deferred giving, alumni directories, parent relations, and regional conferences, whereas those at public institutions placed heavier emphasis upon special graduate school programs and legislative efforts. Both types of institutions had similar size program budgets, but the private colleges with fewer alumni had more dollars-per-alumnus. When these institutions were compared on the basis of fund raising success to AAC figures for 1,033 institutions in 1965-1966, the fifty colleges exceeded the AAC sample in all five observation categories: percent participation in the fund, amount contributed per donor, amount contributed per alumnus, average amount contributed by alumni per institution, and the percent of total institutional support which comes from the alumni. Based on the selection criteria, the perceived quality of the alumni relations program does appear to make a difference in fund raising success.

Barcus (1968) has suggested nine areas for additional research: the criteria used in allocating staff and funds to projects; staff assessment techniques used by presidents and alumni boards; changes in the relative effectiveness of clubs, classes, and publications with changes in age, position, and vocation of alumni; the level of understanding possessed by segments of the alumni regarding the institution's current educational program; the relationship of "interest," "understanding," and "action" to specific goals; the effectiveness of the alumni association as a forum for faculty, administrators, and alumni in improving education; a comparison of the ratings of presidents with those of trustees, alumni association officers, students, faculty, and alumni; the amount and kinds of nonfinancial assistance received from the alumni; and the effectiveness of the institution and the alumni association in stimulating the alumni to apply their backgrounds and expertise as responsible citizens of their communities.

PROGRAMS

Alumni Publications

Since the earliest days of alumni relations some form of a regular magazine has been the primary method of maintaining contact with alumni. Because of its importance the publication should be of high quality and produced as economically as possible (Barcus, 1968; Currant, 1969; Sailor, 1944).

There is considerable variety of style, format, and content among the approximately 930 college alumni periodicals currently published in the United States. Singer (1974) has identified four major types of such publications. First, are publications of general interest, representing an attempt to appeal to intellectual readers who are interested in the relation of the institution to the rest of the world. Such magazines increased their prestige by accurately reporting campus events of the 1960's. Now, "the best magazines are trying to suggest what the world will look like tomorrow" (Singer, 1974, p. 308).

A second major type of alumni publications are tabloids, which carry more news items and fewer features than the first kind, and are generally printed on newsprint. Specialty publications which are related to the nature and sponsorship of the institution comprise the third type. Singer's fourth major group are "the rest," which are neither stimulating nor creative, suffer from insufficient financial resources, and are edited by persons having other responsibilities as well (Singer, 1974).

Many writers believe that the alumni magazine should serve as a sounding board for alumni (Dehne, 1972) and that it is essential for administrators to react to alumni letters and alumni-authored articles. Publications are also showing renewed interest in journalism as opposed to blatant public relations.

> We are charged with the responsibility of telling the story of higher education. Therefore, to my mind, our independence from the college is highly important if our audience is to have any respect for what we say. Alumni are skeptical of propaganda (D. Fenn quoted in Dehne, 1972, p. 248).

As interest in accurate journalism is increasing, so too is the frequency and degree of student participation in alumni publications. Some feel that by involving students, their interest may be maintained as alumni. Thus, the *Simmons* (College) *Review* is written, laid out, and partially edited by students for "the entire Simmons family." Other use student columnists to infuse life and interest into the publication, believing that they are better able to probe young minds than would be true for older editors (Dehne, 1972).

At least one publication, *Harvard Magazine*, is sent only to paying subscribers, rather than to all former students. Many publishers of alumni magazines attempt to strike a balance between these extremes by sending the magazine only to dues-paying members of the alumni association or to those alumni members who have expressed a desire to receive the magazine.

Finally, many alumni associations are seeking to discover from the alumni themselves what they desire to read about in their publication. Considerable variation in preference has been found among the alumni of different institutions, with interest having been expressed in current educational concerns and general intellectually stimulating topics (Carter & Lyle, 1962; Currant, 1969), news of the college and classmates (Currant, 1969), policy decisions of trustees and administrators, activities and concerns of students and other alumni, and plans of the institution for building and construction (Dehne, 1972).

The Continuing Education of Alumni

Writers in alumni relations have long stressed the responsibility of the institution to supply the motivation as well as the opportunity for continued education of its graduates. Essentially equal emphasis has been placed upon continued education in both professional and cultural matters (Shaw, 1929; Weeks, 1965). In a survey of an unspecified number of Indiana University alumni, it was found that over 76 percent desired alumni programs dealing with contemporary issues in society and nearly 60 percent requested projects related to national and world affairs (Dehne, 1972).

Reporting on a 1956 survey conducted jointly by the AAC and the Fund for Adult Education, Danilov (1959) notes that both groups agreed that the continuing education of adults is a major responsibility of colleges and that each has an obligation to provide such an opportunity to its alumni. This agreement was followed in 1957 by an AAC resolution to that effect, stressing cooperation rather than competition with existing institutional programs, such as extension. Nevertheless, by 1960 only 10 percent of the 800 AAC members had any form of continuing education for alumni, and these were clouded by skepticism and lack of any real direction or purpose (Eklund, 1961). They seemed to be simply another means to increase the size of the annual donation. With these observations in mind, Eklund called for

creation by universities of an organized and systematic program for their postgraduates which would provide guidance and counseling and sequential and systematic educational experiences, both credit and noncredit, technical and cultural, throughout their productive lifetimes — in short, a true Alumni University (p. 161).

He also noted that this idea had been voiced fourteen years previously by Houle and remained unaccomplished.

Griswold, in his 1962 address to the graduating class of Yale, said that it was "the special purpose of liberal education" (p. 359) to instill in them a sense of responsibility to society to assume voluntary control of their own continuing education "Self-education of Alumni," 1962). Brown (1961) in a study of 290 college alumni drawn from a sample of over 800 colleges and universities found a strong suggestion, particularly among women and older alumni, that the quantity and quality of continuing education pursued is directly related to the quality of undergraduate education received.

With such an apparently high degree of consensus regarding the importance of education during the years following graduation, the singular failure of institutions to develop viable programs seems paradoxical. Weeks (1965) considers the geographical dispersion of the alumni as the primary debilitating factor and suggests institutional cooperation as a possible remedy. Additional factors include the high costs involved and an apparent lack of effectiveness on the part of many alumni directors in developing attractive programs (Eklund, 1961). As solutions, Eklund suggests cooperative efforts between work and study to fill gaps in individuals' past education and to deal with new information as it arises, and utilization of college and community resources, media, and all forms of class experience, both traditional and nontraditional.

Opportunities for alumni education have usually been on-campus alumni institutes, "circuit riding faculty," refresher programs in specialized fields, and a variety of miscellaneous programs. Somewhat more original attempts have included week-long, in-depth programs at an Ozark resort, a nationwide program including both technical and intellectual content, as well as information concerning university plans, and "a clinic to examine the physician as a Man" (Danilov, 1959). Others have included training members of the Alumni Council to lead discussions among alumni in their areas (Weeks, 1965); a monthly day-long meeting to discuss literature and values under the direction of a noted English professor (Carlson, 1959); and a lecture series entitled "Man Faces Change" at two alumni clubs (Looby, 1964).

As an alternative to the traditional forms of postgraduate education, formalized graduate programs, the limited offerings of conferences and institutes, and the superficial efforts conducted in conjunction with reunions and football weekends, Eklund (1961) offers his program at Oakland University, Rochester, Michigan. Emphasis is placed upon systematic opportunities for continuing education, not necessarily "at the alma mater, but continuing education wherever it may be found and acquired systematically" (Eklund, 1966, p. 155, italics omitted).

In this program Oakland serves as the counselor and clearinghouse for information concerning the kinds of educational experiences that are available and assists with arrangements. The phases of the program include an undergraduate orientation to the importance of postgraduate education, placement and involvement of the employer in the program, continuing advice and counseling, and ultimately, continuing education for the alumni. The key to the success of this program is the Alumni Education counselors who advise in both the undergraduate and alumni phases and work with the employers (Eklund, 1966).

In reporting the success of the Oakland plan, Eklund calls for regional and nationwide cooperation and reciprocity in the program to reduce overall costs and combat the effects of geographical scattering of alumni. Finally, says Eklund, increased alumni financial support, recruitment, and involvement with the institution would naturally result from such a program.

Alumni Placement Services

A few institutions have been involved for many years in the development of alumni counseling and referral services. However, there was a decided upswing during the early 1970's in the number of alumni who returned to their alma maters for revised career planning and career counseling in response to involuntary career changes related to the depressed state of the economy (Sovilla & Knapp, 1973).

In suggesting that this phenomenon is indicative of a growing trend which can be expected to continue, Sovilla and Knapp (1973) refer to a survey of 234 University of Cincinnati alumni, all of whom were living in the Cleveland area. Most alumni were interested in some form of placement, planning, or counseling service from the university. The most popular options were, notices of vacancies with opportunities for career advancement (76%), regular mailings dealing with new ideas and/or research in their field (74%), and expanded placement services for alumni (70%).

To assist alumni placement offices in handling the anticipated increase in demand, the College Placement Council developed Graduate Resume Accumulation and Distribution ("A New CPC Service," 1965), which is a computerized nationwide referral service. Although the service is centralized, alumni are served through the placement office at their alma mater (see Placement chapter).

Other Programs

In addition to the programs already discussed, a wide variety of minor endeavors are found which are less universally employed. A number of alumni associations sponsor low-cost trips to exotic places for their members in the hope of encouraging a favorable disposition toward the institution at fund drive or student recruitment time (Meyer, 1974). Bowling Green State University has a nationwide "Falcon Network" of alumni who meet recent graduates as they move into new jobs in unfamiliar locations (Kuhlin, 1970) and provide information concerning the cost of living, housing, and schools to aid prospective graduates in making realistic employment decisions. In similar programs alumni of Georgia State University assist the placement office by providing consultative services and an opportunity for "reality testing" on the part of students who are considering

444 *College Student Personnel Services*

entering any of a wide variety of business or professional occupations (Upchurch & Thomas, 1975), and recent women graduates of Purdue University provide role models and sources of information for present students (Slavens, 1975).

At least one public community college, Delta College in Michigan, has established a self-sufficient revenue-producing alumni program, dispelling the notion that such a feat was impossible for institutions of this type. Bypassing the usual preliminary steps (identifying the alumni, rearousing their interest in the institution, and securing involvement in its activities), the effort began by asking alumni to contribute to a program which was only in planning. Utilizing such innovative techniques as a recorded telephone message from the college president, three giving campaigns produced over $26,000 (Krafft, 1974).

In proposing a new area of alumni involvement, Smith (1973) suggests that too many institutions accept the notion that alumni are noncontributors for the first ten years after graduation. What is required is a broadened definition of the types of contribution possible, including return to the campus as auxiliary teaching resources and sources of feedback to the faculty with respect to the relevance of the instructional program.

It has been suggested that when alumni are active, this is due to a serious interest in education. Thus, if they are to be expected to provide financial, recruitment, consultative, legislative, and other assistance to institutions, alumni should be encouraged to become involved in the reform and modernization of higher education by granting them real responsibilities and treating them as educated responsible persons (R. E. Nelson, 1962; Sarnoff, 1969). Where the institution is not responsive to the will of the alumni, the graduates have taken matters into their own hands ("The Alums Are Restless," 1974; Feyer, 1973) and have organized to make their opinions known.

ALUMNI GIVING RESEARCH

Of 6.75 million alumni from independent colleges and universities, only 18 percent donate money regularly or often (Laukhuff, 1971), compared to a national average of about 25 percent considering institutions of all types (T. M. Hesburgh in Spaeth & Greeley, 1970). Unless the remaining 5.5 million begin to give to their own or some other institution, the independent institutions are in deep trouble (Laukhuff, 1971). Many of the better-known independent institutions receive contributions from fewer than half of their graduates, and among alumni of public institutions, 86 percent fail to give anything. Not giving is due in part to a lack of awareness on the part of alumni concerning what is happening to their colleges and in part to the fact that some alumni do not like what they see happening (Laukhuff, 1971). Clearly, colleges must do a better job of selling themselves to their own alumni, a frequently cited observation (Barcus, 1968; Dehne, 1972; Laukhuff, 1971; Sailor, 1944; Singer, 1974).

Discovering what it is that induces alumni to donate considerable sums of money in large numbers is a complex task. Carter and Lyle (1964) found at Stanford that giving was highly related to involvement in Stanford through organizational membership, family ties, professional attachments, and participation in activities.

When the criterion was the percent of alumni donating, Long (1963) found in a survey of private schools, that alumnae of women's colleges gave most frequently, followed by alumni from men's colleges and finally, alumni of private universities. However, when the private university alumni did give, they gave the largest amount. Although Catholic institutions followed this pattern, but with lower percentages in all cases, they also ranked among the highest in average dollar size of gift.

Basing his findings upon AAC Annual Reports of Voluntary Support for the years 1958-1959 and 1962-1966, Barcus (1968) concluded that the general increase in alumni support was due primarily to increases in the number of alumni and in per capita disposable income during that period. Additionally, the percent of alumni who were solicited rose from 79 percent to 88 percent for all types of institutions during that period, with the largest gains being made by small private institutions and the smallest gains by large public ones. In general, the Fifty Colleges Study revealed that public institutions had greater increases in alumni annual fund gifts, total annual fund gifts, and total alumni support and greater proportional increases in dollars contributed-per-alumnus solicited, ·while private institutions, especially large ones, had relatively faster increases in the size of average donation-per-donor. The private institutions also induced a larger percentage of alumni to contribute, received larger average donations per alumnus, as well as per alumni donor. In addition, at private institutions, alumni were found to provide a larger portion of the institution's total voluntary support (Barcus, 1968).

Barcus concludes that size of the alumni body seemed to be most closely related to all variables considered, and that the relationship was negative in all cases, except where the criterion was the number of active alumni clubs. The second best indicator seemed to be the amount budgeted per alumnus. He tentatively concludes that, although publications seem to broaden the base of support, club organizations appear to increase the size of the average gift to the fund. The greater overall success which is generally enjoyed by private institutions can perhaps be attributed to a more acute awareness of financial need among alumni from institutions which receive no public support. Barcus found little actual increase in the percent of alumni participating, except at those institutions with extremely low participation in the early years. In short, there appears good reason to believe that gains made during the 1960's could well be temporary (Barcus, 1968).

At least one attempt has been made to predict alumni donations based on demographic information available at graduation (Blumenfeld & Sartain, 1974). Studying 109 donors and 109 nondonors at Georgia State University, the researchers found seven differentiating characteristics with which it was possible to forecast donations with better than chance accuracy. The differentiating characteristics were: male sex, business school students, Georgia State graduates, Master's degree from Georgia State, economics majors, high or low undergraduate GPA, and moderate to high graduate GPA. Based upon these findings, alumni fund raisers may wish to gear appeals differently to different groups of alumni, or to devote more time to certain areas.

A selective solicitation program is already in operation at Stanford University. Based upon their 1962 findings, Carter and Lyle (1964) designed a model alumni development program. Since giving was found to be related to involvement with the institution, all efforts are directed at maintaining and increasing the level of involvement through judicious selection of the sources, content, and channels of communication. Communications are geared to specific groups of alumni and seem to be more personalized with an attempt to avoid irrelevant material. Obviously, such a program requires comprehensive record-keeping, but with computer assistance, it could be rendered cost-effective for many institutions.

Spaeth and Greeley (1970), in their report of one of the largest, most recent studies of a national sample of alumni, reach a conclusion which is nearly the exact opposite of the one just noted. Among their 4,868 respondents (81% of 6,005 1961 graduates sampled), 37 percent donated to their alma mater in 1967-1968, which was considerably more than the 25 percent national average. Giving among the class of 1961 was related to three factors: the school itself, with private schools more likely to receive donations, and among these the better quality schools most likely of all; loyalty to alma mater; and parental income (but not the income of the graduates themselves). Since most of these are factors over which the institution exercises little if any direct control, Spaeth and Greeley conclude with the somewhat unorthodox suggestion that a cost-benefit analysis might indicate that it is more prudent for most institutions to devote time and money to attracting a few well-to-do prospects. The suggested approach would be based upon tax laws favoring large-scale giving, with less time spent in alumni solicitation. As with other areas of higher education, there exists only limited consensus regarding the optimal method to employ.

REFERENCES

Alumni gifts for colleges. *School and Society*, 1966, *94*(2283), 444-445.
The alums are restless. *Time*, May 27, 1974, *102*(21), 80.

Bacon, A. L., & Pride, C. Trends in campus advancement. *College and University Journal*, 1971, *10*(2), 9-12.

Barcus, F. E. *Alumni administration.* washington, D. C.: American Alumni Council, 1968.

Blumenfeld, W. S., & Sartain, P. L. Predicting alumni financial donation. *Journal of Applied Psychology*, 1974, *59*, 522-523.

Brown, M. A. Factors in the continuing education of college alumni. *Adult Education*, 1961, *11*(2), 68-77.

Carlson, E. W. An experiment in alumni group discussion. *Adult Education*, 1959, *9*, 173-175.

Carter, R. F., & Lyle, J. Reasons for alumni giving. *College and University Journal*, 1962, *1*(2), 31-40.

Carter, R. F., & Lyle, J. Publications! Who reads … and why? *College and University Journal*, 1964, *3*(1), 39-45.

Cassell, W. C. (Ed.). *Deferred giving programs: Administration and promotion.* Washington, D. C.: American Alumni Council, 1972.

Currant, H. S. Surveys and opinions. *College and University Journal*, 1969, *8*(1), 46-47.

Danilov, V. J. Continuing education for alumni. *Educational Record*, 1959, *40*, 353-357.

Dehne, G. Responding to the alumni. *NASPA Journal*, 1972, *9*, 247-251.

Eklund, L. R. The alumni university — education's "new frontier." *Adult Education*, 1961, *11*, 161-171.

Eklund, L. R. The Oakland plan for the continuing education of alumni. *Adult Leadership*, 1966, *15*(5), 155-156.

Feyer, T. The revolt of the alumni. *Change*, March, 1973, *5*(2), 42-43.

Finehout, R. L. (Ed.). *Taxation and education.* Washington, D. C.: American Alumni Council, 1966.

Fluckiger, W. L. What determines success for the alumni association? *College and University Journal*, 1962, *1*(2), 15-18.

Fluckiger, W. L. The failure of alumni support. *College and University Journal*, 1963, *2*(2), 23-28.

Krafft, J. H. Earning your alumni endorsement. *Community and Junior College Journal*, 1974, *45*(3), 27.

Kuhlin, M. E. Bowling Green's alumni network. *Journal of College Placement*, Dec. 1970-Jan. 1971, *31*(2), 91-94.

Lang, C. H. Where the action is: Alumni associations band together. *College and University Journal*, 1972, *11*(3), 5-8.

Laukhuff, P. Do alumni care if their colleges fail? *College and University Business*, 1971, *51*(5), 40.

Long, W. R. Is alma mater on their gift list? *National Catholic Education Association Bulletin*, 1963, *59*(4), 19-23.

Looby, L. A university's responsibility for alumni education. *Adult Leadership*, 1964, *13*(2), 47-48.

Massey, J. W., & Fawcett, J. R. Junior college presidents in the south view problems and responsibilities of office in differing ways today. *College and University Journal*, 1969, *8*(3), 46.

Meyer, J. W. Personal communication, December 26, 1974.

Microfilm keeps alumni only seconds away. *College and University Business*, 1972, *53*(3), 50.

Miller, J. Storing frequently used alumni records for easier access "downs" cost and "ups" giving. *College Management*, 1972, *7*(12), 34.

Nelson, J. L. Follow-up study of graduates. *Improving College and University Teaching*, 1964, *12*(2), 111-112.

Nelson, R. E. Alumni? *College and University Journal*, 1962, *1*(4), 23-26.

New Alumni Council President. *School and Society*, 1969, *97*(2319), 350.

A New CPC Service — GRAD. *Journal of College Placement*, Dec. 1965-Jan. 1966, *26*(2), 32-33+.

Radock, M., & Rhodes, R. M] Long road to unity: AAC/ACPRA. *College and University Journal*, 1974, *13*(2), 17-20.

Rowland, A. W. The management of the institutional advancement program. *College and University Journal*, 1974, *13*(2), 4-12.

Sailor, R. W. *A primer of alumni work*. New Brunswick, N. J.: American Alumni Council, 1944.

Sarnoff, R. W. Academic bankruptcy. *Vital Speeches of the Day*, Feb. 15, 1969, *35*(9), 282-284.

Self-education of alumni. *School and Society*, 1962, *90*(2214), 336+.

Seller, M. C. The history of the ACPRA: 1915-1950. *College and University Journal*, 1964, *3*(4), 43-48.

Shaw, W. B. *Alumni and adult education: An introductory survey*. new York: American Association for Adult Education, 1929.

Singer, M. Alumni magazines: The editors reach out. *The Nation*, Oct. 5, 1974, *219*(10), 306-308.

Slavens, P. J. 0075. *Journal of College Placement*, 1975, *36*(1), 72-75.

Smith, V. W. One man's answers. *College and University Journal*, 1973, *12*(4), 24-25.

Sovilla, E. S., & Knapp, R. W. Service to alumni is needed and can be rewarding. *Journal of College Placement*, 1973, *33*(4), 75-78.

Spaeth, J. L., & Greeley, A. M. *Recent alumni and higher education: A survey of college graduates*. New York: McGraw-Hill, 1970.

Turner, F. H. *An adventure in alumni relations*. Nashville, Tenn.: Vanderbilt University Alumni Association, 1947.

Upchurch, B. L., & Thomas, J. M. Answers that work. *Journal of College Placement*, 1975, *35*(2), 67-69.

Weeks, R. W. An alumni secretary looks at continuing education. *Journal of Education*, 1965, *147*(3), 32-35.

Weisman, S. S., Snadowsky, A., & Alpert, e. Alumni feedback and curriculum revision. *Improving College and University Teaching*, 1970, *18*(2), 120-121.

CHAPTER 16

JUNIOR COLLEGE SERVICES

LYNETTE DANIELS SCHNEIDER

HISTORY

OVER the past seventy years the junior college has emerged as a permanent element of the American educational system. The first successful junior college established in this country was in Joliet, Illinois in 1901. By 1975 approximately 1,200 junior colleges had been established with a total student enrollment of over four million (Drake, 1976).

Student personnel work and junior colleges are both comparatively new phenomena in the American educational system. The post-World War II years were a period of expansive growth for junior colleges (Thornton, 1972), while the student personnel profession and counseling specialities experienced a spurt of growth in the post-World War I era. By 1972 student personnel programs were well established in American two-year colleges (Matson, 1972a). However, in many junior colleges personnel programs have received only lip service and too few have made the effort to develop comprehensive student personnel programs to fit their needs (Weatherford, 1965).

DEFINITION

"Junior College" is a generic title which includes all two-year postsecondary institutions. In common usage "junior college" usually refers to independent, private two-year colleges, half of which are denominationally controlled, while "community (junior) college" refers to the larger, publicly controlled institutions (Thornton, 1972).

The 1976 *Directory* of the American Association of Junior Colleges lists 216 independent junior colleges with an enrollment of 147,737 students (Drake, 1976). Most of these colleges are east of the Mississippi River in New England, middle, and southern states. The independent junior colleges tend to be smaller than the average public junior college with a median size for the private college of about 380 students compared with about 1,950 in public institutions. The independent college also enrolls a smaller proportion of part-time and unclassified students than the public institutions (Thornton, 1972).

Public junior colleges listed in the *Directory* totalled 1,014, enrolling 3,912,542 students (Drake, 1976). Public junior colleges are heavily concentrated in the western and central sections of the country and account for 78 percent of all junior colleges listed. Nearly half of all public college enrollments are part-time and adult students. While the median enrollment of the public college is five times as large as that of the private college, there is an equally wide variation in size among both types of colleges (Thornton, 1972).

Thornton (1972) cites two future developments in junior college growth which have not been fully realized. One is the development of the rural community college which devotes its attention to the special educational needs of its own clientele: the rural poor who "derive different educational disqualifications from their cultural isolation and distance from colleges" (p. 87). Second, is the trend toward the establishment of central city colleges (sometimes referred to as urban community colleges) designed to serve the educational needs of the poor and to "upgrade the economic and social potential of the under-educated" (p. 87). In the future a large proportion of public junior colleges will be in urban settings in order to attract larger numbers of disadvantaged youth who cannot afford or cannot get into other colleges (Schlossberg, 1966).

Description

In 1965 the American Association of Junior Colleges (AAJC) published the findings of an extensive study for the Carnegie Corporation on student personnel programs in 123 junior colleges. The study defined a junior college student personnel program as a "series of related functions designed to support the institutional program, respond to student needs, and foster institutional development" (p. 15).

The basic program is implemented through seven major functions which include twenty-one essential student personnel services:

> *Orientation* to college and career opportunities and requirements includes: (1) precollege information; (2) student induction or orientation to college; (3) group orientation; and (4) career information.
>
> *Appraisal* of individual potentials and limitations includes: (1) personnel records; (2) educational testing; (3) applicant appraisal including health appraisal.
>
> *Consultation* with students about their plans, progress, and problems includes: (1) student counseling; (2) student advisement; (3) applicant counseling.
>
> *Participation* of students in activities that supplement classroom experience includes: (1) cocurricular activities; (2) student self-government.
>
> *Regulation* to provide an optimal climate for social and academic development includes: (1) student registration; (2) academic regulation; (3) social regulation.
>
> *Services* that facilitate college attendance and further education or employment include: (1) financial aid; (2) placement.
>
> *Organization* that provides for continuing articulation, evaluation, and improvement of student personnel services includes: (1) program articulation; (2) in-service education; (3) program evaluation; (4) administrative organization (AAJC, 1965; Collins, 1967; Raines, 1966).

At the heart of any student personnel program should be a concern for student needs and an understanding of student characteristics (McDaniel, 1962; Santa Fe Junior College, 1967). One primary goal is to facilitate the education of all junior college students (Blocker, Plummer, & Richardson, 1965). Education encompasses the development of the student's intellectual, social, personal, and vocational capabilities to their fullest (George & George, 1971; Higgins & Thurston, 1963). Ideally, student personnel programs are designed to sort, identify, and develop potential (Higgins & Thurston, 1963) for each student so that the educational experience is individualized and organized around the individual's needs (Maryland Association of Junior Colleges, 1969). O'Banion (1971) concluded that student personnel programs in junior colleges should be the most significant force in the institution for humanizing the educational process.

The focus, then, of student personnel programs is not on the efficient functioning of services, but rather on the student and changes in behavior (O'Banion, Thurston, & Gulden, 1970). Programs aim to assist students in self-understanding, understanding others and society, and the integration of this understanding into a system of values (Dolan, 1969; Maryland Association of Junior Colleges, 1969). Student personnel work should be directed at making improvements in certain behaviors such as identification of goals, decision-making, and integrating the classroom experience with the outside world (Matson, 1967). Overall, the task of the student personnel program is to individualize the college's contact with students, to represent student interests in policy formations, and to coordinate in-service education of college staff in student personnel functions (McDaniel, 1962).

Differences from the Four-Year College

Kirkman (1969) and others agree that student personnel programs in junior colleges modeled after those in senior institutions are rarely appropriate or satisfactory. Because of its open door policy and a commitment to providing universal education up to the fourteenth year, the junior college hosts a student population which is highly diverse and covers a broad spectrum of interests and abilities. The nature of the student body is reflected in a unique student-centered educational philosophy which aims to individualize its education to fit the needs of every student. The junior college is also a unique educational institution in that it provides a variety of types and levels of education, organized into transfer and terminal-vocational programs, which are not found in the traditional four-year liberal arts colleges.

Adoption of inappropriate four-year college models is most evident in the trend toward the establishment of the four-year-counseling service model in the junior college. Adoption of this model may result in too much concern with therapy to the detriment of its vocational and educational counseling program (Matson, 1968) and may constrict efforts to provide individual attention to each student (Matson, 1972b).

The Junior College Student

In some ways junior college students are similar to those in the senior institutions. They are still in need of basic services such as admissions, orientation, and placement traditionally provided in senior colleges. Yet, as a group, junior college students tend to be more diverse than their four-year-college counterparts. Junior college students are more likely to live at home and to commute to college. Consequently, students may be reluctant to stay on campus after class for library work, extracurricular activities, or any other reason (George & George, 1971). Also, students tend to come from middle and lower-middle class families who often do not value education highly or are unaware of many of the opportunities and programs it can provide. This lack of familial support affects the student's motivation and desire to succeed (Richardson & Blocker, 1968).

Generally, junior college students are less academically able than those in four-year colleges and less realistic in their aspirations and expectations of college. The counseling function takes on special importance to these students with mismatched hopes and abilities (Richardson & Blocker, 1968). In addition, a large portion of the student population works part-time while attending college. As with the commuter student, the working student has less time on campus for out-of-classroom activities (George & George, 1971).

The student population as a whole also differs in that one group will continue their education in senior institutions while the other will leave immediately for the working world. For the latter group, junior college spans a critical period in their lives in terms of vocational choice. Terminal education at the two-year college is geared to specific careers with little opportunity to try out various alternatives in the two-year period. Educational programming and counseling is critical for both student groups (Blocker et al., 1965). To deal with a heterogeneous student population, a student personnel program must be able to mediate between students' needs and the requirements of the institution (Blocker et al., 1965). The student personnel worker should consider the student as a whole and as an individual and be able to humanize the educational experience (Lahti, 1968).

ADMINISTRATION

Organization of student personnel programs should not center on officers, but should spring from the functions to be performed (Thornton, 1972). In fact the name Student Personnel Program or Student Personnel Service should not be used, says Harvey (1968), because it projects too narrow an image for the program. Student Development Program would be preferable.

The organizational structure of student personnel programs in junior colleges varies. In 1960 Medsker found that about one half of 243 institutions had a centralized plan. Only 22 percent had a special administrator for the whole student personnel program who devoted full time to personnel. Another 33 percent had an assistant general administrator, usually an academic dean or vice-president of the college, to serve as coordinator for the program. And 45 percent reported that the only person responsible for student personnel programs was the chief administrator of the whole institution. As institutional size increased there was a greater tendency to appoint a special administrator for personnel services (Medsker, 1960).

By 1972 Matson (1972b) concluded that there was a clear trend toward a centralized organizational plan. The umbrella organization which groups related student personnel functions was most common. While chief administrators were found to have various titles, there was an increasing likelihood that this administrative position was supervisory over all the traditional student personnel services and that the administrator reported directly to the chief officer of the college. Matson (1972a) also found that most student personnel administrators prefered the separate but equal organizational model where the chief administrator was on the same level as the chief academic administrator and the chief business administrator.

Administrative Units

The Carnegie Report (AAJC, 1965) organized the basic student personnel program under a centralized organizational structure that had five essential administrative units. These included (a) admissions, registration, and records; (b) placement and financial aid; (c) student activities; (d) guidance and counseling; (e) central administrative unit which is responsible for program articulation, in-service education, program evaluation, and general administrative organization. In some cases, an additional unit may be established for special services.

Availability of Services

Since the Carnegie Report in 1965, the range of student personnel services provided neither increased nor decreased by the 1970's (Matson, 1972a). Peer counseling, tutoring, instruction in special curriculums for high-risk students, and housing were the only services Matson (1972a) did not find available in 20 percent or more of 589 colleges. Financial aid experienced the greatest increase in services, followed by group work and job placement. Size of the institution related to the extent to which student personnel services were added to the program. Although the Carnegie study reported that the services were not effective, Matson (1972a) found that no services had been dropped since 1965.

Clientele

All student personnel services are available to full-time day students, but the junior college student population is not limited to students in this group. One national study found that services were open to part-time and evening students as well as the full-time day students (Hinko, 1971b). The Carnegie study (AAJC, 1965) found that most junior colleges gave little or no attention to evening students as far as counseling was concerned. They reported that this was a result of a personnel shortage. Since the junior college is a community-oriented college, it would seem that student personnel services should be extended to the nonstudent. Matson (1972a) found that three fifths of 589 colleges said that some services were provided for nonstudents. This was usually in the area of counseling services and testing and may primarily be a reflection of precollege counseling activities in the high schools. Matson (1972a) notes, though, that there is no large ground swell to extend student personnel functions to nonstudents.

Centralization Versus Decentralization

Centralization is critical, says Richardson (1965) if the goal is to implement an overall plan of development for student personnel services. Without centralization individual services tend to develop as semiautonomous entities which do not understand the way each is linked to the other.

Blocker et al. (1965) state that despite the need for coordination, the rigid line-staff model is not the most effective organizational pattern. The most appropriate organization is decentralization of services where the responsibility and authority is shared throughout the college (O'Banion et al., 1970). Services could be grouped into "clusters of related, mutually interdependent activities [which would improve] communication and cooperation without sacrificing coordination" (Blocker et al., 1965, p. 244).

Matson (1972b) found that in most colleges where decentralization had been tried, student personnel functions still remained under the chief student personnel administrator. Matson (1972a) also discovered that decentralization was most often mentioned in reference to a particular service rather than the whole program: 37 percent of the colleges reported that some area of their program, usually the counseling services, had been decentralized. No other service had yet been decentralized to a significant degree. Decentralization occurred through physical location of services (see Dockus, 1972) rather than by a change in administrative responsibility in two thirds of the colleges where it occurred. Not surprisingly, larger institutional size usually led to decentralization.

Budget

Overall cost for a student personnel program is difficult to compute since there is great variation in the extent and nature of student personnel services available (Medsker, 1960). In general, each college should commit funds from 10 to 15 percent of its operating budget to allocate for student services, primarily for salaries, materials, and program expenses (Harvey, 1968).

ESSENTIALS FOR AN EFFECTIVE PROGRAM

The Carnegie Report (AAJC, 1965) defined ten critical needs for junior college student personnel programs: (1) staffing standards must be established that will enable the development of effective programs; (2) the nature, purpose, and requirements of satisfactory programs must be effectively interpreted to all members of the college community; (3) colleges should provide adequate training programs for leadership development; (4) a stepped-up program of recruitment and training of junior college counselors is necessary; (5) programs should conduct research and establish criteria pertaining to the development of student personnel programs; (6) student personnel specialists must be made available as field consultants to junior colleges; (7) junior colleges with strong programs should be provided with resources to become demonstration and development centers; (8) better provision for obtaining and disseminating career information is needed; (9) colleges should experiment with the development of community outreach centers; (10) programs should provide centralized coordination for the implementation of these recommendations.

Other specific suggestions and recommendations have been made. (1) Institutional coordination. The student personnel program should reflect the basic philosophy and objectives of the institution (Matson, 1968). Programs should be organized so that they reach out to all students on the entire campus. Regardless of whether the program is centralized or decentralized, the overall direction of the program is important (Medsker, 1972). To achieve this there must be a conscious effort to include faculty, students, and administrative input in the planning stage (Medsker, 1960). It is the administration's task to interpret student personnel objectives and services to students, staff, and community (Fordyce, 1970) and it is the president's task to establish the structure for communication and interaction (Lewis, 1965). There needs to be greater coordination and cooperation between student personnel workers and faculty (Fordyce, 1970) in order to integrate student personnel work with the instructional program (Lahti, 1968). If the instructional and student personnel programs are effectively integrated, it will be demonstrated in the nature and quality of their cooperative activities (Raines, 1967).

(2) Favorable climate for student personnel programs. In order for a student personnel program to be established and successful, a favorable climate of opinion is necessary at all levels. Acceptance and appreciation of student personnel programs should be apparent in the attitudes held by faculty and students (Medsker, 1972). It is hoped that faculty will appreciate the corollary relationship between institutional services and student personnel programs (Collins, 1967). This should be facilitated by cooperative working relationships between faculty and student personnel workers (Medsker, 1972).

A favorable climate of opinion also needs to prevail at both the state level (Collins, 1967) and the local governing level. The attitudes of the governing boards are instrumental in the establishment of such programs, yet board members often are not aware of the total scope of student personnel activities and their importance (Medsker, 1972).

(3) Qualified personnel. Aside from the necessity to upgrade

present student personnel workers' training and provide adequate graduate training programs, there is an additional need for personnel with a willingness to admit deficiencies, to be inquisitive, and to experiment. With a heterogeneous student population, student personnel workers must be flexible in order to achieve excellence with meaning for an individual, and not in relation to standard norms (Medsker, 1972).

Greater attention needs to be given to staff development. This would require increases in in-service supervision, encouragement of professional organization membership, and opportunities to attend workshops, conferences, and further graduate work (Raines, 1967).

(4) Staff roles. As part of their recommendation to develop staffing standards, the Carnegie Report (AAJC, 1965) noted that clarity of staff roles was essential to a sound student personnel program. Staff should have specific assignments of responsibility for implementing the program as should faculty who also need to receive training for their counseling duties and sufficient released time from their other duties. If student personnel workers are responsible for making education more individualized, then they must assume a more creative role (Higgins & Thurston, 1966). Fordyce (1970) suggests that student personnel workers should model behaviors as teachers and counselors, as people interested in humanizing the entire educational system. Student personnel workers should be leaders in providing a positive environment for students who come with a scarred educational background and who have experienced the greatest frustration and failure (Fordyce, 1970).

Student personnel workers should also increase their participation in the governance of the college if they hope to affect the entire educational system at the college (Fordyce, 1970). To be effective in the total college community student personnel workers need to communicate with each other through institutional and statewide conferences, otherwise a coordination program cannot be accomplished (Lahti, 1968).

(5) Programs. Student personnel workers are responsible for establishing meaningful developmental programs. They have the responsibility for developing programs and services to reach

special student groups like part-time students and potential or actual dropouts (Lahti, 1968).

(6) Research. Any program designed for specific goals and purposes can only be declared successful and effective if a continuous program of evaluation and research is conducted (Matson, 1968).

A thorough research program in the junior college should include program follow-ups, studies of dropouts, transfer, employed, and graduate students, and systematic appraisals of the learning being provided (Blocker et al., 1965). The most essential research is that which has implications for learning and the design of the curricula (Matson, 1968). Studies of students should involve students as individuals, in groups, in counseling and student organizations, and in their relationship to their parents (Klitzke, 1960).

As students are not the only members of the junior college community, research should not be limited to them. Colleges could benefit from research on staff members, on the general philosophy and administrative organization, the curricula, and on the college's relationship to the community through their community services programs (Klitzke, 1960). Research is necessary to provide better services and aid faculty and student personnel workers in their work with students, but it is also valuable in helping to evaluate controversial programs. At present a common request is for experimental research comparing faculty and counselors as academic advisors (Medsker, 1960).

The student personnel department, argues Klitzke (1960), should definitely handle the research responsibility. This centralization of research with the student personnel department frees the faculty from this responsibility, but it also requires that student personnel workers receive graduate training with adequate preparation to do research. Hoyt (1965) also feels that student personnel workers should have responsibility for research. They are best suited to do research because they are primarily responsible for facilitating student growth and development and they are the only staff members who perceive the student as their special area of interest, says Hoyt. Student personnel workers, especially counselors, can get a better picture of the student as an individual than a faculty member can. Hoyt also argues that student personnel workers, compared to other staff members, will have at least minimal research training and will be relatively free from departmental alignments.

In conducting research the investigators should provide for student participation not just as subjects, but as partners in the evaluation and conduct of the research (Fordyce, 1962). Investigators should also take advantage of cooperative research efforts, such as the programs offered by the American College Testing Program (Hoyt, 1965).

Despite wide acceptance of the necessity for research, there are obstacles, mainly attitudinal. Administrators often give research low priority. While student personnel workers may be more likely than other staff to have had research training, few have actually acquired real research skills. Finally, there are always insufficient funds (Hoyt, 1965).

(7) Physical essentials. The best programs can fail if sufficient and convenient physical facilities are not provided. The counseling offices and student activity and lounge areas require the most attention, especially as far as privacy, comfort, and a relaxed atmosphere are concerned. Work-saving equipment such as data processing facilitates research and evaluation and may help ease some clerical shortages (Collins, 1967).

Problems

The Carnegie study (AAJC, 1965) prefaced its report with the conclusion that "when measured against criteria of scope and effectiveness, student personnel programs in community colleges are woefully inadequate" (p. IV). "Three-fourths of the junior colleges have not developed adequate student personnel programs" (p. 20). The report further noted that "functions designed to coordinate, evaluate, and upgrade student personnel programs are ineffective in nine out of ten institutions" (p. 22). Apparently, many student personnel programs "lack the professional leadership that might enhance development"

(p. 23). Student personnel programs may be inadequate, stated the report, because "favorable climates" (p. 27) for development cannot be found in most states and because graduate training programs do not give sufficient attention to the special needs of junior colleges.

Others have noted deficiencies in the student personnel programs, such as lack of institutional policy formulation, planning, and professional direction of student personnel programs (Medsker, 1960); lack of differentiation and specialization of services (Richardson & Blocker, 1968); and lack of research on students (Medsker, 1960). Matson (1972a) reported that one fourth of 589 institutions said that support was lacking from either the administration, faculty, governing board, or community and most of these said faculty were mainly lacking in understanding and support. This might be attributable to the appointment of good teachers, who lack training in personnel theory and practice, to counseling positions (Thornton, 1972), the general lack of adequate in-service training programs (Medsker, 1960), or the refusal to cut faculty workloads for those who participate in the counseling program (Medsker, 1960).

Familiar problems also plague the student personnel program. A shortage of clerical help (Dolan, 1969) forces professional staff to perform clerical functions and complicates the serious lack of professional student personnel workers, especially counselors (Matson, 1972a). Financing always remains a problem (Blocker et al., 1965). As junior colleges continue to expand, more funds may be allocated to basic student needs of shelter, study, and food and less will be available for student personnel services (Higgins & Thurston, 1963). In sum, there are inadequate facilities, improvements needed in staff competency levels, and communication difficulties within the college (Matson, 1972a).

The Carnegie Report (AAJC, 1965) concluded that the basic student personnel functions were not being performed adequately in the majority of the junior colleges studied. Among both large and small colleges, the majority reported that all twenty-one functions were being performed, but too often were not considered the administrative responsibility of the student personnel staff (Collins, 1967). "Excellent" ratings for almost every function were reported in fewer than 10 percent of the colleges and only 5 percent of the basic twenty-one functions were found to be satisfactorily performed by two thirds or more of the colleges. The five top rated services were in institutional management: academic regulations, precollege information, student registration, student self-government, and cocurricular activities. The Carnegie Report (AAJC, 1965) viewed these results as an indication that the advising-counseling program was not the major attribute of the junior college it was claimed to be.

The Carnegie study (AAJC, 1965) also showed that students did not praise their student personnel programs highly. Individual functions may have been rated highly, but overall, students were not very enthusiastic. A study of the Council of Deans in 1969 confirmed the Carnegie Report's conclusions. Students, faculty, and administration rated student personnel services as less than "good" (Dolan, 1969).

Ineffective programs may have been due, notes the Carnegie study (AAJC, 1965), to inadequate preparation of student personnel workers, most of which is not geared to the junior college and is too narrowly concerned with counseling. Yet, the study discovered a lack of significance in the relationship between graduate training level (but not the type of training) of either student personnel workers or supervisors and the effectiveness or performance ratings of the twenty-one basic functions. O'Banion (1971) also places the reason for poor student personnel programs with the student personnel workers, but he suggests that it is due to their lack of personal and professional identity.

The Carnegie study (AAJC, 1965) was able to pinpoint those functions which, when provided, could discriminate between a strong and a weak student personnel program. These included applicant appraisal, student counseling, applicant consulting, social regulation, academic regulation, student self-government, financial aid, in-service education, and administrative organization. Student personnel functions would be more effective, concluded the Carnegie Report (AAJC, 1965), if there were strong support from the administration and faculty, if roles were clearly established for all members of the college participating in the student personnel program, and if research was conducted and utilized to enhance and evaluate the program.

SERVICES

On the whole the individual student personnel services in the junior colleges are similar in purpose and function to their parallel services in four-year institutions of higher education. Due to the student-centered philosophy and the demands of a heterogeneous population, different emphases and functions are apparent in junior college student personnel services.

Counseling

While counseling is a large part of the student personnel program in four-year colleges, it is considered the key to the whole student personnel program in the junior college (Fordyce, 1962; Matson, 1968; O'Banion, 1971). O'Banion (1971) reported that counseling is listed among the five or six major services of almost all the colleges surveyed. Despite its prominence, counseling functions were inadequately provided in more than one half of the colleges surveyed in the Carnegie Report (AAJC, 1965; Raines, 1966).

The junior college philosophy, with its stress on student individuality, is reflected in a greater commitment to providing counseling opportunities to the whole student body, rather than limiting it to those who seek it as is often the case in four-year colleges (Collins, 1971). Junior colleges also strive for greater interaction and cooperation with the educational and local community. This philosophy is reflected in a greater commitment of junior college counselors to participation in institutional activities, cooperative efforts with faculty, and contacts with local community groups (O'Banion, 1971).

Specific counseling activities found in the junior college are not unusual in the four-year college counseling service, but several are given greater prominence. A study of Michigan junior colleges (Michigan State Board of Education, 1967) reported that over 95 percent of twenty-one colleges viewed the counselor as directly responsible for five major activities: (a) Applicant consulting: In a study of eighty-six junior colleges in the West, 80 percent reported having some kind of precollege counseling and 90 percent gave standardized admission tests to high school students (Yoder & Beals, 1966). (b) Educational testing (see discussion below). (c) Group orientation: Medsker (1960) found that the most common (70%) group program was the regularly scheduled orientation course which continued for varying lengths of time. In a nonresidential college like the junior college, groups can be used to help large numbers of commuter students to facilitate their adjustment to college (O'Banion, 1971). Groups can also be used by counselors as a means to fulfill the counseling obligation to all students by providing an economical means of spreading the available counseling talent. While counseling groups have been used effectively in the junior college, Matson (1972b) feels that too many counselors have seen group work as a panacea for all their problems. (d) Career information: Information regarding transfer institutions is a unique feature of this part of the counseling program. (e) Student Advisement: In their advising capacity, junior college counselors are also more likely to deal with problems of inadequate study skills and habits. Institutions in Medsker's (1960) study tended to classify all formal advisement programs as part of the counseling service. The major concern of the counseling services in junior colleges is with vocational and educational counseling, whereas counseling services in four-year colleges generally deal with three areas of concern: vocational, educational, and personal counseling (Blocker et al., 1965; Fordyce, 1962; Matson, 1968; O'Banion, 1971).

Students generally initiate counseling in either junior or senior institutions, but in the junior college the counselor will also initiate counseling for students receiving failing grades or violating a college regulation (Blocker et al., 1965). Providing counseling programs to special target populations is also not unique to the junior college, but since the majority of minority and educationally disadvantaged students attend junior colleges, there is a greater emphasis on providing special services, especially remedial and study skills programs (O'Banion, 1971).

Counseling the junior college student may raise problems more particular to the junior college situation. A counselor may have to deal with value systems that conclude that an inexpensive, nonselective college or any formal education has little value. Arranging the curriculum in a transfer-terminal dichotomy has resulted in high positive values placed on the transfer program and negative values on the vocationally oriented part of the curriculum. As a result, three fourths of the students place themselves in the transfer program but only one third of those actually transfer. Counselors too often have to convince students of the value of their junior college education (Collins, 1970).

A survey of students and counselors in Michigan junior colleges found that counselors feel they should discuss with students their strengths and weaknesses, job opportunities, personal and social problems. They noted that career information and educational goals need to be discussed more frequently. Students, on the other hand, felt that discussions should center on advising students into appropriate programs and consultation regarding career plans, educational goals, and probable chances of achieving them. Counselors seem to have greater interest in social and personal problems than students, since 38 percent of the students and 58 percent of the counselors replied that greater emphasis was needed on social and personal problems. Also, 38 percent of the students and 51 percent of the counselors also said greater emphasis was needed on helping students develop effective study skills. Students expressed greater interest in preadmission counseling than did counselors (Michigan State Department of Education, 1969).

Testing

Testing programs in the junior college are primarily used for initial student assessment which helps the counselor and student find a place in a program that is most appropriate for his or her interests and abilities (Matson, 1972b).

In eighty-six western junior colleges, 85 percent had a well-organized testing program with adequate facilities and equipment and 97 percent had a single, well-trained individual to coordinate testing and interpret test results (Yoder & Beals, 1966). A variety of tests are available on a voluntary and mandatory basis. Medsker (1960) found that most of 243 colleges gave a scholastic aptitude test and many used tests for aptitude and ability. Medsker (1960) also reported that 73 percent of the colleges used achievement tests; over 70 percent used an interest inventory; 30 percent used personality scores. Most of the colleges did not use the results in preregistration interviews with students. But a study of Michigan junior colleges found that over 90 percent of the college student personnel workers in responding colleges viewed test interpretation in counseling interviews as part of the counselor's task (Michigan State Board of Education, 1967). Some colleges have been experimenting with new techniques and activities for testing. One has used television to help with mass testing and another has developed a program of consultation for instructors regarding classroom testing and research (O'Banion, 1971).

In an open door institution that takes in large numbers of minority and educationally disadvantaged youths, it is not surprising that there is some resistance to testing as used in the admissions process. Many question the need for selection devices in an open door college. Too often, says Collins (1970), testing has been used by the "haves" to make the "have-nots" doubt their competencies and compound their failures. There is a great need to take the threat out of testing and demonstrate its positive values (Collins, 1970).

Academic Advising

The task of academic advisement in its narrowest sense is the choice of specific courses to meet the requirements of a particular curriculum. Advisement may also include helping with the choice of curricula and plans for making adequate progress within the course of study (Fordyce & O'Banion, 1971). Its major concern is with educational programming (Richardson, 1965).

Academic advisement is usually the assigned responsibility of the faculty (O'Banion, 1971). In a study of eighty-six western junior colleges 54 percent said faculty were designated as advisors for educational counseling (Yoder & Beals, 1966). As more colleges are able to hire professional counselors, there is less use of faculty for advisors. There is considerable conflict over who should be responsible for advising.

Using Faculty as Advisors

Allen (1971) says that faculty advisors improve the relationship between teachers and counseling personnel. When faculty are responsible for advising, they become more aware of and take a greater interest in what other departments are doing. The gap between faculty and counselors may be avoided if each performs some function the other usually performs, i.e. counselors can teach a course on a regular basis and faculty can advise students.

If faculty are used as advisors, steps can be taken to make their efforts more effective. First, academic advising needs to be recognized by the college administration, academic dean, and student personnel dean as an important activity for the institution and, therefore, instructors should be rewarded for their participation. If they are to take time out from their classroom instruction to advise, then faculty should be given sensible student loads (O'Banion, 1971) and teaching loads (Allen, 1971). Perhaps the most important factor is to provide continuous in-service programs for faculty and more intensive orientation programs for new instructors (Allen, 1971; O'Banion, 1971). Faculty can help themselves by guarding against using the system to recruit students for their courses (Fordyce & O'Banion, 1971). Additional counselors to handle personal life and vocational counseling problems and sufficient clerical help would mean more time for advising. Finally, a program of evaluation by students, instructors, and counselors would provide necessary feedback on faculty effectiveness (O'Banion, 1971).

Using Counselors as Advisors

In 1960 Medsker reported that professional counselors used as advisors were generally limited to larger institutions. Smaller colleges are probably unable to supply funds for hiring more counselors and out of necessity and tradition use faculty for advising. There are several arguments in favor of using counselors for advising. First, faculty cannot possibly keep up with the changing curricula requirements of many colleges, especially the larger ones (Harvey, 1967). Also, if the counselor can develop a good rapport with the student during an advising contact, the student is more likely to return if he has a counseling problem (Harvey, 1967). Third, the counselor has knowledge of the counseling process itself, which the faculty member does not (Fordyce & O'Banion, 1971). Fourth, the counselor has knowledge of tests and other diagnostic instruments which the faculty member lacks unless he or she receives extensive inservice education (Fordyce & O'Banion, 1971).

Counselors seem more appropriate especially if one takes a broader view of academic advisement. The task is to insure that students do have appropriate goals and have made appropriate curricula and vocational choices. O'Banion (1971) proposes a model in which the students make the decisions and the advisor simply provides information and a climate of freedom in which the student can best make these decisions. The counselor can offer the most assistance in helping the student explore life and vocational goals as a first step, then follow through in helping the student make program choices and course choices. Exploration should come first and students should not be divided into personal, academic, and vocational parts. For many there is no difference between advising and counseling.

Using Both Counselorors and Faculty for Advising

A well-planned advisory program can be designed to utilize

both the specialist trained in counseling and the faculty acting as general advisors (Robinson, 1960). If counseling is an integral part of the educational process, then every educational worker has a part to play within this total scheme. Both the counselor and faculty have valid roles to play. Faculty role involves intensive personalized teaching, close and direct contact with students. They should be primarily resource persons for the fields their own disciplines represent (Fordyce & O'Banion, 1971).

Other Approaches to Advising

Educational advisors, who are neither faculty nor counselors, are selected for warmth, maturity, open mindedness and potential for working with counselors and students in the junior college setting (O'Banion, 1971). The use of these educational advisors is a new phenomenon and not widespread.

Individual academic advising is giving way to several group methods. One college integrated academic advising with a one-hour required orientation course, "Seminar on College Life." Another used video-tape programming for classes and individual interviews to deal especially with program and course selection. These and other innovations in academic advising are profiled in O'Banion (1971).

Orientation

In eighty-six western junior colleges 88 percent had orientation programs (Yoder & Beals, 1966). Most junior colleges utilize the one to two day summer retreat or an orientation course which includes activities to disseminate information about the college, do mass testing (if it is required), discuss study skills, prepare four-semester schedules, explore value systems, and meet people (O'Banion, 1971).

Admissions

Junior college admissions programs make a greater effort to establish communication and articulation with the entire community. Because of its open door policy, the college needs to insure that its admission process is simple enough so as not to discourage prospective students (Maryland Association of Junior Colleges, 1969). If a college operates under the open door concept, it must offer programs suited to those admitted. Each college needs to establish differential criteria for admissions and the means to clearly interpret them to faculty as well as to prospective students (Blocker et al., 1965). Selection criteria will depend upon what is meant by success and how open the admissions process really is (Higgins & Thurston, 1963). The admissions officer may also find that the quick turnover of students every two years and the large number of part-time and drop-in, drop-out students make record-keeping more difficult, especially in the larger colleges.

Placement

The majority of eighty-six western junior colleges had placement services (Yoder & Beals, 1966). Yet a study of Illinois junior colleges found that only 30 percent of thirty-seven colleges had assumed this responsibility (Johnson, 1966). In 1965 the Carnegie study reported that adequate provision of career information was extremely rare even though junior colleges are supposed to give great consideration to questions of vocational choice.

Junior college placement services usually do not provide the career counseling which is often found in four-year college placement offices. But the college community oriented philosophy is reflected in efforts at continuous contact with all types of employers in the local community. This serves to keep the placement officer more aware of emerging needs for trained employees in the local area (Thornton, 1972) and to facilitate job placement in the community (O'Banion, 1971). Special attention is also given to locating jobs for students who do not complete a program (O'Banion, 1971), to programs designed to provide occupational outlets for students of average ability (Fordyce, 1962), and to helping students with transfer to four-year colleges (Maryland Association of Junior Colleges, 1969).

Health

The Carnegie Report (AAJC, 1965) did not include health services among the list of twenty-one essential functions for junior colleges. Few junior colleges have developed comprehensive health programs. Most simply require a physical exam and provide emergency treatment (O'Banion, 1971). In one study of forty-one junior colleges with over 5,000 students, health services were only open during the day; they provided no psychiatric counsel; and they required physical exams of faculty and staff, but not students (Thurston, Norrie, & Venable, 1970). The same study also showed that junior college health services were organized under the student personnel umbrella and were under the direct supervision of a registered nurse who had earned at least a B.A. or B.S.

Although there is disagreement as to how many functions the health service ought to perform, most studies conclude that the service has been neglected. Neglect has been justified by saying that the student resides at home and, consequently, may use the facilities used before enrollment (Blocker et al., 1965). But since students generally come from lower socioeconomic groups, the assumption of having a family doctor does not hold. Many students do not know when they should seek medical help or what community resources are available to them (Thurston et al., 1970).

Recent literature appears to advocate a more comprehensive health program than is presently provided. Thurston et al., (1970) suggests first, that the nurse in charge be responsible to the dean of students in order to be a full member of the student personnel staff. The service should have a part-time physician who assumes medical responsibility for health programs for the entire community. A psychiatrist or psychologist should also be available for consultation. The nurse in charge should be encouraged to belong to professional groups, attend workshops, and make other efforts to keep training up to date. As with all student personnel programs in the junior college, top administrative support and understanding is needed.

A Michigan State committee (Sharland, 1971) designed a similar, but more explicit, health services program. The first goal was to provide preventive service. This would include providing entrance exams for students as well as follow-ups (Thurston et al., 1970). The staff was responsible for identifying health problems of each incoming student. The committee felt that a good preventive service should also work with physical education instructors, counselors, and financial aid directors to recommend programs that fit needs of the individual students.

The second goal was to provide adequate health care/clinical services. In a manner similar to that in four-year colleges, each junior college should evaluate its own needs. But all should have emergency programs for first aid and some type of infirmary with medical treatment for more ambulatory illnesses. Affiliations should be maintained with hospitals and ambulance services. Thurston et al. (1970) stress that adequate clinical services should provide a health counselor who cooperates with the counseling staff in making referrals and providing follow-up for students and family. The third goal was to provide health education.

Financial Aid

In the eighty-six western junior colleges 95 percent had some kind of scholarship program with scholarships based on scholastic achievement and financial need (Yoder & Beals, 1966). On the whole the junior college financial aid service is similar to its four-year college counterpart. In addition to its standard functions, the junior college service helps recruit students (sometimes in conjunction with the placement service for occupational fields where there is a shortage of trained workers) (Silver, 1968). The junior college service will also make greater efforts to encourage community participation through financial donations (Maryland Association of Junior Colleges, 1969).

Financial aid officers in junior colleges also use a need analysis system to determine eligibility for aid (Silver, 1968). Of sixty-six junior colleges in the Midwest, 88 percent made use of such a system. Also, 56 percent of the junior colleges in that study offered six or more different types of aid and 79 percent provided short-term emergency loans (Hinko, 1971a).

The junior college financial aid officer was profiled in Hinko's (1971b) study of midwestern colleges: 88 percent were male; most were married; their average age was 37.6 years; 95 percent had earned at least an M. A.; 67 percent were considered to be faculty; 82 percent of the officers operated their service by themselves; and 94 percent had to divide their time with other duties, usually in placement, counseling, admissions, or student activities. While 41 percent said that most administrators and faculty members had a good working knowledge of their financial aid service, an almost equal number (39%) said they did not. The overlap of duties may be reflected in the fact that 42 percent of the officers saw themselves as counselors, 35 percent saw themselves as administrators, and 23 percent saw themselves as both simultaneously.

Student Activities

Student activities in the junior college tend to follow the traditional pattern of activities programs in four-year colleges (Graham, 1962; Matson, 1972b) or the pattern set by the high school activity program (George & George, 1971). Few efforts have been made to design innovative programs to fit the specific needs of the junior college student (George & George, 1971; Graham, 1962). Rather, there is a tendency to blame student apathy for poor program development. The incompatability of student and campus environment may explain why in on-campus interviews of six midwestern junior colleges, George and George (1971) found that student participation in campus activities was unbelievably low. Prahl (1968) suggested that students avoid activities they see as highly competitive or open only to the talented, such as chess or math clubs.

The unique situation of the junior college makes it difficult to organize and implement an activities program based on the four-year college model. A successful program needs to be comprehensive in order to serve a heterogeneous population (Maryland Association of Junior Colleges, 1969). Students generally remain at the junior college for only two years and there is also a high withdrawal rate (Thornton, 1972). This is too short a time in which to develop leadership ability. Freshmen and sophomores do not usually have the leadership experience juniors and seniors have in senior colleges (Medsker, 1960). Student leaders also are absent because many high school students with a background of leadership experience choose to attend four-year colleges rather than the junior college (O'Banion, 1971). Thus, a major goal of the activities program should be development of student leadership (Richardson, 1965).

Activity programs also are difficult to organize because a large number of students live at home and there is a tendency for these students to maintain close associations with their established peer groups, rather than seek new friends (Medsker, 1960). Since the junior college is primarily a commuter college, students tend to leave campus once their classes are over for the day. This is especially true for the many students who leave campus to work at part-time jobs (O'Banion, 1971).

On most junior and senior college campuses greater efforts are being made to involve students in formal governance procedures. The "Joint Statement of Student Rights and Freedoms" is being examined to ascertain changes which might make it more appropriate to the junior college setting. Student personnel workers can aid students as they consider newly recognized rights and freedoms (Matson, 1968, 1972b).

Unions

There is a great need, says Reinhard (1967), for unions in the junior college. The union has great potential for bringing the entire community an educational focus. Programs could be designed to bring together community members of different ages, experiences, and educational levels. Food services, either attached to or separate from a union, may provide the only spots on the junior college campus for casual conversation and meeting new people (Blocker et al., 1965).

Housing

A study of thirty-seven Illinois junior colleges showed that there was little concern for student housing among the colleges surveyed (Johnson, 1966). This is not unexpected since most junior college students live at home. But approximately 15 to 20 percent of the student population do not live at home (Fordyce, 1962) and many are not within easily accessible commuting distance. Therefore, the junior college should have responsibility for providing some housing (Blocker et al., 1965).

PERSONNEL

Chief Student Personnel Administrator

The Carnegie Report (AAJC, 1965) found that among forty-nine larger junior colleges only 18 percent of the chief student personnel administrators had earned a Ph.D. in the behavioral sciences, student personnel work, or education and 40 percent of the directors did not have a Master's degree in behavioral science or student personnel work. Matson (1972a) found that one fourth of the 589 student personnel directors held the Ph.D. or Ed.D. and two thirds held an M.A. Two thirds had their highest degree in education, counseling, guidance, administration, or student personnel work. Matson (1972a) concluded that colleges established since 1965 were more likely to attract or require administrators with Ph.D.'s.

The chief student personnel officer may carry several titles. Matson (1972a) found that three fourths of 589 colleges used the title "dean," but 16 percent used "director." While chief administrators tended to have considerable experience in the educational field, they had less background in the junior college as either student, teacher, or administrator (DeCohooter, 1972). In Matson's study (1972a) approximately half of the administrators had advanced from a subordinate student personnel position and the same number of persons came directly from teaching as from counseling. Apparently, the K-12 public school system has declined as the major source of chief administrators. In a national study of 160 junior colleges DeCohooter (1972) found that chief student personnel officers were, on the whole, satisfied with their positions in the college and intended to remain. Despite their intentions, 81 percent saw their present positions as opportunities for advancement in their chosen profession.

As a group, junior college student personnel administrators tend to be male, married, young in the number of years in their present positions, and overworked in terms of the number of hours of work per week (DeCohooter, 1972).

Counselor/Student Ratio

Few studies have reported actual counselor/student ratios. The Carnegie Report (AAJC, 1965) concluded that institutions should develop a ratio and obtain administrative commitment to hire counselors on that basis. In their study about 800 professional counselors were employed in 719 colleges on a full-time equivalency (FTE) basis. This results in a probable ratio of 1:1200 for the colleges surveyed, but it does not represent the disproportionate distribution of counselors among the colleges. The report concluded with a recommendation to provide 2,500 additional counselors. A reasonable and effective counselor/student ratio for each college should be one FTE counselor to each 250 FTE students (Harvey, 1968) or 1:300 (Harvey, 1967). A small ratio of counselor to students seems inherently justifiable in a student-centered college such as the junior college claims to be. Another rationale is that lower student personnel staff to student ratios, especially the counselor to student ratio, have been shown to be related to more favorable rates of completion (Hedlund & Jones, 1970).

Student Personnel Staff

According to the Carnegie Report (AAJC, 1965) there were 3,000 student personnel workers in junior colleges who worked at least half-time. Of these 3,000, approximately 1,800 have at least an M.A. in psychology, sociology, or student personnel work. In the past many student personnel positions were half-time, but increasingly larger numbers are full-time (Matson, 1972b). Also the number of supervisory levels varies. In larger colleges it is common to have at least two levels within a student personnel area. Counseling is usually the first function to require a separate supervisory position.

Teaching was often required of student personnel members in the past, but Matson (1972a) found that in three fourths of the institutions, teaching was not an obligation. This requirement tends to shift with age of the institution, size, and source of support. Teaching was more likely to be demanded in smaller colleges (less than 500) and in all independent colleges. Where teaching was required, the subject taught was less likely to be related to student personnel work. Although student personnel workers are not obligated to teach, some feel they should have full faculty status and participate in all college committees (Harvey, 1968).

Shortages of student personnel workers in junior colleges have been apparent for some years. To help alleviate the short supply, some colleges have made use of trained subprofessionals or support personnel. It has been suggested that junior colleges could themselves establish training programs for these subprofessionals that could lead to an Associate of Arts degree (Matson, 1972b).

If thirty units of graduate work is the minimum necessary for student personnel work in the junior colleges, states the Carnegie Report (AAJC, 1965), then 45 percent of the student personnel workers in larger colleges who work half-time or more and 60 percent in smaller colleges fall below this. The report notes that all workers in the field need upgrading. While junior colleges are in need mainly of counselors, they also must have workers trained in student personnel specialty areas (AAJC, 1965; Collins, 1967).

There is a general consensus on the need for university training programs which are concerned with the kinds of students, community pressures, and societal changes with which the junior college deals and the overall philosophy, psychology, and sociology of the junior college (Clarke, 1972;

Higgins & Thurston, 1963; Raines, 1966). Broad interdisciplinary training might increase good quality relations with faculty, administration, community, and each other (Higgins & Thurston, 1963). In terms of specific skills, graduate training for junior college student personnel workers should emphasize skills in quick diagnosis and testing, skills in working with a heterogeneous population, competence in electronic data processing, research skills, and group skills (Higgins & Thurston, 1966). A good graduate program would also provide well-supervised internships and practicums in junior colleges (Higgins & Thurston, 1966; Raines, 1966).

In the future, suggests Young (1971), the major source for student personnel workers in junior colleges may be instructors, especially those from the behavioral sciences. A major source will continue to be experienced secondary school teachers who receive the proper upgrading and training. A third source may be M.A. level psychology majors with an understanding of higher education and personnel services programs in the broadest sense. It should be noted that Young ignores the M.A. level student personnel workers emerging from the established programs in graduate schools.

Roles

Counselor's Role

The counselor is considered by many to be the key student personnel staff member (Blocker et al., 1965). Counseling the student throughout the college experience is the counselor's major task. It is primarily the counselor who personalizes the induction of students into the college setting, into a curriculum, and into courses (Michigan State Board of Education, 1967).

More specifically, the counselor plays three roles (Collins, 1971). The first role is to provide vocational counseling as opposed to psychotherapy, since counselors are not psychiatrists or clinical psychologists and the counseling obligation is to the whole student population. Most counselors see themselves playing the second role of specialist in educational advisement. Collins (1971) feels that counseling should concentrate on these first two roles, but he also suggests a third. The counselor should enhance the investigation of values by students. To be a successful catalyst the counselor should be accepting and approachable, somewhat urbane and detached, and have a tough logical mind.

Student Personnel Worker's Role

There is an obvious overlap of roles between the student personnel worker and the counselor. Much of the literature discusses the student personnel worker, but seems to refer specifically to the counselor. Student personnel workers' roles appear to be undergoing a change. One switch is from an emphasis on the rehabilitative to the facilitative. *In loco parentis* has less influence and personal freedom is held more desirable. Another change is the shift in style from passive to active. Student personnel workers no longer provide services just for those who seek them. They now develop action-oriented programs that encounter, intervene, and facilitate. Their task is to organize resources to change and direct institutional philosophy (O'Banion, 1971).

Several models have been established to define the student personnel workers' role. The most prominent model is that of the maintenance or serviceman who provides services for those who seek them. With the therapist model, the student personnel worker functions as a psychotherapist, which often results in the counseling service being seen as a place to go only when you have a serious problem. But if higher education is moving toward a student development model, then the student personnel program requires human development facilitators who can facilitate the development of all groups in the educational community (O'Banion et al., 1970). The program concentrates on positive changes in student behavior rather than on efficient functioning of services.

Overlap Roles

Regardless of their specific duties, both the student personnel worker and the counselor are responsible for the facilitation of similar goals. Both work to assist students in making educational and vocational choices and in coming to grips with the philosophical and social questions they may raise (Medsker, 1972). They also provide assistance with realistic self-assessments and choice of appropriate training. Both student personnel worker and the counselor need to communicate effectively with faculty and administration about students' needs (Higgins & Thurston, 1963).

Faculty's Role

Faculty generally participate in student personnel programs in junior colleges more than they do in senior colleges. Their participation is important in the initial phase of development when policy and goals are being set. Faculty should also be represented on continuing student personnel policy-making committees. Involvement should be, and has been, more active than consultative participation. This usually is accomplished through faculty-conducted student advising. In addition to these activities, faculty also benefit from the special talents available through use of trained student personnel specialists (Robinson, 1960).

REFERENCES

Allen, W., Jr. Academic advising? We use faculty members. In W. K. Ogilvie & M. R. Raines (Eds.), *Perspectives on the community junior college.* New York: Appleton-Century-Crofts, 1971.

American Association of Junior Colleges. *Junior college student personnel programs: Appraisal and development* (Report for the Carnegie Corporation). Washington, D. C.: American Association of Junior Colleges, 1965.

Blocker, C. E., Plummer, R. H., & Richardson, R. C., Jr. *The two-year college: A social synthesis.* Englewood Cliffs, N. J.: Prentice-Hall, 1965.

Clarke, J. R. Student personnel work and minority groups. In T. O'Banion & A. Thurston (Eds.), *Student development programs in the community junior college.* Englewood Cliffs, N. J.: Prentice-Hall, 1972.

Collins, C. C. *Junior college student personnel programs: What they are and what they should be.* Washington, D. C.: American Association of Junior Colleges, 1967. (ERIC Document Reproduction Service No. ED 011 459)

Collins, C. C. The community college student and the 1970's. Some student characteristics and their implications for student personnel. In W. A. Robbins & S. V. Martorana, *Proceedings of the conference on student development in the community college: Directions and designs for the seventies.* Albany: State University of New York, Two Year College Student Development Center, 1970. (ERIC Document Reproduction Service No. ED 050 715)

Collins, C. C. Junior college counseling: A critical view. In W. K. Ogilvie & M. R. Raines (Eds.), *Perspectives on the community junior college.* New York: Appleton-Century-Crofts, 1971.

DeCohooter, A. W. A file on the personnel officer. *Community and Junior College Journal,* 1972, *42*(5), 17-19.

Dockus, K. Walk-in counseling service. *Personnel and Guidance Journal,* 1972, *50,* 835-836.

Dolan, R. E. *Strategies for facilitating the development of student personnel programs at Chicago City College.* Chicago: Chicago City College, May, 1969. (ERIC Document Reproduction Service No. ED 030 434)

Drake, S. L. (Ed.). *1976 Community, junior and technical college directory.* Washington, D. C.: American Association of Junior Colleges, 1976.

Fordyce, J. Student personnel policies and the climate of an institution. In Florida State University, Creating the college climate. *Proceedings of the Junior College Administration Teams Institute.* Tallahassee: Florida State University, July 30-August 3, 1962. (ERIC Document Reproduction Service No. ED 013 625)

Fordyce, J. W. The implication of student personnel services for effective instruction. In S. E. Menefee & D. B. Smith (Eds.), *Humanizing education in the junior college.* Washington, D. C.: American Association of Junior Colleges, Program With Developing Institutions, September, 1970. (ERIC Document Reproduction Service No. ED 046 371)

Fordyce, J. W., & O'Banion, T. U. Academic advising: We use counselors. In W. K. Ogilvie & M. R. Raines (Eds.), *Perspectives on the community junior college.* New York: Appleton-Century-Crofts, 1971.

George, R. L., & George, K. A. Meeting the non-academic needs unique to the junior college student. *NASPA Journal,* 1971, *9,* 155-159.

Graham, R. W. A look at student activities in the junior college. *Community and Junior College Journal,* 1962, *33*(1), 43-45.

Harvey, J. The counseling approach at Harper College. *Community and Junior College Journal,* 1967, *38*(2), 38-40.

Harvey, J. Organization and administration of junior colleges. In *GT 70 Student personnel workshop.* William Rainey Harper College, October 1-4-November 1, 1968. (ERIC Document Reproduction Service No. ED

031 200).

Hedlund, D. E., & Jones, J. T. Effect of student personnel services on completion rate in two-year colleges. *Journal of College Student Personnel*, 1970, *11*, 196-199.

Higgins, S., & Thurston, A. J. Challenges in student personnel work. *Community and Junior College Journal*, 1963, *34*(3), 24-28.

Higgins, S., & Thurston, A. Student personnel in the junior colleges in the years ahead. In G. J. Klopf, *College student personnel work in the years ahead*. Washington, D. C.: American College Personnel Association, 1966. (Student Personnel Monograph Series, No. 7)

Hinko, P. M. Financial aid officers and institutional programs. *Community and Junior College Journal*, 1971, *41*(7), 20-23. (a)

Hinko, P. M. A national survey of counseling services. *Community and Junior College Journal*, 1971, *42*(3), 20-24. (b)

Hoyt, D. P. Research and the junior college student personnel program. In F. R. Mealey, Administering community college student personnel services. *Report of the Annual President's Institute, 5th Midwest Community College Leadership Program*. Ann Arbor: Michigan University, 1965. (ERIC Document Reproduction Service No. ED 013 636)

Johnson, J. J. Personnel services in Illinois junior colleges. *Journal of College Student Personnel*, 1966, 7, 236-240.

Kirkman, R. E. Student personnel services in the community junior college: An overview. *Peabody Journal of Education*, 1969, *47*(3), 131-136.

Klitzke, L. L. Needed research in junior college stadent personnel services. *Community and Junior College Journal*, 1960, *30*(8), 452-459.

Lahti, R. E. Student personnel services in the community college. In *GT 70 Student personnel workshop*. William Rainey Harper College, October 1-4-November 1, 1968. (ERIC Document Reproduction Service No. ED 031 200)

Lewis, J. A. The organization for maximizing the effectiveness of student personnel services. In F. R. Mealey, Administering community college student personnel services. *Report of the Annual President's Institute, 5th Midwest Community College Leadership Program*. Ann Arbor: Michigan University, 1965. (ERIC Document Reproduction Service No. ED 013 636)

Maryland Association of Junior Colleges. *The role of student personnel programs in Maryland community colleges*. Author, 1969. (ERIC Document Reproduction Service No. ED 037 194)

Matson, J. E. Student personnel services in junior colleges. *NASPA Journal*, 1967, *4*, 161-164.

Matson, J. E. Emerging trends in junior college student personnel work. *Second Annual Workshop for Junior College Student Personnel Specialists*. Detroit, Michigan, April 7, 1968. (ERIC Document Reproduction Service No. ED 021 255)

Matson, J. E. A perspective on student personnel services. *Community and Junior College Journal,* 1972, *42*(6), 48-52. (a)

Matson, J. E. Student personnel work four years later: The Carnegie study and its impact. In T. O'Banion & A. Thurston (Eds.), *Student development programs in the community junior college.* Englewood Cliffs, N. J.: Prentice-Hall, 1972. (b)

McDaniel, J. W. *Essential student personnel practices for junior colleges.* Washington, D. C.: American Association of Junior Colleges, 1962.

Medsker, L. L. *The junior college: Progress and prospect.* New York: McGraw-Hill, 1960.

Medsker, L. L. The crucial role of student personnel services in the junior college. In T. O'Banion & A. Thurston (Eds.), *Student development programs in the community junior college.* Englewood Cliffs, N. J.: Prentice-Hall, 1972.

Michigan State Board of Education. Direction and emphasis. A survey of guidance and counseling programs in Michigan community colleges. *Final report.* Michigan: State Board of Education, October 1967, (ERIC Document Reproduction Service No. ED 018 830)

Michigan State Department of Education. *A survey of student and counselor perceptions of the emphasis placed on specific counselor functions in Michigan community colleges.* Lansing, Mich.: State Department of Education, June, 1969. (ERIC Document Reproduction Service No. ED 038 685)

O'Banion, T. *New directions in community college student personnel programs.* Washington, D. C.: American College Personnel Association, 1971. (Student Personnel Monograph Series, No. 15)

O'Banion, T., Thurston, A., & Gulden, J. Student personnel work: An emerging model. *Community and Junior College Journal,* 1970, *41*(3), 6-14.

Prahl, M. Student activities in the junior college. In *GT 70 Student Personnel Workshop.* William Rainey Harper College, October 1-4-November 1, 1968. (ERIC Document Reproduction Service No. ED 031 200)

Raines, M. R. The student personnel situation. *Community and Junior College Journal,* 1966, *36*(5), 6-8.

Raines, M. R. Student personnel development in junior colleges. *NASPA Journal,* 1967, *4*, 153-161.

Reinhard, H. F. The union is the center. *Community and College Journal,* 1967, *37*(8), 29-30.

Richardson, R. C., Jr. Developing student personnel programs in newly established junior colleges. *Journal of College Student Personnel,* 1965, *6*, 295-299.

Richardson, R. C., Jr., & Blocker, C. E. A tri-level concept of personnel services in two-year colleges. *Journal of College Student Personnel,* 1968, *9*, 126-130.

Robinson, D. W. The role of the faculty in the development of student personnel services. *Community and Junior College Journal*, 1960, *31*(1), 15-21.

Santa Fe Junior College. *A senior partner in the junior college.* Gainesville, Fla.: Santa Fe Junior College, 1967. (ERIC Document Reproduction Service No. ED 030 424)

Schlossberg, N. K. Challenges for urban community college personnel workers. In M. R. Smith, *Guidance-personnel work: Future tense.* New York: Columbia University, Teachers College Press, 1966.

Sharland, I. B. Health services programs for the student. *Community and Junior College Journal*, 1971, *41*(8), 15-17.

Silver, L. Financial aid in a junior college. In *GT 70 Student personnel workshop.* William Rainey Harper College, October 1-4-November 1, 1968. (ERIC Document Reproduction Service No. ED 031 200)

Thorton, J. W., Jr. *The community junior college.* New York: John Wiley, 1972.

Thurston, A., Norrie, L., & Venable, J. Health services: Who needs them? *Community and Junior College Journal*, 1970, *40*(8), 32-34.

Weatherford, S. The status of student personnel work. *Community and Junior College Journal*, 1965, *35*(5), 21-23.

Yoder, M., & Beals, L. Student personnel services in the west. *Community and Junior College Journal*, 1966, *37*(2), 38-41.

Young, R. J. Some thoughts about staffing for junior college student personnel programs. In W. K. Ogilvie & M. R. Raines (Eds.), *Perspectives on the community junior college.* New York: Appleton-Century-Crofts, 1971.

AUTHOR INDEX

(Italicized numbers indicate citation in Reference lists).

A

Abramson, S. A., 288, *295*
Abt, L. E., *336*
ACU-I: Priorities for effectiveness., 180, *199*
Adams, D. V., 138, *145*
Adams, F. C., 52, 64, 65, 74, 78, 84, *91-96, 98, 99, 101*
Adams, G. A., 398, *414*
Adams, H. J., 342, *365*
Adams, W., 10-12, *43*
Addison, A., 404, *414*
Adelphi University, 24, *37*
Admissions records aren't legally confidential, Maine court rules., 18, *37*
Agnew, S. T., 11, *37*
Aiken, J., 397, *414*
Aiken, L. R., 21, *37*
Albert, G., 20, *37*, 347, 348, 350, 351, 355, 356, 358, *365*
Albertus, A. D., 140, *152*
Alcohol — to serve or not to serve?, 196, *199*
Alexander, R., 191, *199*
Alexander, S. B., 327, *328*
Alfert, E., 130, *145*
Allen, D. J., 57, 65, 72, *91*
Allen, H. E., 210, *216*
Allen, J. G., 135, *145*
Allen, W., Jr., 19, *37*, 469, *482*
Allyn, N. C., 26, 27, *37*
Alpert, E., 433, *449*
Altman, R. A., 92, *120*
Altmeyer, D., 18, *39*
Alumni gifts for colleges., 430, *447*
The alums are restless., 444, *447*
Amada, G., 319, *328*
Amdur, M. J., 314, 322, 328, *339*
Amdur, S. B., 313, *328*
American Association of Junior Colleges., 451, 452, 456-458, 460, 462-465, 472, 473, 477-479, *482, 483, 485*
American Civil Liberties Union (ACLU)., 250, 255, 258, *270*
American College Health Association., 300, *328*
American Council on Education., xix, *101, 121, 122, 271, 422, 426*
American Council on Education Studies., xxiii, *xxvi*
American Medical Association., 298-300, 302, 327, *328*
American Personnel and Guidance Association., 264, *270*, 353, *365*
American Psychological Association., 353, *365*
Amsden, R., 15, 31, *37*
Andersen, D. G., 398, *415*
Anderson, B. D., 86, *91*
Anderson, B. R., 284, 291, 293, 294, *295*
Anderson, D. L., 35, *37*
Anderson, G. R., 165, *175*
Anderson, J. F., 33, *37*
Anderson, S. V., 219, *229*, 230
Anderson, W., 265, *270*, 354, 359, *365*
Andrews, E. E., 141, *145*
Andrews, M. H., 191, *199*
Anker, J. L., 312, *335*
Antes, R., 169, *176*
Anthony, W. A., 143, 144, *151*
Anthony v. Syracuse University., 253, *270*
Apostal, R. A., 74, 86, *91*
Appleton, J. R., 269, *272*
Arbolino, J., 27, *37*
Arbuckle, D. S., 3, *37*, 64, 65, 78, 92, 157, 160, 164, *176*, 385, 400, *415*
Arndt, J. R., 250, 251, *270*
Arthur, S., 36, *37*
Artman, J. M., 157, 160, *177*
Asbury, B. A., 208, *216*
Association of College and University

487

SUBJECT INDEX

A

AAC (*see* American Alumni Council)
AACRAO (*see* American Association of Collegiate Registrars and Admissions Officers)
AAJC (*see* American Association of Junior Colleges)
ACAC (*see* Association of College Admissions Counselors)
Academic achievement,
 and financial aid, 85
 and fraternities, 166
 and housing, 138-140
 and orientation, 117
Academic advising (*see* Counseling)
Academic calendar, 109
Academic credit,
 for career planning, 374, 397
 for community field work, 173
 for orientation courses, 102
 for orientation work, 116
 for student employment, 403
 in the union, 181, 183, 193
Academic deans, 10, 327, 377, 378, 380, 424, 455, 469
Academic departments,
 and counseling, 343, 347-349, 353
 and graduate financial aid, 82
 and health education, 318
 and orientation, 106
 and placement, 357, 377, 378, 380, 386, 394, 403
 and student employment, 403
 ties to the union, 181
Accreditation,
 of junior colleges, 24
 of overseas dependents' schools, 27
ACPA (*see* American College Personnel Association)
ACPRA (*see* American College Public Re-

lations Association)
ACT (*see* American College Testing Program)
Activism (*see* Student protest)
Activities (*see* Student activities)
Acts, 422
ACUCAA (*see* Association of College, University and Community Arts Administrators)
ACU-I (*see* Association of College Unions - International)
ACURA (*see* Association for the Coordination of University Religious Affairs)
Adhesion, contract of, 243
Adjudication, 247
Adjustment (*see* Student development)
Administration (*see* Chief student personnel administrator)
 and admissions, 7, 17
 and financial aid, 52, 53, 57
 and orientation, 105, 108
 and the union, 180, 187, 190, 193
Admissions, 3-50
 and alumni, 433, 434
 application forms, 18
 culminating in orientation, 103
 and financial aid, 30, 36, 64, 89, 475
 and health, 309, 310, 327
 in the junior college, 452, 454, 456, 457, 466, 467, 471-472
 and mental health screening, 323
 and the ombudsman, 226
 and orientation, 103
 and placement, 385, 413
 and the registrar, 36
 requirements, 3, 4
 Statement of Good Practices, 36
Admissions counselor (*see* Counselor, admissions)
Admissions directors,
 composite description, 33-36

509

249, 251
Ethics, 263, 265
  in admissions, 36
  code of, 264, 353, 409
  in counseling, 353
  in financial aid, 90-91
  in health, 300
  in mental health, 324, 325
  in placement, 409
Evaluation (*see* Research)
  and alumni, 432, 433, 444
  of financial aid, 85-89
  of health services, 307-309
  in junior colleges, 452, 456, 461, 465, 470
  of mental health services, 325
  of orientation, 116-119
  of placement, 385-387, 393, 394, 414
  of transfer credit, 24
  of the union, 191, 192
Exhibition Day (*see* Graduation)
Expenses (*see* Financial need, and student expenses)
Experimental Colleges, 141
Expulsion (*see* Discipline)
Extracurricular activities (*see* Student activities)

F

Faculty,
  and admissions, 3, 6, 7, 9, 10, 13, 15
  and admissions interviews, 19
  and counseling, 340, 341, 343, 344, 346, 349, 351-353, 357, 358, 361, 395
  and discipline, 232, 233, 239, 240, 257, 258, 260, 267-269, 279
  and graduation, 424, 425
  and health, 298
  and housing, 127, 137, 138, 141, 144-145
  influence in college choice, 32
  and junior college services, 459-465, 469-471, 480, 482
  and mental health, 321-323, 346
  and the ombudsman, 223-227
  and orientation, 102, 105, 112, 115
  and placement, 368, 369, 372, 374, 375, 377-379, 395, 397, 400, 402, 403, 414
  and security, 282, 289
  and selectivity, 13

and student activities, 153, 154, 169, 174
and student employment, 403, 404
and their health, 302, 304, 314
underpayment and financial aid, 58
and the union, 180, 182, 184, 185, 187-189, 193
Faculty rank (*see* College student personnel professional, faculty rank)
Falcon Network, 443
Fall orientation, 108
Family Contribution Analysis Report, 76
Family Educational Rights and Privacy Act of 1974, 391
Family financial statement, 69
Family life movement, 155
Federal Emergency Relief Administration, 52
Federal funds,
  for counseling, 369
  for employment services, 376
  for financial aid, 52, 53, 57-61, 63, 65, 67, 72, 76-77
  for housing, 133
  for placement, 390
  for private colleges, 253
  for union construction, 179, 188
Federal Housing and Home Finance Agency, 133
Federal Insured Student Loan Program, 74, 75
Federal tax return, 71
Fees (*see* Student fees)
Fellowships (*see* Gift aid)
Fiduciary theory of discipline, 240, 244-245
Fifty Colleges Study, 437, 446
Films (*see* Culture; Cultural affairs)
Financial aid, 51-101
  and academic achievement, 85
  administrative view of, 57
  and admissions, 36, 64, 89, 475
  and business office, 89
  conglomerate model of, 59
  and counseling, 79, 343, 346, 354, 475
  and discrimination, 396
  and food service, 195
  in junior colleges, 452, 456, 464, 474-475
  newsletters, 85
  personnel view of, 57

College and University Food Services)
NAFSA (*see* National Association of Foreign Student Affairs)
NASPA (*see* National Association of Student Personnel Administrators)
National Association of College Admissions Counselors (*see* Association of College Admissions Counselors)
National Association of College and University Food Services, 195
National Association of Foreign Student Affairs, 28
National Association of State Universities and Land-Grant Colleges, 63
National Association of Student Personnel Administrators, 216, 256
National Association of Women Deans, Administrators, and Counselors, 216, 256
National Cancer Institute, 52
National clearinghouse for admissions, 17
National Defense Education Act, 53
National Defense Student Loan, 53, 73, 86
National Merit Scholarship Finalists, 87, 88
National Orientation Bulletin, 113
National Orientation Directors Association, 113
  Handbook, 113
National Science Foundation, 63
National Student Association, 173, 256
National Student Loan Bank, 63
National Vocational Guidance Association, 369
NAWDAC (*see* National Association of Women Deans, Administrators, and Counselors)
NDEA (*see* National Defense Education Act)
NDSL (*see* National Defense Student Loan)
Nebraska Centennial College, 141, 142
Nebraska, University of, 145
Need (*see* Financial need)
Negative dowry theory, 77
Neurosis (*see* Mental health)
New Consciousness Series, 172
New Mexico State University, 413
New York, City University of, 11

New York Media Project, 393
New York, State University of, 190, 219
NODA (*see* National Orientation Director's Association)
Noncategorical Aid, 59, 60
Northern Michigan University, 172
Northwestern University, 382
NSA (*see* National Student Association)
Nurses, 306, 310, 315, 327, 473
Nursing Scholarship Program, 76
Nursing Student Loan Program, 76

O

Oakland University, 442
Oberlin College, 393, 413
Occupational Outlook Handbook, 369, 399
Occupational Outlook Quarterly, 399
Occupational Outlook Report Series, 399
Occupational Outlook Service, 399
Occupational Safety and Health Act, 282, 316
Occupational Thesaurus, 400
Ohio State University, 11, 88, 361, 362, 435
Ohio University, 86
Ombatman, 223
Ombudsman, 219-231
  civil, 219, 220
  and discipline, 220, 256
  evaluation, 228
  ombatman, 223
Open admissions, 10-12
Open door admissions, 14-15, 468, 472
Oregon State University, 86
Organizational development, xi
Organizational structure, place in,
  of admissions, 89
  and alumni, 433
  and counseling, 348
  and discipline, 265
  of financial aid, 64, 89
  and health, 303, 316
  and junior college, 452, 455-457, 464
  and the ombudsman, 223
  of orientation, 106
  and placement, 376
  and religion, 210-211

SAM (*see* Single Application Method)
San Jose State, 219
Sanitation (*see* Health)
SAT (*see* Scholastic Aptitude Test)
Satellite union (*see* Union, satellite)
Scholarships (*see* Gift aid; Loans)
Scholastic Aptitude Test, 4, 19, 26, 28
Scott v. Alabama State Board of Education, 251
Screening, 323
Second curriculum, 153
Secondary education, 3-5
Security (*see* Campus security)
Selective admissions, 12-13
Self-actualization (*see* Student development)
Self-discipline, 233-235 (*see* Student development)
Self-help dormitories, 52
Self-identification (*see* Student development)
Seminar on college life, 471
SEOG (*see* Supplementary Educational Opportunity Grant Program)
Service activities (*see* Volunteer activities)
Service awards (*see* Gift aid)
Service station, 181
Servicemen's Readjustment Act of 1944 (*see* G.I. Bill)
Sex, 312-314
 activity, 268, 312, 314
 and coed living, 135-137
 contraceptives, 172, 312, 313
 counseling, 355
 education, 307, 312-314
 influence in academic prediction, 21
 and mental health, 321, 326
 pregnancy counseling, 313
 revolution, 312
 venereal disease, 299, 312
Sexual discrimination,
 in admissions, 9
 and G.I. Bill, 73
 in gift aid, 56
 in housing, 136
 in placement, 389, 390
 in student leadership positions, 173
 workshops, 109, 174
Sickle-cell, 302

Simmons (College) *Review*, 439
Single application method, 17
Smoking (*see* Drugs)
Social Ethic, 155
Social influence, 104, 105
Social reconstructionism, 157
Social science delivery system, 183
Social Security, educational benefits of, 60
Socioeconomic,
 background and disciplinary cases, 266
 background and financial aid, 60, 61, 63, 67, 68, 70, 74, 77, 81, 86
 background of junior college students, 454, 473
 and college choice, 32
 equalization, 60, 77, 90
 inbreeding of fraternities, 165
 status and admissions, 10, 18
Soglin v. Kauffman, 251
Sororities (*see* Fraternities)
Southern Association of Colleges and Schools, 432
Special Conferences, 430
Sports (*see* Athletics)
Sputnik, 53
Standard Oil, 379
Stanford University, 136, 313, 445, 447
State Employment Agencies (*see* Placement)
Statement of Good Practices, 36
Statement of Principles (*see* College Scholarship Service)
Statement of Purpose (*see* Association of College Unions-International)
Status theory of discipline, 240, 245
Statutory theory of discipline, 240-241
Steinmetz, George, 368
Stephens College House Plan, 140
Storey, Dr. Thomas A., 299
Strict constructionist, 236
Student activities, 153-178
 and counseling, 343, 344
 and cultural affairs, 196
 and discrimination, 390
 and financial aid, 475
 handbook, 163
 information in orientation, 106
 in junior colleges, 452, 454, 456, 464, 475, 476